S A R A H C . C H A M B E R S

FROM SUBJECTS TO CITIZENS

*Honor, Gender, and Politics
in Arequipa, Peru*

1780–1854

Library of Congress Cataloging-in-Publication Data

Chambers, Sarah C., 1963–
    From subjects to citizens : honor, gender and politics in
Arequipa, Peru, 1780–1854 / Sarah C. Chambers.

        p.   cm.
    Includes bibliographical references and index.
    ISBN 0-271-01901-8 (cloth : alk. paper)
    ISBN 0-271-01902-6 (pbk. : alk. paper)
    1. Political participation — Peru — Arequipa — History.
2. Citizenship — Peru — Arequipa — History.   3. Honor — Peru — Arequipa —
History.   4. Arequipa (Peru) — Politics and government.   I. Title.
JS2678.A72C48   1999
306.2′0985′3209034 — dc21   98-37144
                                                                               CIP

It is the policy of The Pennsylvania State University Press to use acid-free paper for
the first printing of all clothbound books. Publications on uncoated stock satisfy the
minimum requirements of American National Standard for Information Sciences —
Permanence of Paper for Printed Library Materials, ANSI Z39.48-1992.

Contents

List of Maps, Figures, and Tables

Maps

Figure

Tables

Acknowledgments

Like the humble folk of Arequipa whose wills I read, I have contracted numerous debts in researching and writing this book. I fear that the only way I can repay those teachers, friends, colleagues, and archivists is by giving them my sincere gratitude. Therefore, being of relatively sound mind and body, let me begin.

I never could have found the stories upon which this book is built without the assistance of numerous archivists in both Arequipa and Lima. Let me thank in particular Guillermo Galdos Rodríguez, director of the Archivo Regional de Arequipa, and Alejandro Málaga Medina, director of the Archivo Arzobispal de Arequipa, and his assistant Roberto Ruelas, and Arlet Ocola of the Archivo del Palacio Arzobispal de Arequipa. In Lima, the directors and staff of the Archivo General de la Nación, the manuscripts division of the Biblioteca Nacional del Perú, and the Archivo Histórico-Militar del Perú were helpful and professional. I am also grateful to Félix Denegri Luna for allowing me access to his private library. Research assistants Rocío Villaverde, Irma Soto, and Magali Muñoz in Arequipa helped me get through the large body of uncataloged documents. I also owe a debt to my friends and colleagues in Peru, among them Pablo de La Vera Cruz, Eusebio Quiroz Paz Soldán, Carlos Contreras, Betford Betalleluz, Armando Guevara Gil, Nelson Manrique, and Carlos Aguirre. Finally, when in Lima, I enjoyed an affiliation with the Instituto de Estudios Peruanos.

This book grew out of my dissertation and I am grateful to my advisers, Florencia E. Mallon and Steve J. Stern. I learned from their overall approach to Latin American history as well as from their careful and detailed reactions to my own work. Let me also express my thanks to Francisco Scarano, who served as a reader on my dissertation committee. In the long process of writing the book, I benefited from the comments of John Chasteen, Nils

Jacobsen, Charles Walker, Carlos Aguirre, Louis Pérez, Judith Bennett, Nancy Hewitt, Judith Allen, and Eileen Findlay, who read various versions of the manuscript. Further, conversations with my fellows at the Institute for the Arts and Humanities gave me valuable insights on gender and republicanism. I would also like to thank readers Peter Guardino and Eric Langer for their insightful suggestions.

If my greatest intellectual debt is to those colleagues, my financial debt is also large. I was fortunate to receive a Fulbright-Hays Doctoral Dissertation Research Grant from the Department of Education. My research was also supported by a grant from the Joint Committee on Latin American and Caribbean Studies of the Social Science Research Council and the American Council of Learned Societies; funds for that program were provided by the William and Flora Hewlett Foundation and the Andrew W. Mellon Foundation. A travel grant from the Institute of Latin American Studies at the University of North Carolina funded a final trip to the archives. Finally, I was able to read comparatively on republicanism thanks to a Junior Faculty Development Grant and a fellowship at the Institute for the Arts and Humanities, both at the University of North Carolina.

I have also incurred debts in the production of the book. My research assistant at the University of North Carolina, Karen Paar, helped in the compilation of statistical material, and Heidi Jensen drew the maps. The copy editor, Anne Collier Rehill, meticulously combed the text and notes. And I am particularly grateful to Sanford Thatcher, the editor at Pennsylvania State University Press, for his own care in reading the manuscript and guiding it to publication.

Last, but not least, are my personal debts. My parents, in addition to a lifetime of nurturing, have also contributed in very concrete ways to this book. My mother, Florence W. Chambers, is a sharp copy editor. It is from my father, Clarke A. Chambers, that I inherited my love of history, and he has been a most committed and constructive adviser throughout my education and career. My husband, Eugene C. Ozasky, has contributed his technical skill in computers. However, it is his support and accompaniment, both at home and in Peru, for which I am most deeply grateful. Our son, Alexander, completed his gestation before this book did, and he has continually reminded me of the joys of the present as well as of the past.

To fellows, friends, and family, I give my thanks. I take full responsibility for remaining flaws. I have no legacy from which to repay my debts, except for this testament to the people of Arequipa, whose story I will try to tell.

Introduction

The Myth of the White City

Arequipa is an impressive sight. Its white buildings dazzle in the bright desert sun as if reflecting the snowcapped volcanoes that stand guard over the city. The twin spires of the cathedral, more like Moorish minarets than Spanish bell towers, rise up from the plaza. Today surrounded by industry and suburban sprawl, the city's center still evokes in the visitor strong feelings of its past. One can imagine, therefore, the enthusiastic reactions of earlier travelers who had to journey two days from the port through the desert before arriving at the "White City."

Flora Tristan, a French feminist whose father was from Arequipa, made the trip in 1833 on the back of a mule. By the time she reached the top of the final peak, she was weary and ill, but her companions coaxed her to take in the view. "Then I looked at the smiling valley and felt so sweet an emotion that I wept," she later wrote, "but these were tears of joy."[1] British merchant Samuel Haigh better withstood the journey from the coast, but he too was

---

1. Flora Tristan, *Peregrinations of a Pariah: 1833–1834*, trans. Jean Hawkes (1874; reprint, Boston: Beacon Press, 1986), 91.

impressed by his first sight of Arequipa: "We saw a vast city with walls as white as snow," he wrote, "shining in the light of the full moon."[2]

When these travelers entered the city, they would discover this external image reflected in a highly politicized regional identity. Arequipa is nicknamed the White City as much for its Hispanic population as for its architectural style, but such racial overtones were only one component of a larger social myth about its role in Peruvian history. Víctor Andrés Belaúnde, a native son who became an eminent intellectual and diplomat, highlighted the "popular, purely civic character" of the frequent rebellions launched from Arequipa during the nineteenth century, rebellions that he attributed to a common identity and solidarity not achievable at the national level: "It is surely the quality of our population, its egalitarian tendency, individualist by its race, affirmed by small property, that has determined its unique participation in the development of Peruvian democracy."[3]

It is tempting to dismiss such an obviously idealized image as mere local pride, but to do so would miss its influence on national politics. Throughout the nineteenth and twentieth centuries, politicians from Arequipa would call for free trade, a reversal of the centralizing tendencies of the Lima state, and a democratization of Peruvian society. Their ability, on numerous occasions, to mobilize common folk to take up arms in support of such a program indicates that it was a vision with deep roots in local society.

Jorge Basadre, one of Peru's most prominent historians, identified Cuzco with the country's Inca past, Lima with the colonial period, but Arequipa with the republican era.[4] Although leaders from Arequipa overemphasized the uniqueness of their homeland for ideological reasons, the region did differ from Lima and Cuzco, its major political rivals, in two important ways. First, according to the late colonial census, whites formed a minority of the population in those cities but a majority in Arequipa. Although such demographic proportions were in part socially constructed, they did make republican elites in Lima and Cuzco less confident about the possibility of assimilating those of African and indigenous descent into the nation.

Second, the timing of elite concerns about urban disorder distinguishes Arequipa from Lima. Attempts to police the population were initiated by

---

2. Samuel Haigh, "Bosquejos del Perú, 1825–1827," in Alberto Tauro, ed., *Viajeros en el Perú republicano* (Lima: Universidad Nacional Mayor de San Marcos, 1967), 19.

3. Víctor Andrés Belaúnde, *Meditaciones Peruanas* (Lima: Biblioteca Perú Actual, 1933), 136.

4. Jorge Basadre, *La multitud, la ciudad y el campo en la historia del Perú*, 3d ed. (Lima: Ediciones Treintaitrés and Mosca Azul Editores, 1980), 200.

Bourbon reformers beginning in the viceregal capitals during the late colonial period. Their extension to provincial cities like Arequipa after independence allowed men greater opportunities to defend themselves from criminal charges, by appealing to their rights as citizens. Within the larger context of Spanish America, Arequipa may prove less unique than representative of provincial cities in regions without major racial conflict.

The myth of the White City, therefore, speaks to historical processes that go far beyond Arequipa or even Peru. Arequipa's proud claims of local democracy are clearly exaggerated, but they reveal that ordinary people did participate in critical ways in the transition from colony to republic. In contrast to much of the scholarly literature on Spanish American independence, this study contends that political culture was dramatically transformed during the formative period between the late eighteenth and the mid-nineteenth centuries, and that the popular classes as well as the elites played crucial roles in this process. Although governments frequently failed to practice professed principles, the political terrain was significantly altered by the new need to claim legitimate authority based upon popular sovereignty as opposed to absolute monarchy. Independence initiated negotiations over citizenship—its respective rights and obligations as well as its boundaries of inclusion and exclusion—that have remained at the center of political movements in Latin America, as throughout much of the world, until today.

My aim in this study, therefore, is to illuminate the gradual and conflictive processes by which Peruvians transformed themselves from colonial subjects into republican citizens. It is not enough to measure the extent of popular participation in the wars of independence themselves, because the formation of new states took place over several decades and within legal and cultural as well as military and electoral arenas.[5]

The languages and rituals of power that had developed in the colonial period, moreover, would continue to shape people's consciousness and actions even as the underlying meanings were gradually transformed. In particular, despite a rich literature on the centrality of honor to colonial society and governance, scholars have missed its continuing importance in

5. For theories that emphasize the "cultural" nature of state formation, see Gilbert M. Joseph and Daniel Nugent, "Popular Culture and State Formation in Revolutionary Mexico," in *Everyday Forms of State Formation: Revolution and the Negotiation of Rule in Modern Mexico*, ed. Joseph and Nugent (Durham: Duke University Press, 1994), 3–23; and Phillip Corrigan and Derek Sayer, *The Great Arch: English State Formation As Cultural Revolution* (New York: Basil Blackwell, 1985).

the political culture of early republicanism.[6] Looking back, Belaúnde identified the essence of the Arequipeño character as "señorío," which he defined as embodying the virtues of traditional nobility but without titles or wealth. This exploration of the intersection of popular culture and politics will demonstrate that such an egalitarian interpretation of honor was rooted in the claims of common folk who, by shifting the emphasis from status to virtue, both made sense of and influenced republican discourse.

A sense of honor was key to colonial governance in Spanish America; public rituals, ornate dress, and official titles were designed to affirm both the legitimacy of Spanish rule and a social hierarchy based upon race and class. More than reflecting internal virtue, honor was a social attribute that increased in value as it was recognized publicly by others. Numerous libel suits testified to its importance in daily life. Elites measured honor by noble lineages, racial purity, and nonmanual professions. Artisans, small farmers, market sellers, and even laborers, however, implicitly challenged such exclusive claims by insisting that their conduct also earned them honorable names. Nevertheless, widespread acceptance of codes of deference, based upon degrees of honor, maintained social peace in Arequipa through the end of the colonial period.

That peace was broken by independence in the 1820s. Fearing disorder during this politically unstable period, republican authorities became more repressive than their colonial predecessors. By reorganizing the judicial system and bolstering the police force, they dramatically intensified the level of criminal prosecution, but they faced resistance from defendants who, with the help of their lawyers, claimed new constitutional protections of civil liberties. Plebeians linked these rights to their understanding of honor, appealing particularly to those articles that called for the protection of public reputations and the upholding of patriarchal authority within the household. Those men who were able to support their pleas with proof of hard work and respectable conduct were granted some rights as "honorable" citizens. Significantly, plebeians not only reacted to but also shaped republican discourse. Prominent politicians from Arequipa, familiar with these courtroom pleas from their training as jurists, promoted at the national level a form of liberalism that emphasized not only discipline but also individual liberties and praise for the honest working man.

6. Or they have limited their analysis to elites, as in Michael P. Costeloe, *The Central Republic in Mexico, 1835–1846: Hombres de Bien in the Age of Santa Anna* (Cambridge: Cambridge University Press, 1993).

That the discourse of republican honor was masculine indicates that gender was central to this political transition. Despite the recent explosion in Latin American women's history, most interpretations of the period of independence continue to ignore gender.[7] Although women were ultimately marginalized within the political sphere, the ideologically defined boundary between public and private space was more porous in practice. Because republican authorities needed men as workers, soldiers, and political partisans, they were willing to reinforce patriarchal privileges in the private sphere in exchange for more respectable male conduct in public. In buttressing the private power of men, the link between honor and citizenship had concrete consequences in women's lives. Moreover, the continuing emphasis on female virtue as private morality both justified the exclusion of women from politics and subjected their behavior to increasing public scrutiny, as republican officials targeted female sexuality in their campaign to restore order. Finally, such conservative norms and traditional gender roles exerted a strong influence upon both the liberal philosophies of Arequipeños and their nostalgic depictions of the White City.

Independence and Periodization

Although independence was disruptive, it did not transform political culture in Peru overnight. This study, therefore, follows a trend toward focusing on a "middle period," in this case from the major late colonial revolts of 1780 to the establishment of a relatively stable liberal state under Ramón Castilla in 1854. Efforts by the Bourbon monarchs during the late eighteenth century to centralize power more effectively were resisted by many of their American subjects. Creole elites did not question the construction of a stronger state, however, as much as they challenged who would control it. Similarly,

7. For the exceptions, see Silvia M. Arrom, *The Women of Mexico City, 1790–1857* (Stanford: Stanford University Press, 1985); Evelyn Cherpak, "The Participation of Women in the Independence Movement in Gran Colombia, 1780–1830," in Asunción Lavrin, ed., *Latin American Women: Historical Perspectives* (Westport, Conn.: Greenwood Press, 1978), 219–34; Mary Lowenthal Felstiner, "Kinship Politics in the Chilean Independence Movement," *Hispanic American Historical Review* 56, no. 1 (1976): 58–80; and Arlene Julia Díaz, "*Ciudadanas* and *Padres de Familia*: Liberal Change, Gender, Law, and the Lower Classes in Caracas, Venezuela, 1786–1888" (Ph.D. diss., University of Minnesota, 1997). By contrast, feminist analyses have dramatically transformed the way we see the North American and French revolutions.

attempts by religious authorities in the late colonial period to rein in what they saw as the disorderliness of popular culture were intensified by the republican officials.

In contrast to many studies of the middle period, however, I emphasize important changes against the backdrop of continuity.[8] On the surface, rituals of power, forms of popular protest, and the use of a language of honor may look similar throughout this period, but their underlying meaning was undergoing significant if subtle shifts. The same ceremonies might be used, for example, to swear loyalty to a king and to a constitution, but their political messages were distinct.

Taking a longer view allows us to reassess the degree to which independence resulted in significant changes. Over the past several decades, social historians have provided a crucial corrective to patriotic tales of national "liberation."[9] Certainly, there was no significant transformation in the economic or social structure, and the reins of power shifted only slightly from royal officials appointed by the crown to the American-born creole elite. This elite attempted to suppress or channel popular unrest, which had been increasing throughout the eighteenth century.[10]

Indeed, this study demonstrates that republican judges and prosecutors in Arequipa intensified repression against what they defined as criminality. For Peru, in particular, fears of a race war in the wake of the 1780 rebellion of

8. For example, see Mark D. Szuchman's introduction to *The Middle Period in Latin America: Values and Attitudes in the Seventeenth–Nineteenth Centuries* (Boulder: Lynne Rienner, 1989). Cheryl Martin proposes that the ethos of colonial governance, which she perceptively analyses for the eighteenth century, likely remained little changed during the first half of the nineteenth century: Martin, *Governance and Society in Colonial Mexico: Chihuahua in the Eighteenth Century* (Stanford: Stanford University Press, 1996), 198. In a review article, Eric Van Young similarly emphasizes continuity in Mexico between 1750 and 1850, but he calls for greater attention to the popular classes and "before and after" studies on the impact of independence: Van Young, "Recent Anglophone Scholarship on Mexico and Central America in the Age of Revolution," *Hispanic American Historical Review* 65, no. 4 (1985): 725–44. For a contrasting interpretation that emphasizes important political changes, see Peter Guardino and Charles Walker, "The State, Society, and Politics in Peru and Mexico in the Late Colonial and Early Republican Periods," *Latin American Perspectives* 19, no. 2 (1992): 10–43.

9. For two overviews, see John Lynch, *Latin American Revolutions, 1808–1826*, 2d ed. (New York: W. W. Norton, 1986); and George Reid Andrews, "Spanish-American Independence: A Structural Analysis," *Latin American Perspectives* 12, no. 1 (1985): 105–32.

10. For Peru, see Alberto Flores Galindo, ed., *Túpac Amaru II: 1780* (Lima: Antología Retablo de Papel, 1976); Scarlett O'Phelan Godoy, *Rebellions and Revolts in Eighteenth-Century Peru and Upper Peru* (Cologne: Böhlau Verlag, 1985); and Steve J. Stern, ed., *Resistance, Rebellion, and Consciousness in the Andean Peasant World* (Madison: University of Wisconsin Press, 1987).

Túpac Amaru II strengthened royalist sentiment among many creoles, and the continuing exploitation and political exclusion of the indigenous population marks the policies of the nineteenth-century state as neocolonial.[11]

Nevertheless, even after the Túpac Amaru rebellion, at least fractions of the creole elite outside of Lima were willing to mobilize cross-class and multi-ethnic alliances in pursuit of independence.[12] This study will trace how such regional alliances reemerged in the frequent civil wars of the early republican period. Moreover, the change from monarchy to republic generated demands from below that could not easily be ignored. In a period during which state institutions were relatively weak and the dominant classes divided, the ability to mobilize the masses, whether at the ballot box or on the field of battle, was crucial.

With the disappearance of the king, *caudillos*, military strongmen with regional power bases, competed to control the emerging national states throughout Spanish America.[13] Recent analyses of the turbulent first half of the nineteenth century have begun to identify a political logic to the apparent chaos. Paul Gootenberg, for example, moves beyond a simple personalistic interpretation of major caudillos in Peru to explore the particular political platforms they represented.[14]

But such studies tell us little about why artisans, small farmers, or workers would rally behind a particular cause. In the absence of political tracts written by such common folk themselves, the usual explanation relies heavily upon the power of "charismatic" leadership and the rewards of clientelism.[15] According to contemporary accounts, however, caudillos in Peru were often

11. Heraclio Bonilla, ed., *La independencia en el Perú* (Lima: Instituto de Estudios Peruanos, 1972); and Timothy E. Anna, *The Fall of the Royal Government in Peru* (Lincoln: University of Nebraska Press, 1979).

12. John R. Fisher, "Royalism, Regionalism, and Rebellion in Colonial Peru, 1808–1815," *Hispanic American Historical Review* 59, no. 2 (1979): 232–57; and Sarah C. Chambers, "The Limits of a Pan-Ethnic Alliance in the Independence of Peru: The Huánuco Rebellion of 1812" (M.A. thesis, University of Wisconsin at Madison, 1987).

13. John Lynch, *Caudillos in Spanish America, 1800–1850* (Oxford: Clarendon Press, 1992).

14. Paul Gootenberg, "North-South: Trade Policy, Regionalisms, and *Caudillismo* in Post-Independence Peru," *Journal of Latin American Studies* 23, no. 2 (1991): 273–308. For Mexico, see Donald Stevens, *Origins of Instability in Early Republican Mexico* (Durham: Duke University Press, 1991); Costeloe, *The Central Republic*; and Torcuato S. Di Tella, *National Popular Politics in Early Independent Mexico, 1820–1847* (Albuquerque: University of New Mexico Press, 1996).

15. For a more complex interpretation that links "charisma" to emerging national identities, see John C. Chasteen, *Heroes on Horseback: A Life and Times of the Last Gaucho Caudillos* (Albuquerque: University of New Mexico Press, 1995).

lacking in personal charisma. Indeed Arequipa's nickname of the "Pueblo Caudillo" highlights the role of the people or community rather than an individual leader. The patron-client model, moreover, has limited explanatory power beyond either military corps or rural regions characterized by large estates with a predominantly dependent population. Despite subtle studies of nineteenth-century caudillos, therefore, the assumptions about their followers remain relatively simplistic.

By conceptualizing the sphere of politics and state building more broadly, we shall see that the urban (and semi-urban) popular classes responded to and helped shape political ideas during the transition from colonial to republican rule. They were exposed to political concepts through speeches, newspapers, and pamphlets, but they could rarely use these media to talk back. The courts, one of the most stable state institutions in this transitional period, provided an arena for dialogue. Numerous studies of the colonial period have demonstrated the central role played by the legal system in buttressing Spanish hegemony, but, once again, we need to extend those insights into the republican period.

In court, people came face to face with officials of the state and their interpretations of rights and obligations under the law. The response of common folk, necessarily shaped by unequal power relations and mediated by lawyers and scribes, was nonetheless recorded. The ensuing negotiations over political notions such as honor and citizenship were far from abstract: freedom, in its most fundamental terms, was at stake.

The ability of leaders to mobilize masses during political rallies or armed revolts can only be understood against the backdrop of such everyday negotiations over the changing terms of governance. Pathbreaking studies, based upon extensive research in local archives, have demonstrated how indigenous peasants engaged discourses of republicanism and liberalism in their attempts to limit the encroachment of state power upon the political and economic autonomy of their communities.[16] In Mexico, their success in at least partially shaping national policies resulted in a relatively hegemonic

---

16. Florencia E. Mallon, *Peasant and Nation: The Making of Postcolonial Mexico and Peru* (Berkeley and Los Angeles: University of California Press, 1995); Peter Guardino, *Peasants, Politics, and the Formation of Mexico's National State: Guerrero, 1800–1857* (Stanford: Stanford University Press, 1996); Mark Thurner, *From Two Republics to One Divided: Contradictions of Nationmaking in Andean Peru* (Durham: Duke University Press, 1997); Cecilia Méndez G., "Los campesinos, la independencia y la iniciación de la república: El caso de los iquichanos realistas," in Henrique Urbano, ed., *Poder y violencia en los Andes* (Cuzco: Centro de Estudios Regionales Andinos [CERA] Bartolomé de las Casas, 1991), 165–88; and Tristan Platt, "Simón

state, but in Peru increasingly exclusive and authoritarian governments marginalized the indigenous population.

The urban popular classes have not received the same attention, yet, especially for Peru, they hold the key to understanding how the republican state was able to garner at least some broader legitimacy. Their heterogeneity and lack of a strong corporate identity, in contrast to the indigenous peasantry, provided possibilities for hegemonic cross-class coalitions as suggested by the regional mythology of Arequipa.[17]

Political Culture and Hegemony

Following the usage of the period, this study sometimes refers to the majority of the working population—rather than just the underemployed and vagrants—as "plebeian," to distinguish them from the landowning and merchant elite.[18] Nevertheless, it is impossible to draw clear boundaries either among social classes or between high and low cultures, especially in the preindustrial, urban context. Popular culture in Arequipa as it emerges from the historical record was dominated by artisans, small farmers, and female vendors and brewers, but poorer general laborers and domestic servants come and go from the stage. Moreover, priests, professionals, and shopkeepers could be found drinking in the taverns one day and attending parties in the homes of the elites the next.

It was in these overlapping areas that culture and politics intersected, particularly in a period in which the formal politics of parties and elections was only beginning to emerge. Jürgen Habermas identifies the ideal bourgeois public sphere as an intermediary arena between the private sphere and the state, where citizens (educated and propertied men) created public

Bolívar, the Sun of Justice and the Amerindian Virgen: Andean Conceptions of the *Patria* in Nineteenth-Century Potosí," *Journal of Latin American Studies* 25 (1993): 159–85.

17. For another case in which proto-nationalist identity was relatively inclusive, see Francisco A. Scarano, "The Jíbaro Masquerade and the Subaltern Politics of Creole Identity Formation in Puerto Rico, 1745–1823," *American Historical Review* 101, no. 5 (1996): 1398–1431.

18. Plebeians were the urban counterparts of *peasants*, a term that similarly covers a range of socioeconomic strata. I will also use the contemporary Latin American term of *popular classes*. While both terms are broad, they reflect the heterogeneity of a preindustrial society without an identifiable working class.

opinion through "rational" debate.[19] Yet political debates were often more raucous than "rational," and they were as likely to occur in taverns and on street corners as in salons and in the press.[20]

Groups officially excluded at various times from the sphere of politics (working-class men, ethnic minorities, and women) were often present in these more broadly defined public spaces. Public festivals and rituals were arenas where power was both constructed and contested. Social contacts established in neighborhoods and taverns could be mobilized in riots or in elections. Popular understandings of monarchy and republic, of rights and citizenship, drew from the language of honor. Such interpretations, in turn, shaped more elite political ideologies and literary representations of the White City.

Arequipa has been identified as the bastion of liberalism within nineteenth-century Peru, primarily because from its dominant classes emerged the country's strongest proponents of free trade.[21] Yet it is difficult to see how economic liberalism, which advanced the interests of the bourgeoisie, could serve as a platform for popular mobilization. Republicanism, with its emphasis upon virtuous citizens acting in public on behalf of the common good, has more appeal, and in many contexts has been used by groups initially excluded from the franchise to advocate broader participation in politics.[22]

In response to pressures from below, therefore, Arequipa's liberals emphasized the protection of civil liberties as well as economic freedoms. They recognized claims to honor, even as they defined virtue as self-discipline in an effort to both maintain a stable labor force and contain the conflict resulting from enlarged participation in politics. Finally, liberalism, like republicanism, defended the autonomy of the private sphere, where the patriarch should

---

19. Jürgen Habermas, *The Structural Transformation of the Public Sphere*, trans. Thomas Burger (Cambridge: MIT Press, 1989).

20. Mary P. Ryan, "Gender and Public Access: Women's Politics in Nineteenth-Century America," in Craig Calhoun, ed., *Habermas and the Public Sphere* (Cambridge: MIT Press, 1992), 264. See also in Calhoun: Seyla Benhabib, "Models of Public Space: Hannah Arendt, the Liberal Tradition, and Jürgen Habermas," 73–98; and Nancy Fraser, "Rethinking the Public Sphere: Models and Boundaries," 109–42.

21. Paul Gootenberg, "Beleaguered Liberals: The Failed First Generation of Free Traders in Peru," in Joseph L. Love and Nils Jacobsen, eds., *Guiding the Invisible Hand: Economic Liberalism and the State in Latin American History* (New York: Praeger, 1988), 63–97; and, also in *Guiding the Invisible Hand*, Nils Jacobsen, "Free Trade, Regional Elites, and the Internal Market in Southern Peru, 1895–1932," 145–75.

22. For a comparison, see Daniel T. Rodgers, "Republicanism: The Career of a Concept," *Journal of American History* 79, no. 1 (1992): 11–38.

govern free from state interference, a stance in which men of various classes had a common interest. Belaúnde would later describe the philosophy elaborated by the politicians of Arequipa and embraced by the people as liberalism "in the noble sense of the word, that is to say in the respect of individual rights, without utopias nor Jacobin radicalism."[23]

The "myth" of the White City, with its claims to economic and racial (but not gender) egalitarianism, was neither a simple reflection of reality nor an elite fabrication. Its power to motivate men to arms depended upon sufficient credibility, built up by the concession of limited rights during the early republican period.[24] It is important, therefore, to see hegemony as a dynamic historical process rather than just an outcome.[25] Even when a governing class remains in control, it is on terms that have been modified through a process of conflict and negotiation with men and women of other classes and ethnic groups. These conflictive origins would only later be erased in elite and literate expressions of the myth, such as the memoirs of Belaúnde.

Sufficient credibility does not necessarily reflect complete consensus. Both within and between societies, the degree of legitimacy accorded to dominant powers by subordinated groups will vary. Similarly, a person's behavior and self-presentation will differ from home to courtroom. Nevertheless, in most cases, and certainly in Arequipa, what James Scott has distinguished as public and private transcripts are interwoven.[26] "What hegemony constructs,"

23. Víctor Andrés Belaúnde, *Arequipa de mi infancia: Memorias, primera parte* (Lima: Imprenta Lumen, 1960), 131. For both an excellent overview of the historical literature on Latin American liberalism and a call to reexamine the inventiveness of nineteenth-century liberals, see the introduction to Vincent C. Peloso and Barbara A. Tenenbaum, eds., *Liberals, Politics, and Power: State Formation in Nineteenth-Century Latin America* (Athens, Ga.: University of Georgia Press, 1996).

24. For a compelling model of the power of myths, see Bruce Lincoln, *Discourse and the Construction of Society: Comparative Studies of Myth, Ritual, and Classification* (New York and Oxford: Oxford University Press, 1989). For a Latin American example, see Emília Viotta da Costa, *The Brazilian Empire: Myths and Histories* (Chicago: University of Chicago Press, 1985). Roland Barthes identifies myth as a "type of speech" with nebulous and timeless qualities that make it difficult to contradict, but he overemphasizes the degree of elite fabrication: Barthes, *Mythologies* (New York: Hill and Wang, 1972).

25. My approach to hegemony is influenced by Antonio Gramsci, *Selections from the Prison Notebooks*, ed. and trans. Quintin Hoare and Geoffrey Nowell Smith (New York: International Publishers, 1971); and Raymond Williams, *Marxism and Literature* (Oxford University Press, 1977), 112.

26. James C. Scott, *Domination and the Arts of Resistance: Hidden Transcripts* (New Haven: Yale University Press, 1990); see also Derek Sayer, "Everyday Forms of State Formation: Some Dissident Remarks on 'Hegemony,'" in Joseph and Nugent, *Everyday Forms of State Formation*, 374.

according to William Roseberry, "is not a shared ideology but a common material and meaningful framework for living through, talking about, and acting upon social orders characterized by domination."[27] It was the relatively flexible concept of honor that provided the common framework during the transition from colonial to republican rule in Arequipa.

Organization of the Book

It is difficult to break down subtle and gradual processes, such as the development of popular culture and the transformation of worldviews, into a series of "subperiods." Therefore, the book is organized thematically rather than chronologically. Chapters 1 through 5 will trace the patterns of change within successive "building blocks" of Arequipa's political culture: its development as a region, identities based on race and class, social networks and rituals at the level of community, efforts at social control, and the transformation in meanings of honor. The final two chapters focus primarily on the period after independence, exploring the limits of citizenship and the construction of Arequipa's republican political culture.

Chapter 1 sets the scene and provides an overview of the political history of the region between 1780 and 1854. Arequipa's transition from a royalist stronghold during the colonial period to a center of liberal revolts in the nineteenth century suggests that independence was an important watershed. Current interpretations, however, do not pay adequate attention to popular participation in the events of this period.

In order to explore the formation of a common identity that underlay cross-class and multi-ethnic alliances, Chapter 2 introduces the cast of characters. The mythical image of social harmony was clearly exaggerated, but an economy based upon agriculture, trade, and small-scale manufacturing provided opportunities that mitigated sharp class divisions. In line with scholarship that is increasingly asserting the fluid nature of racial identities, this chapter analyzes how even "whiteness" was socially constructed.

Chapter 3 analyzes the tension between conflict and cohesion within popular culture at the level of both neighborhood and citywide festivals. Because the city's inhabitants lived, worked, and socialized in close quarters,

27. William Roseberry, "Hegemony and the Language of Contention," in Joseph and Nugent, *Everyday Forms of State Formation*, 361.

the line between household and neighborhood, private and public, was easily crossed. Women were key participants, therefore, in networks of talk and surveillance, especially because they managed the taverns that served as primary gathering spaces for members of the popular and even middle classes. The dynamics of popular culture explored in this chapter are crucial to the later analysis of politics. The language and rituals of disputes within families and between neighbors served as a repertoire for political actions. In all three arenas, moreover—household, neighborhood, and the public sphere of politics—gender conflict provided a potential basis for alliance among men of different classes. Finally, growing elite concerns over disorder and immorality made cultural practices a key terrain of conflict and negotiation during the transition from colonialism to republicanism.

Chapter 4 examines shifting strategies of social control. During the late colonial period, it was the church, under the leadership of a reform-minded bishop, that expressed concern over the "excesses" of popular culture, particularly sexuality. The civil authorities did not share the bishop's belief that such behavior seriously threatened public order, and they frequently declined his requests for assistance in enforcing moral codes. In the early republic, however, the attitudes of civic officials changed markedly. Fearing social disorder after the collapse of colonial rule, they broadened definitions of criminal behavior and increased enforcement through the courts and a new police force. But a reliance upon force could not provide a firm basis for either regional political alliances or the nascent state, over the long term.

Chapter 5 argues that hegemonic ideals of honor, which had helped maintain social peace during the colonial period, had to be refashioned to achieve a new social pact during the early republican era. An analysis of libel suits and other criminal cases demonstrates that eighteenth-century plebeians were already challenging the exclusivity of elite claims to honor, but not the hierarchical basis of their apportionment. The republican discourse of civic virtue, however, was at odds with a system of inherent privileges. Plebeians and their lawyers, therefore, transformed the meaning of honor by linking reputation and patriarchal authority to constitutional rights. It was a defense strategy that increasingly proved successful against criminal prosecution.

Nevertheless, claims to citizenship encountered crucial limits, as explored in Chapter 6. On the one hand, republican judges responded to popular claims of honor based upon conduct by raising the standards of respectable behavior. On the other hand, groups defined as dependent—including slaves, indigenous servants, and all women—were not considered citizens regardless of their behavior. The sexual virtue of women, in particular, was targeted in judicial efforts to restore order. Significantly, the rights granted to some men were inextricably linked to the exclusion of women. If they met their public obligations to work hard and defend the state, men were allowed to govern their households with little interference from the authorities.

The insights gained from the analysis of popular culture and negotiations of citizenship within the courts are brought to a reinterpretation of the more formal politics of rebellion and elections in Chapter 7. Although free trade potentially would have had a negative impact upon many artisans and laborers, liberal politicians and caudillos sought popular support by advocating political and legal reforms as well. By the mid-nineteenth century, these revolts brought to national prominence a generation of liberals from Arequipa. The imprint of demands from below on the philosophies they articulated is evident not only in their advocacy of political as well as economic freedom, but also in their frequent and explicit linkage of citizenship to honor.

From this republican code of honor, the myth of the White City emerged. When Víctor Andrés Belaúnde recalled growing up in Arequipa at the beginning of the twentieth century, he highlighted the same elements that had become important in the wake of independence. For Belaúnde, Arequipa was a city of *hidalgos* (literally the lower Spanish nobility, though invoked in this context to mean men of honor) who were not divided by extreme racial or class differences. The city was also a confederation of families, where a woman maintained the moral sanctity of the home while the patriarch represented the household within the public sphere. Finally, according to Belaúnde, these ideals of egalitarian honor, racial harmony, and familial respectability combined to create the civic spirit that motivated Arequipeños to arms throughout the nineteenth century.[28]

This myth suggests the crucial role of the popular classes of Arequipa in the politics of the early republic, but its appeal to innate characteristics makes it easy to dismiss. Exposing its roots in conflicts and negotiations over the terms of citizenship not only provides a more convincing explanation of Arequipa's role in Peruvian history but also challenges regional claims to a uniquely democratic character. Honor and justice, subject to a variety of interpretations, were central to colonial governance across Spanish America. It is only logical to expect, therefore, that similar struggles over changing

28. Belaúnde, *Arequipa de mi infancia*.

political and legal rights took place on streets and in courtrooms throughout the emerging nations after independence. Although the resulting boundaries of citizenship and dominant myths would vary according to particular contexts, the White City may prove less a unique case than a model for understanding the transformation from subject to citizen.

1

From Loyal City
to Pueblo Caudillo

On the evening of January 13, 1780, a crowd of about six hundred people gathered outside the new customs house (*aduana*) in the center of Arequipa. Shouting epithets against its administrator, Juan Bautista Pando, they expressed their opposition to an increase in the sales tax (*alcabala*) from 4 to 6 percent. The protestors also hurled stones and mud at the building, but they withdrew after making their point. The demonstration did have the desired effect on the *corregidor* (royal governor) Baltasar Sematnat, who, together with the members of the city council, appealed to Pando in the interest of social peace to slow down the implementation of the new tax. Pando, however, was part of a new breed of tough Spanish bureaucrats, and he vowed to continue carrying out his duties according to the letter of the law.

Given the failure of local authorities to address their grievances, Arequipeños took matters into their own hands. Those who gathered the following night broke into the aduana, sending Pando and his retinue into flight. Although the crowd was ready for action, its raid was relatively orderly. They burned the tax records and stole more than two thousand pesos, but they left the merchandise, which was being held pending the payment of duties, untouched. This escalation brought a more decisive response from the corregidor. Sematnat officially pronounced the aduana closed and ordered Pando to leave the city. But it was too late. The wrath of the crowd quickly spread to new targets. On the night of January 15, the corregidor's house was attacked and the store of his close associate was looted. The mob also broke into the jail and freed the prisoners. The next day brought reports that the revolt had spread to the Indian quarter of Miraflores.

Only with this specter of an Indian uprising was Sematnat finally able to muster the militia for a counterattack. And attack they did. Soldiers on horseback charged into Miraflores, setting fire to the homes, killing several Indians, and sending the rest into hiding in the hills. Six Indians and a mestizo were captured, quickly convicted as the instigators, and hung. This repression put an end to open rebellion in the city, but the viceroy remained suspicious about the loyalty even of Arequipa's authorities. The corregidor and the council refused to allow Pando's return and made veiled threats that the entrance of royal troops would only provoke more unrest.

When troops finally did arrive in April, however, they met no opposition. The commander launched an investigation, but it was cut short by the eruption of a much larger rebellion in the highlands under the Indian leader Túpac Amaru. This new threat to Spanish rule gave Arequipeños an opportunity to redeem themselves and prove their loyalty; the city's notable citizens mobilized the populace, which had so recently rioted, and financed an expedition against the followers of Túpac Amaru.[1]

The revolt of 1780 was a dramatic opening to a period of change in Arequipa. Although it came as a surprise, given the city's title of "very noble

1. This account of the 1780 rebellion is drawn from several studies: Guillermo Galdos Rodríguez, *La rebelión de los pasquines* (Arequipa: Editorial Universitaria, 1967); John Frederick Wibel, "The Evolution of a Regional Community Within Spanish Empire and Peruvian Nation: Arequipa, 1780–1845" (Ph.D. diss., Stanford University, 1975), 17–52; Eusebio Quiroz Paz Soldán, "La rebelión de 1780 en Arequipa: Reflexiones para una interpretación," in Luis Durand Flórez, ed., *La revolución de los Túpac Amaru: Antología* (Lima: Comisión Nacional del Bicentenario de la Rebelión Emancipadora de Túpac Amaru, 1981), 342–48; Kendall W. Brown, *Bourbons and Brandy: Imperial Reform in Eighteenth-Century Arequipa* (Albuquerque: University of New Mexico Press, 1986), 197–213; and David Cahill, "Taxonomy of a Colonial 'Riot': The Arequipa Disturbances of 1780," in John R. Fisher, Allan J. Kuethe, and Anthony McFarlane, eds., *Reform and Insurrection in Bourbon New Granada and Peru* (Baton Rouge: Louisiana State University Press, 1990), 255–91. Documents related to the revolt are in Francisco A. Loayza, *Preliminares del incendio: documentos del año de 1776 a 1780* (Lima: Librería e Imprenta D. Miranda, 1947); and Melchor de Paz y Guini, *Guerra separatista: Rebeliones de indios en Sur America*, ed. Luis Antonio Eguiguren, vol. 1 (Lima: Imprenta Torres Aguirre, 1952), 85–166.

and very loyal," there had been warnings in the preceding months. As Pando traveled toward Arequipa late in 1779, his meticulous investigations of local crop production raised concern among the population. The fears of farmers in the Vítor and Tambo valleys were realized when he rejected their claim that payment of property tax exempted them from sales tax on their products. To add insult to injury, the administrator also repudiated the *hacendados'* credit, and thus their honor, holding their merchandise until the duties were paid in full.

There were reports that he similarly disregarded the longstanding privilege enjoyed by Indians to freely sell their crops and handicrafts, and that he charged taxes on basic foodstuffs. As rumors of these "abuses" spread, threatening lampoons began to appear throughout the city, following an honored formula of colonial protest. The anonymous authors proclaimed their loyalty to the king and their willingness to pay the old tax, but they threatened an uprising against his "unfaithful" servants at the aduana.[2]

The increase in the alcabala may have been the proverbial last straw (or, as Pando later put it, the fistful of wheat that broke the mule's back),[3] but it was not the only abuse lampooned in the broadsides. Arequipeños also expressed grievances against the corregidor. Sematnat, like many of his colleagues throughout Peru, carried out forced sales (*repartos*) of mules at inflated prices. At the end of 1779, he was also making preparations for a new census, not only of Indians, but also of persons of mixed race. Such censuses generally preceded taxation, and rumors flew that tribute would be extended to mulattoes and mestizos.

That a threat of extended taxation would cause alarm in the "White" City suggests that many "Spaniards" were unsure of their status. Pando not only asserted that the majority of the plebe was mestizo, but implied that many of Arequipa's notable citizens also carried that "stain." The rebellion had been organized, he charged, by "those who believed that the fallacies of their nobility would be discovered with the inspection of marriage and baptism books."[4] Sematnat continued to blame Pando for inciting the unrest, but he prudently took refuge in a monastery when a *pasquinade* warned him: "watch out for your head."[5]

The targets of the lampoons and the crowd revealed grievances against the

2. Loayza, *Preliminares del incendio*, 40–59.
3. Paz y Guini, *Guerra separatista*, 99.
4. Ibid., 108.
5. Loayza, *Preliminares del incendio*, 43.

abuses of authorities, both old (the corregidor and his repartos) and new (the customs administrator and his higher tariffs). Although Arequipa's leaders blamed the revolt on unruly plebeians and Indians,[6] both contemporaries and historians concurred that prominent creoles were involved. The demands of the city council, such as the exemption for products from Tambo and Vítor, reflected the interests of the dominant class. Even Sematnat came under suspicion for not acting immediately to restore order when the threatening pasquinades first appeared. Nevertheless, given the greater threat posed by Túpac Amaru, royal officials chose not to press charges, and the loyalty of Arequipa in the following years earned it the new title of "most faithful" (*fidelísima*).[7]

The 1780 revolt serves as an early sign of Arequipa's potential for forming broad alliances, which cut across lines of class and race, to assert regional demands. The alarm over a census of persons of mixed race further implies that such alliances rested upon a tacit acceptance of light mestizos and mulattoes into the Spanish group. The uprising also marked Arequipa's arrival at a crossroads. Efforts by the Spanish crown to centralize its control over the colonies and their income posed a potential threat to the prosperous and relatively autonomous economy, based on agriculture and trade. On the other hand, reforms aimed at revitalizing the local economy and political institutions offered opportunities for Arequipa's advancement. Before examining the path that Arequipeños followed in the wake of the 1780 revolt, however, let us turn briefly to the origins and development of this "most loyal" city.

The Development of the White City and Its Region

Before the arrival of the Spaniards, southwestern Peru was less densely populated than other regions, but agriculturalists of various ethnic groups

6. For the blaming of plebeians and Indians by the cabildo and corregidor, see AMA, LCED Num. 6 (Aug. 22, 1782), "Representación del Síndico Procurador General," folios 192–95; and LCED 9, report dated Jan. 8, 1784, from Corregidor Sematnat, praising the efforts of Arequipa's militia against Túpac Amaru. For similar excuses by the cathedral chapter, see "Informe que hace este Dean y Cabildo al Sor. Virrey" (Feb. 18, 1780), in BNP doc. C4329, "Cabildo Eclesiástico de Arequipa."

7. Víctor M. Barriga, ed., *Arequipa y sus blasones* (Arequipa: Editorial La Colmena, 1940), 122–24.

lived and farmed along the river valleys.[8] In the late 1530s, Spanish conquerors Diego de Almagro and Francisco Pizarro passed through the Chili River valley; the latter sent his followers back to establish a town at the mouth of the Majes River from which they could gain control of the region. The Villa of Camaná, however, was hot and infested with mosquitos, and the Indian subjects brought down from the highlands began to die. The settlers petitioned to move their town, and on August 15, 1540, Pizarro's lieutenant Garcí Manuel de Carvajal officially founded Arequipa. During the decade of civil wars that followed, the Arequipeños remained loyal to the crown, one of the actions that later earned them their first title.[9]

The choice of a site for the new town would prove a wise one. About eighty miles from the ocean and at an altitude of seven thousand feet, Arequipa is situated beyond the desert plains of the coast and at the entrance to the rugged cordillera (see Maps 1.1 and 1.2). The city was founded at the base of an impressive conical volcano; on each side of "Misti" tower two others, Chachani and Pichupichu. The valley's climate is mild, with temperatures that barely fluctuate throughout the year. The city is on the edge of one of the driest deserts in the world, and it receives only light rainfall from January to March. Nevertheless, long before Carvajal and his band marched in from Camaná, the native inhabitants had turned the valley into an oasis through elaborate systems of irrigation and terracing.

Although Pizarro had initially chosen the Camaná site for its access to the ocean, Arequipa was well situated to become a crossroads of the south. All travel in the Andes was long and difficult, but in relative terms Arequipa was conveniently tied into several major trade routes. It was a two-day journey across the desert to various ports, where ships came and went from Lima. Heading into the sierra, it took six days to travel to Puno and ten to arrive in Cuzco.[10] Finally, it was an easy journey south to the valley of Moquegua, from where one took the roads toward La Paz and Potosí. Arequipa, therefore, was incorporated into both the trade routes of the southern Andes, with their pole at Potosí, and the larger imperial system oriented toward

8. See Franklin Pease G. Y., ed., *Collaguas I* (Lima: Pontificia Universidad Católica del Perú, 1977); Noble David Cook, *The People of the Colca Valley: A Population Study* (Boulder: Westview Press, 1982); and Guillermo Galdos Rodríguez, *Comunidades prehispánicas de Arequipa* (Arequipa: Fundación M. J. Bustamante de La Fuente, 1987).

9. See Keith A. Davies, *Landowners in Colonial Peru* (Austin: University of Texas Press, 1984), 7–27.

10. Alberto Flores Galindo, *Arequipa y el sur andino, siglos XVIII–XX* (Lima: Editorial Horizante, 1977), 79.

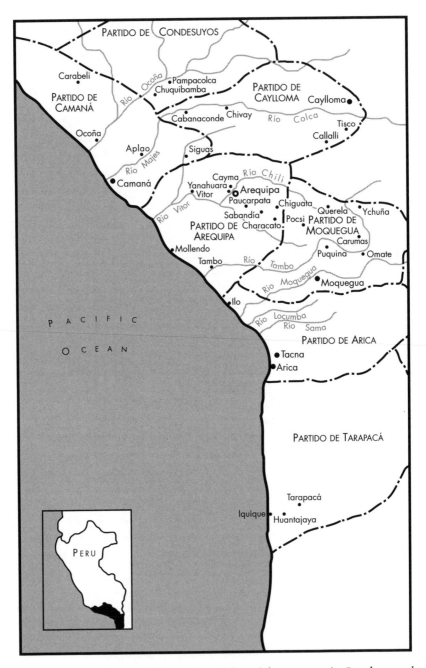

Map 1.1. The intendancy of Arequipa. Adapted from a map in *Bourbons and Brandy* by Kendall Brown, Copyright 1986. By permission of the University of New Mexico Press, 1998.

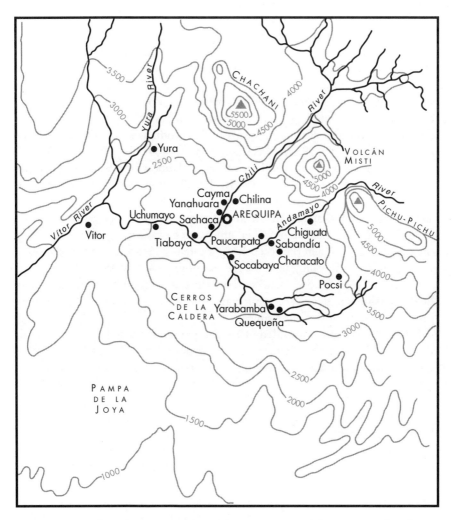

Map 1.2. The valley of Arequipa. Adapted from a map in *Landowners in Colonial Peru* by Keith A. Davies, Copyright 1984. By permission of the University of Texas Press, 1998.

Lima and, ultimately, Spain. By 1784, Arequipa was also the capital of an administrative unit that stretched from the Acari River in the north to the Loa River in what is today part of Chile.

Pizarro had assigned grants of Indians (*encomiendas*) to his followers, but disease and hard labor quickly took their toll on an already sparse native population. Within a quarter century tributes had declined dramatically, and the *encomenderos* began to use their remaining Indians as laborers in agricultural ventures. As the mining center of Potosí grew, Arequipeños recognized its potential as a market for wine and established vineyards along the coastal river valleys near Arequipa.[11] The production of wine and brandy remained the basis of the local economy throughout the colonial period.[12]

As the city grew and food prices rose, landowners also realized the potential of the local market for foodstuffs. The countryside around the city was fertile and produced impressive yields of wheat, corn, potatoes, and alfalfa. By the mid-sixteenth century, Spanish landowners eager to profit from the grain trade had encroached upon much of the indigenous land along the Chili River.[13] When the recently appointed governor Antonio Alvarez y Jiménez toured the valley in 1785, he was impressed that farmers never had to leave their plots fallow: "And so there exists a continuous springtime in its fields, causing wonder to see some mature crops, others in flower and others just budding out at the same time."[14]

When Arequipa was founded in 1540, however, it existed as a city only in the imagination of the Spanish settlers. About fifty of them gathered to witness the formal act at which Carvajal "put a cross on the site that was assigned for the Church, and likewise he put the pillory in the plaza . . . and it was proclaimed that the inhabitants [*vecinos*] and other persons who have lots in this said beautiful town should populate, fence in and build their houses upon them."[15]

The lots were distributed in the grid pattern of sixteen square blocks imposed by the Spaniards throughout the Americas (see Map 1.3). Within a year, the king optimistically elevated Arequipa from the status of town (*villa*) to that of city, but it would be several decades before the first churches and administrative buildings rose up along the Chili River. In 1582, the first of

11. Davies, *Landowners in Colonial Peru*, 12–63.
12. Brown, *Bourbons and Brandy*, 40–50.
13. Davies, *Landowners in Colonial Peru*, 125–30.
14. Víctor M. Barriga, *Memorias para la historia de Arequipa*, vol. 1 (Arequipa: Editorial La Colmena, 1941), 58.
15. Barriga, *Arequipa y sus blasones*, 11.

several devastating earthquakes flattened the city. Nevertheless, the profits from the growing wine industry funded its reconstruction, and by 1609, Arequipa was designated the seat of an extensive new bishopric. The new and sturdier buildings of *sillar* (a white volcanic stone) were decorated in the seventeenth century with the baroque carvings of saints amid abundant flora and fauna that would become a trademark of the mestizo style of architecture.[16]

The plaza was the religious, political, and commercial center of the city. Along the north side stretched the cathedral; it was lighter and more open than the imposing temple constructed in Cuzco, an indication, perhaps, of an easier conquest. Across from it stood the government offices: the *cabildo* (town hall), the treasury, the notary offices, and the jail. In the mid-eighteenth century, a fountain was constructed in the center of the plaza; on top perched a bronze statue of a man sounding a trumpet, dubbed Tuturutú by the townspeople. Around it the market sellers gathered every morning to hawk their wares. Formal shops could be found in the galleries (*portales*) along the west and east sides, from where they continued around the corner and up the aptly named Mercaderes ("merchants") Street. Heading west from the cabildo, more shops lined the three blocks down to the river. After many delays and several earthquakes, a stone bridge was finally completed around 1610 and served as the main entry to the city through the nineteenth century. An inn for visitors and traders was located conveniently by the bridge, but it cannot have been the most pleasant place to stay; on either side artisans took advantage of the river to set up slaughterhouses and tanneries. The Chili also powered several mills and fed irrigation canals that not only watered the surrounding farmland but ran through the streets of the city.

Because of the danger of earthquakes, most houses were built on a single level. Church towers, therefore, dominated the urban landscape. The temples served as landmarks, giving their names to the streets and quarters, and their bells marked the time of day for the townspeople living under their shadows. The Dominicans were the first order to evangelize in Arequipa, and they built their church on the third block east of the cabildo. Around the corner, the city established a hospital that was turned over to the order of San Juan de Dios in the early seventeenth century.

The Mercedarians were the second order to arrive in Arequipa, and they built their church and monastery on the third block south of the cabildo. The

---

16. See Luis Enrique Tord, *Arequipa artística y monumental* (Lima: Banco del Sur del Perú, 1987).

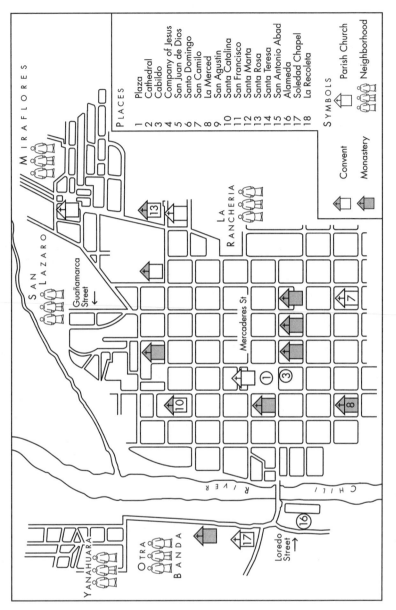

Map 1.3. The city of Arequipa

street of "La Merced" soon boasted some of the finest houses in the city as well. The Jesuits did not arrive until 1573, but they were bequeathed a prime location on the corner of the plaza for their Company of Jesus. When the order was expelled from the colonies almost two hundred years later, the Compañía would house both orphans and soldiers. Continuing around to the northwest quarter, one came upon the monastery of San Agustín, built just one block from the cathedral in the direction of the river. The Agustines held onto their property longer than did the Jesuits, but at independence their cloisters were seized by the new government to serve as an academy; later, the university of Arequipa would occupy that monastery and take its name.

On the third block north of the cathedral, Arequipa's first convent was founded in 1579. Santa Catalina came to occupy two full blocks, and its thick walls of sillar sheltered a miniature cloistered city. Beyond the courtyards, with their requisite cells for novitiates and nuns, the sisters strolled through a labyrinth of alleyways that led to private apartments, each equipped with its own kitchen and servants' quarters. Beyond Santa Catalina was another labyrinthine neighborhood, nestled between the river and a seasonal gully (*lloclla*). San Lázaro had been settled before the arrival of the Spaniards, and Indians continued to reside in its steep, twisting streets throughout the colonial period.

Parallel to the street of Santa Catalina, on the other side of the cathedral, were three blocks that ended at the church of San Francisco. Between the plaza and the Franciscan monastery, one passed the seminary of San Jerónimo, the infamous aduana, and several imposing mansions. After independence, the prefecture would also be established along this street. Turning right at the second corner and continuing four blocks, one arrived at the edge of the original city.

It was here that the church erected the Indian parish of Santa Marta, which initially served not only the natives residing in the city but also the Indian communities to the east. Santa Marta would not remain an exclusively indigenous neighborhood, however, as in the eighteenth century it was joined by the Episcopal Palace and the convents of Santa Teresa and Santa Rosa. Ironically, not far from this cluster of religious institutions was the street of Guañamarca, known for its taverns and exuberant street celebrations during Carnival.[17]

17. For descriptions and brief histories of the various monasteries and churches, see Tord, *Arequipa artística y monumental*, 45–133. I have adapted a map provided by Betford Betalleluz

By the middle of the eighteenth century, the city had begun to grow beyond its initial grid. In honor of the founding of Santa Rosa in 1752, cleric Ventura Travada y Córdova wrote a brief history of Arequipa in which he noted that "one sees the population expanding so much, largely from migrants who come attracted by the vitality and commerce to be found in the city, that soon the edge will withdraw even more to give more extension to the city."[18] The map commissioned by Alvarez y Jiménez in 1784 reflects this haphazard growth, with its drawings of houses spilling out from the neat blocks of the central city.[19]

The main lines of growth were east and west. When Alvarez y Jiménez made his official tour of Santa Marta, the church that had once marked the edge of the city was then part of its center.[20] The Indian neighborhood had extended north and east onto the Pampa of Miraflores, where the parish erected another chapel dedicated to San Antonio Abad. Directly east of the plaza, a new neighborhood was growing up along the extension of Mercaderes Street known as La Ranchería, its name implying that smaller shacks (*ranchos*) outnumbered stone houses. There was less growth to the south, but by 1813 the order of San Camilo had constructed a new church several blocks beyond Santo Domingo.

In the other direction, a neighborhood had extended from the bridge to the other side of the river and was, therefore, named "la otra banda." Houses clustered around the chapel of La Soledad and the Beaterio, a house of lay sisters established for the Indian women who could not enter the convents. Turning left, one passed a couple blocks of homes before entering the countryside. As on Guañamarca, many of the buildings along this "Callejón de Loredo" housed taverns and gambling parlors. In an effort "to prevent the idleness and mischief which carries the commoners away without licit diversions," Alvarez y Jiménez ordered the construction of a promenade, or *alameda*, along the Chili.[21] Not far upstream, and standing in austere contrast to the taverns of Loredo Street, was a second Franciscan monastery built as a retreat and, therefore, named La Recoleta. Continuing along the same road, which, as Alvarez y Jiménez noted, was entirely lined with

---

according to the 1784 map found in Tord, illustration between pages 26 and 27, and a later map from Mariano Felipe Paz Soldán, *Atlas geográfico del Perú* (Paris: Fermin Didot, 1865), xxxi.

18. Ventura Travada y Córdova, *El suelo de Arequipa convertido en cielo* (1752; reprint, Arequipa: Primer Festival del Libro Arequipeño, 1958), 83.

19. Tord, *Arequipa artística y monumental*, 26–27.

20. Barriga, *Memorias para la historia de Arequipa*, vol. 1, 223.

21. Ibid., 64.

houses, one soon arrived at the Indian villages of Yanahuara and Cayma, by then home to many Spaniards, mestizos, and blacks as well.[22] The populated road to the villages on the west bank of the river reveals the difficulty of drawing a strict boundary between the urban and rural areas. Many of those who owned farms in the surrounding countryside maintained their primary residence in the city, where they could enjoy greater comforts and prestige. Others who did live in the villages insisted that they were merely residents there and identified themselves as citizens (vecinos) of Arequipa. Even the more humble villagers who could never claim to be vecinos frequently went to the city, whether for business—to sell their crops or firewood—or pleasure—to visit a tavern or attend a festival.

Likewise, the townspeople enjoyed taking excursions to the countryside, where they might go for a dip in the mineral baths at Paucarpata, Tingo, or Yura.[23] Sabandía was renowned for its pure water, while Cayma boasted of fine views, fresh air, and a miraculous virgin.[24] This two-way traffic was busy enough that contemporaries referred to the city and its "suburbs" in the valley as one geographical unit.

When viceroy Francisco Gil de Taboada ordered a count of his subjects in the 1790s, the city's population was calculated at 23,551; if the surrounding villages were included, that figure reached 37,431.[25] Unfortunately there were no reliable censuses again until 1876, but it is likely that the city's population continued to grow during those years.[26] The *Guia de forasteros* for 1846 gives a figure of 38,543 for Arequipa, extrapolating from an 1827 census.[27] Table 1.1 provides estimates of Arequipa's population between 1792 and 1862, drawn from a variety of sources.

This tour of a growing city brings us back to the fateful year of 1780. Most studies of Peru either end or begin with independence from Spain.[28] Only by

22. Ibid., 247.

23. José María Blanco, "Diario del viaje del Presidente Orbegoso al sur del Perú" (unpublished manuscript in the private library of Felix Denegri Luna, Lima), 281–85, 294.

24. Barriga, *Memorias para la historia de Arequipa*, vol. 1, 188, 274, 284.

25. Günter Vollmer, *Bevölkerungspolitik und Bevölkerunsstruktur im Vizekönigreich Peru zu Ende der Kolonialzeit, 1741–1821* (Bad Homburg: Gehlen, 1967), 253.

26. Based upon excerpts of this "lost" 1827 census, Paul Gootenberg calculated annual population increases in Peru of between 0.6 and 1.3. Although his data does not include Arequipa, there is no reason to believe its population growth differed significantly from that of the rest of Peru. See Paul Gootenberg, "Population and Ethnicity in Early Republican Peru: Some Revisions," *Latin American Research Review* 26, no. 3 (1991), 109–57.

27. Eduardo Carrasco, *Calendario y guía de forasteros de la república peruana para el año de 1847* (Lima: Imprenta de Instrucción Primaria, 1846), 19.

28. A notable exception for Arequipa is Wibel, "The Evolution of a Regional Community."

Table 1.1. Population estimates for Arequipa

Year	Source	City	Valley
1792	1	23,551	37,261
1804	2	28,483	44,234
1824	3	30,000	—
1827	4	38,543	—
1845	5	43,583	—
1862	6	26,472	52,820

SOURCES:

1. Günter Vollmer, *Bevölkerungspolitik und Bevölkerunsstruktur im Vizekönigreich Peru zu Ende der Kolonialzeit 1741–1821* (Bad Homburg: Gehlen, 1967), 253.

2. Francisco Xavier Echevarría y Morales, "Memoria de la Santa Iglesia de Arequipa" (1804), in Víctor M. Barriga, *Memorias para la historia de Arequipa*, vol. 4 (Arequipa: Imprenta Portugal, 1950), 78. Echevarría was a priest and based his figures on reports from the various parishes.

3. Heinrich Witt, *Diario y observaciones sobre el Perú* (Lima: COFIDE, 1987), 13.

4. Eduardo Carrasco, *Calendario y guía de forasteros de la república peruana para el año de 1847* (Lima: Imprenta de Instrucción Primaria, 1846), 19.

5. An extrapolation from the 1827 figure in *ibid.*

6. From the 1862 census in Fernando A. Ponce, "Social Structure of Arequipa, 1840–1879" (Ph.D. diss., University of Texas–Austin, 1980), 81.

looking at the entire period between 1780 and 1854, however, do significant transformations in political culture become apparent against the backdrop of other continuities. Efforts at political consolidation and fiscal rationalization begun by the Spanish empire, for example, were carried on by the republican state. Throughout the period, Arequipeños resisted this centralization and tried to construct their own sphere of influence in the southern Andes. During the late colonial period, elites in Arequipa tried to gain as much autonomy as possible within the existing political system and, therefore, retained their reputation for loyalty to the crown. After independence, however, the broad alliance evident in the 1780 rebellion reemerged in a series of regional revolts.

Elites in Arequipa had specific economic demands; resistance to colonial taxation became the advocation of free trade liberalism during the republican period. Artisans, small farmers, and traders followed their leaders into battle, but popular participation in these movements either has been ignored or taken for granted by historians. Caudillos in Arequipa were not so careless. As emerging ideologies of republicanism and liberalism created new spaces for popular pressure on the state, they praised the hardworking inhabitants of their region and optimistically believed they could be productive citizens.

We cannot understand the region's political culture, therefore, without examining the contribution of the popular classes. But before getting ahead of the story, let us review the significant events of the period from 1780 to 1854.

Colonial Reforms and Rebellions

The Bourbon monarchs, facing threats to their empire from other European powers in the mid-eighteenth century, initiated a process of reforms aimed at tightening their political and economic control first over Spain and then over its colonies. In 1776, the crown removed from Peru the territory that today corresponds to Argentina and Bolivia, in order to create the new viceroyalty of Río de la Plata. A year later, Antonio de Areche was sent to inspect the diminished viceroyalty of Peru and make recommendations for ending the corruption of local officials and increasing imperial revenue. Just as Areche began to investigate charges against the corregidors, such as their abuse of the repartos and their collusion with local rather than imperial interests, rebellions exploded in the highlands and lent credence to his findings.

In 1784, the crown's response was to introduce in Peru a new administrative system that had been copied from France and previously implemented in Spain and other viceroyalties. The fifty-nine *corregimientos* were replaced by eight *intendencias*, divided primarily along the boundaries of the bishoprics. The intendants wielded considerable military, judicial, and financial power and were represented at the local level (in provinces called *partidos*) by new subdelegates, who, in theory, would be directly accountable for their activities. The intendancy of Arequipa stretched down into what is today northern Chile, including the provinces of Camaná, Condesuyos, Caylloma, Arequipa, Moquegua, Arica, and Tarapacá.[29]

The first intendant of Arequipa, José Menéndez Escalada, served only a year before being transferred to Huamanga. Therefore, it was Antonio Alvarez y Jiménez, arriving in 1785, who oversaw the implementation of the

29. On the intendancy system, see John R. Fisher, *Government and Society in Colonial Peru: The Intendant System, 1784–1814* (London: Athlone Press, 1970); and Eusebio Quiroz Paz Soldán, "La intendencia de Arequipa: Organización y problemas económicas," *Histórica* 8, no. 2 (1984), 151–75.

new system. Alvarez was the model of what an intendant should be. He quickly embarked on an inspection of his territory that would eventually take him to even remote districts.[30] In each village he visited, the new governor meticulously questioned civil and religious authorities about every aspect of the local economy, administration of justice, parish matters, and the state of the militia.

Alvarez was particularly concerned with ending abuses against the indigenous population, while simultaneously taking measures to eradicate native languages and integrate Indians into the market economy. If anything, Alvarez was overzealous in his reforms. His requests for more funds to carry out his thorough inspection and map the territory were repeatedly denied, and he was ordered not to pursue reports that Spanish landowners had usurped royal (and, therefore, Indian) properties. Even the Council of Indies became exasperated with his constant reports and told him that in the future, he should communicate only with the viceroy.[31] Alvarez's successor, Bartolomé María de Salamanca (1796–1811), carried on many of his projects, but on a more modest scale.[32]

The economic reforms of the Bourbons had begun before the introduction of the intendancy system. In 1777, a new tax of 12.5 percent was levied on distilled liquors, the primary product of Arequipa. And the increase in the sales tax three years later provoked the revolt against the new customs house. The declaration in 1778 of a "free trade" policy, which allowed direct trade between any ports within the empire, was a more benign measure, but most of its benefits went to the Spanish merchants who emigrated to Arequipa. In the wake of the 1780 protest, Arequipeños accepted the inevitability of the new taxes, but they continued to subvert them clandestinely through evasion and contraband.[33] Nevertheless, the overall record of Alvarez and Salamanca in fiscal matters was good; revenues from all sources rose steadily until 1800 and then held fairly stable, despite the turbulence of the years preceding independence.[34]

---

30. His detailed account of this *visita* is published in Barriga, *Memorias para la historia de Arequipa*, vols. 1, 2.

31. Fisher, *Government and Society*, 162–63.

32. For Salamanca's account of his term, see John R. Fisher, ed., *Arequipa 1796–1811: La relación del gobierno del intendente Salamanca* (Lima: Seminario de Historia Rural Andina, 1968).

33. Wibel, "The Evolution of a Regional Community," 209–17.

34. See John J. Tepaske and Herbert S. Klein, eds., *The Royal Treasuries of the Spanish Empire in America*, vol. 1, *Peru* (Durham: Duke University Press, 1982), 39–63; Barriga, *Memorias para la historia de Arequipa*, vol. 1, 84–117; and Fisher, *Arequipa 1796–1811*, 52–81.

If the intendants of Arequipa improved tax collection, they were markedly less successful at promoting real economic expansion in the region. The Bourbon reforms focused primarily on mining and commerce, the sources of wealth for the empire as a whole, whereas the economy of Arequipa was based upon agriculture. Although the production of wines and brandies expanded from 1700 to 1775, once it had saturated an inelastic market, prices began to fall.[35] The new taxes cut further into profit margins and provoked frequent complaints from the vineyard owners.[36]

In spite of the problems in viticulture, landowners did little to diversify the economy. During his inspection, Alvarez dutifully carried out his instructions to encourage the cultivation of hemp and flax, but he noted, in most cases, that the climate was better suited to other crops. He also reported that the only way to increase agricultural production would be to find new sources of water, not an easy task in the desert.[37] In addition to the lack of irrigation, landowners complained of a labor shortage.[38] In spite of these problems, Arequipa remained, in relative terms, one of the most productive regions in Peru.[39]

Influenced by the European Enlightenment, the intendants also promoted public works and education. In addition to the construction of the alameda, Alvarez drew up plans for the reconstruction of the government offices damaged in the 1784 earthquake, as well as for the establishment of a powder magazine outside of the city, where it would not pose a danger to the inhabitants.[40] In the interest of improving public health, Alvarez prohibited the burial of cadavers within churches and broke ground for a new cemetery in the Pampa of Miraflores.[41] His first priority, however, was in the field of education; in each village he ordered the construction of a small school and

35. Brown, *Bourbons and Brandy*, 52, 103, 192.

36. For example, see AMA, LAC Num. 25, minutes from meeting of Cabildo Abierto on Oct. 16, 1789, to request the king for a reduction in taxes; AMA, LEXP, Num. 1, letter dated Oct. 29, 1803, from the cabildo to the viceroy; and Matheo de Cossío, "Razón circunstanciada que Don Matheo Cossío diputado del comercio de Arequipa produce al Real Tribunal del Consulado de Lima con relación a los ramos de industria de aquella provincia (1804)," in *Revista del Archivo Nacional* 28 (1964): 228–30.

37. Barriga, *Memorias para la historia de Arequipa*, vol. 1, 62.

38. Cossío, "Razón circunstanciada," 220–21.

39. Arequipa had the highest per capita production in Peru, almost double the average. Brown, *Bourbons and Brandy*, 215.

40. Barriga, *Memorias para la historia de Arequipa*, vol. 1, 64–67. For discussions of these projects in the cabildo meetings, see AMA, LAC 25 (Nov. 25, 1789; Feb. 14, 1791).

41. Barriga, *Memorias para la historia de Arequipa*, vol. 1, 64–74. At the end of his term, he asked the cabildo to continue work on the cemetery. AMA, LEXP 2, letter dated Jan. 30, 1796.

appointed a teacher to instruct the Indians, free of charge. In this way, he hoped to eradicate the "ancient and backwards customs" of the native population.[42]

As in other areas of administration, Salamanca was less ambitious but, ultimately, more successful. He actually completed the public-works projects initiated by Alvarez, although on a smaller scale. Arguing that many monasteries offered instruction, Salamanca stopped paying a Latin teacher for the inhabitants of Arequipa. He was more active than Alvarez, however, in the field of public health. In addition to completing the rural cemetery, Salamanca built additions to the hospital, distributed smallpox vaccines, and ordered periodic exterminations of dogs to prevent outbreaks of rabies.[43]

To assist in these public programs, the intendants revitalized the cabildo of Arequipa and improved the collection of municipal funds. Although some of the reforms ran into popular resistance, the council members proved to be enthusiastic allies in the diffusion of enlightened ideas. They and other educated elites presented lengthy reports, laced with references to European studies, on issues such as the proper location of the new cemetery, the prevention of epidemics, and measures to be taken during bad harvests.[44] After noting bookkeeping problems and a decline in conditions at the hospital, they seized the books and appointed an administrator to manage the institution. These measures provoked a lawsuit from the order of San Juan de Dios.[45]

The intendants' revitalization of Arequipa's cabildo would turn out to be a double-edged sword. The council members praised the efforts of Alvarez, especially his promotion of public works, but signs of tension began to surface in 1790.[46] Three members accused the intendant of dispossessing the

42. Barriga, *Memorias para la historia de Arequipa*, vol. 1, 63; and *passim*.

43. Fisher, *Arequipa 1796–1811*, 12, 14, 21, 43–46; BNP doc. D11684 (1806), "Sobre propagación del beneficio de la Bacuna"; and minutes of cabildo meetings between 1804 and 1812 in AMA, LAC 26.

44. AMA, LEXP 2, report dated March 29, 1794, from Juan de Dios López y Castillo, on the most appropriate site for the cemetery; LEXP 2, minutes from a meeting called by Intendant Alvarez for Jan. 12, 1796, to propose measures to prevent the outbreak of epidemics; and AGN, Superior Gobierno, Leg. 31, Cuad. 963 (1804), "Expediente . . . con motivo de la carestia del Trigo."

45. See AMA, LCED 6, report dated April 14, 1790, regarding irregularities in the hospital accounts; AMA, LAC 26 (April 27, 1804); and AGN, Real Audiencia: Causas Civiles, Leg. 132, Cuad. 1349 (1815), "Autos seguidos por el Convento Hospitalario de San Juan de Dios contra el Cabildo."

46. For the council's praise of Alvarez, see letter dated Dec. 19, 1795, from the cabildo to the intendant. In BNP doc. C4288 (1785), "Papeles sobre Alvarez y Jiménez."

cabildo of the right to fill municipal posts, even though these positions had been created by Alvarez.[47] In addition, local elites began to make requests that, even with the support of the intendant, were rejected by Madrid. When a new high court (*real audiencia*) was established in Cuzco in 1787, for example, the cabildo of Arequipa petitioned to join its jurisdiction. Even the Council of Indies supported their request, but the king decided that Lima should not suffer another blow to its authority.[48] The elite of Arequipa also believed that they were entitled to their own university, but their efforts to obtain a license were continually frustrated.[49] Such disappointments damaged not only the educational opportunities for the city's youth, but wounded local pride as well.

Throughout Peru there was a rising tide of resentment, not so much against the reforms themselves as at the unequal distribution of their benefits. In 1808, the abdication of Charles IV and the capture of Ferdinand VII by Napoleon created a crisis throughout the empire. Local assemblies from Spain to Mexico and Argentina began to declare the power to govern until the monarchy was restored, and their initial proclamations of loyalty to Ferdinand VII would prove transitory or superficial. The cabildo of Arequipa, however, fervently swore its allegiance to the king: "They cried out for revenge, they offered and offer now their lives, their property, and all that they possess to defend the Sovereignty so atrociously and ignominiously tread upon."[50]

When rebellions broke out over the next two years in La Paz and Buenos Aires, Arequipeños fulfilled their pledge by raising donations and troops for expeditions under their own Gen. José Manuel de Goyeneche to quell the uprisings.[51] Nevertheless, Arequipeños were most willing "to shed their last drop of blood" when they believed that their own city was directly threatened.[52] In November 1810, for example, the cabildo refused a request from the royal army for 200 rifles, on the grounds that they needed all 450 for the defense of the city.[53] Five years later, General Pio Tristán tried to raise the

47. Fisher, *Government and Society*, 184.

48. AMA, LCED 6, report dated June 20, 1788, from the cabildo to the viceroy, and Fisher, *Government and Society*, 49–52.

49. See Mary Gallagher, "Imperial Reform and the Struggle for Regional Self-Determination: Bishops, Intendants, and Creole Elites in Arequipa, Peru, 1784–1816" (Ph.D. diss., City University of New York, 1978), 139–64.

50. AMA, LAC 26 (Sept. 30, 1808).

51. Minutes of cabildo from Aug. 1809 to Aug. 1811 in AMA, LAC 26.

52. The quote is from the cabildo's original oath of loyalty to Ferdinand VII. AMA, LAC 26 (Sept. 30, 1808).

53. AMA, LAC 26 (Nov. 27, 1810).

morale of soldiers stationed in Puno, apparently in response to their request to return home, by assuring them that he was looking after their families.[54] The fervent regionalism of Arequipeños was already apparent.

Even in the "most loyal" city of Arequipa, there was tension between creoles and peninsular Spaniards.[55] Given the increasing threat of independence, Madrid could hardly ignore the complaints of American subjects. When several members of the cabildo leveled accusations of corruption and despotism against Salamanca, therefore, he was removed from office in 1811. In a gesture of goodwill, a native son of Arequipa, Josef Gabriel Moscoso, was appointed as the new intendant.[56] Moscoso would not serve long. In 1814, a rebellion broke out in Cuzco under the leadership of Vicente Angulo and Mateo Pumacahua that directly challenged Spanish rule. In November the rebels occupied Arequipa; although they soon retreated before royalist troops, Angulo and Pumacahua took Moscoso with them and executed him for his refusal to support their cause.[57]

It is difficult to judge the extent of support for or opposition to the rebels during their occupation of Arequipa; most townspeople probably played it safe by keeping their loyalties to themselves. In August, when news of the revolt in Cuzco reached Arequipa, a small group of men on Guañamarca Street allegedly shouted: "Long live the Fatherland, and death to the hoofed Spaniards [*chapetones pezuñentos*]: no one will reign in Arequipa except for us."[58] Others were tried for collaboration, but most had played minor roles and were pardoned.[59]

The most avowed patriot among the Arequipeños, cleric Mariano José de Arce, managed to escape. He had even criticized Angulo for swearing allegiance to Ferdinand VII rather than openly calling for independence.[60] It was not until after independence that priests and other professionals would be able to rally a greater following for their revolts. Meanwhile none of the city's elite supported the rebels, as some had in 1780.[61] When royalist troops

---

54. BNP doc. D10645 (1815), "Proclama del Brigadier Pío de Tristán."

55. See account of Spanish cleric Antonio Pereira y Ruiz in Enrique Carrión Ordóñez, *La lengua en un texto de la ilustración: Edición y estudio filológico de la noticia de Arequipa de Antonio Pereira y Ruiz* (Lima: Pontificia Universidad Católica del Perú, 1983), 375–76.

56. Fisher, *Government and Society*, 196, 210–11.

57. Fisher, "Royalism, Regionalism, and Rebellion," 232–57.

58. BNP doc. D630 (1814), "Contra Don Mariano Nicolás Salazar por rebelión."

59. BNP doc. D6135 (1815), "Contra Gaspar Esquino"; BNP doc. D6126 (1815), "Contra el esclavo Manuel Santayana"; BNP doc. D6148 (1815), "Contra Domingo Vargas"; and BNP doc. D6149 (1815), "Contra el Cacique de Puquina Manuel Lajo Olin."

60. Wibel, "The Evolution of a Regional Community," 259.

61. BNP doc. D11712 (1814), "Medidas adoptadas por el Ayuntamiento."

retook the city, Doña María Ignacia de Berrogaray y Portu donated to them a diamond ring in gratitude "for having liberated us from the tyrannical captivity and yoke that was oppressing us."[62] In the wake of the rebellion, bishop Luis Gonzaga de La Encina, a fervent royalist, temporarily closed the seminary to purge suspect professors like Arce and made all priests take an oath of loyalty.[63]

The events of 1814 symbolized the attitudes that Arequipeños would take toward independence for the next ten years: revolutionary spirit among a few priests, professionals, and lesser landowners; strong royalism among the elite (especially merchants); and careful neutrality among the rest of the population.[64] Whatever actions pro-republican Arequipeños might be taking in Lima, therefore, the city itself remained a royalist stronghold to the end. When Bolívar's lieutenant José Antonio de Sucre managed to occupy Arequipa for a mere twenty-five days in 1823, he reported that "although the region is patriotic, it resists the service of arms, the people desert frequently, and it is somewhat reluctant to commit itself."[65] Nevertheless, the royalist sentiments of Arequipeños were more out of self-interest and self-defense than a strong conviction. When the liberating army was victorious, they quickly accepted the inevitable and were as enthusiastic as other Peruvians in swearing allegiance to the new republic in January 1825.

Republican Reforms and Rebellions

Local authorities seized the opportunity offered by independence to continue and even expand the reforms begun by the late imperial government. Just as Intendant Alvarez had promoted education in order to "civilize" the indigenous population, new republican officials in Arequipa were equally enthusiastic about its effectiveness in molding citizens. A report from the educational committee of the departmental junta began with the optimistic pronouncement "that learning [la ilustración] was the foundation of the happiness of the people because through it were formed good parents, good children, good magistrates, and good citizens in all the classes of society."[66]

---

62. BNP doc. D6133 (1814) "Expediente sobre el donativo de Doña María Ignacia de Berrogaray y Portu."
63. BNP doc. D11887 (1815), "Edicto del Obispo Encina."
64. See Wibel, "The Evolution of a Local Community," 232–302.
65. Quoted in ibid., 299.
66. *El Republicano*, supplement to Aug. 29, 1829, 2.

The local government, therefore, established several primary schools and experimented with the new Lancasterian method of instruction.[67] The cloisters of San Agustín were seized to house the secondary school, appropriately named El Colegio de la Independencia and later to serve as the long-awaited university.

With the assistance of the private literary society La Academia Lauretana, a public library was established in Arequipa. The departmental junta ensured that it would be stocked with "modern" books. When one of the deputies proposed limiting entrance to subscribers, their guests, and students from the Colegio de la Independencia, another objected that "no one should be impeded the use of [the library]." During a heated debate, one side warned "that if free entrance were permitted, a thousand abuses, thefts and disorders would be committed." Finally, in the interests of "equity," it was agreed that no students would be allowed to use the "public" library until some future date when it was better established.[68] This debate foreshadowed the tension between liberty and disorder that would surface in many areas of public life after independence.

New officials were equally vigilant in the area of public works and health. In addition to continuing the vaccination programs and extermination of rabid animals, local authorities commissioned scientific studies of the mineral baths around Arequipa and built hostels so that the inhabitants could benefit from their medicinal properties.[69] Republican leaders also outdid their colonial predecessors in the construction of a new cemetery, La Apacheta, even farther outside the city. In September 1833 it was officially opened with a ceremonial reburial of the remains of Mariano Melgar, a poet from Arequipa who had joined and died for the 1814 rebellion. According to the local newspaper, the day of patriotic speeches and emotional tears was marred only by the early departure of the bishop.[70]

---

67. For prefect Antonio Gutiérrez de La Fuente's own assessment of his achievements in the field of education, see *El Republicano*, July 25, 1829, 4–6. For discussions on education in the departmental junta, see the minutes from their meetings reprinted in supplements to *El Republicano* from July 25, 1829 to Oct. 3, 1829.

68. *El Republicano*, Aug. 1, 1829, 2–3; supplement to Sept. 12, 1829, 8; supplement to Oct. 10, 1829, 4–6; and Oct. 17, 1829, 3.

69. On vaccination campaigns, see *El Republicano*, April 11, 1829, 2–4; and Aug. 8, 1829, 3. The republican government not only exterminated rabid animals, but fined those persons who refused to cooperate: *El Republicano*, July 18, 1829, 1; and Jan. 5, 1833, 4. On the mineral baths, see *El Republicano*, July 4, 1829, 3; Aug. 8, 1829, 3–4; Nov. 28, 1829, 4–5, and AGN, R.J. (Ministerio de Justicia): Beneficencia, Leg. 130.

70. "Apertura y estreno del Panteón de Arequipa," *El Republicano*, Sept. 21, 1833, 5–8. See also *El Republicano*, May 16, 1829), 3–4.

Finally, republican officials went further in efforts to prevent crime. With the aim "to prevent asylum to Thieves, [and] conserve individual and public security," the government knocked out sections of monasteries that extended into streets and formed narrow alleys, such as the "pocket of the devil" near San Francisco.[71] In a similar effort, the city began to develop a system of public lighting.[72]

In 1829, deputies elected to serve in the new departmental junta gathered to discuss the most important issues facing their provinces. At their opening session, outgoing prefect Gutiérrez de La Fuente gave a speech highlighting his accomplishments but pointing out that much work remained to be done to increase economic production.[73] He could have saved his breath. The region's advancement was already the priority of the local elite represented by these deputies, and they threw themselves into the task with a passion. The agriculture committee praised the hardworking farmers of Arequipa but noted that since they had never studied agricultural techniques, "they have not been able to break out of the narrow limits of mediocrity."[74] They recommended the study of scientific texts, the emulation of successful European methods, and the introduction of new crops.[75]

The junta recognized, however, that the main hindrance to agriculture in Arequipa was the scarcity of water, and it supported a joint private-state venture, called Vincocaya, to divert water from the upper Chili River and bring twelve thousand acres of land under cultivation. An anonymous member declared optimistically in the local newspaper that the project was "the result of the peaceful and enterprising genius of the Arequipeño."[76] But after numerous delays and obstacles, the project was abandoned in 1845.[77]

In addition to improving agriculture, the deputies realized that the economy of Arequipa needed to be diversified. They sponsored measures aimed at reviving mining in the region, but they were particularly interested in promoting industry. In 1829, French entrepreneur Esteban Foleaud offered to demonstrate "the wealth of the country contained in even its most

71. AAA/Civ (24-I-1825), "Expediente sobre la calle nueva de San Francisco"; and *El Republicano*, July 18, 1829, 1.

72. ARAR/Pref (3-I-1851), "Petición de Don Felipe Ramires, contratista de alumbrado"; and (3-VII-1852) "Petición de Don Mariano Cornejo sobre la dificultad de cobrar la pención de serenasgo y alumbrado."

73. *El Republicano*, Sept. 26, 1829, 4; Oct. 3, 1829, 5; and Oct. 10, 1829, 4.

74. *El Republicano*, Oct. 24, 1829, 2.

75. Ibid., and *El Republicano*, Oct. 31, 1829, 1–5.

76. Barriga, *Memorias para la historia de Arequipa*, vol. 1, 348.

77. Wibel, "The Evolution of a Regional Community," 362.

ordinary wools," in exchange for four hundred pesos to help pay the costs of shipping machinery to Arequipa for a textile mill. The assembly was enthusiastic in its support. When the prefect informed them that they were not authorized to make such an expenditure, the deputies agreed to petition the central government on Foleaud's behalf, and one even offered to make a personal loan.[78]

Wool was the future of Arequipa's economy, but most of it would be exported to Europe for processing and then reimported as cloth.[79] As late as 1852, the prefect interceded twice with the central government to help a local company establish a textile mill. In support of the request, the prefect noted: "The industrial and mercantile situation of Arequipa, Mr. Minister, is of a special kind: it possesses infinite men suitable for commerce and industry, and it has in reality neither industry nor commerce—purely agricultural, at a level that does not meet with due proportion the real needs of its inhabitants, since the population grows, while the natural resources remain stationary, due to the lack of new cultivable land."[80] With employment, he warned obliquely, Arequipeños might not be so inclined to cause "scandals." The minister of finance, however, merely filed the letter.

Rather than receiving assistance from the central government to implement their plans, Arequipeños faced a state that was at least as demanding and centralizing as the Spanish crown. In 1832, the deputies complained: "Lacking funds from the imaginary budget awarded by law, one is tempted to believe that its [the assembly's] creation had the object of uniting the representation of the provinces, so that for ninety days they can decry together the ruin of their native communities."[81]

A heavy fiscal burden had been one of the grievances against Spain, but the republican state introduced several new taxes. Whereas only Indians had paid a personal tax during the colonial period, after independence, those of mixed race and clerics were added to the rolls; others were assessed on their income or urban property.[82] The government in Lima seemed insatiable, especially in

---

78. Supplements to *El Republicano*, July 11, 1829, 1; July 25, 1829, 5; Aug. 22, 1829, 4; and Aug. 29, 1829, 1.

79. Manuel Burga and Wilson Reátegui, *Lanas y capital mercantil en el sur: La casa Ricketts, 1895–1935* (Lima: Instituto de Estudios Peruanos, 1981); and Flores Galindo, *Arequipa y el sur andino*.

80. AGN, Hacienda H-1-1, O.L. 372, Num. 287 and 289 (1852), letter dated June 3 from the prefect to the minister of finance.

81. Quoted in Wibel, "The Evolution of a Regional Community," 334.

82. Wibel, "The Evolution of a Regional Community," 336–41. For an overview of the

its military budget. After the first prefect repeatedly protested that there was no surplus in the local treasury to remit for the national defense, the ministry of finance began resorting to forced loans.[83] French visitor Flora Tristan, with her cruel wit, caricatured the wealthy men she watched pass by her window on their way to relinquish their sacks of money. But to the elite of Arequipa, it was no laughing matter.[84] When the government further disrupted the local economy by requisitioning troops, mules, and alfalfa, the burden on all classes became intolerable.[85]

The initial response of Arequipeños to these increasing demands was the same they had taken against colonial taxes: evasion. When the treasury brought charges against sub-prefect Manuel Amat y Leon for failing to collect almost 35,000 pesos in taxes, he protested that there was "a kind of conspiracy that the taxpayers have made," and complained that all his efforts earned him nothing but "a thousand insults and slanderous public papers."[86] It would not be long before Arequipeños, moving from passive to active resistance, jumped into the fray of caudillo warfare in an effort to win more favorable policies from the state.

In 1834, Arequipa erupted in revolt against the conservative caudillo

---

postindependence tax system, see Nils Jacobsen, "Taxation in Early Republican Peru, 1821– 1851: Policy Making Between Reform and Tradition," in Reinhard Liehr, ed., *América Latina en la época de Simón Bolívar* (Berlin: Colloquium Verlag, 1989), 311–39.

83. See the correspondence between the prefect of Arequipa and the minister of finance from Dec. 4, 1827, to Aug. 20, 1829, in AGN, Hacienda H-1-1, O.L. 163, Num. 315; O.L. 174, Num. 79; O.L. 174, Num. 102; O.L. 174, Num. 196; O.L. 174, Num. 235; O.L. 185, Num. 3; O.L. 185, Num. 27; and O.L. 185, Num. 213.

84. Tristan, *Peregrinations of a Pariah*, 158–65. For the opposition of Bishop Goyeneche and other clergy, see AGN, R.J. (Ministerio de Justicia): Ministerio de Gobierno y Relaciones Exteriores, Leg. 162, letters from Goyeneche dated Oct. 4, 1833, and June 1, 1834; AGN, Hacienda H-1-1, O.L. 270, Num. 155 (letter dated July 15, 1839); BNP doc. D11600 (1835), "Los Señores Goyeneche contra el ex-Prefecto Manuel Cuadros"; and BNP doc. D11051 (1841), "El Presbítero Gabino Ullaur contra el prefecto."

85. For numerous complaints, see the correspondence between the prefects of Arequipa and the minister of war from 1828 to 1850, in AHMP (CEHMP), Legs. 3, 4, 6, 8, 9, 10, 13, 14, 16, 25, 29.

86. ARAR/Pref (22-V-1831), "Contra el Sub-prefecto del Cercado Don Manuel Amat y Leon por deudas." For other cases of uncollectible taxes, see ARAR/Pref (11-IV-1829), "Contra el Gobernador del Palomar Jacinto Zevallos Laguna"; (21-I-1843) "Contra el Gobernador que fue de Sachaca Juan Manuel Delgado"; and correspondence between the prefect and the minister of finance in AGN, Hacienda H-1-1, O.L. 163, Num. 272 (Sept. 19, 1827); O.L. 163, Num. 319 (Dec. 18, 1827); O.L. 185, Num. 40 (Feb. 18, 1829); O.L. 185, Num. 83 (Apr. 18, 1829); and O.L. 197, Num. 3 (Jan. 3, 1830). See also AGN, Hacienda H-4-1840, R. 282 (1845), Matrícula del Clero de Arequipa; and H-4-1845, R. 287 (1845), Matrícula de Indígenas de Arequipa.

Agustín Gamarra and in support of elected president José Luis de Orbegoso. The majority of the townspeople supported the latter's alliance with Bolivian president Andrés de Santa Cruz and the resulting Peru-Bolivia Confederation, which made the south an independent state from 1836 to 1839. After Gamarra's return to power, Arequipeños rebelled several times under the banner of Manuel Ignacio de Vivanco. When Vivanco was defeated militarily in 1844 by Ramón Castilla, his supporters turned to the polls. During the presidential campaign of 1849 to 1851, the city was the scene of constant clashes between partisans of Vivanco and those of Castilla's chosen successor, José Rufino Echenique.

During his last stand in Arequipa, Vivanco wrote of the joy he felt "upon seeing it brilliant in the midst of its green countryside like a precious diamond surrounded by rich emeralds."[87] According to tradition, Castilla was said to have replied: "Bah, Arequipa is nothing but a white burro in the midst of an alfalfa field."[88] It seems ironic, therefore, that when Arequipa rose up yet again, in January 1854—this time against President Echenique—it was Castilla who rode into town and claimed the banner of the revolution. Recognizing, perhaps, that Castilla had incorporated many of their demands into his platform, the townspeople pragmatically chose to be on the victorious side, for once. Arequipeños did not abandon their political activism. In the future, however, they would not challenge the hegemony of Lima directly, but rather they would seek the best possible terms for the region's incorporation into the national project.

This overview of the turbulent years between 1780 and 1854, during which the city was transformed from a royalist stronghold to the cradle of liberal revots, raises several questions about Arequipa's participation in national affairs. Its liberalism was, moreover, an unusual blend of free trade with protection of local products, and of conservative Catholicism with populist and egalitarian ideals. Several scholars have attempted to explain these apparent paradoxes. John Wibel has traced the gradual reorientation of local elites from their colonial ties with the southern Andes to the new nation centered in Lima. From a more "macro" perspective, Juan Carpio Muñoz proposes that in the absence of a national bourgeoisie, three competing aristocracies—in Lima, Arequipa, and, in the north, Trujillo—were equally poised to fill the power vacuum created by independence: "If the Arequipeño

---

87. Jorge Basadre, *Historia de la República del Perú*, 6th ed., vol. 4 (Lima: Editorial Universitaria, 1968), 97.

88. Máximo Neira Avendaño et al., *Historia general de Arequipa* (Arequipa: Fundación M. J. Bustamante de La Fuente, 1990), 475.

aristocracy fought against this arbitrary power imposed by force with unruly troops [*soldadesca*], it was because it felt called with as much right as the Limeño aristocracy to create a fatherland—i.e. to gain access to the political direction of the new state."[89] According to his analysis, it was the wealth of guano that ultimately determined Lima's hegemony over the other regions.

New research on liberalism in Peru has shed more light on the economic bases of Arequipa's role in the construction of a nation-state. According to Paul Gootenberg: "Arequipeño liberalism grew from four basic roots: a general market orientation to the south, distance from the colonial institutional matrix of Lima, 'oppression' by monopolistic Limeño commercial policies, and incentives of new British-financed regional exports like nitrates, quinine, and wool."[90] The inability of the southern liberals to form a national alliance after independence, however, meant that they would be incorporated only as junior partners when Castilla adopted their plans after 1844.

All these analyses provide important contributions to an understanding of Arequipa's development during this transitional period, and they take important steps away from earlier Lima-centered interpretations of politics. Nevertheless, these scholars share an elite focus that can provide only part of the story. They demonstrate why Arequipa's elites favored liberal economic policies, but not the attraction of liberalism for the city's popular classes. Even Carpio fails to answer his own question: "What mysterious force made a social conglomerate of artisans, small farmers, domestic servants, landowning aristocrats and merchants fight under one banner and a single caudillo?"[91]

Of course it was elites who mediated between Arequipa and competing regional powers, but they did not act in a vacuum. Local tradition acknowledges the participation of the masses in Arequipa's rebellions, but it attributes their role to an innate love of the law or compares their actions to the unpredictable volcanic eruptions and earthquakes that, similarly, shook the region. Only a deeper analysis of local society can explain the remarkable cohesion of Arequipa's classes in their struggles against central authority, and the emergence of a regional political culture that emphasized social homogeneity and noble equality. The following chapters will examine the popular classes of the White City, both in their own right and in their relationship to local elites. The analysis of popular culture and society will lay the groundwork for a fuller interpretation of Arequipa's role in these political events.

89. Juan Guillermo Carpio Muñoz, "Rebeliones arequipeñas del siglo XIX y configuración de la oligarquía 'nacional,'" *Análisis* 11 (May–Aug. 1982): 36.

90. Gootenberg, "Beleaguered Liberals," 76.

91. Carpio Muñoz, "Rebeliones arequipeñas," 33.

2

Class and Caste:
The Ambiguity of Identities

Arequipeño intellectuals of the nineteenth and twentieth centuries would have us believe that distinctions based upon class and race were so slight that inhabitants of the White City easily united in political movements. By contrast, their colonial forebears considered the natural order of society to be heterogeneous and hierarchical, though still harmonious. The problem, then, is not to show that such differences did not exist but how they could be de-emphasized. In addition to describing as accurately as possible the economic and demographic makeup of local society, this chapter will explore the social perceptions that contributed to class and ethnic identities.

Throughout colonial Spanish America, elites used primarily two models to describe the urban social structure. The first used both economic and cultural considerations to distinguish the elite (variously described as nobles, respectable people, or people of reason) from everyone else, namely plebeians. The division of society into two "classes" had European precedents, but the colonial and multiracial context of America gave rise to a second model. Following the conquest, the crown legally divided the society into two separate parts: the Republic of Indians and the Republic of Spaniards. After a century of miscegenation, however, it became difficult to fit this model with reality. In order to accommodate those of mixed descent, a caste system was created that ranked the various racial groups and assigned them corresponding legal rights and restrictions. Although elites invented elaborate terms to describe numerous racial mixtures, those most commonly used were: Spaniard, mestizo, Indian, mulatto, zambo, and negro (the last three indicating various degrees of African descent).[1]

In the ideal world of Spanish theorists, racial distinctions would divide the exploited population and thereby maintain social peace and equilibrium. But to work effectively, the socioeconomic model of society and the caste system should have overlapped and reinforced each other. Over the last two decades, historians have analyzed census data from various regions to determine whether racial classifications, in fact, coincided with occupational categories, and they have measured rates of intermarriage to test the rigidity of the caste system.[2] These studies have generated a debate over the relative importance of caste (or race) and class in late colonial society.[3]

The ongoing disagreement suggests that social status, or *calidad*, was a

1. *Spanish* will refer to whites unless specified to mean immigrants born in Spain. The term *zambo* was used to describe a mixture of Indian and African ancestry; in Arequipa, however, it was not clearly distinguished from *mulatto*. For an introduction to the caste system, see Lyle N. McAlister, "Social Structure and Social Change in New Spain," *Hispanic American Historical Review* 43, no. 3 (1963): 349–70; and Magnus Mörner, *Race Mixture in the History of Latin America* (Boston: Little, Brown, 1967). For an excellent recent study, see R. Douglas Cope, *The Limits of Racial Domination: Plebeian Society in Colonial Mexico City, 1660–1720* (Madison: University of Wisconsin Press, 1994). On class, see Louisa Schell Hoberman and Susan Migden Socolow, eds., *Cities and Society in Colonial Latin America* (Albuquerque: University of New Mexico Press, 1986), 8–10, 321–25.

2. For a sample, see D. A. Brading and Celia Wu, "Population Growth and Crisis: Léon, 1720–1866," *Journal of Latin American Studies* 5 (1973): 1–36; John K. Chance, *Race and Class in Colonial Oaxaca* (Stanford: Stanford University Press, 1978); Patricia Seed, "Social Dimensions of Race: Mexico City, 1753," *Hispanic American Historical Review* 62, no. 4 (1982): 569–606; and Rodney D. Anderson, "Race and Social Stratification: A Comparison of Working-Class Spaniards, Indians, and Castas in Guadalajara, Mexico in 1821," *Hispanic American Historical Review* 68, no. 2 (1988): 209–43.

3. See John K. Chance and William B. Taylor, "Estate and Class in a Colonial City: Oaxaca in 1792," *Comparative Studies in Society and History* 19 (1977): 454–87; Robert McCaa, Stuart B. Schwartz, and Arturo Grubessich, "Race and Class in Colonial Latin America: A Critique," *Comparative Studies in Society and History* 21 (1979): 421–33; McCaa, Schwartz, and Grubessich, "Measuring Marriage Patterns: Percentages, Cohen's Kappa, and Log-Linear Models," *Comparative Studies in Society and History* 25 (1983): 711–20; John K. Chance and William B. Taylor, "Estate *and* Class: A Reply," *Comparative Studies in Society and History* 21 (1979): 434–42; Patricia Seed and Philip F. Rust, "Estate and Class in Colonial Oaxaca Revisited," *Comparative Studies in Society and History* 25 (1983): 703–10; and Seed and Rust, "Across the Pages with Estate and Class," *Comparative Studies in Society and History* 25 (1983): 721–24.

complex combination of racial identity, occupation, wealth, and cultural practices.[4] Significantly, this cluster of attributes was also central to assessments of honor. Rather than enter the debate over quantitative measurements, this chapter explores the lived experience of class and ethnicity and the implications of identity for political mobilization.

Since the eighteenth century, some provincial creole elites in Peru had been willing to join forces with indigenous leaders against colonial rule, but such multiethnic alliances usually broke down in the heat of battle.[5] After independence, therefore, most elites were pessimistic about incorporating Indians into the nation as citizens. One aim of this chapter, therefore, will be to examine whether there was a potential basis for a strong counter-hegemonic identity among those of indigenous or African descent in Arequipa. The 1792 census officially classified the population of Arequipa as 66.8 percent Spanish, 17.5 percent mestizo, 6.4 percent Indian, and 9.1 percent mulatto and black. Nevertheless, such ethnic identities were not based on precise biological categories and were often ambiguous and changeable.[6] The category of "mestizo" was particularly unstable, tending to blend into either the Spanish or the Indian group, and so it did not serve as the basis for a coherent identity.[7] Of course, Arequipa did not have an egalitarian society, but identities were ambivalent enough to blur both caste divisions and the dichotomy between elite and plebe. The final section of this chapter will explore how most of the population identified themselves, and, more surprisingly, were accepted by local officials as "Spanish" (white).

Measures and Perceptions of Class

To define classes in a preindustrial society is a difficult task, but economic histories of Arequipa emphasize the existence of a significant middle sector.[8]

4. Robert McCaa, "*Calidad, Clase,* and Marriage in Colonial Mexico: The Case of Parral, 1788–1790," *Hispanic American Historical Review* 64, no. 3 (1984): 477–501.

5. John R. Fisher, "Royalism, Regionalism, and Rebellion," 232–57.

6. For census figures, see Vollmer, *Bevölkerungspolitik und Bevölkerungsstruktur,* 253–54. For a warning against the reliability of racial categories in census records, see Robert H. Jackson, "Race/Caste and the Creation and Meaning of Identity in Colonial Spanish America," *Revista de Indias* 55, no. 203 (1995):149–73.

7. David Cahill also wonders what distinguished mestizos from the lower ranks of Spaniards and proposes that the notion of "mestizo culture" would have made no sense in the colonial period. "Colour by Numbers: Racial and Ethnic Categories in the Viceroyalty of Peru, 1532–1824," *Journal of Latin American Studies* 26, no. 2 (1994): 342–45.

8. Davies, *Landowners in Colonial Peru*; Brown, *Bourbons and Brandy*; and Fernando A.

The aim here is to give a general idea of the range of property and income distribution derived from various occupations, in order to introduce the cast of characters and explore how Arequipeños themselves could aspire to or identify with particular socioeconomic groups. Even apparently fine grada-tions could be important in assertions of honor. Moreover, middlemen— from professionals to shopkeepers and artisans—played crucial roles in mobilizing popular participation during rebellions and political movements.[9]

The cutoff for property tax in 1833 was an annual income of fifty to eighty pesos, an amount that probably represented a basic subsistence level.[10] Rural rents varied from about twenty to forty-five pesos per *topo* (.86 acres), with a gradual increase throughout the period from 1780 to 1850. Those with incomes of two hundred to five hundred pesos, therefore, could save enough to purchase property. Land prices in the valley varied from one hundred to two hundred pesos per topo, though an especially fertile topo along the Chili River or close to the city could fetch as much as seven hundred pesos.[11] Some Arequipeños converted their savings into silver or jewelry, but only a few allowed themselves the luxury of purchasing slaves, which cost between two hundred and five hundred pesos.[12]

The greatest earnings for the elite were made in international commerce, particularly when Arequipa benefited from the late colonial reforms that liberalized commerce. The number of merchants importing goods from Spain more than doubled between 1755 and 1787, and in 1784 the most important metropolitan traders represented by the Cinco Gremios Mayores

---

Ponce, "Social Structure of Arequipa, 1840–1879" (Ph.D. diss., University of Texas at Austin, 1980).

9. In a study of Mexico, Torcuato S. Di Tella calls for greater attention to the fine but important socioeconomic gradations among the working and middle sectors, as opposed to a clear gulf between upper and lower classes, and proposes that the urban middle classes were key players in politics. Di Tella, *National Popular Politics in Early Independent Mexico*, 1–26.

10. Ponce, "Social Structure of Arequipa," 107.

11. This data and much of that to follow is taken from a sample of notarial records every five years, from 1780 to 1850, in the Archivo Regional de Arequipa. I chose one notary for each year and recorded every document. There were often other notaries working during the same year, but no evidence that any specialized in a particular type of contract or geographical area. The notaries sampled were: Pedro de Figueroa (1780), Manuel González de La Fuente (1785), Ramón Bellido (1790), Rafael Hurtado (1795), Mariano de Tapia (1800), Josef Alberto de Gómez (1805), Hermenegildo Zegarra (1810), Rafael Hurtado (1815), Francisco Xavier de Linares (1820), José Nazario de Rivera (1825), Pedro Mariano Araujo (1830), Francisco de Linares (1835), Casimiro Salazar (1840), Miguel José de Chávez (1845), and Mariano Bolaños (1850).

12. In the sample of 290 wills, about 36 percent of the testators left silver or jewelry to their heirs, while only about 8 percent declared slaves.

de Madrid announced that they would open an outlet in Arequipa.[13] Arequipa remained an important commercial center after independence, as a market developed in Europe for wool from southern Peru, and foreigners continued to dominate the highest levels of the export-import trade, although the British and other northern Europeans began to displace the Spaniards.[14] While merchants were among the wealthiest Arequipeños, however, their incomes in the late colonial period were low by viceregal standards.[15]

Throughout the colonial period, viticulture was the other important basis of both wealth and status for the elite of Arequipa.[16] Most vineyards, as well as sugar, rice, and cotton plantations, were located close to the coast along the Majes, Vítor, and Tambo rivers, but the owners preferred to live in Arequipa, and often they rented out their estates or left them under the care of managers. Although large estates were rare, vineyards yielded up to twelve thousand pesos in annual income. Elite families often owned more than one vineyard, which, when combined with other properties and enterprises, could provide a sizable income. Women, who under Spanish law enjoyed equal inheritance rights to men, were prominent in commercial agriculture. One quarter of the landowners who paid the Vítor wine tithe in 1789 were women, and they produced proportionately more wine than the men.[17]

While most of the urban elite owned coastal plantations, only their modest farms close to the city were visible to their more humble neighbors. The archetypal character in memoirs and novels about Arequipa is the *chacarero*, the small farmer, as opposed to the "feudal" hacendado. In the countryside (*campiña*) surrounding the city, grains and other food crops were cultivated on small and medium-size properties (*chacras*). Of the 377 landowners who

13. There were only five outlets throughout the colonies. See Brown, *Bourbons and Brandy*, 88–94; and Wibel, "The Evolution of a Regional Community," 146–47. For a case study of a successful merchant family, the Goyeneches, see Carlos D. Malamud, "El fin del comercio colonial: Una compañía comercial gaditana del siglo XIX," in Alberto Flores Galindo, ed., *Independencia y revolución* (Lima: Instituto Nacional de Cultura, 1987), 37–120.

14. See Flores Galindo, *Arequipa y el sur andino*; Burga and Reátegui, *Lanas y capital mercantil en el sur*; and Wibel, "The Evolution of a Regional Community," 364–74.

15. Wibel, "The Evolution of a Regional Community," 147–48.

16. Brown, *Bourbons and Brandy*, 112–14. On the origins of the wine economy in the sixteenth century, see Davies, *Landowners in Colonial Peru*.

17. Brown, *Bourbons and Brandy*, 113–14. See also Davies, *Landowners in Colonial Peru*, 58, 114; and Wibel, "The Evolution of a Regional Community," 96–112.

paid property tax in 1784, 60 percent had no more than sixteen topos, and a mere 6 percent had more than forty.[18]

A similar picture emerges from the notarial records, which included properties exempt from taxation. In a sample of 220 recorded land sales, more than half involved one topo of land or less, and about another third involved between one and five topos. There was only one sale of a property of more than fifty topos. In terms of cost, in 42 percent of the sales, no more than two hundred pesos changed hands, and only 16 percent of the buyers paid more than one thousand pesos for their property. Although the large estates may have changed hands less frequently and, therefore, may have been underrepresented in the documents, such data still reveal an active land market among smallholders.

Throughout the period under study, there was a trend toward even further land division. Analyzing the rural property-tax records in 1843 and 1852, Fernando Ponce found that the number of units increased by 11 percent, while the average size decreased by 8 percent. This trend did not necessarily mean a fractioning into subsistence plots, however, as the greatest increase (20 percent) was in medium-size properties (5 to 9.9 topos). Although Ponce estimates that almost one half of the rural proprietors were small farmers, he defines a sizable 38 percent as middle income (annual earnings of 50 to 499 pesos). Moreover, one could argue that given his wide range for upper incomes (500 to 18,000 pesos), some at the lower end could be considered part of the middle sector.

The most successful farmers used a combination of strategies: farming some of their own land, renting out other properties, and leasing parcels from other landowners.[19] Such a land-tenure pattern lent credence to the image of the honest chacarero, and many of these modest farmers were mobilized during revolts.

Arequipa was a provincial, agricultural city, where it was difficult to draw strict boundaries between urban and rural areas. Some who owned agricultural property lived in the city, either farming their own land or renting it out. In 1790, for example, Felipa Urrutia sued master silversmith Matías Martínez for a debt of two hundred pesos; the court impounded fourteen topos of his land just outside the city planted in corn, wheat, and potatoes.[20]

18. Brown, *Bourbons and Brandy*, 28–30. This pattern was set early; see Davies, *Landowners in Colonial Peru*, 122–34, 140, 160.

19. Ponce, "Social Structure of Arequipa," 117, 228–34.

20. ARAR/Cab/Civ (28-IV-1790), "Doña Felipa Urrutia contra Matías Martínez."

Furthermore, evidence suggests that a similar pattern of widespread property ownership existed within the city itself. The grand houses of the central city were owned by prestigious families who carved their coats of arms into the stone portals. Nevertheless, ownership of urban property was accessible to a large segment of the population. In a sample of 290 wills, two-thirds of the women and half of the men claimed at least shares of buildings or urban lots. By excluding those too poor to leave wills, such figures do not reflect the true rate of home ownership in Arequipa, but they do suggest that it was higher than the mere 1.7 percent of the population in Mexico City who owned homes in 1813.[21] When the republican government established a new tax of 3 percent on urban property, it was notoriously difficult to collect. In 1831, the sub-prefect of Arequipa, who owed 4,500 pesos in uncollected taxes, explained that although there were numerous taxpayers on the rolls, the majority owned small houses and were assessed only a few reals.[22]

Of the 89 sales of urban lots (*solares*) included in the sample of notarial records, almost half (47 percent) were valued at 200 pesos or below, and another 39 percent cost between 200 and 500 pesos. Only 13 percent of the purchasers paid more than 500 pesos. Another 133 sales of urban property included buildings, either houses or shops; of these, 35 percent were valued below 500 pesos, and 23 percent cost between 500 and 1,000 pesos. These transactions represented a broad cross section of local society. In 1780, for example, mulatta Bernarda Barreda sold the lot that her father, a freed slave, had inherited from his former masters; the wife of the *cacique* (chief) of Yanahuara paid her 600 pesos.[23] In 1815, María Cansino, an indigenous woman from the urban parish of Santa Marta, sold a lot in San Bernardo Street to Francisco Talavera for 1,080 pesos.[24] The highest price found in the sample was the 7,500 pesos paid in 1850 by Dr. Miguel Abril, the judge for the province of Caylloma, for a house across the street from the convent of Santa Catalina.[25]

A variety of urban occupations could provide enough earnings to invest in small properties. Many earned their income from the agrarian sector indi-

21. Steve J. Stern, *The Secret History of Gender: Women, Men, and Power in Late Colonial Mexico* (Chapel Hill: University of North Carolina Press, 1995), 35.

22. ARAR/Pref (22-V-1831), "Los Administradores del Tesoro contra Don Manuel Amat y Leon." The situation had changed little by 1844; see AGN, Hacienda H-4-1865, R. 306, Predios Urbanos.

23. ARAR, notary Pedro de Figueroa, Dec. 11, 1780.

24. ARAR, notary Rafael Hurtado, June 17, 1815.

25. ARAR, notary Francisco Paula Gonzales, Sept. 17, 1850.

rectly. Women, in particular, were prominent not only in farming, but also in the sale and processing of the harvested products. Many, for example, listed debts of grain in their wills. Much of the corn grown in the campiña was made into the traditional fermented drink known as *chicha*. Women both made the chicha and sold it in the taverns. They also produced bread from the local wheat harvest; of the ninety-four bakeries operating in 1780, sixty-nine were owned or managed by women.[26] When Isidora Gutiérrez filed for an ecclesiastical separation from her husband in 1819, she could claim ownership of their bakery, since it was an "occupation proper to women and not to men."[27] By contrast, bakeries in Lima were relatively large enterprises employing slave and convict labor.[28]

The commercial sector also included a wide range of incomes. Below the international merchants was a significant middle sector of traders in local products. The importation of foodstuffs from the highlands was dominated by indigenous traders. The Indian *forasteros* (migrants or their descendants) in Yanahuara and Cayma, for example, claimed that the native inhabitants (*originarios*) of those communities were jealous of their success in commerce.[29] In 1804, the Protector of Indians complained that a highland cacique was harassing Indians who went from the parish of Santa Marta to graze their cattle in the sierra and returned with goods to sell. Several had even abandoned their trade, according to the protector, and "as a consequence this City [is] suffering a shortage of provisions."[30] Although many of these Indian traders made only enough in profits to pay their tribute, some managed to accumulate savings.[31]

In addition to international and regional traders, numerous local merchants supplied the urban market; they ranged from shopkeepers dealing in

26. AMA, LAR, Num. 1 (1780), report dated June 19, 1780, on the amount of wheat consumed each month in the bakeries.

27. ARAR/Int/Crim (5-VII-1819), "Isidora Gutiérrez contra Patricio Texada."

28. Alberto Flores Galindo, *Aristocracia y plebe: Lima, 1760–1830* (Lima: Mosca Azul Editores, 1984), 165–67.

29. ARAR/Int/Ped (24-XI-1807), "Los indios forasteros de Yanahuara protestan los abusos de los originarios."

30. ARAR/Int/Ped (21-VII-1804), "José Gervacio de Lastarria protesta los abusos del Cacique de Layo y Pichigua." See also ARAR/Int/Ped (12-IX-1785), "Antonio y Gregorio García piden que se le mande al Cacique de Azángaro que no les cobre tributo."

31. See, for examples, ARAR/Int/Crim (22-VII-1802), "Prueba por parte de Pascual Calderón en la causa que le sigue Sebastiana Vera"; (5-I-1820) "Don José Felix Delgado contra José Leon Aro"; and ARAR/Int/Adm (10-XI-1810), "Don Josef Jacobo Casaperalta, Cacique de Chivay, pide que Manuel Guanturo se traslade al pueblo."

luxury imports to the women who sold fruits and vegetables in the plaza. From 1827 to 1848, between 236 and 536 shopkeepers registered annually to pay taxes, and the 1859 census listed 700 merchants (for an average of 8 per block).[32] Although tax evasion likely led to an underreporting of both the number of businesses and their earnings, the records provide at least relative data. Shops ranged from the few large import warehouses (*almacenes*), owned almost exclusively by foreigners who declared average annual earnings of 3,360 pesos, to shops called *tiendas*, which probably sold some imports and reported on average 168 pesos, to *pulperías* (general stores), which reported a lower income of 106 pesos. Women were very prominent in retail commerce, owning about one-half of the shops, but they were concentrated in the smaller pulperías and declared lower annual earnings.[33] These stores provided a comfortable living for many men and women in Arequipa and, we shall see, also served as social centers in the neighborhoods.

While shopkeepers could consider themselves part of the middle sector, other "merchants" eked out a living on the fringes of local retailing. The streets of Arequipa were as crowded with informal vendors in the eighteenth and nineteenth century as they are today. According to Father José María Blanco, who visited Arequipa in 1835, all levels of commerce were represented in the main plaza. The stone buildings housed more than forty shops, including several taverns, a café, and an ice-cream parlor. Outside their doors, along the arcades, gathered peddlers who set out a variety of wares on tables, in stalls, and hanging from ropes. Blanco was struck, in particular, by the women who sold shoes: "All day they remain seated there, surrounded by dogs and by their small children, aggravating the eyes and ears with their filth and the shrieks of these [children]. They do not have the shoes grouped together or in baskets, but rather scattered across the ground, and the peasant buyers go through them many times to try them and see if they fit their feet."[34] Meanwhile, those who sold foodstuffs sat under canvas awnings in the center of the plaza, where they were organized according to their products.

Of course, not everyone could make a living selling goods; some people had to make them. Wealthier citizens patronized the shops of specialized

---

32. The data on taxes was provided by Betford Betalleluz, who got his statistics from the *matrículas de patentes de los gremios* in AGN, Hacienda H-4, Sección de Contribuciones. The 1859 census data is from Ponce, "Social Structure of Arequipa," 172.

33. These statistics are based on Betalleluz's data.

34. Blanco, "Diario del viaje del Presidente Orbegoso al sur del Perú," 147.

artisans such as watchmakers and silversmiths, but there were many more shoemakers, tailors, hatters, and carpenters who catered to a broader clientele. Arequipa's agricultural economy also demanded the services of numerous blacksmiths and saddlers. And although the city imported much of its cloth, it had its own spinners, weavers, dyers, and tanners, many of them Indians and women.[35]

As in agriculture and commerce, the manufacturing sector had a range of income levels, and some artisans did earn a comfortable living. The most highly skilled occupations provided the highest incomes; according to the republican tax records, watchmakers declared earnings approaching those of professionals.[36] Earnings in most trades fluctuated from day to day, depending upon demand. Master tailor Don Antonio Morales testified in 1834 that the income of his journeyman probably averaged 6 reals a day.[37] At that rate, an artisan's annual income could easily reach 200 pesos. By 1862, the British consul reported that laborers in Arequipa earned 6 to 8 reals a day, while artisans had annual salaries as high as 400 pesos a year.[38] At the bottom end of the scale, the women who spun thread and dyed cloth made minimal profits of 1 or 2 reals a day, which was enough to supplement their household income.[39]

Guilds potentially could have fostered an identity based upon trade, or even an incipient working-class solidarity. Certainly, men in the same trade frequently socialized together, as we learn from those occasions when some dispute marred the conviviality. Cobbler Carlos Champi, for example, took his mistress to a dinner given by master shoemaker Hermenegildo Anaya, but the master's wife refused to set the adulterous couple a place at the table.[40]

Nevertheless, the rare appearances of guilds in official documents suggests

---

35. Barriga, *Memorias para la historia de Arequipa*, vol. 1, 53; and Alejandro Málaga Medina, *Arequipa: Estudios Históricos*, vol. 1 (Arequipa: Biblioteca Arequipa, 1981), 68–75.

36. Watchmakers reported annual incomes of around 185 pesos, compared with 140 pesos for solicitors and 160 pesos for surveyors.

37. ARAR/CS/Crim (19-VIII-1834), "Contra Mariano Villegas por rapto y estupro." Barber Alfonso Linares reported that his daily earnings varied from nothing to one peso; AAA/Pen (25-I-1790), "Contra Alfonso Linares por amancebamiento."

38. Heraclio Bonilla, ed., *Gran Bretaña y el Perú*, vol. 4, *Informes de los cónsules: Islay, Mollendo, Arica e Iquique, 1855–1913* (Lima: Instituto de Estudios Peruanos, 1976), 137.

39. Brown, *Bourbons and Brandy*, 70.

40. AAA/Pen (20-X-1784), "Paula Cáseres contra su esposo Carlos Champi y Rafaela de Tal por sevicia y adulterio."

that at least their formal activity in Arequipa during this period was weak. The only references to examinations required to reach the rank of master come from records on the most skilled professions, such as those of assayers, watchmakers, and surveyors.[41] Even the officials of the silversmiths' guild had to ask the intendant for assistance in making members comply with their ordinances. They complained that apprentices moved from one shop to another and, therefore, never received the required six years of training followed by an examination. Worse yet, the masters charged, unlicensed journeymen were receiving work on their own, an "abuse" that they associated with the fencing of stolen silver. When the intendant ordered all silversmiths to comply with the regulations, four journeymen filed an indignant protest, claiming that they had always had the right to work independently.[42]

In trades that required less training, the social distance between masters and journeymen was even less marked and relations more informal. Gregorio Ramos, an Indian migrant to the city, had been told that it was easy to find a job in the suburbs. It was good advice. Tailor Matías Talavera hired Gregorio without even knowing his last name, and they began to take meals together. Talavera may have regretted his decision, however, when Ramos got in a fight at a local *chichería* and accidentally killed the proprietor's husband.[43] When tailors Mariano Goysueta and Ignacio Molina argued over military contracts in 1824, Goysueta claimed to be a master "in whom various persons of first rank in this city deposit the confidence of their work." Molina countered that they were both journeymen. Whatever their rank, both had independently accepted contracts.[44]

The influence of the guilds was eroded further by craftsmen who worked in a variety of trades. As early as 1814, Felipe Beltrán claimed earnings as a painter, embroiderer, saddler, buttonhole maker, carpenter, blacksmith, and

41. ARAR/Int/Ped (5-V-1803), "Mariano Zevallos pide que se le examine en el oficio de albeitería"; ARAR/Int/Adm (23-XI-1805), "Don Juan de Dios Salazar pide título de agrimensor público"; (30-I-1807) "Don Mariano Blas de Tapia, medidor y tasador, pide título"; (3-III-1809) "Don Francisco Gámez, Teniente de Cosmógrafo Mayor, pide que se le confirme en su puesto"; and (19-V-1809), "Don Juan de Dios Salazar reclama el puesto de Teniente de Cosmógrafo Mayor."

42. ARAR/Int/Adm (9-VI-1808), "Sobre que los Maestros Plateros cumplan sus deberes." For a similar case among blacksmiths, see ARAR/Int/Adm (19-XI-1803), "Recurso del Gremio de Herrería." Guilds were also weak in colonial Chile; see Mario Góngora, "Urban Stratification in Colonial Chile," *Hispanic American Historical Review* 55, no. 3 (1975): 442–44.

43. ARAR/Int/Crim (24-XI-1803), "Contra Gregorio Ramos por homicidio."

44. ARAR/Int/Crim (17-VIII-1824), "Mariano Goysueta contra Ignacio Molina."

tanner.[45] After independence, when cheap imports may have cut into a market already disrupted by ongoing warfare, this tendency toward multiple occupations increased. When Colombian Pedro Pontón was brought into court on assault charges in 1828, he reported that "his occupation is that of tailor, shoemaker, merchant and whichever of those activities that proves most worthwhile."[46] Pedro Romero was accused of theft in 1831; although identified as a tailor, he had previously worked as a chocolate maker and as a laborer on a farm in the Tambo valley.[47] Cobbling, in particular, seemed to be a trade that was easy to learn and combine with a variety of odd jobs. José María Madaleno and José Torres were migrant laborers, working both in the coastal plantations and in the farms around the city; when they were arrested for vagrancy in 1831, however, they had been making shoes for two weeks.[48]

Less skilled artisans, such as shoemakers, may have found themselves close to the ranks of general wage laborers, who earned four reals on the days when they could find work.[49] The region's population had grown throughout the eighteenth century, and by the 1760s, seasonal wage labor had overtaken slavery on the coastal plantations.[50] Vineyards required workers for both the pruning and the harvest, and the farms of the campiña, which had several harvests each year, also hired seasonal help.[51] In 1829, the prefect of Arequipa reported that it was difficult to compile tax registers, because so many people were migrant workers.[52]

The courts also had a hard time finding suspects and witnesses. As one defense lawyer pointed out: "Among Poor People principally there is a continual ebb and flow of arrivals and departures from the city, for short or long journeys, aimed almost always to look for their subsistence."[53] Further-

45. AAA/Pen (3-X-1814), "Felipe Beltrán contra Teresa de La Torre."

46. ARAR/CS/Crim (28-X-1828), "Contra Pedro Pontón."

47. ARAR/CS/Crim (25-XI-1831), "Contra Pedro Romero por robo."

48. ARAR/Pref (21-XI-1831), "Sobre investigarse la conducta de Ramón Llerena, José María Madaleno y José Torres."

49. AMA, LCED 6 (1788), "Cuenta y razón de lo que se va gastando en la fábrica de las covachas del puente."

50. Brown, *Bourbons and Brandy*, 48.

51. For a list of workers' names, days worked, and wages, see ARAR/Int/Adm (14-I-1816), "Cuentas para 1815 de Doña Gabriela de Benavente y Silva, hacendada de viña, Valle de Vítor."

52. AGN, Hacienda H-1-1, O.L. 185-40, letter dated Feb. 18, 1829.

53. ARAR/CS/Crim (12-VIII-1833), "Contra Juan Ibáñez y Casimiro Corrales." See also ARAR/CS/Crim (20-IX-1829), "Contra Pablo García"; (4-X-1831) "Contra Dionicio Molina y Don José María Landa"; (10-IX-1833) "Contra Micaela Salas"; (3-IX-1848) "Contra Faustino Corrales y Manuel Delgado"; and (5-II-1840), "Contra Pedro Flores, Martín y Manuel Sanabria."

more, a growing pool of landless Indians joined the ranks of wage workers. As early as 1796, the Indian community of Characato complained that a shortage of communal land forced many of its members to migrate to the valleys in search of work, "abandoning their poor wives and children from which has resulted great suffering and miseries."[54]

Research on economic trends in Arequipa between 1780 and 1850 is still only suggestive and reveals a mixed picture. Throughout this period Arequipa was one of the most economically dynamic regions in Peru, but it was not immune to problems. By the late colonial period, rising taxes and falling demand for the region's liquors led to a decline in viticulture that was only gradually reversed by diversification into sugar, cotton, and rice. Plantation owners further complained that labor shortages held down production.[55] The frequent wars of the nineteenth century also disrupted the economy, as reflected in the numerous complaints about the destruction caused by the troops and military requisitions of mules, horses, and alfalfa (all necessary for the transportation of goods). By 1852, the city even had to import food-stuffs.[56]

The effect of European imports on local manufacturing has not been decisively demonstrated, but the predominance of cloth over finished clothing may have mitigated its impact on the livelihood of tailors and seamstresses if not that of spinners and weavers. Finally, the demand for agricultural workers meant that displaced artisans could at least find employment, even if it resulted in a potential loss of respect as well as earnings.[57]

Clearly, significant disparities in wealth separated migrant workers from

54. ARAR/Int/Adm (6-IV-1796), "Contra el cacique de Characato por deudas por tributos."

55. See Wibel, "The Evolution of a Regional Community"; Brown, *Bourbons and Brandy*; Ponce, "Social Structure of Arequipa"; Flores Galindo, *Arequipa y el sur andino*; Cossío, "Razón circunstanciada," 219–33; Alfonso W. Quiroz, "Estructura económica y desarrollos regionales de la clase dominante, 1821–1850," in Alberto Flores Galindo, ed., *Independencia y revolución*, vol. 2 (Lima: Instituto Nacional de Cultura, 1987), 201–68; and Marcel Manuel Haitin, "Late Colonial Lima: Economy and Society in an Era of Reform and Revolution" (Ph.D. diss., University of California at Berkeley, 1983), 11–20.

56. On requisitions, see letters between local authorities and military officials from 1839 to 1845 in AHMP (CEHMP), Leg. 3, 6, 9, 13, 14. See also requests for exemptions from tithes because of crop losses due to wars, in ARAR/Pref (23-I-1839), "Petición de José Mateo Arse"; (11-VIII-1840) José Gregorio Valdivia; (30-VII-1842) Lorenzo Zegarra; (7-X-1843) Buenaventura Rondón; and (1-III-1845), "El Juzgado de Diezmos expone sobre deudores." On importation of food, see AGN, Hacienda H-1-1, O.L. 372-480, letter from prefect to minister of treasury, Dec. 17, 1852.

57. "Informe del Cónsul interino, Sr. Cocks, sobre el comercio de Islay, 1862," in Bonilla, ed., *Gran Bretaña y el Perú*, vol. 4, 128–38; and Ponce, "Social Structure of Arequipa," 171.

merchants and owners of vineyards, and the social gap may have been widening. Contemporaries regarded such differences as natural, but they also measured their status by more than income. An artisan, petty merchant, or small farmer may not have been far from a general laborer or domestic servant, in material terms; in their own eyes, however, their possession of some property, skills, and a sense of independence were important marks of distinction. While the mythical image of a middle-class city is clearly exaggerated, moreover, class divisions were less stark in Arequipa than in the major capital cities.

In Lima, home to the viceregal court, the ranks of the titled nobility were increasing in the late eighteenth century, and they publicized their status with ostentatious displays of luxury. Mansions were cut off from the street by elaborate wrought-iron fences, and when prominent families ventured out, it was in showy carriages driven by richly liveried slaves. Such splendor was possible only at the expense of widespread underemployment among the majority of the population.[58] The social gulf was even more marked in Mexico City. The largest city in America in 1803, its population of 137,000 had been swelled by migrants fleeing increasing impoverishment in the countryside. Many of them joined the ranks of the chronically unemployed, which contemporaries estimated as close to one-fifth of the inhabitants. Alexander von Humboldt, for example, described 20,000 to 30,000 who lived on the streets and were virtually naked.[59] Many among the other three-fifths identified as "plebeian" were only a step away from such abject poverty. Yet in the midst of all this misery, the city's prominent families were amassing enormous fortunes from a booming economy in mining and commercial agriculture.[60]

Only a few families in Arequipa even approached the wealth of the nobility of Lima and Mexico City. The patriarch of one, Juan Crisóstomo Goyeneche, migrated from Pamplona, Spain, to Peru in the 1760s and became one of the largest importers of European goods to Arequipa as well as one of the largest exporters of wine products from the coast to the highlands. He married creole María Josefa Barreda, who inherited properties worth almost one hundred thousand pesos, including one of the largest

58. Flores Galindo, *Aristocracia y plebe*, 73, 79–81; Haitin, "Late Colonial Lima," 122–25.

59. Alexander von Humboldt, *Ensayo político sobre el reino de la Nueva España*, ed. Juan A. Ortega y Medina (Mexico City: Editorial Porrua, 1966), 86. For further descriptions, see 69–73.

60. See D. A. Brading, *Miners and Merchants in Bourbon Mexico, 1763–1810* (Cambridge: Cambridge University Press, 1971); Doris M. Ladd, *The Mexican Nobility at Independence, 1780–1826* (Austin: Institute of Latin American Studies at the University of Texas Press, 1976); and Arrom, *The Women of Mexico City*, 5–10.

vineyards in Vítor. Throughout his career Goyeneche acquired more properties, including the largest estate (five hundred acres) within the valley of Arequipa, Guasacache, which he rented out to forty tenants. His sons were also successful: Pedro Mariano studied law and eventually was named to the high court of Lima, José Manuel entered the military and reached the rank of brigadier general, and José Sebastián became the bishop of Arequipa and later archbishop of Lima. Meanwhile a fourth son, Juan Mariano, married local heiress María Santos Gamio and managed his father's enterprises, ensuring that the family would remain one of the wealthiest in Arequipa well into the nineteenth century.[61]

But success stories like that of the Goyeneches were rare. Only Juan Mariano Goyeneche and Pio Tristán had net wealth over one million pesos by the mid-nineteenth century, and a handful of families had fortunes of about three hundred thousand.[62] By contrast, at least nineteen families in Mexico City from 1770 to 1830 were worth between one and four million pesos.[63] As early as the seventeenth century, Arequipa had a large "second-rank aristocracy" who possessed only moderate wealth and property but copied the social practices of the high elite.[64] To avoid partitioning estates, sons of notable families often entered the professions, both civil and ecclesiastical. Arequipa had the largest representation of lawyers of any provincial city in the professional association of Lima.[65] And these jurists would play a central role in the development of local political ideologies.

The city also had its share of clergy, notaries, surveyors, assessors, and doctors who, observed a priest, "kill here with the same liberty as in Paris or London."[66] The professional sectors of the elite began to merge into Arequipa's middle sector of shopkeepers, petty traders, artisans, and small farmers. Finally, the accounts of locals and visitors alike lack the shocking descriptions of poverty and crime common in larger cities. Intendant Sala-

61. On the Goyeneches, see Wibel, "The Evolution of a Regional Community," 87–88, 138, 168; Brown, *Bourbons and Brandy*, 93, 105, 108–9, 120–22, 146, 200, 257; and Carlos Malamud, "Relaciones familiares, comercio y guerra de independencia (1808–1828), Los Goyeneche" (tésis de licenciatura, Universidad Complutense, Madrid, 1978).

62. Wibel, "The Evolution of a Regional Community," 100–101, 139–40, 360. The prefect in 1829 complained that it was difficult to collect forced loans, because there were only four or five wealthy persons in the city. See AGN, Hacienda H-1-1, O.L. 185, Num. 3c, Jan. 3, 1829. See also Brown, *Bourbons and Brandy*, 109–11.

63. Ladd, *The Mexican Nobility*, 184–85.

64. Davies, *Landowners in Colonial Peru*, 156.

65. Wibel, "The Evolution of a Regional Community," 161–97.

66. Juan Domingo de Zamácola y Jáuregui, *Apuntes para la historia de Arequipa* (1804; reprint, Arequipa: Primer Festival del Libro Arequipeño, 1958), 31.

manca, for example, assured his superiors that he never tolerated vagrants but added, "although I suppose that very few of that class would have presented themselves in this city."[67]

Rather than featuring a stark divide between elite and plebe, therefore, the social structure of Arequipa was characterized by subtle gradations of wealth and status. It is difficult, for example, to separate wills into clear socioeconomic categories. Many testators who put the honorific of Don or Doña before their names had few belongings to leave to their heirs. Don Ildefonso Uria, for example, declared that he had no goods "because he finds himself entirely poor, without even enough to buy medicine."[68] Some may have come from respectable families that had fallen on hard times.

Don Juan de Dios Delgado, on the other hand, probably felt that he had earned his Don throughout his successful life as an almost archetypal small farmer. Delgado stated that he and his wife had started with only forty-five bushels of corn and a mule; by the end of his life he could declare a house in the city, a soap factory in Yura, several chacras, numerous animals, and several silver items.[69] Even if a clearly elite landowner did not derive his primary wealth from his local properties, moreover, his more humble neighbors might still identify him as a fellow chacarero. And artisans, petty merchants, and small farmers (if not servants and day laborers) could identify socially and culturally with a middling sector of society. It was members of these groups who significantly influenced changing meanings of honor and played a key role in local politics. And just as class boundaries in Arequipa were blurred, so were ethnic divisions.

The Indians of Arequipa

The 1792 census identified 16.8 percent of the population in the valley of Arequipa as indigenous, the majority in the villages surrounding the city.

67. Fisher, *Arequipa 1796–1811*, 17.

68. ARAR, notary Hermenegildo Zegarra, testament dated Feb. 8, 1810. For a few similar examples, see notary Manuel González de La Fuente, Doña Marcela Velásquez, Jan. 10, 1785; notary Mariano de Tapia, Doña Micaela Espinosa y Diez, June 16, 1800; notary Francisco Xavier de Linares, Doña Sebastiana Rivera y Recalde, July 7, 1820; and notary José Nazario de Rivera, Doña Micaela Valencia y Bedrigal, Feb. 21, 1825.

69. ARAR, notary Casimiro Salazar, Feb. 21, 1840. This extension of the Don began in the seventeenth century. See Davies, *Landowners in Colonial Peru*, 154–56.

Although they made up a large and distinct minority, various dynamics worked against the formation of cohesive communities that could have served as the basis for political mobilization. During his inspection tour, Intendant Alvarez y Jiménez noted that Indians in the villages around the city were very acculturated, and that the priests did not need to know their language, Quechua.[70] Indeed, in both the countryside and the city, the indigenous population lived alongside and mingled with other ethnic groups.

Indians were aware of their special status under Spanish law, particularly their access to community land, and they made every effort to use it to their greatest advantage. As those advantages declined over the course of the period of this study, however, so too did the number willing to publicly embrace an indigenous identity. In contrast to some other regions of Latin America, therefore, those Indians who participated in republican politics would do so primarily as individuals, rather than because they were represented by communal authorities.

Despite early colonial regulations that forbad persons of mixed race to reside in Indian communities, the villages around Arequipa were ethnically diverse. Indeed, in some cases Indians formed a minority of the population (see Table 2.1). The priest of Cayma, Juan Domingo de Zamácola y Jáuregui, approved of such mixing, arguing that urban lots should be sold to "Spanish mestizos" who could keep an eye on the Indians and teach them good habits. There were already enough non-Indians in Cayma that Zamácola also proposed integrating the parish so that all residents, rather than just Indians, would attend the local church. He pointed out that "in the same family, it happens that the husband is a parishioner of Cayma and his wife of the cathedral, or the opposite." Even his own servants, he complained, attended mass at the cathedral in Arequipa.[71] Zamácola's statement also implies that there were marriages between Indians and members of other ethnic groups. Similarly, the apparent homogeneity of Yanahuara was only on paper. An earlier ecclesiastical census taker had noted that he did not count the numerous "Cholos, Mestizos, Sambos, Negroes, and Spaniards" in Yanahuara, because they were parishioners of the cathedral in Arequipa.[72]

---

70. Barriga, *Memorias para la historia de Arequipa*, vol. 1, 163, 204, 209, 226, 249, 278.

71. Zamácola y Jáuregui, *Apuntes para la historia de Arequipa*, 42, 45. For a comparative case of the controversy over whether to define parishes by race or territory, see Karen Vieira Powers, "The Battle for Bodies and Souls in the Colonial North Andes: Intra-ecclesiastical Struggles and the Politics of Migration," *Hispanic American Historical Review* 75, no. 1 (1995): 31–56.

72. AAA, "Padrón General de los Feligreses de esta Doctrina de San Juan Baptista de la Chimba, hecho por su Cura Propio el Doctor Don Pedro de Otazú, en este año de 1785."

Table 2.1. Population of the rural parishes, Valley of Arequipa, 1792

	Indigenous	Spanish	Mestizo	African Descent
Yanahuara	1,466 (100.0%)	0 (0.0%)	0 (0.0%)	0 (0.0%)
Cayma	812 (25.8%)	2,336 (74.2%)	0 (0.0%)	0 (0.0%)
Tiabaya	287 (21.6%)	918 (69.0%)	118 (8.9%)	8 (0.6%)
Paucarpata	756 (22.5%)	2,096 (62.5%)	420 (12.5%)	81 (2.4%)
Chiguata	508 (59.8%)	255 (30.0%)	78 (9.2%)	8 (1.0%)
Characato	273 (16.1%)	636 (37.6%)	63 (3.7%)	719 (42.5%)
Pocsi	2,866 (85.7%)	224 (6.7%)	203 (6.1%)	51 (1.5%)
Total	6,968 (45.9%)	6,465 (42.6%)	882 (5.8%)	867 (5.7%)

SOURCE: Günter Vollmer, *Bevölkerungspolitik und Bevölkerungsstruktur im Vizekonigreich Peru zu Ende der Kolonialzeit (1741–1821)* (Bad Homburg: Gehlen, 1967), 253–54.

Despite the diverse population, each Indian community had its own political and religious authorities, apart from (but subordinate to) the Spanish mayor of a given village. At the highest level, the indigenous population was under the authority of caciques, the hereditary nobility known in Quechua as *kurakas*, who, ideally, protected the interests of their subjects. By the eighteenth century, however, the power and legitimacy of these ethnic lords had declined throughout Peru. Those who had used their position as mediators with Spanish society in order to enrich themselves found it increasingly difficult to demand respect and services from their indigenous subjects. On the other hand, kurakas suspected of supporting Túpac Amaru in 1780 found themselves stripped of their office if not executed. With the establishment of the intendancy system in 1784, the duty of tribute collection (and its corresponding salary of 1 percent of the total amount) was officially separated from the post of cacique. Although some loyal caciques were reaffirmed in that position, subdelegates could appoint anyone they deemed most reliable, often Spaniards or mestizos.[73]

During the intendant's visit in 1788, the priest complained that the numerous non-Indian residents relied on his services but paid tithes to the cathedral. Barriga, *Memorias para la historia de Arequipa*, vol. 1, 250.

73. For a copy of the new regulations, see Carlos J. Díaz Rementería, *El cacique en el Virreinato del Perú: Estudio histórico-jurídico* (Sevilla: Universidad de Sevilla, 1977), 235–36. On the erosion of cacique authority throughout Peru, see Núria Sala i Vila, *Y se armó el Tole Tole: Tributo indígena y movimientos sociales en el Virreinato del Perú, 1790–1814* (Huamanga: IER José María Arguedas, 1996), 66–96; Karen Spalding, *Huarochirí: An Andean Society Under Inca and Spanish Rule* (Stanford: Stanford University Press, 1984), 226–38; Christine Hünefeldt,

The majority of the caciques in the valley of Arequipa had remained strongly royalist and, therefore, continued in their posts.[74] The Condorpusas of Yanahuara, the Alpacas of Cayma, and the Cusirramos of Paucarpata had intermarried to form a local ethnic elite.[75] In return for their loyalty, these communities were even allowed to form militia corps with their own officers; during his inspection, Intendant Alvarez y Jiménez decided to approve these technically illegal companies, noting the great pride and enthusiasm of the soldiers.[76] Evidence of the legitimacy of these caciques in the eyes of the indigenous commoners is mixed.

In 1810, the *cacica* of Yanahuara, María Tone Esquiagola, along with the local council, was pursuing several lawsuits on behalf of the community.[77] Two years later, however, several Indians accused Tone and her son of usurping extra land.[78] In 1812, the caciques of Cayma and Yanahuara, fearing that the rebellions erupting in the highlands might take root among the Indians in their communities, had to request measures to reinforce their authority.[79] A few months later, Cacique Condorpusa again complained that

---

Lucha por la tierra y protesta indígena: Las comunidades indígenas del Perú entre colonia y república, 1800–1830 (Bonn: Bonner Amerikanistische Studien, BAS 9, 1982), 27–33; Víctor Peralta Ruíz, *En pos del tributo en el Cusco rural, 1826–1854* (Cuzco: CERA Bartolomé de las Casas, 1991), 21–22; Luis Millones Santa Gadea, "Los ganados del señor: Mecanismos de poder en las comunidades andinas, siglos XVIII y XIX," *América Indígena* 39, no. 1 (1979): 107–45; Charles Walker, "Peasants, Caudillos, and the State in Peru: Cusco in the Transition from Colony to Republic, 1780–1840" (Ph.D. diss., University of Chicago, 1992), 76–91; and Nils Jacobsen, *Mirages of Transition: The Peruvian Altiplano, 1780–1930* (Berkeley and Los Angeles: University of California Press, 1993), 97.

74. See the reports of Intendant Alvarez y Jiménez in Barriga, *Memorias para la historia de Arequipa*, vol. 1, 176, 206, 235.

75. ARAR/Cab/Civ (21-I-1795), "Partición y liquidación de cuentas entre los herederos de Don Juan Bautista Tone Esquiagola y Doña Marcela de Rosa"; ARAR/Int/Crim (4-X-1800), "Contra Matías Alpaca, Manuela Cusirramos, Ylario Quispe y Matías Chagua por el robo de la Caja de Comunidad de Paucarpata"; and David Noble Cook, "La población de la parroquia de Yanahuara, 1738–1747: Un modelo para el estudio de las parroquias coloniales peruanas," in Franklin Pease G.Y., ed., *Collaguas I* (Lima: Pontificia Universidad Católica del Perú, 1997), 30.

76. Barriga, *Memorias para la historia de Arequipa*, vol. 1, 206, 262–64, 297–99.

77. ARAR/Int/Adm (27-III-1810), "El Alcalde de Españoles, la Cacica y el Cabildo de Naturales de Yanahuara piden permiso para usar los fondos de la Caja de Comunidad para litigación."

78. ARAR/Int/Crim (14-V-1812), "El Cacique de Yanahuara y el Subdelegado del Cercado se acusan mutuamente de abusos de autoridad."

79. ARAR/Int/Adm (1812-1813), document dated March 5, 1812, in "Expedientes cortos, y escritos sueltos sin giro."

two members of the indigenous council of Yanahuara were "interfering" in the distribution of communal land.[80]

In many communities throughout Peru, the elected mayors and council members had been gaining authority and prestige at the expense of caciques. Such tensions were particularly clear in the village of Paucarpata. During his inspection in 1788, Intendant Alvarez y Jiménez uncovered several abuses of power by the cacique Lorenzo Cusirramos. He was benefiting from the unpaid labor of community members and illegally collecting tribute from widows, while declining to collect it from young men, so that he would not have to give them a share of communal land. He was occupying 27½ topos of that land himself, well above the 12 assigned to caciques as compensation for their duties. The intendant ordered that the extra land be rented out and the funds used to establish a community chest, with keys to be held by the cacique, the Spanish mayor, and the Indian mayor.

But signs of conflict reemerged ten years later, when the cacique's widow, Rosalía Rojas, unsuccessfully petitioned to veto the recent council elections, on the grounds that the mayors showed her disrespect and either were unable to collect the tribute or refused to turn it over to her.[81] The dispute over power reached a peak in 1800, when Manuela Cusirramos (Rojas's daughter) and her husband, Matías Alpaca (the son of the cacique of Cayma), seized control of the community chest under the ruse that it had been stolen. According to Alpaca's testimony, his wife "said publicly that the money was hers, because her deceased father as cacique of the village had collected it and enjoyed the use of it, and that it was an insult to her that it had now entered into the benefit of the community."[82] Alpaca was ultimately pardoned, in the light of petitions from the community of Cayma and documentation of his father's great services to the crown, but no appeals were filed on behalf of Cusirramos. Clearly, the legitimacy of at least some ethnic lords was under question.

Others Indians chafed under the authority of appointed tribute collectors, who falsely claimed the title of cacique.[83] The greatest complaints arose from the indigenous communities of Quequeña and Mollebaya, which were

---

80. ARAR/Int/Adm (13-V-1812), "Petición de Don Mariano Zeballos y Condorpusa al intendente."

81. ARAR/Int/Adm (4-I-1798), "Petición de Doña María Rosalía Rojas al intendente."

82. ARAR/Int/Crim (4-X-1800), "Contra Matías Alpaca, Manuela Cusirramos, Ylario Quispe y Matías Chagua por el robo de la caja de comunidad de Paucarpata."

83. See ARAR/Int/Adm (1795), entry dated June 19, 1795, in "Libro de Causas ante Rivera," "Los indios originarios de Tiabaya quejan del nombramiento de cacique en la persona del

attached to the parish of Pocsi within the jurisdiction of Moquegua until 1824. When Intendant Alvarez y Jiménez arrived for his inspection in 1791, he found conflicting land claims despite a recent redistribution. Numerous Spaniards who had built homes on and cultivated lands belonging to the indigenous communities were allowed to continue in possession, by paying modest annual fees. Another fifty-five topos identified by the intendant as extra were rented to three Spaniards: Pedro Rodríguez, Francisco de Paula de Arenas, and Pablo José de Rivera. These same men and their relatives (joined later by the Málaga family) also held positions as Spanish mayors, militia officers, and collectors of Indian tribute (also frequently referred to incorrectly as caciques), resulting in a significant concentration of political and economic power.[84] Over the following decade, several complaints against them surfaced in various documents.[85]

In 1811, with the abolition of tribute by the liberal Spanish parliament, the simmering discontent boiled over in one of the rare instances in the valley of indigenous unrest. The Indian council of Pocsi accused the "cacique" Pedro Rodríguez, really the Spanish mayor who had been appointed as tribute collector, of usurping more than sixteen topos of land, which they ordered to be distributed among community members. They argued in court that with the abolition of tribute, Rodríguez lost any authority he might have had. The subdelegate authorized the council to oversee the distribution of lands but specifically prohibited them from taking land from any individual "on the pretext that he is Spanish."[86]

Nevertheless, the fears of non-Indians apparently were not assuaged. In 1812, Rodríguez charged that Pedro Quispe, a member of the Indian council,

---

mestizo Buenaventura Quispe"; and (18-X-1823), "Los Originarios Principales de Santa Marta protesta que Don José Manuel Arana continue en el puesto de Cobrador."

84. Barriga, *Memorias para la historia de Arequipa*, vol. 2, 109–28.

85. ARAR/Int/Crim (20-I-1798), "Doña María Torres contra Don Norberto Arenas por injurias"; (7-VI-1799) "Don Carlos Málaga contra Doña Melchora Viscarra y su hijo Vicente Rivera por injurias"; and ARAR/Int/Adm (4-V-1803), "Sylverio Coaila, indio tributario de Pocsi, queja contra el cacique recaudador Don Pedro Rodríguez."

86. ARAR/Int/Adm (31-X-1811), "Sobre si el Cabildo de Naturales de Pocsi puede hacer la repartición de tierras." See also ARAR/Int/Adm (4-V-1803), "Sylverio Coaila contra el cacique recaudador Don Pedro Rodríguez"; and (12-III-1822), "Rosalía y Leonarda Mamani contra Don Bartolomé Málaga." For similar actions by indigenous councils in other parts of Peru, see Hünefeldt, *Lucha por la tierra*, 157–82; Sala i Vila, *Y se armó el Tole Tole*, 152–88; David Cahill and Scarlett O'Phelan Godoy, "Forging Their Own History: Indian Insurgency in the Southern Peruvian Sierra, 1815," *Bulletin of Latin American Research* 11, no. 2 (1992): 125–67; and Chambers, "The Limits of a Pan-Ethnic Alliance in the Independence of Peru."

had tried to foment a riot against the local Spaniards and mestizos.[87] A potential crisis was averted by higher Spanish officials through the judicious reaffirmation of the respective rights of both indigenous and Spanish local authorities, as well as through a new distribution of lands carried out in 1813 by the official Protector of Indians.[88] Just as tribute was quickly reestablished, the success of the indigenous council members to assert greater authority was also short-lived.[89]

Within the valley, then, there were neither hereditary caciques with enough support nor indigenous councils with sufficient clout to serve as strong ethnic leaders. In Cuzco, by contrast, even creole rebels sought the support of the indigenous nobility for both their material and symbolic power.[90] Divisions within and among the communities further limited the emergence of wider, ethnically based movements in Arequipa. The division in Pocsi between the traditional Andean moieties (*parcialidades*) of Anansaya and Urinsaya was particularly marked. A 1785 dispute between two Indian villages, Mollebaya and Piacca, over irrigation rights likely reflected such differences.[91] Although the Spanish tribute collectors of each were at various times accused of abuses by Indians under their authority, at other times they defended (out of self-interest) the water rights and land base of their respective moieties.[92]

87. ARAR/Int/Crim (31-V-1812), "Pedro Rodríguez, Alcalde de Quequeña, contra Pedro Quispe y otros por azonada." For a similar case, see ARAR/Int/Adm (5-VIII-1813), "Don Juan de La Cruz Quenaya, indio principal de Pocsi, queja que el Alcalde de Españoles de Yarabamba Don Bartolomé Málaga quiere despojarle de un solar."

88. See sentence of Intendant Moscoso in ARAR/Int/Crim (31-V-1812), "Rodríguez contra Quispe y otros por azonada," and the testimony of indigenous officials to have been satisfied with the new land distribution, in ARAR/Int/Adm (3-IV-1813), "El Protector de Naturales Dr. Don José Salazar se defiende de un cargo de mala conducta."

89. For a complaint against tribute collector Bartolomé Málaga for usurping a plot granted to an indigenous family in the 1813 distribution, see ARAR/Int/Adm (12-III-1822), "Petición de Rosalía y Leonarda Mamani." By contrast, the indigenous communities of Cuzco effectively used the legal system to limit abuses of power; see Walker, "Peasants, Caudillos, and the State in Peru," 69–104.

90. Pumacahua, one of the indigenous leaders of the 1814 rebellion, is the most famous, but two creole conspirators in 1805, Gabriel Aguilar and Manuel Ubalde, also sought an "Inca" for their movement; see Alberto Flores Galindo, *Buscando un Inca* (Lima: Editorial Horizonte, 1988), 176–242.

91. ARAR/Int/Adm (28-X-1785), "Petición de los originarios de Mollebaya."

92. ARAR/Int/Crim (16-X-1794), "Don Ignacio Evia contra Don Anselmo Josef de Rivera, Alcalde de Yarabamba, por azonada para cegarle una asequia"; (7-VI-1799) "Don Carlos Málaga contra Doña Melchora Viscarra y su hijo Vicente Rivera por injurias"; ARAR/Int/Adm (4-V-1803), "Sylverio Coaila, indio tributario de Pocsi, queja contra el cacique recaudador Don

Finally, the members of each indigenous community were divided into the two categories of originario and forastero. Technically, the former descended from those Indians assigned to each village by Viceroy Toledo in 1570, while the latter were the descendants of those who had left their communities and migrated to another. These forasteros apparently broke ties with their native communities to escape the obligations of tribute and forced labor (*mita*); in their new communities of residence, they might rent land or integrate themselves through marriage.[93]

More recently, some historians have asserted that many forasteros maintained contact with their communities of origin and even paid tribute to their ethnic caciques.[94] Beginning in 1734, forasteros lost their exemption from tribute, and by 1778 the official distinction for tax purposes was that originarios enjoyed usufruct of communal lands while forasteros did not, and, therefore, the latter paid a lower rate.[95] In nineteenth-century Bolivia, originario status became completely dependent upon the occupation of communal lands rather than one's lineage, and individuals of the same family could be alternately identified as either originarios or forasteros.[96]

Despite such shifting definitions, the distinction between originarios and forasteros remained important in late colonial Arequipa. In some cases, the latter clearly maintained ties to their natal ethnic groups. From the time of the Toledan reductions, communities in the valley of Arequipa and those in the highlands (particularly the neighboring province of Caylloma) retained rights to land within each region, possibly based upon the pre-Columbian strategy of settling colonists in various ecological zones. For example, Intendant Alvarez y Jiménez was informed during his official visit to

---

Pedro Rodríguez"; and (26-VIII-1813), "Don Juan Isidro Cárdenas, Alcalde de Pocsi, queja de los procedimientos del Alcalde de Urinsaya Don Bartolomé Málaga."

93. Nicolás Sánchez-Albornoz, *Indios y tributos en el Alto Perú* (Lima: Instituto de Estudios Peruanos, 1978), 43–53; and Ann M. Wightman, *Indigenous Migration and Social Change: The Forasteros of Cuzco, 1570–1720* (Durham: Duke University Press, 1990).

94. Thierry Saignes, "Indian Migration and Social Change in Seventeenth-Century Charcas," in Brooke Larson and Olivia Harris, eds., *Ethnicity, Markets, and Migration in the Andes* (Durham: Duke University Press, 1995); and Ann Zulawski, *They Eat from Their Labor: Work and Social Change in Colonial Bolivia* (Pittsburgh: University of Pittsburgh Press, 1994), 127–41.

95. Sánchez-Albornoz, *Indios y tributos*, 36–45; Díaz Rementería, *El cacique en el Virreinato del Perú*, 30–31; Carlos Contreras, "Estado republicano y tributo indígena en la sierra central en la post-independencia," *Histórica* 13, no. 1 (1989): 13.

96. Tristan Platt, *Estado boliviano y ayllu andino* (Lima: Instituto de Estudios Peruanos, 1982), 51–62.

Yanahuara that the cacique had jurisdiction over the highland herding community of Llapa, more than twenty-five leagues from the parish church, yet only four leagues from the community of Callalli in the province of Caylloma.[97]

Conversely, the caciques of several highland villages filed claims on territory within the valley. Gaspar Coaguila of Ubinas, Moquegua, claimed possession of a house built upon an urban lot where Indians of the community could stay when they went to the city to sell their products.[98] Therefore, disputes arose over where forasteros should pay their tribute. In 1810, Josef Jacobo Casaperalta, the cacique of Chivay in Caylloma, requested that Manuel Guanturo, recorded in the tribute census as an originario of his community, be ordered to reside there. Guanturo, who claimed to be the son of the previous cacique, protested that he had been born in Yanahuara and had married a local woman. Nevertheless, like other migrants, he cultivated land belonging to the highland community but that was located in the valley, while he continued to pay tribute to the cacique of Chivay. "If the Spaniards can establish their domicile wherever they want, why should it be prohibited to the Indians?" he proclaimed. "Are they not as free? Do they not enjoy equal and even greater privileges?"[99]

Although classification as a forastero for tribute purposes did not necessarily mean one was a migrant, in Arequipa many were. Of those on the 1785 parish census of Santa Marta, 40 percent had been born outside the city. The majority of these had migrated from the provinces of Chucuito (10 percent), Lampa (37 percent), Azángaro (13 percent), and Tinta (22 percent) in the

---

97. Barriga, *Memorias para la historia de Arequipa*, vol. 1, 250–51.

98. ARAR/Int/Ped (26-I-1785), "Don Gaspar Coaguila, indio principal de Ubinas, protesta el despojo de un solar en la ciudad por el actual Cacique Don Bernardo Ysaguirre." See also AGN, Derecho Indígena, Leg. 23, Cuad. 398 (1781), "Los indios de Yanque contra Joaquín Gárate, cacique interino, sobre reivindicación de ciertas tierras"; ARAR/Int/Adm (23-VII-1792), "Don Ildefonso Gutiérrez, Cacique de Callalli, contra los herederos de Don Juan Cárdenas sobre la posesión de dos topos y cuarto de tierras en Sachaca"; ARAR/Int/Adm (24-X-1811), "Petición de Doña Gregoria Pacsi Mosquera y compartes sobre 5 topos de tierras en Yanahuara"; and ARAR/Pref (5-V-1826), "Don Simón Nieto denuncia tierras en Sachaca como usurpadas del estado por el Cacique de Callalli."

99. ARAR/Int/Adm (10-XI-1810), "Don Josef Jacobo Casaperalta, Cacique de Chivay, pide que Manuel Guanturo, matriculado en la última revista, se traslade al pueblo." See also ARAR/Int/Ped (18-XII-1784), "Don Carlos Achircana, Cacique de Forasteros, pide que se le mande a Manuel Cavana pagar tributo"; (12-IX-1785) "Antonio y Gregorio Garcia, indios tributarios de Santa Marta, piden que se le mande al Cacique de Azángaro que no les cobre tributo"; and (21-VII-1804), "El Protector de Naturales protesta los abusos del Cacique de Layo y Pichigua Don Clemente Zapata contra los indios de Santa Marta."

intendancies of Puno and Cuzco, while a mere 15 percent had come from Caylloma or other districts within Arequipa.[100] About 22 percent of adults on the 1785 parish census of Yanahuara were also identified as migrants. Their places of origin were similar to those in Santa Marta, but with a larger proportion from Tinta in Cuzco (43 percent) as compared with Lampa (31 percent) and Azángaro (6 percent).[101]

Such patterns mark a notable change from the 1645 census of Arequipa, when almost 20 percent of the forasteros hailed from the nearby highland region of Caylloma (Collaguas), another 15 percent from other provinces of Arequipa, and only 11.5 percent from Collao (Azángaro, Lampa, Chucuito, and Paucarcolla).[102] It seems that the combination of growing land scarcity and post-1780 repression had launched a second wave of migrants to Arequipa from provinces linked by trade routes yet more distant from the city. Such recent arrivals may not yet have integrated into local communities as effectively as those from Caylloma.[103]

Whether long-term residents or more recent migrants, forasteros sometimes came into conflict with originarios. Those in Yanahuara and Cayma, for example, claimed that the originarios of those communities discriminated against them in the appointment of officials and asked to be assigned their own cacique.[104] During the 1813 land distribution in Pocsi, the members of the indigenous council of Quequeña disdainfully identified the Indians of Yarabamba as "recent migrants [*forasteros advenedisos*], servants of the Spanish residents [vecinos] and not originarios of the Parish."[105] The greatest source of conflict was undoubtedly access to land. In Characato, those who lived in the valley with access to cultivable land were categorized as originarios, while those who lived in the hills and eked out a livelihood from herding were identified as forasteros, despite their long residence in the community.[106] Although there is evidence that at least a few forasteros in

100. AAA, "Padrón de la Feligresia de Santa Marta," 1785.

101. AAA, "Padrón General de los Feligreses de San Juan Baptista de la Chimba," 1785.

102. Nicolás Sánchez Albornoz, "Migración urbana y trabajo: Los indios de Arequipa, 1571–1645," in *De historia e historiadores: Homenaje a José Luis Romero* (Mexico City: Siglo Veintiuno Editores, 1982), 272–75. See also Cook, "La población de la parroquia de Yanahuara," 30–31.

103. For conditions in Azángaro, see Jacobsen, *Mirages of Transition*, 87–90, 101–2.

104. ARAR/Int/Ped (24-XI-1807), "Los indios forasteros de Yanahuara protestan los abusos de los originarios."

105. ARAR/Int/Adm (3-IV-1813), "El Protector de Naturales se defiende de un cargo de mala conducta."

106. Barriga, *Memorias para la historia de Arequipa*, vol. 1, 147.

Tiabaya were shifted to the category of originarios (and, presumably, assigned corresponding usufruct plots), in other cases forasteros were denied available land.[107] When Alvarez y Jiménez made his official tour of Pocsi, for example, he repossessed twenty-five topos that had been assigned to forasteros and rented them out, instead, to Spaniards.[108]

As late as 1830, several noble originarios of Yanahuara complained that the sub-prefect was redistributing land to forasteros that rightly belonged to them. Manuel Amat y Leon countered that he had distributed small plots of unused land to destitute Indians who had been paying tribute for years without enjoying any corresponding plot, and he proposed "that we should abolish those titles of forasteros and originarios, since all are now Peruvians, and reduce taxpayers to those at full or half rate graduated according to their allotment of land."[109]

In a region and period where sustained contact between Indians and Spaniards had resulted in significant acculturation, the prestige and authority of caciques was in decline, and the indigenous population was internally divided by ethnic origin and tribute status, the strongest common denominator among, at least, originarios was their right to a plot of land in exchange for paying tribute to the king.[110] Most Indians who lived in the villages earned their livelihood in agriculture, and their most secure access to land was through the periodic distributions (called *repartimientos* in Arequipa) of communal holdings. In fact, the rare instances when state officials in Arequipa feared that rebellion was brewing among the native population were during these repartimientos. In 1812, Pedro Rodríguez, the Spanish mayor and tribute collector of Quequeña, reported that discontent over the land distribution had erupted in a riot; he cited rumors that "more blood than water would flow and no mestizo would be left alive in the Village."[111]

---

107. ARAR/Int/Adm (13-II-1795), "El Protector de Naturales defiende Miguel y Agustín Castro, indios originarios de Tiabaya."

108. Barriga, *Memorias para la historia de Arequipa*, vol. 1, 119–20.

109. ARAR/Pref (16-VI-1830), "Los indígenas de Yanahuara quejan de los procedimientos del Sub-prefecto durante la revisita." By contrast, in Huaylas, a region that did produce strong indigenous movements, Indian mayors at least defended the access of forasteros to alpine commons. See Thurner, *From Two Republics to One Divided*, 39–41.

110. This exchange resembles what Tristan Platt has identified as a colonial "pact" in Bolivia. Platt, *Estado boliviano y ayllu andino*, 40.

111. ARAR/Int/Crim (31-V-1812), "Pedro Rodríguez contra Pedro Quispe y otros por azonada." See also ARAR/Int/Adm (3-IV-1813), "El Protector de Naturales se defiende de un cargo de mala conducta"; (5-VII-1813) "Don Juan de La Cruz Quenaya queja que el Alcalde de Españoles de Yarabamba quiere despojarle de un solar"; and ARAR/Pref (16-VI-1830), "Los

This right to land in exchange for paying tribute was attractive enough during the colonial period that even persons of mixed race might claim an indigenous identity. After the tribute census of 1786, there was not enough community land for each Indian in Tiabaya to get a plot. Agustín Alpaca, the cacique of Cayma who had jurisdiction there, protested that land had been assigned wrongfully to the mestizo sons of Bernardo Pucho. The Puchos initially were expelled from the land in question, but they were reinstated by the intendant, who undoubtedly did not want a decline in tax revenue. Alpaca continued the case on appeal for at least eight years, but apparently without any success.

Legally, children acquired their caste from the maternal line; the dispute in this case, therefore, centered on the identity of the Puchos' mother. Alpaca insisted that she was reputed as Spanish or mestiza. The Puchos' lawyer admitted that she was mestiza but argued that, as the daughter of a Spanish man and an Indian woman, she (and her children) were legally Indian.[112] Nine years later, the Protector of Indians still asserted that mestizos should be included on the tribute rolls, so as not to defraud the state of tax revenue.[113]

Since indigenous identity in Arequipa was strongly rooted in the land, it was relatively weak among urban Indians, even though they, too, had their own religious and political authorities. Alvarez y Jiménez noted in 1788 that there were two *ayllus* (lineages) of originarios within the parish of Santa Marta: San Lázaro, made up of 39 originarios with land, and Chichas, where none of the 15 originarios owned land, because the mere seventeen topos of communal land was distributed among the cacique and other indigenous officials. Another 198 (about 80 percent of the total) were recorded on the tribute census as landless forasteros, although 72 of these were dead or absent, while more recent migrants were making up the lost revenue.[114]

The vast majority of urban Indians made their living in a variety of occu-

indígenas de Yanahuara quejan de los procedimientos del Sub-prefecto y Apoderado Fiscal durante la revisita."

112. The case "Don Agustín Alpaca, Cacique de Cayma, contra los hijos de Bernardo Pucho que como mestizos tratan de usurpar tierras de repartimiento" exists in several pieces in two archives: BNP Docs. C2648 (1786), C2629 (1788), C3532 (1793), and C3455 (1794); and AGN, Derecho Indígena, Leg. 24, Cuads. 431 and 434 (1788–93).

113. ARAR/Int/Adm (20-III-1795), "Sobre que José Condorpusa y Taco debe entrar en el padrón de tributarios."

114. Barriga, *Memorias para la historia de Arequipa*, vol. 1, 235–43. The proportion between originarios and forasteros remained the same on later tribute censuses; see BNP doc. D6603

pations other than agriculture. Many used their connections in the highlands to work as traders. And while they were more prevalent in certain fields— such as domestic service, general labor, weaving, tanning, and butchering— Indians could be found working in almost any trade. There was even an Indian silversmith with his own shop.[115]

The priest of the urban parish of Santa Marta counted a total of 1,822 parishioners in 1785, while according to the 1792 census, there were 1,515 Indians living in the city.[116] Therefore, they made up between 6 and 8 percent of the urban population. Although many lived in the neighborhood of Miraflores near their parish church of Santa Marta, they were scattered throughout the city. As early as 1788, Intendant Alvarez y Jiménez noted that it was difficult to distinguish the Indians of Santa Marta from Spaniards.[117] By 1834, the prefect proposed dividing the parishes by neighborhood rather than by race, because the Indians had mixed with Spaniards throughout the city.[118]

Because so few of the urban Indians were assigned land, there was little incentive for them to pay tribute, as Pascual Vargas, the cacique of forasteros in Santa Marta, complained in 1803. Not only had many of the Indians in his district died or moved away, he reported, but those who remained were trying to exempt themselves by passing into other ethnic groups: "All the Indians . . . want to become Spaniards, some because they dress in the Spanish style, others because they learn Spanish trades such as Barbers, tailors etc., or because their color is somewhat pale, or because they style their hair, or because their godparents are Spanish and have them baptized in

---

(1813), "Matrícula de indios tributarios del Cercado de Arequipa"; and AGN, Hacienda, Sección Contribuciones, H-4-1623, R. 068 (1828), Matrícula de Indígenas.

115. For tanners, see ARAR/Int/Adm (22-I-1799), "El Síndico Procurador General de Arequipa protesta que las tenerías contaminan el agua." For a list of other occupations, see ARAR/Int/Adm (20-I-1803), "Don Pascual Vargas representa las dificultades de enterar los reales tributos." For the silversmith, see ARAR/Int/Crim (7-I-1823), "Domingo Medina contra el Comisario de Barrio Don José Ariscain." Indians in the cities of Oruro and Potosí held similar occupations (in addition to mining); see Zulawski, *They Eat from Their Labor*, 122–27; and Enrique Tandeter et al., "Indians in Late Colonial Markets: Sources and Numbers," in Brooke Larson and Olivia Harris, eds., *Ethnicity, Markets, and Migration in the Andes* (Durham: Duke University Press, 1995), 196–223.

116. AAA, "Padrón de la Parroquia de Santa Marta." The 1792 census data is from Vollmer, *Bevölkerungspolitik und Bevölkerungsstruktur*, 253.

117. Barriga, *Memorias para la historia de Arequipa*, vol. 1, 244, 333.

118. AGN, R.J. (Ministerio de Justicia): Prefectura de Arequipa, Culto, Leg. 143.

the Cathedral, and finally because they change their Indian surnames and take on Spanish ones."[119]

Even the nephew of the Indian mayor of Santa Marta allegedly dropped the family surname and refused to recognize his uncle's authority.[120] If measures were not taken immediately to end such abuses, Cacique Vargas warned, "the day will arrive in which there will be no Indian left, much less anyone to pay Royal Tribute."[121] Surprisingly, little help was forthcoming from the state. The intendant was deluged with petitions from persons complaining that Vargas was forcing them to pay tribute even though they were not Indians; after a presentation of witnesses, most of them were exempted.[122] Most likely, the intendant thought it wise to give up some revenue in order to prevent political unrest.

Indeed, Vargas's dire warning may have sounded ridiculous to the intendant, because overall tribute revenue had risen during the late eighteenth century.[123] Nevertheless, a steady decline in indigenous communal landholdings throughout the period under study presaged a later decrease in tribute. As early as 1786, the Protector of Indians protested that the Indians were going to be cheated out of their land because the surveyors were using the smaller indigenous topo as a measurement instead of the larger Spanish topo, as was customary.[124] Meanwhile, the state was renting out about 220 topos of prime land, which it had classified as "left over" from the repartimientos in Yanahuara and Pocsi.[125] Two years later, influential Spaniards and creoles such as José Joaquín Tristán, Manuel Flores, Francisco Abril, and Juan de Goyeneche denied rumors that they had been usurping property belonging

---

119. ARAR/Int/Adm (20-I-1803), "Don Pascual Vargas representa las dificultades." His predecessors had also encountered such problems; see ARAR/Int/Ped (18-XII-1784), "Don Carlos Achircana pide que se le mande a Manuel Cavana pagar tributo"; and (22-VIII-1785), "Gregorio Flores protesta que el Cacique de Forasteros intenta cobrarle tributo aunque no sea indio."

120. ARAR/Int/Crim (7-VI-1805), "Mariano Solórsano y José Leon Choquetupa se acusan mutuamente de injurias."

121. ARAR/Int/Adm (20-I-1803), "Don Pascual Vargas representa las dificultades."

122. See petitions in ARAR/Int/Adm (28-V-1802), Melchor Acosta y Pinto; (1-VI-1805) Miguel Oblitas y Ramos; (5-III-1806) Gregorio Silva; (24-IV-1806) Tomás Cosme; (26-I-1807) Blas Plácido Ortís y Gallegos; (18-XII-1807) Pascual Bargas Espinosa y Giles; and (19-XII-1808) Bernardo Rocha.

123. See Tepaske and Klein, *The Royal Treasuries of the Spanish Empire in America*, vol. 1, 39–63; Brown, *Bourbons and Brandy*, 178; Sala i Vila, *Y se armó el Tole Tole*, 36–38, 279–87.

124. AGN, Derecho Indígena y Encomiendas, Leg. 24, Cuad. 419 (1786), "El Protector de Naturales en Arequipa protesta lo actuado en la revista y remensura de tierras."

125. ARAR/Int/Adm (20-IV-1787), "Informe de Don Juan Manuel Bustamante."

to indigenous communities, and they opposed the remeasurement of lands along the fertile west bank of the Chili River.[126] They had nothing to fear. The community of Cayma was left without enough property for each tribute-paying male to enjoy his customary 4 topos.[127] By the turn of the century, the size of the communal share had declined further. In the 1801 distribution, young men received only 2 topos in Yanahuara (which included their house lot in town) and a mere three-quarters of a topo in Tiabaya.[128]

After independence the Indians' loss of lands accelerated, especially on the west bank.[129] Landowners in Arequipa seized upon the change in government and laws as an opportunity to make gains. In early 1826, the new republican state in Lima sent an investigator to Arequipa to hear denunciations of state property being illegally occupied; those lands would be auctioned off to raise revenue. There were so many claims filed, most of them by Spanish landowners against Indians, that by September, the prefect ordered that all cases not clearly in the state's favor be discontinued.[130]

Two days later, however, several Spaniards who occupied urban lots belonging to the Indian community of Pocsi asked to purchase the property from the state. The community protested that the petitioners had used their connections to the caciques (that is, Spanish tribute collectors) to acquire the best lots, on which they built large homes and shops, while the Indians were forced to live on their agricultural plots or in the hills. The case ended abruptly, after the judge gave the Indians nine days to prove their title to the land.[131] At the same time, rather than continue to rent land "left over" from

---

126. AGN, Derecho Indígena, Leg. 40, Cuad. 838 (1788), "Fragmento de un expediente promovido por los Alcaldes, vecinos y hacendados de la ciudad de Arequipa sobre repartimientos de tierras."

127. ARAR/Int/Adm (18-VIII-1788), "El Común de Indios de Cayma pide copia de los autos sobre el repartimiento de tierras."

128. ARAR/Int/Adm (30-V-1801), "Sobre la mensura, asignación, y reparto de tierras vacantes."

129. Ponce, "Social Structure of Arequipa," 128–34; and Betford Betalleluz, "Fiscalidad, tierras y mercado: Las comunidades indígenas de Arequipa, 1825–1850," in Henrique Urbano, ed., *Tradición y modernidad en los Andes* (Cuzco: CERA Bartolomé de las Casas, 1992), 160.

130. AGN, Hacienda H-1-1, Leg. O.L. 145, Exp. 237 (1826), "Informe del Visitador al Sur Don Juan Evangelista de Yrigoyen y Zenteno." The prefect's order was dated Sept. 21, 1826.

131. ARAR/Pref (28-IX-1826), "Solicitud de Don Juan Isidro Cárdenas y otros que se les venda unos solares en Quequeña y Yarabamba." Presumably these were the urban lots for which Alvarez y Jiménez had charged a modest rent, payable to the community chest. See Barriga, *Memorias para la historia de Arequipa*, vol. 2, 124–25.

repartimientos, the state began to pay off its debts with land grants calculated at two-thirds of their value.[132]

By the repartimiento of 1830, each tribute-paying Indian was assigned only one topo of land, and this was to be the last distribution. In compliance with decrees emitted by Simón Bolívar, Indians were granted full ownership of their parcels, with the right to pass them on to their heirs. As for their right to sell the land, the laws were confusing: the initial 1824 decree granted them full title, an 1825 decree prohibited the sale of these plots until 1850, and a law passed by the Peruvian congress in 1828 allowed literate Indians to sell their land.[133] It is impossible to know exactly how many Indians sold their land, but there are hints that the Spanish governor of Yanahuara "encouraged" them to do so.

Indian Rosa Taco complained that governor José Butrón convinced her stepmother to give him power of attorney and then secretly sold a half topo that rightfully belonged to Taco.[134] Indian Manuel Mamani testified in his will that following Butrón's advice, "which seemed legal," he had sold his topo for nine hundred pesos. Butrón acted as the intermediary and was paying Mamani in installments; so far Mamani had received only six hundred pesos.[135] During the tribute censuses of 1843 and 1852, moreover, several Indians asked to be exempted because they had sold their land shares to support themselves.[136] In 1843, officials asked the indigenous authorities of

132. AGN, Hacienda O.L. 144-126 (1826), "Razón de los ingresos anuales que aproxima-damente tiene este Tesoro Público"; ARAR/Pref (3-XII-1826), "Sobre que . . . se proceda a la devolución de las tierras que se remataron en Don Pedro José Toranza"; (1-VII-1828) "Don José Benigno Frías, Don Manuel Marcó del Pont y Don Evaristo Mamani protestan el despojo de sus tierras sin ser oídos"; (4-IX-1829) "Autos entre Don Felipe Santiago de Velarde y Don Juan de Dios Medina con Doña Melchora Lopes sobre el derecho a un estanque de agua en el Pago de Umacollo"; and (9-II-1846), "Sobre el arreglo definitivo de las aguas del Pago de Umacollo."

133. Bolívar's decrees are reprinted in Simón Bolívar, Decretos del Libertador, Sociedad Bolivariana de Venezuela, ed., vol. 1 (Caracas: Imprenta Nacional, 1961), 295–96, 410–11; see also Jacobsen, Mirages of Transition, 122–25.

134. ARAR/CS/Crim (17-X-1831), "Contra Santos Obando por haber estropeado a María Josefa Coronado."

135. ARAR/Pref (16-X-1835), "Juan Manuel Caisa Mendosa protesta que Manuel Mamani murió intestado." The sub-prefect charged that Indians in Yanahuara had sold or rented out their plots; see ARAR/Pref (16-VI-1830), "Los indígenas de Yanahuara quejan de los procedimientos durante la revisita." In 1835 the indigenous community of Pocsi sold eighteen topos. See ARAR, notary Francisco de Linares, land sale dated Oct. 23, 1835.

136. Petitions from Mariano Guamani (May 16, 1844) and Matías Quispe (May 26, 1844) in AGN, Hacienda H-4-1845, R. 287 (1843), Matrícula de Indígenas de Arequipa; and María Paco (March 11, 1852) in AGN, Hacienda H-4-2191, R. 631 (1852), Matrícula de Indígenas de Arequipa.

Paucarpata why two entire ayllus had disappeared from the tribute rosters, and they replied that a Señor Romaña had acquired their land in a lawsuit.[137]

Whatever amount was sold or lost, by the mid-nineteenth century, it was clear that there was no communal land available in the Arequipa valley to distribute to Indians. When Mariano Quispe, the son of a forastero in Yanahuara, asked to be assigned a plot in 1839, the district governor reported that there was not even enough land for the originarios.[138] In 1846, the Indians of Pocsi argued that because there were no community lands left, the exemption from tithing should extend to private land inherited from their parents.[139] Manuel Quispe of Cayma could not even hold onto the quarter topo he had been assigned as a disabled member of the community; because he did not pay tribute, the state agreed to sell the land to a retired accountant from the treasury who had denounced the "misappropriation."[140] Indians in many other regions of Peru did not experience as much loss of land, but the market value of agricultural land in the campiña of Arequipa and the collection of property taxes likely outweighed potential tribute revenues.[141]

The total number of registered tributaries (males between eighteen and fifty) in the province of Arequipa varied only slightly from 1789 to 1828, averaging about 1,150.[142] Beginning in the 1790s, however, it became increasingly difficult to collect the full amount of tribute owed in the countryside as well as the city.[143] When the sub-prefect was sued for debts in 1830, he

137. AGN, Hacienda H-4-1845, R. 287 (1843), "Matrícula de Indígenas de Arequipa." See also ARAR/Pref (12-VII-1849), "Francisco Escalante denuncia un despojo de José María Benavides."

138. ARAR/Pref (25-XI-1839), "Don Mariano Quispe pide probar que es indígena originario contribuyente de Yanahuara."

139. ARAR/Pref (9-VII-1846), "Unos indígenas de Pocsi protestan que el rematador de diezmos trata de cobrarles indebidamente."

140. ARAR/Pref (25-VI-1847), "Don Fernando Pacheco hace denuncia de un retazo de tierras."

141. Contrast with Jacobsen, *Mirages of Transition*, 125–27; Walker, "Peasants, Caudillos, and the State in Peru," 271–84; Gootenberg, "Population and Ethnicity in Early Republican Peru," 109–57; Peralta Ruíz, *En pos del tributo en el Cusco rural;* and Erwin Grieshaber, "Survival of Indian Communities in Nineteenth-Century Bolivia: A Regional Comparison," *Journal of Latin American Studies* 12, no. 2 (1980): 223–69.

142. Vollmer, *Bevölkerungspolitik und Bevölkerungsstruktur*, 286; BNP doc. D6603 (1813), "Matrícula de indios tributarios del Cercado de Arequipa"; AGN, Tributos, Leg. 5, Cuad. 160 (1817), "Tributo en la Intendencia de Arequipa"; AGN, Hacienda H-4-1623, R. 068 (1828) "Matrícula de Indígenas"; Betalleluz, "Fiscalidad, tierras y mercado," 152–53; and George Kubler, *The Indian Caste of Peru, 1795–1940* (Washington, D.C.: U.S. Government Printing Office, 1952), 11.

143. According to figures compiled by Sala i Vila, between 1795 and 1807, there was

complained that during the census of 1828, forasteros without land had initially been told incorrectly that they only had to pay three pesos, making it impossible to later collect the full rate of more than seven pesos.[144] Furthermore, while the first republican tribute census in 1828 showed an increase in the indigenous population, there were already indications of future declines: among the youth, females far outnumbered males, suggesting evasion.[145]

As the land available for this younger generation declined, there is evidence that Indians began trying to escape their ethnic identification. Between 1828 and 1836, the number of indigenous taxpayers in Tiabaya dropped by more than half.[146] Although the final counts from the tribute census of 1843 are missing, census takers repeatedly questioned community authorities about the high numbers of Indians listed as dead or absent. The answer they received over and over was that the men had gone off in search of work and often died far from home in the coastal valleys.[147] Undoubtedly many Indians did work in the valley plantations, but, as noted in the previous section, most were only seasonal migrants. A more intriguing clue to their "disappearance" can be found in the lists of marriages examined by the census takers; suddenly there appeared many villagers listed as "mestizos," which was a term rarely used in Arequipa.[148]

---

consistently a shortfall by about half of the approximately 8,500 pesos owed annually by Indians in the province of Arequipa. See Sala i Vila, *Y se armó el Tole Tole*, 304–8. There are numerous lawsuits against officials for failing to collect all tribute owed: see, for example, ARAR/Int/Adm (6-IV-1796), "Contra Don Mariano de Loredo, Subdelegado del Cercado, por descubierto al Ramo de Tributos" (case continues in several *cuadernos* until 1812); (15-III-1799) "Petición de Don José Osnaya, cacique recaudador de tributos de Characato"; (20-V-1802) "Contra Don Mariano Chalco de Figueroa, indio principal de Yanahuara"; (28-V-1802) "Contra Don Alfonso Osnaya, recaudador de Characato"; (4-IX-1816) "El Subdelegado del Cercado ordena que los recaudadores de tributos comparezcan y paguen las deudas"; ARAR/Pref (22-V-1831), "Los administradores del tesoro público informen que el subprefecto del cercado Manuel Amat y Leon debe 34,480 pesos"; (13-I-1844) "Contra el Recaudador de Miraflores Don Mariano Pinto"; (8-X-1846) "Contra Don Mariano Chávez, Gobernador de Chiguata"; (10-III-1847) "Contra Francisco Menéndez de Yanahuara."

144. ARAR/Pref (22-V-1831), "Contra el Subprefecto del Cercado Don Manuel Amat y Leon por deudas."

145. Betalleluz, "Fiscalidad, tierras y mercado," 152–53.

146. ARAR/Pref (15-IV-1836), "Contribución de Indígenas del Pueblo de Tiabaya."

147. AGN, Hacienda H-4-1845, R. 287 (1843), "Matrícula de Indígenas de Arequipa."

148. For a brief period after independence, mestizos had to pay a personal *casta* tax; in Arequipa, as elsewhere, it was notoriously difficult to collect. By this time the tax had been abolished, providing another economic incentive to declare oneself mestizo rather than Indian.

By the time the last tribute census was taken in 1852, the early warning from the cacique of Santa Marta was echoed by the authorities of Yanahuara, who lamented "that they believed with great reason that very soon that caste would disappear." The reason given is revealing: "Since many years ago, the Indians have been disappearing because of the lack of communal land, because since their Fathers obtained private ownership of these plots and sold them, the sons once they reach the age of ten or twelve flee."[149] Once again, however, the officials ignored the increasing proportions of non-Indians, who were now referred to as either Spanish or white rather than mestizo, in the parish marriage registers. As there is no evidence to suggest a demographic decline among Indians, they were probably making every effort to avoid being registered on the tax rolls.

In Tiabaya, the census takers in 1852 "did not order the censuses required by law to be drawn up because there did not exist any future or present taxpayer."[150] This apparent resignation of even the local officials to the disappearance of the Indians is particularly striking. They probably knew that it would be politically risky to force landless villagers to pay tribute and calculated that the inclusion of valuable property in the local land market would outweigh revenue losses.

The way that individual Indians in Arequipa perceived their ethnic identity when they were not dealing with the state may never be known. In a rare glimpse, onlookers unsuccessfully tried to break up a fight between Indians from different villages on the grounds that they were all "people" (likely translated from the Quechua term *runa*).[151] Nevertheless, it is clear that the incentives for publicly claiming to be Indian or organizing along ethnic lines were declining; the availability of communal lands was steadily decreasing, and neither ethnic caciques nor indigenous councils had much effective power, given the proximity in Arequipa of high officials of the crown and, later, the republican state.

The advanced degree of acculturation, moreover, made it relatively easy for Indians to blend into the mixed populations in both the villages and the city.

It is also possible that some Indians who did have land, but now with private title, also declared themselves mestizos to census takers.

149. Entry dated June 14, 1852, in AGN, Hacienda H-4-2191, R. 631 (1852), "Matrícula de Indígenas de Arequipa."

150. Entry dated June 12, 1852, AGN, Hacienda H-4-2191, R. 631 (1852), "Matrícula de Indígenas de Arequipa."

151. ARAR/CS/Crim (30-IV-1834), "Contra José Tola y Casimiro Velásquez por la muerte de Gabino Flores."

By the turn of the century, the urban authorities were complaining of Indians passing into other ethnic groups. Several decades later, that trend had spread into the countryside. The days had passed when mestizos like the Puchos would claim to be Indians in order to maintain access to communal land. As the Indian share of land in the campiña decreased, so too did the tribute-paying population. It is unbelievable that the "disappearance" of the Indians was due only to migration. Rather, landless Indians began to declare that they were mestizo, and, in some cases, even Spanish.[152] The terms of the dominant political discourse in the White City, therefore, would be Hispanic rather than incorporating elements of indigenous culture.

Slaves in Arequipa

Slaves, like Indians, were legally considered a separate group, and even free people of African descent were more often identified by race than were mestizos. African slaves had been brought to the region to work in the vineyards.[153] By the late eighteenth century, they were increasingly replaced by free workers of various races, but in the coastal valleys the descendants of slaves still made up a significant part of the population. Within the province of Arequipa, the districts of Vítor and Tambo toward the coast had the highest proportions of people of African descent: 66 percent and 29.5 percent respectively.

Such demographics may have contributed to the perception that people of color came primarily from outside the central valley. Nevertheless, in terms of absolute numbers, more blacks, mulattoes, and zambos lived in the city of Arequipa, according to the 1792 census: there were 2,164 people of African descent, almost evenly split between slave and free and constituting 9 percent of the urban population.[154] In the eyes of French traveler Flora Tristan, however, fully one-quarter of the population seemed black or mulatto.

Local histories of Arequipa generally ignore the population of African descent, but Tristan constantly remarked upon the omnipresent slaves, such

152. For similar cases of ethnic passing, see María Isabel Remy, "La sociedad local al inicio de la república: Cusco, 1824–1850," *Revista Andina* 6, no. 2 (1988): 451–84; Jackson, "Race/Caste," 164–71; and Kubler, *The Indian Caste of Peru*, 36–37.
153. Davies, *Landowners in Colonial Peru*, 89–91; and Brown, *Bourbons and Brandy*, 48.
154. Vollmer, *Bevölkerungspolitik und Bevölkerungsstruktur*, 253–54.

as the young girl her relatives assigned to wait on her during her visit.[155] In the city, slaves served as both status symbols and servants for their masters. Others were trained as artisans, like Manuel de Quintana, who hoped to use his earnings as a carpenter in order to purchase his freedom.[156] A few slaves were freed by their masters or allowed to purchase their liberty, but it was a rare opportunity; a sample of notarial contracts between 1780 and 1850 turned up 117 sales of slaves and only thirteen letters of manumission (six of which had to be purchased).[157] María de Cáceres, for example, asked that her shop be sold and the money used to buy freedom for her grandchildren.[158] Even a grant of freedom was often conditional and tenuous. In 1780, for example, the reverend mother of Santa Catalina convent appeared before a notary to sign a document that would free the slave María, age twenty-two, after the nun's death. She confessed that although her own mother had actually freed María at birth, she had sold her; only when she thought "that it might later weigh on her conscience" did the reverend mother buy back María and pledge her future manumission.[159]

Lawsuits and petitions provide evidence of other masters who failed to keep their word. In 1777, for example, a dying woman asked that money be taken from her estate to free a friend's slave for whom she had served as godmother; over fifty years later, the slave's grandchildren were still trying to acquire their freedom.[160] Most slaves undoubtedly would have agreed with the sentiment expressed in María Rosa Arróspide's plea for mercy: "What reason can there be, Lord Intendant, for the unfortunate slaves, men as rational as their masters, to be considered as beasts of burden, untiring in

155. Tristan, *Peregrinations of a Pariah*, 92–97, 107, 127, 175, 187–90, 209–12.

156. AAA/Civ (31-I-1794), "Manuel de Quintana pide que el Sr. Don Lorenzo de La Quintana le pague." Vicente Torre had managed to purchase his freedom from his earnings as a shoemaker, as he stated in his testimony in the lawsuit ARAR/Int/Crim (5-VII-1819), "Doña Isidora Gutiérrez contra su esposo Don Patricio Texada por robo."

157. Compare with Carlos Aguirre, *Agentes de su propria libertad: Los esclavos de Lima y la desintegración de la esclavitud, 1821–1854* (Lima: Pontificia Universidad Católica del Peru, 1993); Christine Hünefeldt, *Paying the Price of Freedom: Family and Labor Among Lima's Slaves, 1800–1854* (Berkeley and Los Angeles: University of California Press, 1994); and Lyman L. Johnson, "Manumission in Colonial Buenos Aires," *Hispanic American Historical Review* 59, no. 2 (1979): 258–79.

158. Notary Manuel González de La Fuente, testament dated July 25, 1785.

159. Notary Pedro de Figueroa, Oct. 18, 1780.

160. ARAR/CS/Crim (11-II-1831), "Don Bartolomé Pedrero contra Don Toribio Gómez por injurias."

their service and without the slightest liberty to complain of their sad fate?"[161] Clearly, Arequipa was not a "racial democracy."

Although urban slaves did not enjoy lenient treatment, they did have relatively more freedom of movement than those who worked on plantations. Masters sent their slaves on errands throughout the city and hired them out as workers or artisans.[162] Those who had complaints against their owners, therefore, could seek refuge in the homes of other wealthy patrons who had offered to buy them.[163] Slaves who were far from their masters' sides also appeared as witnesses in a variety of criminal trials. Juan de Dios Bello, the slave of one of the church canons, was out watching the carnival celebrations when he saw a gentleman attack a young man.[164] Gregorio Pérez had to be bailed out of jail by his master after the games of chance he was watching in the plaza were broken up by the authorities.[165] Two slaves were called to court when the owner of one was the victim of a robbery; they testified that they had not been at home at the time, because they had gone to eat dinner in a café.[166] In one of the most surprising cases, the slave of the governor of Salta walked into a store to sell two pistols. When the shopkeeper could not get them to work, the slave (thinking they were unloaded) fired them at the ground, causing minor injuries to an Indian boy. He was absolved on the grounds that the shooting was accidental.[167]

Such freedom of movement allowed slaves to integrate themselves into broader plebeian networks, which came to the attention of authorities when they were mobilized to plan thefts and fence stolen goods. In 1778, for

161. ARAR/Int/Crim (23-VII-1819), "María Rosa Arróspide contra su amo Don Juan Bautista Arróspide por maltrato."

162. For studies of urban slavery, see Aguirre, *Agentes de su propria libertad*; Hünefeldt, *Paying the Price of Freedom*; Frederick P. Bowser, *The African Slave in Colonial Peru, 1524–1650* (Stanford: Stanford University Press, 1974); and Mary C. Karasch, *Slave Life in Rio de Janeiro, 1808–1850* (Princeton: Princeton University Press, 1987).

163. See ARAR/Cab/Civ, Leg. 15, Cuad. 401 (13-XI-1782), "Capitán Don Josef Medina contra Doña Agustina Castro Viejo y Doña Baleriana Ripa por robo de una esclava"; ARAR/Int/Ped (8-II-1797), "Don Francisco Sánchez pide que Doña Gabriela Benavente preste declaración sobre la esclava del primero"; (3-VIII-1798) "Don Mariano de Benavides pide que Don Bruno de La Llosa le devuelva su esclavo"; and ARAR/Pref (2-VII-1825), "Ursula Hurtado, esclava de Don José María Flores, pide que se la venda a otro amo."

164. ARAR/Pref (20-II-1828), "Contra Don Mariano Arróspide por heridas a Marcelo Arayco."

165. ARAR/Int/Crim (26-V-1806), "Don Manuel Pérez contra el Alcalde de Cárcel por injurias a su criado."

166. ARAR/Int/Crim (19-III-1806), "Sobre el robo a Don Pedro Yansen."

167. ARAR/Int/Crim (27-I-1812), "Don José Butrón contra Juan de Dios de La Cruz."

example, Don Juan Fermín de Errea caught his slave María del Carmen stealing from his wife, but not before she had sold dozens of pearls to at least seven women, including a free mulatta, an Indian, and a *chichera*.[168] An investigation into the robbery of Doña Manuela Dias's house uncovered a large network of slaves and free persons, black and white, artisans and shopkeepers. One defendant, Francisco Valdivia, who worked rolling cigars, claimed that he had been recruited by Dias's own slave but confessed that he had sold various items from his share of the loot to three shopkeepers, two slaves, and a silversmith. Agustín Salamanca, a black man nicknamed "the soap maker," went all the way to the city of Tacna to sell some rosaries to Francisca the *"mulata pulpera."*[169] In 1808, Juan Antonio Manrique, absent from his master, who lived in the Majes valley, said that he had been recruited into robbing some silver after getting drunk with a laborer and two tailors (one of them a free mulatto) at the shop of "the Negro Miguel."[170]

Of course, slaves did not rely on their contacts in plebeian society only for criminal purposes. In 1780, Ramón Arguedas asked the vicar of Arequipa to make María Ramírez fulfill her promise to marry him. María admitted their engagement but backed out by saying that she had not realized Ramón was a slave.[171] But others did not share María's objections; marriage petitions reveal several cases of slaves who married free persons.[172] Even when they chose to marry other slaves, they sometimes presented free persons, apparently friends or coworkers, as witnesses. For example, two tailors and a shoemaker stood up for slaves Joaquín Palacio and Petronila Lancho.[173]

Less information has survived about free people of color, because neither were they valuable commodities like slaves nor did they enjoy the legal rights of Indians. Nonetheless, people were more frequently identified in the documents by the terms *black*, *mulatto*, and *zambo* than *mestizo*. Even though they apparently stood out by race in local eyes, they worked in a variety of occupations.[174] There is no evidence, moreover, that their social

168. ARAR/Corregimiento/Crim, Leg. 26, Exp. 439 (18-VIII-1778), "Causa seguida por Don Juan Fermín de Errea sobre las perlas que robó María del Carmen."
169. ARAR/Int/Crim (3-XII-1796), "Causa seguida sobre el robo de las joyas de Doña Manuela Dias."
170. ARAR/Int/Crim (1-VII-1808), "Contra Juan Antonio Manrique y otros por robo."
171. AAA/Mat (11-I-1780), "Ramón Arguedas pide que María Ramírez se cumpla con sus esponsales."
172. See AAA/Mat.
173. AAA/Mat (26-III-1800), "Joaquín Palacio y Petronila Lancho, esclavos de Don Lorenzo Murguía."
174. At least one mulatto, Bernardo Portugal, worked as a silversmith. See ARAR/

relations were limited to others of African descent. Like slaves, free people of color married or formed relationships of godparenthood with persons of distinct ethnic descent. Vicente Torre, a zambo and a freed slave, identified himself as a good friend of merchant Patricio Texada, who presented him as a witness in a dispute.[175] Official records cannot reveal whether people of African descent felt a common affinity, but they do indicate that they never organized socially or politically around a distinct ethnic identity. Further, when they attempted to defend their conduct against negative stereotypes, they used (even as they subtly modified) the dominant Hispanic notion of honor.

Perceptions of Ethnicity

If the aim of the caste system was to "divide and rule," there is little evidence that it succeeded in late colonial Arequipa.[176] To a certain extent, the indigenous population was still officially separated into a Republic of Indians, backed up by a legal structure that assigned them special obligations and rights, such as tribute and access to communal land. When such rights were not honored, however, indigenous authorities complained that the persons under their charge were passing into other castes. Many people of African descent, whether slave or free, were also identified by their color, but race did not segregate them from other plebeians. The social dynamics examined at the beginning of the chapter, however, also prevented the formation of multiethnic alliances along class lines in opposition to local elites.

Nowhere in colonial Spanish America did the caste system function according to the ideal, but it is particularly striking that in Arequipa, many authorities began to give up even trying to classify people by race. When someone appeared in court, for example, she or he was legally obliged to

---

Corregimiento/Crim, Leg. 26, Exp. 433 (21-I-1773), "Don Juan Joseph de Valcarcel contra Bernardo Portugal."

175. ARAR/Int/Crim (5-VII-1819), "Doña Isidora Gutiérrez contra su esposo Don Patricio Texada por robo." For examples of intermarriage, see AAA/Mat.

176. Flores Galindo asserts the opposite for late colonial Lima, though, in this case, the differences in our interpretations are not merely regional. I think that his reliance upon criminal records leads to an overemphasis on ethnic conflict. See Flores Galindo, *Aristocracia y plebe*, 168–79.

provide pertinent personal data such as occupation, age, civil status, and ethnicity. In Arequipa, however, that last item was recorded haphazardly, and the only terms that appeared with any frequency were *Indian, black, mulatto,* or *zambo.* Occasionally witnesses were identified as Spanish in the smaller villages (where it may have been more important to maintain divisions), or in cases where their testimony was being contrasted with that of Indian witnesses or defendants.[177]

Even more surprising—and revealing—was the absence of ethnic identifications in the parish registers, since it was at baptism that a person was, theoretically, assigned to the proper caste.[178] A clue to the reason behind such a glaring omission appears in a letter from Bishop Gonzaga de La Encina to the king in 1815, in which he explained: "This classification is odious to the parish priests, since having been ordered by the courts to do it, the priests found themselves obliged either to tell the truth or to lie. If they did the former, all those who judged themselves to be Spanish citizens, not being such, believed they had been insulted, and they rose up against the priests, they insulted, scorned and slandered them. If the latter, it weighed upon their consciences."[179] This statement also reinforces the argument of the cacique of Santa Marta that a baptismal certificate from the cathedral was no proof of racial purity.

Significantly, the term *mestizo* was rarely used in local documents. Although the 1792 census officially identified 17.5 percent of the population as mestizo, it was compiled either by authorities from outside Arequipa, or at least under the pressure of Bourbon officials.[180] Similarly, foreign visitors identified the majority of the population as mestizo or *cholo* (which referred to acculturated Indians), rather than white.[181] On the rare occasions that

177. See ARAR/Int/Crim (4-X-1800), "Contra Matías Alpaca y otros por el robo que hicieron de la caja de Comunidad de Paucarpata"; (21-V-1803) "Contra Isabel Portugal por maltratos a su esposo Rudecindo Megía"; and (2-II-1804), "Sebastian Valencia contra María Laguna por injurias." For an example of using the testimony of Spaniards against Indians, see ARAR/Int/Crim (7-X-1807), "Contra Antonio Dias por concubinato con la Casica de Yanahuara."

178. One may assume that those baptized in Indian parishes were de facto classified, but the cathedral administered sacraments to all non-Indians, and its records list no racial classifications during the period under study.

179. BNP doc. D11883, "Copiador del Obispo Gonzaga," letter dated July 7, 1815.

180. Vollmer, *Bevölkerungspolitik und Bevölkerungsstruktur,* 253.

181. Ernst W. Middendorf, *Perú,* vol. 1 (Lima: Universidad Nacional Mayor de San Marcos, 1973–74), 164; Middendorf, *Perú,* vol. 2, 170; and Heinrich Witt, *Diario y observaciones sobre el Perú* (Lima: COFIDE, 1987), 13.

locals did use the term *mestizo*, it was associated closely with the indigenous population, or else its meaning was clarified, as when the priest of Cayma advocated settling "Spanish mestizos" in the village.[182]

Legally, a mestizo with a Spanish father and an Indian mother had to pay tribute. The Puchos of Tiabaya tried to use this law to their advantage in order to claim a share of communal land; they argued that although their mother was a mestiza, her mother was Indian, and she and her children should follow that caste.[183] Similarly, Francisco Luis de Sosa petitioned the departmental junta in 1829 to be assigned a share of land—"as a mestizo"—and reappointed as a tribute collector.[184] Indian Asencio Huerta, on the other hand, tried to get his sons exempted from tribute because his wife was Spanish. He successfully claimed that it was customary "that the mestizos like my sons, always have been reputed and considered in the class of Spaniards."[185]

When it was used, therefore, *mestizo* had a meaning closer to *cholo*. One of the few witnesses identified as "of the mestizo caste," for example, was also credited with being an "expert in the Spanish Language."[186] Clearly, the assumption was that mestizos were virtually Indians. Given its association with "Indianness" and the obligation to pay tribute, most people of mixed race probably tried to avoid being labeled with the term at all. The sudden appearance of mestizos during the tribute census of 1843 marked a transitional stage that led to the prevalence of Spaniards and whites during that of 1852. The important legal distinction, therefore, was between Indians and everyone else.

182. Zamácola y Jáuregui, *Apuntes para la historia de Arequipa*, 45.

183. BNP doc. C2629 (1788), "Apelación de Agustín Alpaca, Cacique de Cayma, contra los hijos de Bernardo Pucho." For similar debates in Colombia, see Frank Safford, "Race, Integration, and Progress: Elite Attitudes and the Indian in Colombia, 1750–1870," *Hispanic American Historical Review* 71, no. 1 (1991): 14.

184. *El Republicano*, supplement to Oct. 3, 1829, 4. For other references to land being distributed to mestizos, see ARAR/Pref (9-VII-1846), "Unos indígenas de Pocsi protestan que el rematador de diezmos trata de cobrarles indebidamente"; and (25-VI-1847), "Don Fernando Pacheco hace denuncia de un retazo de tierras en Cayma."

185. ARAR/Int/Adm (5-III-1807), "Expediente para que se declare a los hijos de Asencio Huerta, Indio, y Rosa Vílchez, Española, por mestizos." See also ARAR/Int/Adm (26-I-1807), "Blas Plácido Ortís y Gallegos pide se le declare exento de tributar." For similar claims in Colombia, see J. Jaramillo Uribe, "Mestizaje y diferenciación social en el Nuevo Reino de Granada en la segunda mitad del siglo XVIII," *Anuario Colombiano de historia social y de la cultura* 2, no. 3 (1965): 36.

186. ARAR/Int/Crim (3-VII-1815), "Doña María Zenteno y Capas contra Cayetana Riberos y otros por injurias."

In fact, when claims to Spanish status were investigated for racial purity, few held up under scrutiny. In the 1770s, for instance, the children of Miguel Gerónimo de Medina petitioned to be declared legally Spanish; even their own witnesses, however, identified their race as mixed. Although they confirmed that Medina was Spanish, one called his wife, Andrea Ati, *cuarterona* (one-quarter black), and the other called her *media Asambada* (roughly half zambo).[187]

Pascual Bargas Espinosa y Giles ran into the same problem when he tried to exempt himself from paying tribute on the grounds that he was Spanish. His witnesses described his father variously as zambo, half zambo, and cholo, and his mother as "seeming Spanish," zamba, and mulatta; as for Pascual, one concluded he was Spanish, another zambo, and the third mulatto. The cacique seized upon these inconsistencies and pointed out: "If we should judge on appearances, the sentence would come out against Pascual, because in addition to being an Indian he seems like one, as has been said."

Pascual later prevaricated that "it is a question of name that my father seemed cholo to him because he was white, and my mother mulatta because she had somewhat curly hair, but blonde." The judge also investigated whether Pascual's wife was Spanish; witness Bernardo Torres testified that he considered her Spanish "although she does not appear to be, since her aunts . . . are acknowledged as Spaniards." When the lawsuit entered its third year, a frustrated Pascual accused the cacique and his cohorts of plotting to catch "the persons who are wheat-colored [*del color trigueño*] in order to arrest and oppress them." Ultimately, the intendant exempted him from paying tribute as a non-Indian even if not a Spaniard.[188]

When it came to ethnic identity in Arequipa, as in many areas of Latin America, appearances could be deceiving.[189] Once factors such as dress or customs were considered along with color, categories could become very ambiguous. In 1807, the Spanish mayor of Yanahuara accused the cacica of keeping her Indian lover, Antonio Dias, off the tribute rolls. The witnesses performed linguistic feats. Ignacio Paderes testified that he knew Antonio's father by sight as a "mestizo medio cholo" and that his mother was an Indian

187. AAA/Civ (1772), "María Petrona y María Nieves Medina piden que se les declare españolas."

188. ARAR/Int/Adm (18-XII-1807), "Pascual Bargas Espinosa y Giles queja que el Cacique de Forasteros le cobra tributo aunque sea español."

189. In addition to the literature on race and class cited at the beginning of the chapter, see Martin Minchom, *The People of Quito, 1690–1810: Change and Unrest in the Underclass* (Boulder: Westview Press, 1994), 153–97.

"according to what people said," which made Antonio a "choloized Indian" (*indio acholado*). Simón Corrales described his parents' appearance in a similar fashion, concluding that Antonio "in his judgment is more Indian than cholo."[190]

Even at the highest levels of society, color was in the eyes of the beholder. The colonial priest and chronicler Travada y Córdova admitted that the creoles of Arequipa had a few drops of noble Indian blood in their veins, but he argued that it was more the sun that had darkened their skin.[191] Eighty years later Flora Tristan noted, with a touch of her characteristic sarcasm: "In aristocratic parlance 'white' means anyone with no negro or Indian ascendants, and I saw several ladies who passed as white, although their skin was the colour of gingerbread, because their fathers were born in Andalusia or Valencia."[192] The elites of Arequipa, therefore, were probably sensitive to suspicions about their racial purity from outsiders, including officials from Spain or Lima. The Bourbon-appointed customs administrator Juan Bautista Pando had made precisely that charge when accusing elite creoles of instigating the tax revolt of 1780.[193]

Because two-thirds of the population was officially identified as Spanish in the 1792 census, whiteness did not automatically confer elite status in Arequipa. Therefore there were, likely, fewer efforts to maintain exclusive standards. In one case, a witness testified that because a woman had claimed that the father of her illegitimate child was Spanish, "therefore her daughter Francisca was Spanish *enough*, and well born."[194] Given that few in Arequipa could claim to be absolutely "pure" Spaniards, Bishop Gonzaga probably reflected a general consensus that in the interest of social peace, it was better not to stir up the hornet's nest of racial labels. After all, rumors that tribute would be extended to those of mixed race had helped trigger the 1780 revolt. This unspoken agreement could explain the numerous Arequipeños who appeared in official documents without any indication of their caste. Perhaps the scribes could not bring themselves to identify "wheat-colored" witnesses

190. ARAR/Int/Crim (7-X-1807), "Contra Antonio Dias por concubinato con la Casica de Yanahuara Doña María Tone."

191. Travada y Córdova, *El suelo de Arequipa*, 93.

192. Tristan, *Peregrinations of a Pariah*, 127.

193. Paz y Guini, *Guerra separatista*, 108.

194. The emphasis is mine. See BNP doc. C3532, "Don Agustín Alpaca, Cacique de Cayma, contra los hijos de Bernardo Pucho." By contrast, Haitin asserts that few mestizos were absorbed into the Spanish category in Lima; see Haitin, "Late Colonial Lima," 305.

as Spanish, but leaving their race off the record entirely kept everyone happy and tacitly allowed the majority to consider themselves white.

Such discretion does not mean that Arequipeños were free from racism. Many expressed prejudices, common throughout Peru, that identified non-whites as dishonorable. Those of African descent—and particularly the racially mixed mulattoes and zambos—were widely believed to be devious, crafty, and prone to criminal activities. In 1773, for example, Juan Joseph de Valcarcel sued Bernardo Portugal for slander after the silversmith accused him of theft. Portugal was a mulatto, and, therefore, it was he, according to Valcarcel, who was "by nature inclined toward the offense of Spaniards, and with a propensity for employment in only the occupation of Thieves."[195] Others accused mulattoes of lacking in respect. As Josef Antonio García commented in one case: "Those Zambas have as a custom to stir up quarrels."[196]

Indians, on the other hand, were tagged with the vices of laziness, ignorance, and drunkenness. When Vicente Vilca and Isabel Condori, Indians of Santa Marta, complained that their mayor was abusing them, the intendant appointed Dr. Mariano Larrea to investigate the charge. Larrea upheld the mayor's authority and belittled the Indians' complaints: "The leisure and desires of these poor Natives end in drink for which reason one should not pay attention to their outcries and bragging."[197] This stereotype was still strong after independence. Several members of the departmental junta argued that Indians must be forced to work, because they were "inclined toward laziness, apathetic, without aspirations to better their sad means of existence, and with only the need to provide themselves a scanty and crude nourishment."[198]

Such stereotypes led Arequipeños to enrich their fighting vocabulary with racial insults. One colorful exchange in 1819 was provoked when Juan de Mata Núñez scolded some boys for throwing garbage from their house into

195. ARAR/Corregimiento/Crim, Leg. 26, Exp. 433 (21-I-1773), "Don Juan Joseph de Valcarcel contra Bernardo Portugal." See also Leg. 26, Exp. 434 (18-III-1773), "Antonio Zúniga e Ignacio Gordillo contra Diego Navarro, mulato."

196. ARAR/Corregimiento/Crim, Leg. 26, Exp. 445 (19-XII-1782), "Don Faustino Biamonte y su esposa Petronila de Carpio contra Sebastian Bedoya."

197. ARAR/Int/Crim (13-XI-1798), "Vicente Vilca e Isabel Condori, indios de Santa Marta, piden su libertad."

198. "Propuesta a la Junta Departamental del Diputado Juan de Dios Ballón para impulsar la minería," in *El Republicano*, Oct. 3, 1829, 3–4.

his neighboring lot. Their aunt, Lorenza Escudero, reportedly came out and called him a "black dog."

"The Indian calls [me] a Negro?" Núñez retorted.

Escudero escalated the exchange by threatening that "the Blacks [should] get ridden out of town on the back of a mule."

Not to be outdone, Núñez countered with "Indian women [should] get ridden out tied to a llama like a sack of potatoes."[199] Even if not meant literally, such insults associated the person's behavior with the stereotypes of the slurred group. Arequipeños were sensitive to that implication, because it could strip away the tacit consent that they were, more or less, white.

Although Arequipeños expressed the racist attitudes of other Peruvians, they did not seem to share their fear of the Indian or African masses.[200] According to the 1792 census, Indians in Cuzco and people of African descent in Lima made up almost 45 percent of the respective populations of those cities. By contrast, Arequipa's population included only 6.4 percent Indians and 9 percent of African descent.[201] Because the nonwhite population in and around the city was relatively small and did not claim a distinct, politically charged identity, these groups were not considered a dangerous threat.

The indigenous communities of Yanahuara and Cayma had even been allowed to form militia companies. There were also elites who defended "their" Indians. Although the priest of Cayma hoped to rid his parishioners of their superstitions, he still referred to the Indians living around Arequipa as "very civilized."[202] And when one member of the departmental junta proposed forcing the Indians to work, the deputy from the province of Caylloma protested that "the Indian worked when he was treated and paid well, as can be seen in practice in various plantations of Vítor and Majes."[203]

---

199. The original quotes were: "Que a los negros se sacaba en un aparejo," and "que a las indias se sacaba en una llama con costal y soga." ARAR/Int/Crim (5-I-1819), "Juan de Mata Núñez contra Doña Lorenza Escudero por injurias."

200. On racial fears in Lima, see Hünefeldt, *Paying the Price of Freedom*, 60–61, 180; and Haitin, "Late Colonial Lima," 284–85, 339.

201. Vollmer, *Bevölkerungspolitik und Bevölkerungsstruktur*, 248, 261. The population of Lima had been between 40 and 50 percent of African descent since 1593; see Bowser, *The African Slave*, 339–41.

202. Zamácola y Jáuregui, *Apuntes para la historia de Arequipa*, 26–27. See also quote by Intendant Alvarez y Jiménez in Barriga, *Memorias para la historia de Arequipa*, vol. 1, 57.

203. Minutes from the meeting of July 20, 1829, reprinted in *El Republicano*, supplement to Oct. 10, 1829, 1. There were a few elites outside of Arequipa who espoused similar views; see Charles Walker, "Voces discordantes: Discursos alternativos sobre el indio a fines de la colonia,"

More important than debating the relative importance of class or caste, therefore, is examining the social and political implications of the ambiguities that existed in both categories. The society of eighteenth- and nineteenth-century Arequipa was ranked hierarchically, but neither the wealth of the elite nor the poverty of the lower classes was as extreme as that in larger capitals, such as Lima and Mexico City. The middling economic sector included fractions that blended into the city's more clearly elite and plebeian families. As families with honorable surnames fell on hard times, it was difficult to distinguish them from more successful upstarts who proudly affixed a Don or Doña to their own names.

The ambiguities of class were matched by those of caste and, similarly, could be used as a basis for broad claims to honor. When people were called upon to classify their neighbors, the confusion over appearances usually prevented a definitive identification of their ethnicity. By discreetly avoiding the use of racial labels in most situations, a majority of Arequipeños could claim to be white.

Although officials in Arequipa were, apparently, less strict in their use of racial categories than those in Lima and Cuzco, there are likely parallel cases in politically important provincial cities throughout Spanish America. The rare use of the term *mestizo* also suggests the need to rethink the timing and process in the emergence of *mestizaje* as a basis for national identity in Spanish America. In the colonial and early republican periods, mestizos were defined legally by what they were not (tribute-paying Indians). Rather than developing a unifying identity of their own, they tended to be grouped, in cultural terms, with either Spaniards or Indians.

The dominant identity as white that emerged in Arequipa, therefore, had both exclusive and inclusive dynamics. Casting the racial other as primarily from outside Arequipa—blacks from the coast or Indians from the high-lands—denied the cultural contributions of these groups to the local society. Nevertheless, many who under legal examination might prove to be of mixed race were treated as Spanish in daily life. Moreover, even some who were identified as of indigenous or African descent, if they accepted dominant Hispanic norms and codes of behavior, were incorporated into the broader community networks that formed the basis for political mobilization.

---

in Charles Walker, ed., *Entre la retórica y la insurgencia: Las ideas y los movimientos sociales en los Andes, siglo XVIII* (Cuzco: CERA Bartolomé de las Casas, 1996), 89–112.

3

Families, Friends, and Festivities

Ties of Community and Culture

Late colonial and early republican Arequipa was home to a significant intermediary social group made up of artisans, traders, and farmers, as well as shopkeepers and professionals. In addition, the erratic fortunes of an agricultural economy meant that many prominent families did not have the wealth to match their social status. Ethnic identity, like social class, was often fluid. Almost by implicit agreement, all but the most absurd claims of being Spanish went unquestioned. Even those Arequipeños who were identified by their African or Indian ancestry did not face rigid social segregation. With the exception of the very rich and socially exclusive on the one hand, or the very poor and dark-skinned on the other, Arequipeños lived, worked, and spent their leisure time together, in close quarters.

Of course, not everyone appreciated crowded urban living. When the prefect wanted to knock down part of the wall around the Dominican monastery in order to straighten out the street, the friars objected to his plan: "To join our cells to a numerous neighborhood, of generally vulgar and uneducated people, in which some sing, others dance, those argue, these shout, the kids cry, the dogs bark, the workshops hammer, the guitars play impure and profane songs, and all this within our earshot . . ."[1]

As anyone who has lived in a small town or a crowded neighborhood knows, relationships within communities include both cooperation and conflict. Arequipa was no exception. Neighbors kept track of each other's personal as well as professional business, and, by sharing this knowledge with others, they affected the reputations that were so important in a face-to-face society. During disputes, each side appealed to the court of public opinion by claiming to abide by codes of honor, although specific interpretations of those values could vary. In this sense, community implied not an absolute moral consensus, but rather participation in an ongoing argument using a common language.[2] The language and rituals developed at the neighborhood level, moreover, served as a repertoire for riots and other political actions.

Indeed, just as the physical boundaries between private and public were relatively fluid, there was no clear division between domestic and community concerns. Women, therefore, were prominent in social networks of talk and surveillance. Cases of adultery, for example, provoked conflict between rival women and their respective allies, and the ensuing fights were staged for maximum public effect. Despite—or perhaps because of—the central role of women in influencing popular opinion at the neighborhood level, they would be increasingly marginalized within the public sphere after independence. Republican and liberal political theories defined public opinion as resulting from "rational" debate among educated male citizens, not the "gossip" of women.[3]

The social networks that made up the local community were strongest at the neighborhood level and among those of fairly close socioeconomic status. Nevertheless, ties of kinship, place of origin, and occupation did extend throughout the city and even to neighboring villages. Townspeople frequently left their neighborhoods on business, and they also roamed widely in their free time. Leisurely walks downtown or on the alameda along the river allowed the status-conscious to see and be seen. During the summer and on holidays, moreover, Arequipeños extended their *paseos* to the smaller villages and mineral baths of the immediate countryside. Just as households blended

1. Petition dated April 29, 1828, in AGN, R.J. (Ministerio de Justicia): Prefectura de Arequipa, Culto, Leg. 143 (1829).
2. See David Warren Sabean, *Power in the Blood: Popular Culture and Village Discourse in Early Modern Germany* (London: Cambridge University Press, 1984), 29.
3. Habermas, *The Structural Transformation of the Public Sphere*, 89–102.

into neighborhoods, these broader contacts knit together a larger community. Leisure activities, especially civic celebrations and religious festivals, brought together Arequipeños from all walks of life and marked the fullest expression of a shared regional culture. Even strangers who met one another on the street or in a tavern brought with them the repertoire of common experiences and values built up daily in the overlapping communities. Such occasions, therefore, could affirm a common identity among Arequipeños and forge the broad alliances that, subsequently, were mobilized in times of political turmoil. Nevertheless, such an outcome could not be guaranteed. The social mix, with its latent class, ethnic, and gender conflicts, could also prove divisive. This chapter will explore both the potential for social and cultural cohesion and the tensions that threatened to pull it apart.

Households and Neighborhoods

Households, the smallest units of the urban community, varied greatly in size and composition, as two sources allow us to examine. One is the 1811 census from the urban parish La Ranchería, which includes a total of 2,035 inhabitants grouped by household.[4] Some of the findings from this parish census are confirmed by a sample of 290 wills taken from the notarial records at five-year intervals between 1780 and 1850.[5] One of the most surprising aspects of both the census and the wills is the gender imbalance; approximately 60 percent of the inhabitants counted in La Ranchería and an equal proportion of the testators are women. Because the census was for religious and not military or tax purposes, this imbalance is difficult to explain; it may be that many of the men (especially younger, single men) were off working in agriculture. Whatever the cause, this striking result underlines the important social and economic role played by women in the city.

4. Because this parish was on the outskirts of the city, elite households may be underrepresented. AAA, "Padrón de los Feligreses designados a la Vice-Parroquia del Sor. Sn. José de La Ranchería erigida el año de 1811."
5. ARAR, Notarios Públicos. Those notaries sampled were: Pedro de Figueroa (1780), Manuel González de La Fuente (1785), Ramón Bellido (1790), Rafael Hurtado (1795), Mariano de Tapia (1800), Josef Alberto de Gómez (1805), Hermenegildo Zegarra (1810), Rafael Hurtado (1815), Francisco Xavier de Linares (1820), José Nazario de Rivera (1825), Pedro Mariano Araujo (1830), Francisco de Linares (1835), Casimiro Salazar (1840), Miguel José de Chávez (1845), and Mariano Bolaños (1850).

Men rarely lived alone, even if single, and a mere 4.5 percent of the male testators were widowed. The small number of widowers may have resulted partly from demographic factors, but men were also more likely to remarry than were women; 24.7 percent of the male testators who were married or widowed had been married more than once, compared with 14.3 percent of the women. Such a pattern is no surprise, given the male advantages within marriage. Overall, nonetheless, households headed by single or married men made up only 43.6 percent of those in La Ranchería.

But male-headed households were larger, with 3.9 persons compared with an average of 3.2, and therefore they encompassed slightly more than half (52.6 percent) of the parish population. Of course, few men could hope to be patriarchs on the scale of Don Diego Oyanguren, who, in addition to a wife and five children, could boast of having seven domestic servants. But of those who resided permanently in the city, most had at least a wife (common-law if not legal) and, probably, children.

Women in La Ranchería had a more varied experience. While a slight majority lived under the authority of a husband or father, 14 percent of the households were made up of women living alone. Furthermore, there were virtually the same number of female-headed households (43.8 percent) as there were households controlled by patriarchs; however, they were smaller, on average (2.6 members), and they included only 35.2 percent of the parish population.[6] Unfortunately, the census taker did not record whether these matriarchs were single, widowed, or separated. But in 64.6 percent of the female-headed households with children, those children carried their mothers' last names, which implies they were illegitimate.

Such a large number of independent women was not unique to La Ranchería parish. Of the women from the sample of wills in Arequipa, 24.7 percent were widowed, and another 33.1 percent had never married. Moreover, 57.6 percent of those single women had illegitimate children. The criminal documents also reveal cases of adult women continuing to live with, and often work with, their mothers. For example, Bernarda and Juana Torres ran a bakery with their mother, María, while Francisca Corrales was assisted in her tavern by her daughters.[7]

---

6. Such a large proportion of female-headed households was not unusual in Latin American cities during the nineteenth century. See Arrom, *The Women of Mexico City*, 129–34; and the articles by Barbara Potthast-Jutkeit, Elizabeth Anne Kuznesof, Donald Ramos, and Arlene J. Díaz and Jeff Stewart in the *Journal of Family History* 16, no. 3 (1991).

7. ARAR/CS/Crim (12-XII-1832), "Doña María Beltrán contra Doña Bernarda, Doña

Finally, 12.6 percent of the households in La Ranchería (with 12.2 percent of the population) had no clearly identified head and were probably made up of relatives or friends. In particular, adult siblings often lived together. For example, when Nicolás Carbajal sneaked into his lover's house, her older, married sister threw him out and called the night watchman to accompany him home; once there, Carbajal called upon his two sisters, brother, and sister-in-law to protect him.[8] Sisters Manuela and Juana Carpio also lived in the same house with their husbands, who had a hard time getting along together.[9]

Even those Arequipeños who lived alone or in nuclear families often had other relatives nearby who could serve as a larger support group. A conservative count of people with the same last name living close together in La Ranchería parish turned up at least eighty-five households (13.5 percent of the total). For example, Tereza Pantigoso, age eighty, lived with her daughter, age forty-eight, and a younger girl (probably her granddaughter). Marcela Pantigoso, age forty-eight, lived next door with her three children. Not far away were Ramón Pantigoso, age twenty-five, with his wife; and Rafaela Pantigoso, age forty-seven, with two children.

The extension of family beyond the household is one indication that most households were not private and isolated, but rather incorporated into the larger neighborhood. Only the wealthiest families of the city occupied entire houses, with relatives, servants, slaves, and other dependents. Homeowners of more middling status needed the extra income that rents could provide, and consequently many "households" in late colonial and early republican Arequipa were actually only rented rooms. The large stone houses of the central city were built around two or three interior patios. The rooms that faced directly onto the street were often rented out as commercial stores or artisan workshops. Those around the patios, on the other hand, were occupied as residences, and there were sometimes shacks built right in the courtyards to house even more people.[10]

Because artisans often worked out of their rooms, these houses were not

---

Juana, y Doña María Torres por injurias"; and (7-III-1827), "Contra Francisca y María Josefa Corrales por puñaladas a Pedro Moscoso."

8. ARAR/CS/Crim (7-V-1836), "Contra el sereno Lorenzo Velasco por heridas a Nicolás Carbajal."

9. ARAR/CS/Crim (12-V-1829), "Don Antonio Sans contra Don Miguel Cárdenas por injurias."

10. See, for example, ARAR, public notary Pedro de Figueroa (contract dated March 3, 1780).

simply residential units. On the contrary, these crowded, multiunit dwellings functioned like miniature neighborhoods and represented a fairly broad cross section of society. In 1788, for example, the old Treasury was rented out to a variety of tenants. Doña Evarista Arroya, whom witnesses described as "of illustrious birth," lived in a room next to a mulatta pastry cook. When the two women got into a fight over a kettle left out in the patio, there was nowhere for Arroya to escape from the insults of someone whom she felt was beneath her.[11]

Despite the turnover among tenants, residents quickly got to know each other—and each other's business. When Doña Nicolasa Rodríguez accused her husband, Don Juan José Mostajo, a merchant, of having an affair, it turned out that his lover, Ignacia Calula, was living in his brother's house. Among the witnesses in the case were six other tenants: a tailor, a blacksmith, and four women whose occupations were not identified. Only the tailor, Andrés Rodríguez, claimed to know nothing of the affair, but he explained that he always left the house early and returned late. The others, even if they had lived there for only a few months, testified that they had seen Juan José enter Ignacia's room at all hours, sometimes with friends and musicians. Catalina Valdivia and Tomasa Lozana added that they had seen him leave early in the morning—though not early enough, apparently, to escape detection. Ignacia's neighbors had no qualms about revealing the secrets of her life; perhaps they resented her lack of participation in their little community. Lozana testified that Ignacia kept to herself, staying out of the main patio, and that she "did not make friends with the neighbors—men or women—of the house."[12]

These houses were a microcosm of the larger society, but they were not isolated from the rest of the neighborhood. Many people were called as witnesses in criminal cases because they had been sitting or standing in their doorways, from where they could keep an eye on the block and learn the habits and activities of their neighbors. As Francisco Velasco explained, the reason that he had witnessed a brawl that led to one death was that he "was accustomed to go out frequently into his doorway."[13] Shopkeepers, in particular, stood in their doorways when not waiting on customers, and they

11. ARAR/Int/Crim (17-V-1788), "Doña Evarista Arroya contra Tomasa 'la Piqueña' por injurias."

12. AAA/Pen (18-IX-1784), "Nicolasa Rodríguez contra Juan José Mostajo."

13. ARAR/CS/Crim (17-IV-1833), "Contra Mateo Chávez por homicidio."

were probably among those who best knew the business of the neighbor-hood.[14] Such daily contacts built and maintained communities.

Arequipeños had an irrepressible curiosity. After master silversmith José Salazar looked up from his work to witness a quarrel in the street, he had a hard time getting his journeyman to stay out of the doorway. José Herrera later testified that he watched the fight until his master ordered him back to work and told him—prophetically—"not to be so curious because then they would take him as a witness."[15] He obeyed briefly but soon was back in the doorway. Salazar did not want to lose work time having his assistant go off to court to give testimony, but years later, when his wife got in a fight with the neighbors, he would be thankful for such witnesses. Seamstress Francisca Vercolme de Aranivia was sitting in her doorway and sewing, on that Saturday afternoon, when she heard Salazar's son crying and so became a witness to a fight between the two families.[16]

Even those neighbors who were not in their doorways were quick to gather at the sound of any commotion. As Melchora Viamonte explained in one case: "She heard voices in the house of Doña María Lopes, and since the witness is from the neighborhood she went closer and heard that Marcos Torrelio was insulting said Doña María in her own home."[17] Shocked at such insolence, Viamonte put herself between the two and received a blow meant for Lopes.

The same dynamic was at work in the villages around Arequipa. Eugenia Rodríguez of Tiabaya testified that "upon seeing another neighbor running, she came out of her room figuring there must have been some fire [quema-zón]."[18] As it turned out, people had gathered in the plaza to witness a row among several women. A fight between Juan Montoya and Manuel Lazo, in which the latter was mortally wounded, attracted almost everyone from the neighborhood around the convent of Santa Catalina; some neighbors helped

---

14. See ARAR/Int/Crim (4-VIII-1789), "María Zeballos contra Don Mariano Villanueva por injurias"; ARAR/CS/Crim (11-XI-1827), "Contra Miguel Ramos por la muerte de Francisco de tal"; and (20-IV-1836), "Contra Benito González por heridas a María del Rosario Condorpusa."

15. ARAR/Int/Crim (22-II-1820), "Don Ignacio Severiche contra Don José Pozo por injurias."

16. ARAR/CS/Crim (16-VIII-1838), "José Salazar contra Teresa Gutiérrez."

17. ARAR/Int/Crim (1-VI-1792), "Doña María López contra los sambos Marcos Torrelio y Pedro Pastor por injurias."

18. ARAR/CS/Crim (12-XII-1832), "Doña María Beltrán contra Doña Bernarda Torres y otras por injurias."

carry Lazo home, while the others chased down Montoya.[19] A big enough commotion could arouse people from bed, as happened when a fight broke out between a shopkeeper from Spain and his neighbors.[20]

Usually neighbors and bystanders watched a dispute without talking sides, but they would intervene if violence threatened to get out of hand. There were certain members of the neighborhood who had greater authority as mediators. Because many fights erupted between renters in the same house, it was often the owner of the house or the chief tenant who intervened. When two tenants got into a fight over whether to close the outside door for the night, for example, young Javiera Velasco ran to get her grandmother, who owned the house.[21] Shopkeepers also intervened to protect people from injury. When Lorenso Garcia and Asencia Hurtado saw Don Mariano Villanueva hitting a street seller with a sword, they went to her defense and took her back to the former's shop to treat her wounds.[22] Doña Isabel Rosa hid merchant Miguel Reyes in her shop and even brought charges against the angry crowd who was after him.[23] Finally, in the most serious cases of violence, someone would summon the local authorities (usually the neighborhood *alcalde* or *comisario*).

This constant contact and surveillance among neighbors built up a community of shared experience and knowledge that could be tapped even when members were not eyewitnesses to an event. Hermenegilda Villafuerte lived alone with her two servants, so no one saw them kill her on the night of June 22, 1808. The next morning at eight, Petrona Aransaez arrived to accompany Villafuerte to mass and found a boy knocking on the outside door to her house. When he told her that the door to Villafuerte's room was open, she explained that that meant it was all right to go in. Aransaez was shocked to

19. ARAR/CS/Crim (12-VI-1830), "Contra Juan Montoya por la muerte de Don Manuel Lazo."

20. ARAR/CS/Crim (8-VII-1833), "Contra Julián Martínez por la muerte de Lorenso Yepes."

21. ARAR/CS/Crim (14-V-1834), "Contra Juana Palacios y Julián Mantilla por dar una puñalada a Mariano Cárdenas." See also ARAR/Int/Crim (9-IX-1803), "Don Mariano y Don Melchor Tapia contra Domingo 'el Estre' por injurias"; (9-XII-1815) "Doña Micaela Begaso contra María de tal por injurias"; and (22-II-1820), "Don Ignacio Severiche contra Don José Pozo por injurias."

22. ARAR/Int/Crim (4-VIII-1789), "María Zevallos contra Don Mariano Villanueva por injurias." See also ARAR/CS/Crim (20-IV-1836), "Contra Benito González por heridas a María del Rosario Condorpusa."

23. ARAR/Int/Crim (24-IX-1803), "Doña Isabel Rosa contra Josef Savala y otras por injurias."

find Villafuerte's dead body, and she rushed back into the street, shouting for help. She later reported that the only neighbor around was tailor Bernardo Benavente, who was sewing across the street from Villafuerte's house, but she added that soon a crowd of people from farther away had gathered. It did not take long for them to realize that Villafuerte's servants were missing and to provide a description of them to the authorities; meanwhile, someone went to inform the victim's niece. Within two days, a search party caught the suspects on the road to Puno. Thus, even an old woman who lived alone and did not appear to have much to do with her neighbors was not a stranger to the community.[24]

Even the less crowded living conditions in the rural areas around the city of Arequipa did not prevent the formation of such communities of knowledge. As many of the agricultural parcels were small, people out working in the field could observe what was going on in neighboring plots. When a dispute occurred, therefore, these witnesses could recount the events even if they had not heard all the words that had passed between the participants. If it looked like a particularly interesting fight, the inevitable crowd would gather. Mariano Talabera, who witnessed a fight between Melchora Viscarra and the tribute collector of Pocsi, explained that he heard some shouting from about two blocks away, "and since he saw that many people were running toward the voices he did the same."[25] Finally, even those neighbors who had not seen such a dispute had all heard about it by the next day.

Talk, then, as well as direct observation, constructed communities.[26] The high degree of familiarity among neighbors facilitated the circulation of information, as the following case demonstrates. When Andrea Barbachano went to the shop of Josefa Valencia to collect on a small debt, the latter said

24. ARAR/Int/Crim (23-VI-1808), "Contra Leandro Quispe y Luisa Chaves por la muerte de Hermenegilda Villafuerte."

25. ARAR/Int/Crim (7-VI-1799), "Don Carlos Málaga contra Doña Melchora Viscarra por injurias."

26. For a survey of the large ethnographic literature that examines gossip, particularly as a means for holding a community together and regulating the behavior of its members, see Sally Engle Merry, "Rethinking Gossip and Scandal," in Donald Black, ed., *Toward a General Theory of Social Control*, vol. 1, *Fundamentals* (New York: Academic Press, 1984), 271–301. For Mediterranean societies, see F. G. Bailey, ed., *Gifts and Poison: The Politics of Reputation* (Oxford: Basil Blackwell, 1971); and J. K. Campbell, *Honour, Family, and Patronage: A Study of Institutions and Moral Values in a Greek Mountain Community* (Oxford: Clarendon Press, 1964), especially 263–320. David Garrioch asserts that gossip could define the boundaries of community even in eighteenth-century Paris: *Neighborhood and Community in Paris, 1740–1790* (London: Cambridge University Press, 1986), 33.

that she could not pay until her husband got home. In frustration, Barbachano called Valencia a "whore." Neighbor Francisco Carbajal and passerby Juana Gil witnessed the argument firsthand, while another woman overhead two strangers discussing the event: "Look what shameful women (speaking about the Barbarchanas) who have discredited this woman (speaking of Doña Josefa Valencia) of whom they have said that while her husband is at work she is prostituting herself."[27]

This witness added that she was scandalized to hear such accusations against a woman whom she had considered honorable. Barbachano had achieved the desired effect of spreading rumors about Valencia's reputation; on the other hand, Valencia struck back by using the same network to support her charges of slander.

Talk could even create communities of knowledge that extended far beyond the level of neighborhood or village. When the body of Camilo Calla was discovered in an irrigation ditch in Sabandía, the authorities first called it an accidental death. His nephew, however, suspected foul play by Don Valentín Origuela, a merchant from Arequipa on whose property Calla's body had been found. Origuela had hired Calla to repair the roof of his granary, but they had argued over whether he should be paid in advance. No one had actually witnessed Calla's death, but detailed and gruesome rumors about his murder had traveled as far as the village of Characato. Once called into court, witnesses were unwilling to admit to having started or spread the rumor, and, therefore, Origuela was absolved.[28] It is remarkable, however, that he was put on trial with such slim evidence. That gossip could occasionally affect even members of the elite is a testament to the power of talk in Arequipa. It was a lesson that public officials and their rivals would remember during times of political turmoil.

People repeated those stories that most closely touched their lives, and in the process, they highlighted those values they considered most important. Rumors about murder, for example, were rare. Most gossip discussed personal honor—an issue that will be explored in Chapter 5—and domestic matters. Values such as honor, fidelity, and responsibility provided a shared language of discussion, even if there was not a consensus on their precise

27. The name of the last witness is missing from the document; the parenthetical statements are in the original. ARAR/Int/Crim (10-VI-1786), "Doña Josefa Valencia contra Doña Andrea Barbachano por injurias."

28. ARAR/CS/Crim (8-III-1827), "Contra Don Valentín Origuela por la muerte de Camilo Calla." Compare with a similar case in Sabean, *Power in the Blood*, 174–98.

meaning. Certain kinds of behavior, such as married women taking public lovers or beating their husbands, provoked widespread censure.[29] Most cases, however, were more ambivalent, and members of the community often took different sides.

The thin line between private concerns and public issues and the role of talk in creating communities are best exemplified by marital disputes. Although women's reputations were especially vulnerable, it was usually wives who publicized such conflicts. Apparently, given their relatively weak position within the home, they were willing to submit themselves—and their husbands—to the judgment of their neighbors. Masculine honor depended, in part, on the image of a patriarch in control of his household. As the public sphere became increasingly identified with politics after independence, however, republican authorities would reemphasize the privacy of the home, a position favorable to husbands, as we shall see in later chapters.

The Private Is Public

Although it did not predominate numerically, the patriarchal family was certainly the dominant norm promoted by both the church and the state. Moreover, particularly during the colonial period, it was a model that linked family, society, and the state. The king and, by extension, other royal and ecclesiastical officials were depicted as stern yet benevolent fathers of the people, and the obligations of spouses reflected the idealized relations between a sovereign and his subjects.[30] The wife was to serve her husband faithfully, while, in turn, he was to protect and support her. No one in Arequipa openly questioned this basic code of behavior, which was closely tied to the central value of honor.

But what might appear to be a simple exchange was subject to a range of interpretation. Most men believed their privileges to be absolute, while they defined their wives' neglect of housekeeping, much less sexual infidelity, as

29. See ARAR/Int/Crim (21-V-1803), "Contra Isabel Portugal por maltratos a su esposo Rudecindo Megia."
30. Stern, *The Secret History of Gender*, 189–213; Richard Boyer, "Women, *La Mala Vida*, and the Politics of Marriage," in Asunción Lavrin, ed., *Sexuality and Marriage in Colonial Latin America* (Lincoln and London: University of Nebraska Press, 1989), 252–86; Habermas, *The Structural Transformation of the Public Sphere*, 4–11; and Susan Dwyer Amussen, *An Ordered Society: Gender and Class in Early Modern England* (New York: Basil Blackwell, 1988).

illegitimate, regardless of the circumstances. For the most part, women also recognized their duties and the superior position of their husbands, but they emphasized the "reciprocal" nature of the marital pact.[31]

One of the most frequent complaints filed by a woman against her husband was the failure to provide financially for the family or, worse yet, to have dissipated the property that she had contributed to the household.[32] Juana Calderón complained that she provided her husband with food and clothing, "turning on their head the obligations that bind him and me."[33] When Isidora Gutiérrez made similar charges against her husband, Patricio Texada, her witnesses concurred that "she is the one who, taking the place of the husband, maintains and dresses him and their children which is almost public in the neighborhood."[34]

Women often cited such financial irresponsibility as grounds for separation. María Micaela Torre, who claimed that her husband had wasted her dowry and inheritance in mismanaged farms and failed commercial enterprises, concluded that she could do better on her own: "In spite of being a woman I will work my hacienda, and always industrious I will take care of my children, and I will leave them with enough to support themselves, free from crying over the ruin to which the bad conduct of their father exposes them."[35]

Most men recognized their responsibility to maintain their families, but they emphasized their absolute authority to control both the people and the property within those households. When Domingo Llerena claimed the right to manage his wife's property, for example, he pointed out that he had always supported her, that he neither drank nor gambled and was "applied to my work, and to the advancement of my household."[36] But his final argument

---

31. Compare with Stern, *The Secret History of Gender*, 70–111; and Arrom, *The Women of Mexico City*, 232–38.

32. Under Spanish law, a woman was entitled to both her dowry and half of the common property acquired during marriage. See Asunción Lavrin and Edith Couturier, "Dowries and Wills: A View of Women's Socioeconomic Role in Colonial Guadalajara and Puebla, 1640–1790," *Hispanic American Historical Review* 59, no. 2 (1979): 280–304.

33. AAA/Ped (18-VIII-1813), "Doña Juana Calderón pide divorcio de su esposo Don Martín Salazar."

34. ARAR/Int/Crim (5-VII-1819), "Doña Isidora Gutiérrez contra su esposo Don Patricio Texada por robo."

35. AAA/Civ (11-XII-1810), "María Micaela Torre pide divorcio de Mariano Rodríguez." See also AAA/Pen (24-XI-1800), "Teresa Velásquez pide divorcio de José Vegaso." Ecclesiastical divorce did not end a marriage, but it did permit a legal separation.

36. Case dated Mar. 23, 1807, in ARAR/Int/Adm (1795), Libro de Causas de Rivera.

was that the laws supported him. Similarly, merchant Patricio Texada could barely contain his anger when his wife not only asked the church for a separation but accused him of stealing her belongings. In an appeal to the judge, Texada indignantly proclaimed: "I am the Husband, I am the Father, and I am the owner of the goods that were removed. . . . The time has come that the authority of Justice makes my Wife understand that she is a married woman, and that as such she should live subject to my orders and administration, treating me with love and reverence, it is time that she mend her ways and recognize the power [*potestad*] and privileges of her husband."[37]

The source of greatest contention between spouses was over the mobility of women. Many women worked outside the home to help support the family. While poor husbands may have accepted such activities out of economic necessity, they generally demanded that their wives stay home during the evenings. When Tomasa Talavera complained that her husband, Mateo Cornejo, was not supporting her or their son, he replied that he would be happy to do so if she would agree to live in peaceful subordination. Cornejo explained to the judge that he had tired of her company because she stayed out late at night; as a result, he complained, he was often stuck out in the street after finding their house locked and empty.[38] Men asserted that the boundary between house and street, between private and public, was an important one that should be respected by their wives.

Efforts by husbands to control their wives' mobility reflected both their anger that domestic duties went unfulfilled and their suspicion that the women were using the opportunity to be unfaithful. In such cases, men felt perfectly entitled to "correct" their wives through physical punishment.[39] Toribio Gutiérrez, who lived in the village of Paucarpata, sent his wife, Ignacia Flores, into the city to sell firewood. When she did not return until the next day, he became angry and refused to accept her excuses. He later explained to the judge that they often fought over such matters, and that their

<hr>

37. ARAR/Int/Crim (5-VII-1819), "Doña Isidora Gutiérrez contra su esposo Don Patricio Texada por robo."

38. AAA/Civ (22-VIII-1792), "Doña Tomasa Talavera pide que su esposo Mateo Cornejo le pague los alimentos."

39. Evidence on domestic violence was gathered from 77 cases in various jurisdictions: 41 complaints to ecclesiastical authorities, 6 libel suits, 13 cases of assault, and 17 murder trials. Statistical analysis would be difficult, because such violence tends to be significantly underreported. For a more developed analysis of this issue, see Sarah C. Chambers, " 'To the Company of a Man Like My Husband; No Law Can Compel Me': Women's Strategies Against Domestic Violence in Arequipa, Peru, 1780–1854," *Journal of Women's History* 11, no. 1 (spring 1999), 31–52.

arguments usually ended with his kicking and beating her. On the night in question, Gutiérrez went further, hitting Flores with a shovel and pushing her outside to spend the night in the patio. The next morning he found her dead. When the judge asked if he had a reason to be jealous, Gutiérrez replied that he did not suspect any particular person but often told his wife: "You must stay with someone when you don't come back and spend the night in the city."[40]

The prerogative of the husband to "correct" his wife was generally recognized, and neighbors were hesitant to intervene directly in such a case. When Manuel Dávila was beating his wife, Rosalía, for example, witnesses were shocked when he suddenly turned on the bystander Lorenso Aguirre, even though Aguirre "did not even defend the wife of said Manuel while he was beating her."[41] Similarly, when Benito González was hitting his lover, María del Rosario Condorpusa, a witness intervened only after Condorpusa said that she was not his wife.[42]

Imminent danger of death could also justify intervention. Martina Tapia claimed that when her husband tried to drown her, she was saved by a master locksmith who lived in the neighborhood.[43] But when violence occurred in the home, it was difficult for neighbors to judge its severity, even as they listened to arguments from the other side of walls and doorways. When landlord Manuel Pacheco heard a common-law couple arguing in their room, he shouted to them to be quiet or they would have to move; shortly thereafter, the woman was mortally wounded.[44] In another case, Santos Flores thought his advice to a neighbor to stop beating his wife and daughter had been heeded, but, in fact, their cries stopped only because the wife had escaped and the daughter had died.[45] To the degree that the privacy of the domestic sphere was respected, therefore, it worked to the detriment of women; violence that resulted in the murder of wives and lovers usually took place within the home.

Men's recourse to violence during marital disputes reflects both their

40. ARAR/CS/Crim (11-IV-1836), "Contra Toribio Gutiérrez por la muerte de Ignacia Flores."

41. ARAR/Int/Crim (23-X-1787), "Lorenso Aguirre contra Manuel Dávila por heridas."

42. ARAR/CS/Crim (20-IV-1836), "Contra Benito González por heridas a María del Rosario Condorpusa."

43. AAA/Civ (15-XII-1800), "Doña Martina Tapia pide divorcio de Don Pedro Reynoso."

44. ARAR/CS/Crim (21-VIII-1832), "Contra Mariano Mercado por la muerte de su amasia Manuela Barrios."

45. ARAR/CS/Crim (26-VIII-1834), "Contra Celedino Portillo por la muerte de su hija."

assertion that patriarchal privileges were absolute and that such matters should be settled privately. Women had less power to make their husbands fulfill their responsibilities, and when private rebukes failed, they aired their domestic problems in public. Women were aware that they were taking a serious step in exposing their husbands' misconduct. María Ignacia Baldivia asserted that her husband failed to provide, but that "I bore it all patiently in order to conserve his honor and so that the Public watching our operations would not notice his misconduct and the ruin caused by his contraction to vices."[46] Only when he also began to beat her did she complain to the vicar.

Tomasa Castillo was able to present older gentlemen from her neighborhood as witnesses to her husband's financial irresponsibility and public affair with another woman; one testified that her husband "had entirely lost modesty and shame and what is more the Holy Fear of God."[47] It is difficult to know whether such talk would affect a man's reputation enough to induce a change in behavior, but simply having his wife talking about their private problems would have revealed that he did not have his household under control.

Furthermore, a woman's complaints, if convincing, could induce intervention on her behalf. Couples' godparents, in particular, tried to reform husbands who displayed excessive misconduct, even if they were often unsuccessful.[48] Although neighbors were hesitant to intervene directly between couples, they often provided refuge to women fleeing abuse. When Mariano Delgado accused sisters Teresa, Manuela, and María Díaz of sheltering his wife after she stole several baskets of coca from him, they denied any knowledge of the theft but said she had probably taken it in order to support her children. The Díaz sisters asserted that Mariano's scandalous mistreatment of his wife was well known throughout the neighborhood and that they, like others, had sometimes fed her or taken her in "so that her Husband would not mistreat her more than was customary, an act demanded by Christian charity and neighborliness."[49]

An aggrieved wife could further heighten the degree of publicity, and,

46. AAA/Ped (3-XI-1823), "Doña María Ignacia Baldivia queja sobre los procedimientos de su esposo Don Manuel Postigo."
47. ARAR/Int/Crim (24-III-1817), "Tomasa Castillo contra su esposo Narsiso Tinta por adulterio y homicidio en conato."
48. AAA/Pen (20-X-1784), "Paula Cáseres contra su marido y Rafaela de tal por adulterio y sevicia"; and AAA/Civ (29-X-1794), "María Rodríguez contra su esposo por sevicia."
49. ARAR/CS/Crim (3-XI-1817), "Mariano Delgado contra Teresa, María y Manuela Díaz por injurias."

thereby, expose the connection between the private and public spheres, by complaining to local civil or religious authorities. When Tomasa Castillo took her case all the way to the intendant, she tried to exert pressure by claiming that her neighbors were "murmuring" about why the mayors had failed to punish her husband and his lover.[50] Public officials did recognize that domestic peace was key to general social order, and they might be willing to put an offending husband in jail overnight or issue a warning to improve his conduct. It seems unlikely, however, that such measures had much effect on the most violent or profligate men. In fact, the authorities were often satisfied with promises and excuses. For example, a justice of the peace reported to the court that tailor Luis Barrionuevo had injured his wife's head and, on an earlier occasion, had broken her arm. When asked if he habitually beat her, Barrionuevo replied no, although he did remember laying hands on her once, when she had not washed the clothes. The judge, noting that it was not his custom to mistreat his wife, let him off with a mild warning.[51]

Many wives blamed their husbands' lack of financial support and abuse on affairs with other women. In fact, the evidence of adultery mirrored the marital relation: a woman who cooked and cleaned for a man was presumed to be his lover even if they were not caught in the act. Paula Cáseres, for example, claimed that her husband, Carlos Champi, had a two-year affair with a Rafaela "So-and-So," and that they had a child whom he supported. He caused further scandal by taking his mistress to public functions and dressing her in expensive clothes. In return, Rafaela provided Carlos with "food and all other necessities, and he has had the custom of dining every night in her house."[52] In the worst cases, a lover literally usurped the wife's place, as María Rodríguez complained: "The boldness of this woman is so extreme that when I go to Chiguata to work and look for a living to support myself and my child, she comes to live with my husband in my own house, and with much impudence as if she were his proper wife, she comes and goes in front of everyone, and is cooking for him."[53]

While it was difficult to reform their husbands' behavior, wives knew that

---

50. ARAR/Int/Crim (24-III-1817), "Tomasa Castillo contra su esposo Narsiso Tinta por adulterio y homicidio en conato."

51. ARAR/CS/Crim (1-X-1832), "Contra Luis Barrionuevo por heridas a su esposa Juana Salas." See also ARAR/CS/Crim (12-VIII-1834), "Contra Antonio Vilca por puñaladas a su esposa."

52. AAA/Pen (20-X-1784), "Paula Cáseres contra su marido y Rafael de tal por adulterio y sevicia."

53. ARAR/CS/Crim (24-I-1826), "Contra María Rodríguez por puñaladas a Pascuala Santayana."

the reputations of other women were more vulnerable to gossip. Just as there was always some concerned neighbor to inform a wife of her husband's infidelities, there were others to convey a wife's accusations back to the alleged mistress or her family. Jacinta Dias and Bernardina Llerena, who lived in rooms next to Manuela Calderón, heard the latter arguing with her husband and accusing him of having an affair with María Salazar, to whom she referred in very dishonorable terms. They repeated the conversation to Teresa Aranibar, and eventually it got back to María's father, Manuel Salazar. He promptly filed charges against Calderón for publicly slandering his virgin daughter. Although he had not heard the insults himself, he explained, he had learned of them from the neighbors, "who scandalized came to report them to me."[54] Finally, if someone was too naive to get the hint, some kind soul would explain it. María Arispe testified that she had heard Teresa Villalobos say that "if there were no whores, there would be no bad men." It was only later that a relative explained that the words were meant for her.[55]

Although women were affected by gossip, especially if it provoked male violence, words were not always sufficient to change their behavior. Such cases could escalate into dramatic disputes reminiscent of the charivaris of early modern Europe. The charivaris were usually made up of the young men of a village who ritualistically poked fun at newlyweds, especially if one was marrying for a second time.[56] Like the charivaris, such disputes in Arequipa often related to sexual matters; as in the case of gossip, however, it was primarily women—rather than young men—who tried to ridicule their rivals.

In 1809, for example, Rafaela Gómez accused María Santos Salazar and her relatives of attacking her and calling her a "housebreaker," among worse insults; although her body was bruised, Gómez insisted that she was more concerned about her honor and reputation. Salazar responded that ever since some people had secretly informed her that her husband was carrying on an affair with Gómez, she had been trying to put a stop to it. First she asked her husband to stop going to Gómez's house "because of the scandal it caused in

54. ARAR/Int/Crim (25-XI-1807), "Don Manuel Salazar contra Manuela Calderón por injurias a su hija María."

55. ARAR/CS/Crim (12-VII-1838), "Doña Rosalía Delgado contra Doña Teresa Villalobos por calumnia a su hija Doña María Arispe."

56. See Natalie Zemon Davis, "The Reasons of Misrule," in *Society and Culture in Early Modern France* (Stanford: Stanford University Press, 1975), 97–123; and, for a critique, Suzanne Desan, "Crowds, Community, and Ritual in the Work of E. P. Thompson and Natalie Davis," in Lynn Hunt, ed., *The New Cultural History* (Berkeley and Los Angeles: University of California Press, 1989), 47–71.

the neighborhood." When the affair continued, her mother-in-law left a message for Gómez that she had an important matter to discuss with her. Finally Salazar, accompanied by her mother-in-law, her sister-in-law, a female friend (*comadre*), a black woman (perhaps a slave), and several Indian servants (*cholas*), went to challenge her husband's lover directly.[57]

Surprisingly, the attacks could also go in the other direction. Bernarda Velarde complained that when she convinced her husband, Mariano Vásquez, to stop seeing Brígida Santayana, the latter came with her mother, her sister, and other people from her "faction" (parcialidad) to attack her and rip off her clothes. According to a witness, as soon as the women entered the house, they began "making an uproar and provoking both Don Mariano as well as his wife for which purpose they carried in their hands bull horns and stones." The horns, undoubtedly, were meant to symbolize cuckoldry, in this case directed at the woman rather than her husband. When María Beltrán went to the bakery of sisters Bernarda Torres and Juana Torres and accused them of an affair with her husband, they threw flour in her face "to better open her eyes," and, lifting her skirt, threated "to introduce hot peppers in her private parts" (in the polite language of the scribe).[58]

Although the core of these groups usually was made up of female relatives, occasionally they could become larger crowds of friends and neighbors. For example, in 1815, when Micaela Begaso went to rebuke her husband's alleged lover, María "So-and-So," the young woman's family attacked her "with sticks, a knife, scissors and stones." Some bystanders went for Begaso's family, and, according to one report, her brother José came to her rescue accompanied by "some chicheras [brewers] known vulgarly as the Tincalos, the Delgados disguised with blankets and other inhabitants of the neighborhood toward los Arces." Maria's mother tried to influence the judge by accusing Begaso, "the ringleader of that rabble," and her allies of supporting a recent revolt against the crown. Another witness saw the group as it crossed the bridge into the city and reported that it was preceded by a crowd of boys who shouted "advance guerrillas."[59] This cry suggests the potential politicization of domestic and neighborhood disputes.

---

57. ARAR/Int/Crim (29-V-1809), "Doña Rafaela Gómez contra Doña María Santos Salazar por injurias."

58. The first example comes from ARAR/Int/Crim (4-I-1790), "Bernarda Velarde contra Brígida Santayana, su madre y sus hermanas por insultos y provocaciones." See also ARAR/Int/Crim (2-II-1804), "Sebastian Valencia contra María Laguna y sus parientes por heridas a su mujer." The second example comes from ARAR/CS/Crim (12-XII-1832) "Contra Bernarda Torres y Juana Torres por herida a María Beltrán."

59. ARAR/Int/Crim (9-XII-1815), "Doña Micaela Begaso contra María de tal por injurias."

Such ritualized conflicts demonstrate the porous boundary between private and public space, domestic and community concerns. Even issues that on the surface seemed to have little to do with domestic affairs could be sexualized, especially when women were involved. Angered when she was evicted from a rental property, Cayetana Riveras went with her nephews, son, and daughter-in-law to protest outside the house of her landlady, María Senteno y Capas. Rather than calling attention to the rental dispute, however, the crowd shouted out that Senteno y Capas was unfaithful to her husband and that was why she lived outside the city (in Yanahuara).[60]

Ritual disputes were rooted in communities that had been built up by observation and talk. Participants knew that the insults they flung at their opponents would be repeated and diffused. Some even appealed directly to their audience, by crying out: "May you all be witnesses."[61] Such calls appealed, as well, to a core of common values, centered around honor and sociability, by which people were judged and evaluated, at least if they wanted to be recognized as part of the respectable sector of local society. The object was to win over as many neighbors as possible, in order to broaden one's network of support.

Those connections could prove decisive when seeking contracts, clients, employment, or loans, and they could increase one's social or political influence in the community. Conflict, therefore, far from reflecting a breakdown in community, was inseparably intertwined with gossip in the process of making and remaking social and, potentially, political networks. Moreover, the language and ritual of neighborhood disputes echoed during political mobilizations.

Taverns

The prominent role of women in the public life of communities included their management of the central gathering places in the neighborhoods. Taverns were named chicherías after the traditional Andean drink made from fermented corn, but they also served (usually spicy) food. Ventura Travada y

60. ARAR/Int/Crim (3-VII-1815), "Doña María Senteno y Capas contra Cayetana Riveros y otros por azonada."

61. See, for example, ARAR/Int/Crim (22-II-1820), "Don Ignacio Severiche contra Don José Pozo por injurias"; ARAR/CS/Crim (7-III-1827), "Contra Francisca y María Josefa Corrales por puñaladas a Pedro Moscoso"; and ARAR/Pref (20-II-1828), "Mercedes Tapia contra Don Mariano Arróspide por heridas a su hijo."

Córdova, writing in 1752, claimed that there were three thousand chicherías in the city and its suburbs. More than eighty years later, José María Blanco counted two thousand, some with very colorful names such as The World Upside Down (El Mundo al Revés), Hell (El Infierno), The Show-off (La Fachenda), and Poison (El Veneno).[62] People from the neighborhood, especially single men, often stopped in at the local chichería for an inexpensive lunch or dinner. But on weekends and holidays, drinking became the main focus, as both men and women emptied communal carafes of chicha.

More than a simple tavern or restaurant, however, the chichería was a primary locus of community life. Observers were ambivalent in their estimation of those who frequented the chicherías. Travada y Córdova and Blanco asserted that the clientele tended to be from the lower classes, but French visitor E. de Sartiges noted that all but the very elite drank chicha.[63] Artisans, laborers, and farmers—but also priests, professionals, and petty merchants—were sure to find someone they knew in the local tavern, so they could relax and visit with their friends.

Someone usually pulled out a deck of cards or pair of dice, and the games of chance determined who would buy the next round of chicha. Others brought their guitars to serenade the customers with a *yaraví*, the characteristic song of Arequipa that blended Andean and Spanish harmonies. The plaintive lyrics usually told of the loss or betrayal of love, but they also evoked local scenes such as the volcano and the green campiña.[64] Although the clientele was relatively diverse, for plebeians the chichería was a particularly welcome refuge that promised, as the aptly named tavern Quitapesares, to take away their sorrows. Rarely could a chichera afford to let a customer get away without paying his or her half-real for a jug of chicha, but she might accept a pledge or an odd job in exchange for a drink.[65] When people had nowhere to stay, moreover, chicheras often let them spend the night, perhaps under the pretext of guarding the premises.[66]

62. Travada y Córdova, *El suelo de Arequipa*, 127; and Blanco, "Diario del viaje del Presidente Orbegoso al sur del Perú," 277.

63. Etienne Gilbert Eugène, comte de Sartiges, "Viaje a las repúblicas de América del Sur," in Raul Porras Barrenechea, ed., Emilia Romero, trans., *Viajeros en el Perú*, vol. 2, *Dos viajeros franceses en el Perú republicano* (1834; reprint, Lima: Editorial Cultural Antártica, 1947), 16–17.

64. Juan Guillermo Carpio Muñoz, *El Yaraví arequipeño: Un estudio histórico-social* (Arequipa: Editorial La Colmena, 1976).

65. ARAR/CS/Crim (11-XI-1827), "Contra Miguel Ramos por la muerte de Francisco de Tal."

66. See ARAR/Int/Crim (4-X-1800), "Contra Matías Alpaca y otros por robo"; ARAR/CS/Crim (22-V-1826), "Sobre la muerte de Pascual Quispe"; (4-VII-1848) "Contra José Quispe

While the atmosphere of the chicherías was generally congenial, it was not uncommon for tempers to flare after heavy drinking. A typical fight started with an exchange of insults, which quickly escalated into physical violence; if one or more of the aggressors had a knife, the results could be serious. Nevertheless, the chances of defusing a conflict in a chichería were probably greater than if the fight took place in a private home or a back alley. Others present, and often the owner herself, usually intervened, especially if the brawlers were well-known locals.[67] People under attack frequently escaped into chicherías, apparently with the expectation that they would be welcome and find protection.[68]

By contrast, neighbors were hesitant to enter a private home to mediate disputes. On August 25, 1834, Celedonio Portillo spent the day with his wife and daughter in the chichería of Bartola Nuñes. Reportedly he had treated them with much affection; as soon as they got home, however, Portillo began to beat the two women because there was nothing to eat. His wife, Melchora, rushed back to the chichería for help. Unfortunately, the chichera was less eager to interfere outside of her business. When the daughter's screams subsided, Nuñes assured Melchora that the trouble had passed and invited her to spend the night at the chichería. But the next morning, the daughter was found dead.[69]

Their role as refuges from everyday hardships does not distinguish chicherías from taverns in other cultures.[70] As the case above implies, however,

---

por maltrato e ilícita amistad con su hija Petrona Suñi"; and ARAR/Pref (21-XI-1831), "Sobre investigarse la conducta de Ramón Llerena, José María Madaleno, y José Torres."

67. See ARAR/Int/Crim (29-II-1816), "Doña Josefa Rodríguez contra Petrona Romero y otros por injurias"; (24-III-1817) "Tomasa Castillo contra su esposo"; ARAR/CS/Crim (15-V-1825), "Contra Julian Zegarra por puñaladas a Hermenegilda Vera"; and (7-IV-1836), "Contra Rafael González por puñaladas a tres hombres y una mujer."

68. See ARAR/Corregimiento/Crim, Leg. 26, Exp. 445 (19-XII-1782), "Don Faustino Biamonte y su esposa contra Sebastian Bedoya por lesiones"; ARAR/Int/Crim (28-V-1806), "Doña María Valdivia contra el Alcalde de Socabaya por atropellamientos"; ARAR/CS/Crim (22-V-1826), "Sobre la muerte de Pascual Quispe"; (1-II-1849) "Contra Pedro José Vargas por homicidio de un niño"; and (24-IV-1850), "Contra Carlos Herrera por maltratos a su mujer."

69. ARAR/CS/Crim (26-VIII-1834), "Contra Celedino Portillo por la muerte de su hija Petronila."

70. On taverns in Mexico (*pulquerías*), see William Taylor, *Drinking, Homicide, and Rebellion in Colonial Mexican Villages* (Stanford: Stanford University Press, 1979), 66–68; Michael C. Scardaville, "Alcohol Abuse and Tavern Reform in Late Colonial Mexico City," *Hispanic American Historical Review* 60, no. 4 (1980): 643–71; and Juan Pedro Viqueira Albán, *¿Relajados o reprimidos? Diversiones públicas y vida social en la ciudad de México durante el Siglo de las Luces* (Mexico City: Fondo de Cultura Económica, 1987), 169–219. On taverns in Paris, see

in Arequipa they also served as safe havens for women. While women were often targets of violence within their own homes, they seemed to have felt safer, rather than more vulnerable, when they were drinking and socializing in the chicherías. Although they still might be assaulted, they usually were protected—often by other women, including the chichera.

In May 1825, for example, Julián Zegarra suspected his sister-in-law Hermenegilda Vera of being a go-between for his wife in an extramarital affair. When he found her in a chichería, he took out his knife and attacked her. Teresa Barriga, who had been drinking with Vera, went out to find help. Meanwhile another friend, Feliciana Gutiérrez, tried to stop Zegarra, first by yelling that the police were coming and then by throwing a rock at him. Vera did end up with some cuts on her arm, but the consequences probably would have been much worse if her friends had not been there to protect her.[71]

Dramatic cases reveal the confidence many women felt when they were in a chichería. In 1806, María Valdivia brought charges against the mayor of Socabaya for trying to jail her without just cause. According to witnesses, she took refuge in the chichería of Isabel Medina. The mayor ordered his deputies to go in and get Valdivia, but she put up such a fight that none were able. When the mayor finally gave up, Valdivia triumphantly challenged the male deputies "to put on her skirts and give her their pants."[72]

A few women even acted as aggressors rather than victims. Manuela Chalcotupa and Pascual Quispe were drinking together in a chichería when he insulted her "in the most delicate part of her honor." Enraged, she took the knife that she used as a butcher and stabbed him. Quispe, who was not so lucky as Vera, died from the knife wound.[73]

The small neighborhood general stores also sold food and liquor and thus became gathering places as well, but they were significantly different from the chicherías. Shopkeepers enjoyed a higher economic and social status than did chicheras, they sold hard liquor (*aguardiente*) rather than chicha, and their clientele tended to be male. But the most pertinent contrast between shops and chicherías, for an understanding of popular culture, is their

Garrioch, *Neighborhood and Community*, 23–27; and Thomas Brennan, *Public Drinking and Popular Culture in Eighteenth-Century Paris* (Princeton: Princeton University Press, 1988).

71. ARAR/CS/Crim (15-V-1825), "Contra Julian Zegarra por puñaladas a Hermenegilda Vera."

72. ARAR/CS/Crim (28-V-1806), "Doña María Valdivia contra el Alcalde de Socabaya por atropellamientos."

73. ARAR/CS/Crim (4-IV-1829), "Contra Manuela Chalcotupa por la muerte de Pascual Quispe."

differentiation between public and private spaces: although both were often located in the owners' homes, only the former enjoyed the corresponding rights of privacy. The proprietors closed up shop whenever they wished— whether because it was getting late, they wanted to have a private party, or they feared an outbreak of disorder.[74] When alcohol fueled their customers' tempers, therefore, shopkeepers were quick to remove the aggressors from their premises and close the door.

Although some were run by female proprietors, moreover, these stores were no refuge for women. Mariano Domingo Quirós hired Margarita Ascuña to work in his sisters' shop only on the condition that she be single and unattached. When a man turned up one night and began to cause a ruckus by claiming Ascuña was his common-law wife, Quirós scolded her for not telling him the truth. Despite her pleas that she feared for her life, Quirós turned her over to a night watchman and closed the store. Apparently the officer was not very watchful, because shortly thereafter, Ascuña was fatally wounded.[75]

Before removing the offenders, by contrast, chicheras generally tried to mediate fights that broke out in their establishments. Even if they tried to evict unruly patrons, they might run into legal difficulties. When Juan Galiano was sentenced to exile for violently forcing his way into a chichería and punching the owner, his defense lawyer appealed on the grounds that "he entered the chichería, a public place, where everyone has the right to enter just like going to the plaza to drink from the public fountain."[76] Galiano's sentence was reduced to six months' service in the police force.

Similarly, when several men were charged with impersonating the police in order to force their way into the home of the shoemaker Julian Lazo, the defense implied that the house was, in fact, a chichería and brothel, and,

74. See ARAR/Int/Crim (24-IX-1803), "Doña Isabel Rosa contra Josef Savala y otros por injurias"; (1-VII-1808) "Contra Juan Antonio Manrique y otros por robo"; (15-XI-1824) "Causa sobre la muerte de Manuel Vilca"; ARAR/CS/Crim (28-X-1828), "Contra Pedro Ponton por puñaladas a Doña María Dolores Ureta"; (22-VI-1829) "Contra Don Santiago Le Bris por la muerte de Miguel Linares"; (7-VIII-1830) "Contra Eusebia Ortiz por puñaladas a José María Poblete"; (22-VII-1833) "Contra Pedro José Madueño por estropear a Ramón Esquivel"; (29-III-1836) "Contra Mariano Martín Cañoli por expresiones contra unos soldados Bolivianos"; and (10-VI-1836), "Contra Inocencio Pardo por heridas a Pablo Rosado."
75. ARAR/CS/Crim (7-XI-1854), "Contra Francisco Sanches Murguía por heridas a Margarita Ascuña." See also ARAR/Int/Crim (23-X-1787), "Lorenso Aguirre contra Manuel Dávila por heridas."
76. ARAR/CS/Crim (20-X-1831), "Contra Juan Galiano y Matías Bedoya por haber portado armas prohibidas, entrado a fuerza a una chichería y estropeado a las dueños de ella."

therefore, "the quality of the house which they wanted to enter, by its nature frequented by all classes of men and at all hours, makes [the imputation] disappear."[77] The men were absolved.

That chicherías were regarded as public places rather than private businesses turns on its head the traditional separation of spheres into public/male and private/female. Here were public taverns run by women, catering to women as well as to men, and, often, serving as refuges for women against male violence. A woman was safer in a chichería, despite the potential for alcohol-related violence, than in the privacy of her own home. As we shall see, however, after independence, chicherías would increasingly come under attack by liberal reformers who decried the disorder caused by "public" women. In addition, the public character of chicherías points to a potential distinction by class. The elite of Arequipa could hold parties in the privacy of their homes, while the poor to middling classes socialized in public: in the chicherías or in the streets.

Festivals

Tavern culture in Arequipa incorporated a relatively broad spectrum of society but did tend to exclude the upper crust. Religious and civic festivities, however, further blurred the boundaries between public and private, popular and elite. During holidays, parties overflowed from houses into the streets, as revelers carried their celebrations across the city. Despite the latent potential for class conflict, such occasions provided opportunities for forging a common regional identity.[78]

The year was filled with religious festivals, from the many saints' days to the major holidays, such as the Epiphany, Easter, Corpus Christi, the Assumption of the Virgin, All Saints' Day, the Immaculate Conception, and Christmas. With the exception of the anniversary of the city's Spanish foundation, on August 15, and, later, commemorations of independence victories, civic holidays conformed less to a calendar than to ad hoc celebra-

77. I found no other references to chicherías as formal houses of prostitution; the lawyer was probably trying to play upon elite stereotypes. ARAR/CS/Crim (12-VIII-1833), "Contra Juan Ibáñez y Casimiro Corrales por fingirse de la Policía."

78. For comparative studies of festivals in Mexico, see the essays in William H. Beezley, Cheryl English Martin, and William E. French, eds., *Rituals of Rule, Rituals of Resistance: Public Celebrations and Popular Culture in Mexico* (Wilmington: Scholarly Resources, 1994).

tions of a birth or marriage in the royal family, the reception by the city of a new royal honor, the arrival or departure of a political or religious figure, or oaths of loyalty to new authorities.[79]

The centerpiece of civic festivities was the pomp and spectacle organized by the cabildo or municipality, using the visual symbols of honor. The formula for such celebrations remained virtually identical throughout the period studied, whether the city's corporations were swearing loyalty to a king, constitution, or president. The event generally began with a parade of the royal standard—or, later, the national flag—in which the civil authorities, the military, and the guilds wound their way through the city, stopping to read proclamations at the four main plazas (the central plaza as well as those of Santa Marta, San Francisco, and La Merced). The march ended at the cathedral, where the notables entered to hear a thanksgiving mass and a sermon suitable to the occasion. Throughout the day the church bells rang, and at night the city was illuminated. After the public events, the city's elites adjourned to banquets, where they continued to make speeches and to toast one another.

The town council was always publicly enthusiastic about the success of these functions, as reflected in the secretary's description of the oath of loyalty to the Spanish constitution of 1812:

> They regarded the constitution at the head of the most sumptuous and illustrious accompaniment that they had ever seen, many arches— most of them triumphal—the repeated cries of "long live" which were heard from all sides: in short, a murmur of people of both sexes and all ages, from plazas, balconies, rooftops, windows, streets, restaurants, cafés, it seems the watchword was given so that this function would be the most august which had come to the most faithful Arequipa, the memory of which will be transmitted from century to century to the furthest posterity.[80]

This description differs little from the observations made by Father José María Blanco twenty-three years later, on the occasion of President Or- begoso's entrance to Arequipa. It took two hours, Blanco reported, for the

79. For the colonial period, the cabildo records refer to civic celebrations. Records of civic functions before and after independence in the BNP include Docs. D8234, D11879, D11258, D11257, D11896, D11557, and D10779.
80. AMA, LAC 26 (December 26, 1812).

president to reach the main plaza, passing through more than eighty decorated arches where he was praised in speeches and in verse: "At the distance
of one step, one could not understand what was being said: the murmur and
the cries of 'long live' of more than twenty thousand people, the music, the
camaretas and rockets, and the general bell-ringing, spread throughout the
air a tangle which acutely hurt the ear and made the head faint."[81]

Although artisan guilds were invited to construct arches and march in
processions, the primary role scripted to plebeians in these festivities was that
of spectator and cheerleader. The crowd was rewarded not only with a good
show, but often with an outflowing of patronage as well. In its report on the
swearing of loyalty to King Charles IV in 1789, the cabildo noted that during
the parade, silver coins were thrown to the people, who grabbed them up
"joyfully and with many cries of 'Long Live the King.'"[82] It was no secret
that the function of these civic events was to legitimate the social and political
order. As the cabildo pointed out, the purpose of celebrating the city's
Spanish foundation was to "recall the glory of the conquest, and to revive the
homage that justly should be rendered to the sovereign."[83] On another level,
civic celebrations could reinforce a common regional identity, despite differences of class and race. Nevertheless, members of the crowd might interpret
the meanings of such rituals in distinct ways. Privately, councilors complained that the city's annual celebration on August 15 was sparsely attended.[84]

However flashy the civic functions, they could not match the significance
of the religious holidays, which were closer to the heart of the people. The
only record left of the parades and oaths of loyalty are the descriptions of the
cabildo or those of an occasional visitor, whereas references to Easter,
Christmas, or the numerous saints' days crop up in all kinds of documents.
Even the members of the town council implicitly recognized the greater
import of the church festivities; they were in almost continuous litigation
among themselves or with church officials over the honors due them during
such celebrations.[85]

Officially, the main events differed little from the civic functions, with the

---

81. Blanco, "Diario del viaje del Presidente Orbegoso al sur del Perú," 130.
82. AMA, LAC 25 (December 21, 1789).
83. AMA, LAC 26 (August 16, 1810).
84. AMA, LCED 9 (August 16, 1783); and LAC 26 (August 16, 1810).
85. See, for example, AMA, LEXP 1 (April 28, 1791), "Expediente sobre las Procesiones de
Semana Santa"; and (December 5, 1794), "Expediente sobre si en pie, o de Rodillas ha de recibir
la Bendición Episcopal"; and minutes from cabildo meetings in AMA, LAC 26.

parishes rather than the cabildo organizing the processions and masses. But evidence suggests greater popular participation. By 1803, many blacksmiths were trying to get out of their customary role of accompanying the image of the Virgin during the celebration of the Immaculate Conception, because of the expense.[86] On the other hand, the women of the "guild of hot pepper vendors" were indignant when the indigenous mayor of Santa Marta removed their arch from its central location in order to favor the coca sellers, during the festivities for the patron saint.[87] Perhaps enthusiasm was higher for more local festivals and among women compared with men. During Holy Week of 1789, the bishop ordered that women be relegated to the back of the procession in the parish of Santa Marta. His assistant reported that he had successfully prevented a woman from carrying a banner at the head of the march, but that he had had more trouble keeping the sexes apart, "because of the great crowd."[88]

Nevertheless, the principal role of the population during religious celebrations was, again, that of spectator. Arequipeños undoubtedly appreciated a good show, as Flora Tristan acidly observed: "The Arequipans are very fond of all kinds of spectacles and flock to them with equal enthusiasm whether they are theatrical or religious. They need such diversions because of their total lack of education, which also makes them very easy to please."[89]

The heart of the holidays, however, was the unofficial revelry that took place after mass. Many men and women went straight from church to a shop or chichería, where they began drinking. Others flocked to the cockfights and bullfights or to gambling parlors, which were allowed to operate only on weekends and holidays. In the evenings the celebration moved to the streets, where people visited the altars built and decorated by parish societies and listened to musicians who gathered to serenade and entertain the revelers. Finally the day was concluded with another spectacle: the very popular fireworks display.[90]

86. ARAR/Int/Adm (19-XI-1803), Recurso del Gremio de Herrería.
87. BNP doc. D6052 (1805), "El Gremio de Ajiceras contra el Alcalde de Naturales sobre despojo."
88. BNP doc. C4146 (1789), "Sobre Procesiones de Semana Santa."
89. Tristan, *Peregrinations of a Pariah*, 124; see also 107–8.
90. These details on festivals come from the testimony of witnesses in criminal trials. See ARAR/CS/Crim (22-V-1826), "Causa sobre la muerte de Pascual Quispe"; (10-VI-1836) "Contra Inocencio Pardo por herir a Pablo Rosado"; (7-VIII-1832), "Don Estanislao Bravo contra Don Mariano Montañez por rapto"; (4-VIII-1833), "Para determinar quienes hirieron y robaron a Don Mariano Espinoza"; and (1-VII-1836), "Contra Diego Pacheco por robo."

The quintessential annual holiday was Carnival, a celebration that lasted for several days and served as an emotional release before the more ascetic and "penitential season of Lent. There was no holiday in which the celebrations were more concentrated in the streets, where, at least, male plebeians and patricians intermingled. The principal game was to throw eggshells filled with paint or dye at the other masked gambolers bedecked in white costumes. Tristan noted with surprise that even "the slaves too share in the fun."[91] Juana Flores gave her slave Alberto Flores permission to go out and enjoy himself as long as he went in good company, explaining that it was "an inevitable custom," and she regretted only that her servant was attacked and wounded by another reveler.[92]

At the other end of the social scale, apparently even Anglo immigrants joined the celebration with gusto. In 1832, José Bennet Crane and Juan Jayman were seen drunkenly roaming the streets "with their clothes apparently soaked with chicha, [and] Jayman was carrying an empty jug under his arm (which did not seem strange to the witness because in those days [of Carnival] there is no decency)."[93]

José María Blanco was so impressed with Carnival that he devoted several pages of his diary to a description of the event. According to him, even the distinguished ladies participated in the free-for-all mock battle, albeit from the advantaged position of their balconies and rooftops. In the evening, observed Blanco, they continued entertaining themselves "with the song and dance sponsored by the nobility in their homes, and carried out by the plebe in the streets which have served them as a theater in the afternoon so that those [streets] which by day were a battleground, are converted by night into showy malls where, by the light of the torches, they sell sweets, meads and liquors."[94]

During Carnival, elite Arequipeños contributed briefly to the blurring of class boundaries as they frolicked in the public streets, where all but the ladies played. But they reasserted social divisions in the homes to which the "nobility" could retreat for private entertainment. According to Blanco, this mingling of the classes and races in an atmosphere of mock conflict did not get out of hand: "Perhaps this public adornment [*paramento*] has no equal in

91. Tristan, *Peregrinations of a Pariah*, 126.
92. ARAR/Int/Crim (1-III-1816), "Doña Juana Flores contra Bernardo Pastor."
93. As reported by witnesses called to testify in a murder trial against Crane: ARAR/CS/Crim (19-III-1832), "Contra José Bennet Crane por la muerte de Asa Bourne."
94. Blanco, "Diario del viaje del Presidente Orbegoso al sur del Perú," 292.

any other country, as neither does the simplicity, good humor and frankness with which they enjoy themselves without offending public decency and morality."[95]

The criminal records, however, tell a different story. Holidays were a time when drinking and revelry could easily escalate into disorder, and Carnival led the list in numbers of offenses. In general, fights and other violent crimes occurred among plebeians, who did not direct their anger against the patricians. The only evidence of the politicization of Carnival, a satirical program in 1842 mocking General Vivanco and other local notables, undoubtedly was penned by a highly literate author.[96]

Nevertheless, the latent possibility for class conflict did, occasionally, erupt into violence, most notably after independence had introduced at least an egalitarian rhetoric. In 1828, for example, merchants Mariano Arróspide and the Portuguese José López were tried for stabbing Marcelo Arayco, a carpenter. Apparently, a group of boys carrying a makeshift flag tried to break through Arróspide and his friends, who were walking arm in arm and taking up much of the street. Accounts of the ensuing fight differed. Arróspide, who claimed that the boys also threw mud, admitted taking their flag but denied stabbing anyone. Arayco insisted that he was not part of the gang and was unarmed, except for his dye and a pomander of scented water; he asserted, therefore, that Arróspide attacked him for no reason. Several plebeian witnesses did report seeing a young gentleman, whom some identified as Arróspide, beating Arayco.[97]

The incident revealed significant gender as well as class dynamics. As in the ritual disputes at the neighborhood level, it was a group of women who called for justice, shouting to the bystanders: "Be witnesses that Arróspide has stabbed him."

Arayco's aunt Magdalena Tapia said she saw Arróspide pass the dagger to his friend López. She fished the knife out of the latter's pocket and cried out: "Observe you all the weapon with which he wounded my nephew."

Finally, it was the carpenter's mother, Mercedes Tapia, who filed charges,

---

95. Ibid., 292.

96. BNP doc. D1927 (1842), "Gran espectáculo para el lunes de carnavales." A case of collective disorder did occur when the inhabitants of the Yarabamba valley (both Indians and Spaniards) were incited to riot on Carnival Sunday and destroyed the canal that carried water to Chapi. See ARAR/Int/Crim (16-X-1794), "Don Ignacio Evia contra Don Anselmo Josef de Rivera por azonada."

97. ARAR/Pref (20-II-1828), "Mercedes Tapia contra Don José López y Don Mariano Arróspide por puñaladas a su hijo Marcelo Arayco."

insisting "that such a public crime not remain unpunished, since even if I am poor, and the delinquent from a good family with money, we are all equal before the law."[98] The accused did suffer in jail for several months, but in the end, the court proved more sympathetic to the pleas of the merchants' families and lawyers than to the calls for justice of poor women. The charges were dropped.

This fight between two young merchants and a carpenter appears to have been an exception. Most likely, the rules of deference were only loosened, but not abandoned, during festivals. While this case pitted members of two classes against each other, moreover, it remained at a personal level and never directly challenged the social order. In this sense, Carnival in Arequipa seems to have acted primarily as a "safety valve," an escape from daily efforts to make a living, rather than as a true world turned upside down.[99] Just as Juana Flores allowed her slave to join in the festivities, the authorities in Arequipa generally tolerated the "inevitable" drinking and disorders that accompanied holidays. Moreover, there were signs of a growing separation between the high and low cultures, as elites increasingly emulated European models.[100]

Popular and Elite Cultures

Although the rules were relaxed on holidays, the elites of Arequipa did express concern over the disorderly conduct, drunkenness, and crime that occurred within the chicherías. Intendant Alvarez, for example, supported the cabildo's request to increase the tax on grinding corn, much of which was used in the production of chicha. In addition to raising revenues, he argued, it would have the beneficial effect of reducing "the drunkenness that causes so many spiritual and temporal ills within the plebe which is so corrupted by

98. The quotes are from the testimony of Mariano Arostegui on Feb. 23 and that of Magdalena Tapia on Feb. 27, and from the petition of Mercedes Tapia dated Feb. 21, in ARAR/Pref (20-II-1828), "Mercedes Tapia contra Don José López y Don Mariano Arróspide."

99. See Davis, *Society and Culture*, 124–51.

100. Such a division and efforts to control popular culture had begun earlier in Lima and Mexico City; see Juan Carlos Estenssoro Fuchs, "Modernismo, estética, música y fiesta: Elites y cambio de actitud frente a la cultura popular, Peru 1750–1850," in Henrique Urbano, ed., *Tradición y modernidad en los Andes* (Cuzco: CERA Bartolomé de las Casas, 1992), 181–95; Viqueira Albán, *¿Relajados o reprimidos?*; and Pamela Voekel, "Peeing on the Palace: Bodily Resistance to Bourbon Reforms in Mexico City," *Journal of Historical Sociology* 5, no. 2 (1992): 183–208.

[chicha] that it disturbs the peace within families that use it and even between neighbors."[101] After independence, letters to the local official newspaper *El Republicano* echoed the intendant's concerns with complaints about the "pestiferous chicherías in the best streets."[102]

Although chicheras were respected by their customers and neighbors, they were often the object of derision by their social superiors, who associated them with disorder, immorality, and dishonor. Gregoria Rodríguez, for example, opposed the marriage of her son Juan Muños to Brígida Valencia on the grounds that she was "a mulatta chichera by trade and of a dishonest conduct which degrades her," and that her work "serves no purpose other than congregating drunk and dissolute men, which will make married life tormented and worrisome."[103] Similarly, when Martina Tapia brought suit against Rafael Salas, requesting that he fulfill his promise to marry her, he argued that he could never marry Martina because she was a chichera, "which brings with it a disorderly [*desastrada*] life, and because she is of lower lineage than I."[104]

The differing views of chicherías clashed in 1830, in a dispute between Toribio de Linares, the municipality's deputy for police, and María Escalante, the proprietor of a chichería. According to Linares, he was out doing his rounds, trying to get residents to clean up their sections of the street of La Ranchería. When he told Escalante not to throw out the fetid water from her chichería, she replied insolently "that she didn't recognize me as her Judge." Escalante claimed that she had simply tried to explain to Linares that a recent rainstorm, not her chichería, had made the street muddy, and that she would appeal her case to a higher authority.

It was not an empty threat, for she brought charges against Linares for violently arresting her without cause, "since she was honorable, and a *mujer de bien*, and had not committed any crime for which she should be taken away with scandal." As we shall see, *hombre de bien* referred to honorable

---

101. AMA, LPA 2 (May 14, 1785). For a similar argument by the cabildo, see AMA, LCED 6 (February 20, 1786). Nevertheless, the taverns in Arequipa were never regulated to the extent of those in Mexico City; see Scardaville, "Alcohol Abuse and Tavern Reform," 643–71; and Viqueira Albán, ¿*Relajados o reprimidos?* 169–219.

102. "Aviso" in *El Republicano*, Jan. 7, 1826. See also *El Republicano*, Nov. 2, 1833, 8; and Dec. 21, 1833, 7.

103. AAA/Mat (9-VI-1790), Juan Muños y Brígida Valencia.

104. AAA/Civ (18-V-1795), "Martina Tapia pide que Rafael Salas cumpla su palabra de casamiento." See also ARAR/CS/Crim (22-VII-1826), "Don Pedro Rivera contra Doña María Valdivia por injurias."

men, and it is striking that Escalante uses this term. Several witnesses who had been in the chichería, apparently respectable citizens, backed up Escalante's story. Escalante won the first round when Judge Zavala freed her from jail and ordered Linares to appear in court, despite his position on the city council, "since all Peruvians are equal before the law."

Linares would not give up so easily, however, and took his case to the prefect. The city council complained that the court should uphold the authority of the police, so that they would not become "the laughing stock of even chicheras like Escalante." Linares played upon the elite perception of chicherías in his argument to the prefect, calling Escalante's story "the imagined supposition of a person who runs, exercises and foments a tavern both morally and physically harmful; because it is clear that in all such establishments young people and servants are corrupted, and they are in the end offices of prostitution and shelters for criminals, vagrants and ne'er-do-wells."

He continued by citing all the ordinances that he was attempting to enforce and arguing that if she was let off, "no authority will be respected nor free from criminal prosecution, insubordination and anarchy will reign, and only disobedience and disorder will prevail." When questioned by the judge whether he had violated the asylum of her home, Linares replied "that he was convinced that no chichería deserved the name of asylum." By appealing to new liberal principles of order as well as to existing elite stereotypes of chicherías, Linares managed to have jurisdiction transferred to the executive branch, where he won a favorable settlement from the prefect.[105]

By the early nineteenth century, those offended by the public atmosphere of the chicherías could withdraw to more exclusive establishments, such as cafés or billiards salons.[106] In 1833, for example, Don José Urrutia opened a café to serve coffee, tea, fine liquors, and ice cream, guaranteeing his clientele that "they would be treated with the appropriate cleanliness, neatness and punctuality."[107] His provision of a full meal service for six reals a day was

---

105. All the quotations for this case come from ARAR/CS/Crim (4-I-1830), "Contra Doña María Escalante por resistir al Diputado de Policia D. Toribio de Linares."

106. For references, see ARAR/Int/Crim (19-III-1806), "Causa sobre el robo de pesos a Don Pedro Yansen"; ARAR/CS/Crim (28-VIII-1830), "Don Joaquín de Otero contra Don Valerio de Arrisueño por injurias"; and (19-III-1832), "Contra José Bennet Crane por la muerte de Asa Bourne."

107. *El Republicano,* July 27, 1833, 6; and Sept. 7, 1833, 7. French immigrant Desidero Girard had earlier advertised a shop selling imported sweets, sorbets, and wines; see *El Republicano,* Dec. 31, 1825, 24.

well beyond the reach of a laborer's wages of four reals, but such restaurants might have drawn some professionals or wealthy artisans away from taverns. Ever more often, the city's patricians, preferring to socialize among their equals in the exclusive parties known as *tertulias*, left the street to the crowd. Particularly after independence, as Arequipa was opened up to European ideas and immigrants, elites tried to model their behavior on more cosmopolitan and "enlightened" norms.[108] One letter to the editor chastised townspeople for riding their horses on the sidewalks, behavior that the author expected from "rustic" country people but considered insufferable among gentlemen who were "enlightened and civilized in the drawing rooms and tertulias."[109] Tristan, who, like other travelers, was questioned about the latest fashions from Europe, noted that at the balls: "French dances are replacing the fandango, the bolero and the native dances which decency condemns."[110]

Finally, the construction of a theater allowed the elites both to separate themselves more from the masses and to feel as if they were part of an international high culture.[111] By 1853, the prefect noted favorably of the city's inhabitants "the rapid refinement of their customs, and their full entrance into the terrain of culture and good taste."[112]

As the dispute between police chief Linares and the chichera Escalante suggests, this trend was accompanied by a growing effort to control popular culture, an effort in which women were especially targeted. As early as the 1780s, the disorder associated with religious festivals was of great concern to bishop Pedro José Chaves de La Rosa, who did his best to make them solemn and dignified. He received little support, however, from the civil authorities, perhaps because they, too, were the target of the bishop's reforms. This attitude began to change after independence. In 1826, the central government reduced the number of official religious holidays, on the grounds that: "Far from being consecrated to the pious ends for which they were instituted, they

---

108. In 1838 a tailor from Lima opened a shop that, he advertised, would provide the latest fashions from Paris and London; see *El Republicano*, Feb. 10, 1838, 6. This frenchification of the Mexican upper classes had begun in the eighteenth century; see Viqueira Albán, *¿Relajados o reprimidos?*, 15. European visitors still found Arequipa lacking in refinement; see Haigh, "Bosquejos del Perú, 1825–1827," 29; and Tristan, *Peregrinations of a Pariah*, 132.

109. "Policía," *El Republicano*, May 18, 1833, 8.

110. Tristan, *Peregrinations of a Pariah*, 127.

111. *El Republicano*, Apr. 12, 1828, 65; May 31, 1828, 95; June 21, 1828, 110; Aug. 2, 1828, 135; Oct. 4, 1828, 3; Nov. 1, 1828, 5–6; Nov. 8, 1828, 4; and Nov. 22, 1828, 4.

112. In a letter dated July 16, 1853, reprinted in *El Republicano*, July 20, 1853, 3.

are destined for nothing but vice and immorality, keeping paralyzed meanwhile the course of justice, in the courts and tribunals, deserted the labors of the countryside, and abandoned the workshops of the artisans."[113]

This decree would be faithfully carried out by authorities in Arequipa, who added to it many of their own. Republican officials recognized the connection between popular culture and the need to control both labor discipline and political mobilization. Moreover, they used the language of honor to discuss and define these problems.

---

113. Letter dated October 20, 1826, from the minister of ecclesiastical affairs to the bishops in BNP doc. D11555, "Sobre reducir a menor número las fiestas de la Iglesia."

4

From the Church to the Courts

Efforts at Social Control

The depiction of social activities and festivals in the preceding chapter gives rise to questions of social control. The chicherías and stores selling distilled liquors, never lacking for customers, were frequently the scenes of disorderly and even violent behavior. Gambling, despite its illegality, was popular among members of every social class. And the crime rate increased on holidays, when heavy drinking was common and revelers took to the streets. The apparently topsy-turvy world of Carnival may have served as a release mechanism, ultimately reaffirming the social order. Nevertheless, every society must have a way to ensure that deviant activities do not get out of control.

In late colonial Arequipa, it was the church that expressed alarm at what it defined as sinful and immoral behavior among the populace. Initially, local elites and civilian authorities did not share these concerns; in their eyes, a little drinking, gambling, and "illicit" sex were enjoyed by people at all levels of society and posed no threat to public order. After independence, however, political instability made republican officials increasingly uneasy and, along with the growing influence of liberalism, colored their perceptions of the "excesses" of popular culture.

The Bishop's Morality Crusade

At the end of the eighteenth century, a zealous reformer arrived in Arequipa to take leadership of the church. Bishop Pedro José Chaves de La Rosa, who brought from Spain the new Enlightenment influence of the Bourbons, worked persistently from 1788 to 1805 to reform both his own church and what he saw as the lax morality of the population.[1] Some of his projects, such as the establishment of a foundling home and the reorganization of the seminary, enjoyed relative success. His efforts, however, were continually undermined by both the civil authorities and his own subordinates, so that his campaign to change the behavior of nuns and priests, as well as that of plebeians and creole elites, was markedly less successful.

When Chaves de La Rosa arrived in Arequipa in 1788, he immediately embarked upon a pastoral tour of his diocese. He was not impressed with the state of affairs.[2] In a 1790 report on his visita, he noted that there was much ignorance and vice even among his own clergy.[3] The bishop traced the origin of these problems to the miserable state of the local seminary and to its graduates' consequent lack of education. Upon inspection, he found only a rector, a vice-rector, professors of Latin and logic, and twenty-odd students, many of whom, he claimed, were ineligible because they were marked by the dishonor of illegitimacy or of mixed race. (His views on race undoubtedly differed from those of most Arequipeños.)

He immediately shut down the school for reorganization. When it re-opened two years later, it had a new, "enlightened" curriculum, better qualified instructors, and more disciplined students. Under his tutelage, the Seminario de San Jerónimo came to be regarded as a fine institution of higher learning and educated many of the region's notable citizens, including some who later fought for independence.[4]

Chaves de La Rosa found the situation in the city's convents to be little better. The bishop was disturbed by a lack of commitment—particularly in the convent of Santa Catalina—to the simple and communal lifestyle to which the nuns had pledged themselves. Women from the wealthiest local families entered Santa Catalina, and they were not eager to give up the

---

1. Compare with Kathy Waldron, "The Sinners and the Bishop in Colonial Venezuela: The *Visita* of Bishop Mariano Martí, 1771–1784," in Asunción Lavrin, ed., *Sexuality and Marriage in Colonial Latin America* (Lincoln and London: University of Nebraska Press, 1989), 156–77.

2. BNP doc. C4058 (1788), "Carta Pastoral del Obispo Chaves de La Rosa."

3. BNP doc. C4192 (1790), "Informe sobre la visita pastoral."

4. Gallagher, "Imperial Reform and the Struggle for Regional Self-Determination," 150; and Wibel, "The Evolution of a Regional Community," 224–25.

comforts in which they had been raised. Although they were supposed to surrender their possessions to the community upon taking their vows, the women of Santa Catalina asserted their right to control private allowances known as *peculios*.[5] Many of the nuns lived in private apartments that could hardly be called "cells," where they were waited upon by servants and slaves.

Such customs not only violated the rules of communal living, but the presence of large numbers of secular women—who were free to leave the convent on errands—also compromised the cloisters. Even for nuns, then, the boundary between private and public could be bridged. During the Easter season of 1789, the bishop sent a warning to the convents to ensure that the servants were modestly dressed and observed the holiday with dignity, and especially that they did not go out onto towers or rooftops, where they could be seen from the street.[6] In December of that year, he also warned the mother superior of Santa Catalina not to allow men into the convent under any circumstances, not even the gardener nor the artisans who built special altars for Christmas.[7]

In his report of 1790, the bishop noted only "the weak resistance by a small number of poorly advised religious to my loving remonstrances for their temporal and spiritual well-being."[8] In fact, he would find the opposition of a majority of nuns to his reforms to be both strong and persistent. At first the nuns demurely assured the bishop that they were following his advice as faithful daughters.[9] When Chaves suspended the 1790 elections for a new prioress and appointed a nun he knew would carry out his orders, however, the sisters mobilized their connections outside the convent by writing letters of protest.[10] The bishop struck back by imposing penances on those who resisted his reforms, going so far as to deny the Eucharist to five of the ringleaders.

Far from humbled, the nuns took their case to the audiencia (high court) of Lima. Their lawyer denounced the bishop's abusive interferences in the elections, his appointment of confessors, and his management of finances, but complained just as bitterly about the reforms that targeted the nuns' lifestyle. The rigorous schedule of religious exercises, he maintained, "does

---

5. See Gallagher, "Imperial Reform," 89–92.

6. BNP doc. C4173, "Pastoral de Chaves de La Rosa sobre lo que deben hacer las religiosas en lo tocante al culto."

7. Letter dated Dec. 21, 1789, in BNP doc. C947, "Santa visita del Monasterio de Santa Catalina."

8. BNP doc. C4192.

9. Documents dated Feb. 28, 1788; and May 7, 1790, in BNP C947.

10. See Gallagher, "Imperial Reform," 97–102, on the dispute.

not allow the nuns to rest." Depriving them of the occasional sweets to which they were accustomed, he continued, would establish a perfect communal life at the cost of "making the nuns perish from hunger."[11] Whether it was through the persuasiveness of their arguments or the influence of their powerful families, the women achieved a resounding victory.

In 1795, the king himself upheld their right not only to internal self-government, but also to resist with a clear conscience "the new method of communal living."[12] French traveler Flora Tristan visited Santa Catalina in the 1830s, where she was entertained with concerts and sumptuous banquets. The nuns questioned her about the latest French fashions and even lifted her skirts to inspect her corset and drawers. Given Tristan's lively descriptions of Santa Catalina, one may assume the nuns were not challenged again.[13]

While Bishop Chaves was fighting for reforms within his own church, he simultaneously pursued the battle on another front. In his pastoral letter to the convents in 1789, he also asked the nuns to pray for the sinners outside the convent. "With great sorrow in our heart," he wrote, "we have heard about the preparations for and beginnings of the disorders which are repeated every year in Arequipa." He went on to compare the popular celebrations associated with Lent and Easter to "the very infamous Bacchanalia of pagan Rome."[14]

That same year, he required parishes to apply for licenses to hold processions, which he granted only under the strict condition that they conclude before dark and that men and women be kept separated.[15] Over a decade later, he had to repeat his admonitions in a general pastoral letter to the diocese. He complained of idolatries and other superstitions, noting that even Spaniards emphasized exterior and pagan shows of religiosity rather than true internal faith. He ordered his priests not to allow processions to continue after sunset, in order to prevent disorders; further, he prohibited bullfights, dramatic presentations, and dancing on feast days, even if not directly part of a procession. Finally, he specifically denounced private celebrations during the festival of the Holy Cross, including "the so-called native dances, indecent and provocative in themselves, as well as the excesses of the plebe of both sexes."[16]

11. Document dated March 9, 1792, in BNP doc. C947.
12. Document dated June 13, 1795, in BNP doc. C947.
13. Tristan, *Peregrinations of a Pariah*, 193–204.
14. Letter dated Feb. 14, 1789, in BNP doc. C4173.
15. BNP doc. C4146 (1789), "Sobre las procesiones de semana santa."
16. BNP doc. D11627 (1801), "Pastoral expedida por el Obispo Chaves de La Rosa,

While the bishop may have been particularly concerned about pagan activities that occurred in Indian villages far from his watchful eye, there were certainly instances within the city and its suburbs of mixing profane elements into religious celebrations. Revelers dressed in satirical costumes, for example, parodied ecclesiastical rites and authorities. During the Holy Cross festival in May 1794, the indigenous mayor of Yanahuara and his deputy reported that while on patrol, they had encountered a crowd of people in costume, celebrating with music and dance. Most of the crowd dispersed, but they arrested two men—a tailor and a barber—who were dressed as a cardinal and a bishop and playing guitar and flute. They took the offenders to the local priest, who, furious at this mockery of the church, shouted that they were "thieves" and ordered them whipped.[17]

Forty years later, however, the church had made little headway toward making religious celebrations more solemn. In her description of the procession for Our Lady of Ransom, Tristan was shocked to see costumed "negroes and *sambos*" dancing at its head: "There must have been forty or fifty of them, writhing and gesticulating in the most shameless and indecent fashion, arousing the excitement of the coloured women and negresses who lined the route calling out obscenities to them." Unknowingly, she echoed the words of the late Bishop Chaves, likening the festival to "pagan bacchanals and saturnalia."[18]

Another issue that had long been of great concern to the church in Arequipa was the way parishioners dressed. Bishops railed against indecent outfits, which they saw as calculated by the devil "to conquer not only the Weak Men who habitually fall short in matters of purity and chastity, but also those cedars highest in fortitude and virtue."[19] They threatened both the

prohibiendo la celebración de . . . ceremonías reñidas con el rito cristiano." Similar efforts to control religious festivities were implemented in Bourbon Mexico City, but with the cooperation of secular authorities. See Linda A. Curcio-Nagy, "Giants and Gypsies: Corpus Christi in Colonial Mexico City," in William H. Beezley, Cheryl English Martin, and William E. French, eds., *Rituals of Rule, Rituals of Resistance* (Wilmington: Scholarly Resources, 1994), 27–46.

   17. BNP doc. C4144 (1794), "Expediente de unos soldados que se vistieron de Obispo y Cardenal en la Festividad de la Santa Cruz." For such satirical celebrations in Mexico, see Irving A. Leonard, *Baroque Times in Old Mexico: Seventeenth-Century Persons, Places, and Practices* (Ann Arbor: University of Michigan Press, 1959), especially 117–29.

   18. Tristan, *Peregrinations of a Pariah*, 107. See also Sartiges, "Viaje a las repúblicas de América del Sur," 20.

   19. BNP doc. C4185 (1739), pastoral letter of bishop Juan Cavero de Toledo; see also BNP doc. C4186 (1750), pastoral letter of bishop Juan Bravo de Rivero.

women who wore such fashions and the tailors who sewed them with excommunication. No matter what the proscriptions, however, women seemed able to make small yet clever changes in their outfits to expose a little more skin or to accentuate the shape of their bodies.

On more than one occasion, the effort to enforce greater modesty back-fired. During the Advent season of 1792, for example, friar José Neves gave a fiery sermon in the central plaza, condemning provocative female attire and singling out hoopskirts for special censure. He advised young men who passed a woman so dressed to cry out "Ave María," an order they eagerly took to an extreme. On December 11, Agustín de Abril, the attorney general for the cabildo, informed Intendant Alvarez that gangs of lower-class boys had taken to the streets, where they were snatching hoops (*aros*) from women's skirts. Perhaps they saw it as an opportunity to retaliate against women, who carried out the public shaming rituals analyzed in the previous chapter.

The intendant immediately issued a proclamation announcing that he would send out troops to patrol the city and imprison anyone caught ripping women's garments. He also sent a note about the incident to Bishop Chaves, who launched his own investigation into the matter. Friar Neves explained to the bishop that he had not mentioned the hoopskirts by name, and he claimed that reports of the riot were exaggerated. He insisted that it had all started the night of the sermon, when some repentant women set fire to a pile of their hoops in the plaza. The next morning, the boys started dragging the remaining hoops through the streets, shouting "Death to the hoops" and attacking women only of the "lowest plebe."

The "excesses" of the crowd quickly passed, but there remained some discomfort between the civil and religious authorities. The bishop took offense at the implication that the church was to blame for the incident; one of his assistants pointed out that "if parents educated their children well there would not be such atrocious disorders." The intendant assured Chaves that he had never meant to accuse him of irresponsibility. But he also warned him not to underestimate the gravity of the affair, and insisted "that the serious excesses of the young men were not limited only to the plebe but also extended to persons of considerable prominence."[20]

There were no further reports of such clothing riots—which, undoubtedly,

---

20. The account of this incident is in BNP doc. C4130 (1792), "Sobre graves escándalos a raiz del uso de vestidos indecorosos." The minutes of the cabildo refer to a similar case in 1783; AMA, LAC 25 (Oct. 6, 1783).

pleased the intendant and cabildo—but neither was there any move toward more modest fashions. In spite of all the warnings and admonitions issued from the pulpit, Chaves, like his predecessors, felt compelled in 1801 to issue a pastoral letter on proper attire. The bishop complained of the indecency of many outfits worn to church "which would be detestable in the theaters of civilized nations." He further condemned the great expense and luxury that was bankrupting families. For the first time he also chastised men, for wearing tight pants that signified "a feminization opposed to our national character." He went on to detail what fashions would be proscribed and instructed the upper classes to set a better example.

By diminishing the strict punishments such as excommunication set by his predecessors, however, Chaves seemed to acknowledge at least a partial defeat. The rules applied only to clothing worn to mass, and those who broke them would be politely asked to leave the church and refused communion.[21]

Of all the reforms, Bishop Chaves probably threw the most energy into his crusade against sexual "immorality." In his reports and correspondence, he often lamented the high number of illegitimate births and the consequent abandonment of many infants.[22] He was not exaggerating; more than one-third of the children in sampled baptismal records were born out of wedlock, though many of their parents likely lived in consensual unions. In 1780 and 1790, such children were identified as "of unknown parents," but by 1800, the new explicit category of "illegitimate" may have reflected an order from the bishop.[23]

One way that the bishop addressed at least the consequences of this problem was by establishing a foundling home, where parents could abandon unwanted infants, thereby protecting the honor of the mothers. His eye fell upon the Compañía, the Jesuit monastery that had been expropriated by the crown when the order was expelled in 1767. For several years the city's elites had been trying to gain approval to found a university on the property, but Chaves moved quickly. The doors of the Compañía were opened to found-lings in December 1788, a mere three months after the bishop's arrival in

21. BNP doc. D11728 (1801), "Pastoral del Obispo Chaves de La Rosa por la cual invoca a los fieles sencillez y recato en el uso de vestidos."
22. BNP doc. C4192 (1790); and doc. D11643 (1801), "Exposición elevada por el Obispo Chaves de La Rosa al Virrey."
23. Baptismal books for the cathedral and the indigenous parish of Santa Marta in the Archivo del Palacio Arzobispal for the years 1780, 1790, and 1800 reveal illegitimacy rates of 27 to 50 percent. Rates were also high in seventeenth-century Lima; see María Emma Mannarelli, *Pecados públicos: La ilegitimidad en Lima, siglo XVII* (Lima: Ediciones Flora Tristán, 1993).

Arequipa. In 1790, the Compañía housed fifty-six children; by 1804, a total of 1,431 infants had been admitted. Many of them had also died.

Chaves committed considerable funds to the foundling home, but he still came up short of the six-thousand-peso annual budget. He complained that the local populace refused to support the charitable project because of a "lack of enlightenment;" more likely their refusal to contribute to the bishop's cause stemmed from their resentment over losing their opportunity for a university.[24] In spite of the financial problems, however, the children stayed on in the Compañía, and the bishop could proudly point to the foundling home as one of his great achievements.

If Chaves de La Rosa addressed one of the consequences of extramarital sexuality, his efforts to attack the problem at its root did not have a chance. His failure, nevertheless, did not come from lack of trying. In 1791, he wrote to assure the viceroy that the population was calm in spite of the appearance of some political broadsides, but added: "What I do fear is that the Epidemic of fevers that is growing . . . is punishment for the public sins of concubinage, and the lack of the administration of Justice."[25] In another letter to the viceroy in 1801, he complained that these "illicit" affairs included people who were married and "visible for their circumstances and employment."[26]

The bishop preferred not to wait for God to punish such sins and, therefore, repeatedly called upon the civil authorities to take measures against the offenders.[27] In 1791, for example, Chaves sent a note to Intendant Alvarez informing him that the public treasurer of Moquegua Apolinar de Carbonera was living scandalously with a plebeian woman known as Tomasa "la Longaniza" (the sausage).[28] The intendant forwarded the note to the parish priest, undoubtedly hoping the matter could be dealt with locally.

---

24. See BNP doc. C4192; and doc. D11643, "Exposición elevada por el Obispo Chaves de La Rosa al Virrey"; and Gallagher, "Imperial Reform," 119–29.

25. Letter dated June 20, 1791, in BNP doc. C4003, "Correspondencia cursada por el Virrey al Obispo de Arequipa"; for another reference to the broadsides, see AMA, LAC 25 (April 25, 1791).

26. BNP doc. D11643 (1801).

27. Chaves's predecessor had tried to prosecute some sinners in ecclesiastical court, and Chaves's own shift to the secular courts may be an indication of the failure of that strategy. See AAA/Pen (2-V-1783), "Contra Corregidor Don Baltasar Sematnat por excesos escandalosos y concubinato público"; and (31-VIII-1784), "Sobre el escándalo de Catalina Nates con diversos sujetos."

28. AGN, Real Audiencia/Crim, Leg. 70, Cuad. 839 (1791), "Contra Don Apolinar de Carbonera y Peralta por ilícito comercio."

When the priest wrote back asking for instructions, Alvarez ordered a private investigation.

After nine witnesses acknowledged the affair (though they said they had noted no public scandal), the intendant ordered Carbonera to appear before him. Several months later, the subdelegate of Moquegua reported that the affair must have ended, because Tomasa had left the city. He warned, moreover, that if the intendant really wanted Carbonera to report to Arequipa, he had better send soldiers to escort him, because none of those in Moquegua would willingly carry out such orders. At the end of the month the bishop again wrote to the intendant, protesting that Carbonera had simply sent his mistress to a nearby village to avoid her punishment. But Alvarez took no further action.

Chaves may have been discouraged by the intendant's reluctance to discipline a royal official, but he did not give up his efforts. In 1800, the bishop reported to the new intendant, Bartolomé María de Salamanca, that Tomás Quintanilla, the tribute collector in the village of Carumas, was cheating on his wife. Chaves asked that Quintanilla be removed from the village so that, as bishop, he could attend to "the marriages he has disrupted and the other spiritual ruin he has caused by his abandonment."[29] In this case, the bishop chose a better target: witnesses testified not only to Quintanilla's adultery, but also to his general abuse of the indigenous inhabitants.[30] Quintanilla was arrested twice, but each time he was quickly released on bail. Although the case was sent to the royal attorney on the first of March, it was not considered until 1810, when it was filed away on the assumption that the affair must have concluded.

In 1803 Chaves tried once again, with a slightly different strategy. When he informed Salamanca that the customs officer in Tambo, Juan Bautista Villanueva, was living sinfully with Juana Portugal, he asked that *she* be removed from the village so that Villanueva would return to his wife. Even when the mayor of Tambo protested that the bishop had the wrong girl, the intendant insisted that she be sent to Arequipa, where she was detained in the Casa de Recogidas.[31] Only when her mother presented several witnesses, including

29. ARAR/Int/Crim (31-I-1800), "Contra Don Tomás Quintanilla por los excesos que se expresan, por su mujer Doña Melchora Torres."

30. ARAR/Int/Crim (15-II-1800), "Contra Don Tomás Quintanilla por amancebamiento en el Pueblo de Carumas."

31. This institution was roughly a house of correction for women, but with highly religious overtones; some women entered voluntarily for devotion or to escape abusive husbands. For a thorough study, see Nancy Elena Van Deusen, "*Recogimiento* for Women and Girls in Colonial

the local priest of Tambo, who testified to her proper conduct, was Juana absolved. In his sentence, the intendant said he feared that Villanueva would continue to make his wife suffer; nevertheless, he did nothing to punish his behavior.[32]

After trying unsuccessfully for more than a decade to get the courts to take action against sexual offenders, Chaves was fed up. He complained to the viceroy that the intendant offered no assistance and even had refused the "simple measure" of placing the mistresses of royal officials—mere plebeian women—in the Casa de Recogidas. "The mayors," he added, "have lent me legal assistance with regard to wretched persons, but do not dare to do so with the Powerful and their relatives."[33]

The charge was undoubtedly true. When Doña Rafaela Ure filed for an ecclesiastical divorce because her husband, Don Santiago Rodrigues, was having an affair with her sister, mayor Pio Tristán was ordered to testify. He acknowledged that he had known of the affair but had taken no action at the time, "because of the status of [Rodrigues] and until acquiring more information in order to remedy the situation without scandal."[34] For elites, it was public scandal, rather than private peccadilloes, that brought dishonor.

As for the "wretched persons," Chaves may have been referring to the project of mayor Mariano de Bustamante in 1797 "to go out to patrol the city every night in order to cut down in some way on the many recognized concubinages among the Plebe."[35] Because there were no budgeted funds, Bustamante came up with a plan to pay the deputies' salaries out of the fines collected from the delinquents. Most, if not all, of the couples apprehended were probably living in common-law marriages; several were repeat offenders (with the same partner), and Bustamante referred to one "notorious" couple who had numerous children from their long relationship.

They were charged from two to six pesos, depending upon their means—a

---

Lima: An Institutional and Cultural Practice," (Ph.D. diss., University of Illinois at Urbana-Champaign, 1995).

32. ARAR/Int/Crim (5-V-1803), "Causas seguidas a pedimento del Obispo Chaves de La Rosa contra Juana Portugal por crear un escándalo con Don Juan Bautista Villanueva."

33. BNP doc. D11643.

34. See AAA/Pen (7-VII-1808), "Doña Rafaela Ure pide divorcio de su esposo Don Santiago Rodrigues."

35. AMA, LEXP 1 (January 11, 1797), folio 272. In fact, only adultery—and not cohabitation—was prohibited by Spanish law. See Alamiro de Avila Martel, *Esquema del derecho penal indiano* (Santiago, Chile: Seminario de Derecho Público de la Escuela de Ciencias Jurídicas y Sociales de Santiago, 1941), 101.

substantial amount, considering that a laborer would earn only one-half peso a day on construction projects. Some were imprisoned as well, and Bustamante reported that six couples had been brought to trial. The project turned quite a nice profit; after subtracting salaries and other expenses, the mayor had almost one hundred pesos left over, which he applied to repairs on the public fountain. Nevertheless, Bustamante suspended the vice squad after only three months. He lamented that because so many men refused to pay the fine, claiming their exemption (*fuero*) as soldiers, he could not afford to pay the deputies. More likely the project had become extremely unpopular among the "lowly plebe," many of whom cohabited outside of marriage.

Chaves's charge that he received little cooperation from the civil authorities to carry out his reforms is certainly true. This inaction should have come as no surprise, however, since many among the region's dominant classes were implicated in the very types of behavior that the bishop was trying to eradicate. They did not enjoy being preached to about wasting too much money on finery, when being seen in public in the latest and most luxurious fashions added to their social status and honor. They saw nothing wrong in men having affairs with lower-class women, as long as they did not cause a public scandal. Although none would have defended blasphemy, they enjoyed the secular entertainments that went along with religious festivities. Furthermore, cabildo members were angered when their own processions were canceled simply because they had not applied to the bishop for a license.[36] And finally, while they may have been scornful of the "excesses" of the plebe, they did not consider a little wine, women, and song as a threat to the social order. On the contrary, they were more likely to fear the consequences of a backlash if such behavior were repressed.

In fact, the cabildo members and other local notables harbored resentment against Bishop Chaves, whom they saw as coming from the outside to impose unwanted changes, much like the royal officials sent to carry out the Bourbon reforms. They were angered when he thwarted their efforts to establish a local university and spent money instead on wretched orphans. In 1794, the city's attorney general complained to the king that the fees charged by priests for religious services were arbitrary; he won a favorable decision, and the bishop was forced to set new rates.[37]

The intendants, though also representatives of central power, had conflicts with the bishop over their right of patronage, that is, to oversee the appoint-

36. See AMA, LEXP 1 (May 28, 1791).
37. BNP doc. C4062 (1799), "Real Cédula y aranceles formados en su razón."

ment of priests and other church officials. Bishop Chaves did not even have the support of his own cathedral chapter; only a couple years after his arrival, he complained that they were opposing his reforms and spreading gossip about him. Already stinging from the new rules that two-thirds of the body be composed of peninsulars, the creoles on the council resented the bishop's contention that their seminary was inadequate.[38]

These conflicts in Arequipa reflected the general weakening of the church's power in Spanish America during the eighteenth century.[39] At the local level, Intendant Alvarez, the cabildo, and the cathedral chapter joined forces in a campaign to drive out Bishop Chaves. The viceroy sympathized with Chaves, but simply advised him to be patient and ignore the slanders against him.[40] In 1805 the bishop, tired of fighting, asked to resign his post. By the time his successor, Luis Gonzaga de La Encina, arrived in 1810, the independence crisis was underway and Encina concentrated his efforts on opposing insurgency rather than immorality.

Chaves could look back with satisfaction on certain institutional reforms, such as the foundling home and the seminary, but he had had no perceptible success in changing the morality or behavior of his flock. Local officials and prominent citizens could claim part of the credit for Chaves's defeat, but the popular classes as well simply chose to ignore his admonitions and to carry on with their lives as they wished. It is impossible to know exactly what they thought of the bishop and his reforms. Plebeians probably considered themselves more or less good Catholics; they certainly attended mass, especially on holy days.[41]

Chances are that they simply did not share all the bishop's definitions of sin. If you could not afford a marriage service, you simply set up a household and lived "as if you were married." You probably owned only a few changes of clothing and, therefore, ignored the bishop's admonitions against indecent dress. And you celebrated religious festivals as you had learned them in your community. What was "ignorance and superstition" to the bishop was tradition to most plebeians.

---

38. Gallagher, "Imperial Reform," 60–76, 119–50, 173–75, 206–26; and Wibel, "The Evolution of a Regional Community," 224–26.

39. Josep M. Barnadas, "The Catholic Church in Colonial Spanish America," in Leslie Bethel, ed., *The Cambridge History of Latin America*, vol. 1 (Cambridge: Cambridge University Press, 1984), 536–40. For Arequipa, see Brown, *Bourbons and Brandy*, 127–46.

40. BNP doc. C4192 (1790).

41. Testimonies in the criminal records include numerous references to going to church; see also Antoine Tibesar, "The Peruvian Church at the Time of Independence in the Light of Vatican II," *The Americas* 26, no. 4 (1970): 359–60.

Colonial Law Enforcement

Although the bishops of Arequipa could not count upon their colleagues in government for assistance in policing the morality of their flock, it was certainly in the interest of the latter to maintain general law and order. The civil authorities may have overlooked harmless carousing among the plebe, but they could not afford to let thievery and violence get out of hand. One would expect concern over social control to have been particularly high in the late colonial period. In addition to rural indigenous uprisings in the eighteenth century—which reached a peak during the widespread rebellion lead by Túpac Amaru in 1780 and 1781—insurrections with the apparent goal of political independence shook several Andean cities during the first decades of the nineteenth century.[42]

Arequipa's elites witnessed rioting and looting during the tax revolt of 1780, and the city was occupied in 1814 by troops from Cuzco supporting the rebellion in that city. Nevertheless, there are few indications that they were worried about a threat from below. In fact, the leading citizens—who themselves probably were involved in the 1780 revolt—defended the fidelity of the city's inhabitants. In a letter to the viceroy, a municipal official blamed the uprising on the lower classes, and especially the Indians, but pointed to their repentant participation in expeditions against the supporters of Túpac Amaru: "See there erased with tears and blood the indiscretions of an ignorant plebe, who let themselves be seduced."[43] When viceroy José Abascal sent out an urgent order in 1807 to apprehend vagrants, moreover, Intendant Salamanca apparently did not share his concern. Whereas other intendants replied that they would take immediate measures, Salamanca responded with numerous questions about the order's feasibility.[44]

The lack of concern about disorder among the city's authorities is reflected in their ad hoc approach to law enforcement. Larger cities such as Lima and Mexico City established police forces in the late eighteenth century in response to growing concerns about crime.[45] Although Arequipa's city

---

42. For an introduction to late colonial rebellions in Peru, see Stern, *Resistance, Rebellion, and Consciousness*; and Godoy, *Rebellions and Revolts*.

43. AMA, LCED 6 (Aug. 22, 1782), folios 192–95, "Representación del Síndico Procurador General."

44. BNP doc. D5914 (1807), "Orden . . . circulada a todas las intendencias para la aprehensión de vagos y malhechores."

45. Though it took some time for the police to become effective. See Flores Galindo, *Aristocracia y plebe*; Michael C. Scardaville, "Crime and the Urban Poor: Mexico City in the Late Colonial Period" (Ph.D. diss., Unversity of Florida, 1977); and Gabriel James Haslip,

council had a commissioner for police, there is no record of his having a regular force at his disposal, and his primary responsibility was to make sure city streets were maintained in good condition and cleaned up for special occasions.[46] Commissioners were also appointed at the neighborhood level, where their duties included overseeing cleanliness and repairs, intervening in disputes among neighbors, enforcing standard weights and measures in local businesses, maintaining calm at night, and keeping track of all those living in or visiting the *barrio*.[47]

There is little evidence, however, that they complied with all these regulations. Most delinquents who were apprehended probably had an oral hearing before a local justice of the peace. Those who committed more serious offenses were tried before the city's mayor or the intendant, but there was no independent court system set up to handle criminal litigation.[48]

The lack of an institutionalized police force became evident in a 1794 petition from the mayors of Arequipa to Intendant Alvarez y Jiménez, in which they lamented: "All your indefatigable zeal to see that this city is to the extent possible purged and free from troublemakers, vagrants, and harmful elements; and all our desires for the greater honor to God, good service to the Sovereign, and fulfillment of our duties, all are found to be sadly frustrated."[49] Because the jail fees generated so little income, they explained, there was not enough money to pay officers to serve on patrols. The mayors asked the intendant to establish a force of four deputies with an annual salary of fifty pesos each, to be paid out of other municipal funds. The cabildo, in supporting this request, claimed that "the lowly plebe is almost unbridled in its excesses without this assistance."[50]

The intendant, believing that he did not have the authority to make such a decision, forwarded the request to the real audiencia of Lima, which waited

---

"Crime and the Administration of Justice in Colonial Mexico City, 1696–1810" (Ph.D. diss., Columbia University, 1980).

46. AMA, LPA 3 (May 21, 1792).

47. AMA, LAC 25, folios 24–25.

48. For an introduction to the colonial system of criminal justice, see H. H. A. Cooper, "A Short History of Peruvian Criminal Procedure and Institutions," *Revista de derecho y ciencias políticas* 32 (1968): 215–67; Colin MacLachlan, *Criminal Justice in Eighteenth-Century Mexico: A Study of the Tribunal of the Acordada* (Berkeley and Los Angeles: University of California Press, 1974); and Haslip, "Crime and the Administration of Justice."

49. BNP doc. C1196 (1794), "Expediente promovido por los alcaldes sobre que se establezcan esbirros para las rondas de la ciudad."

50. Ibid.

more than ten years to issue a ruling. When the justices did announce their approval, in March 1805, it was only provisional; if the king did not ratify their decision, the cabildo of Arequipa would have to refund any money spent on the patrols. The council appealed this condition, but it was not lifted until 1808. Although this request reflected the concern of local authorities with maintaining public order, their willingness to wait fourteen years to establish the police force reveals that law enforcement was not their first priority.

While strict regulations may have existed, therefore, enforcement was often lax. For example, authorities often looked the other way when it came to gambling. In one lengthy case, a woman accused her neighbors of personal injuries and invasion of privacy; the origin of her problems, she maintained, was their operation of gaming tables, which attracted a bad class of people. She had complained to the intendant the year before, but his orders to suspend the games had been ignored. The neighborhood commissioner backed up her assertions, testifying that it was a well-known house of gambling in which games often lasted late into the night despite warnings by judges, the mayor, and the former intendant. The accused did not deny that gambling took place in his house, but insisted that he allowed only card games played for small stakes, and only among "persons of judgment, honor, and distinction."

"In this city in all places of recreation," he boldly added, "there has been gambling, and there is gambling now, and neither your Lordship, nor your predecessors have prohibited it."[51] A year and a half after charges were brought, the intendant ordered that the house in question close at eight every evening and prohibited any games of chance. Given the record on enforcement, however, it is likely that the gambling continued and that the neighbors simply had to put up with any noise or inconvenience.[52]

Gaming was a popular pastime among all classes, and authorities undoubtedly hesitated to put their peers on trial. Even in prosecuting plebeians for robbery, however, the record is uneven. There is little in the records about petty thefts; most likely these were dealt with at the neighborhood level and punished with restitution of the goods and/or a few days in jail. Nevertheless,

51. ARAR/Int/Crim (14-XI-1806), "Contra Ignacio Canano y su mujer Teresa Gonzales por desórdenes de malversación en su casa."

52. For a similar case that resulted in a simple warning to stop, see ARAR/Int/Crim (22-VI-1815), "Doña María Josefa de Silva y Zaconeta contra Don Atanacio Trujillo por injurias."

of the twelve surviving larceny cases that did make it to trial between 1784 and 1824, only four reached the sentencing stage. One reason for inconclusive prosecution was the slow pace of justice; several robbery trials lasted for years, while the lawyers and justices attended to the higher priority and more lucrative civil suits. By the time these cases reached sentencing—if they did—the punishment was often less than the time the defendant had already spent in detention. For the most part, criminals were not the targets of vindictive condemnations, and pardons to commemorate civic occasions were not uncommon.[53] Although harsh penalties such as mutilation existed in the written law, they were rarely applied in practice, especially by the eighteenth century. Jails were to serve only for temporary detention and security, not for punishment, although defendants were often sentenced to the time they had already served during the trial.[54]

In the late colonial period, then, accused criminals suffered as much from neglect as from serving out actual sentences. Although some prisoners languished in jail—or even died—others had been released on bond or escaped long before their trials concluded or were discontinued.[55] Inefficiency was probably the primary cause of the frequent escapes in Arequipa, but it would be difficult to argue that security was a high priority in the late colonial period. In 1789, for example, an accused murderer left through the front door of the jail; the jailkeeper admitted that he had invited the prisoner to his birthday party and then let him leave, believing that his offer to fetch musicians was sincere.[56]

On the eve of independence, security was even more lax. When three prisoners escaped in 1821, an investigation uncovered that their shackles and cell doors were defective. The jailkeeper insisted that he had tried to get the cabildo's deputy for jails to repair them, but that latter official only joked that "the prisoners were not birds who could fly over such high walls," and he asserted that the Spanish constitution (reestablished in 1820) had put an end to prisons.[57]

---

53. See ARAR/Int/Crim (4-X-1800), "Contra Matías Alpaca y otros por robo"; (24-XI-1803) "Contra Gregorio Ramos por la muerte de José Fuentes"; and AMA, LAC 26 (Aug. 1, 1808).

54. For similar trends in Chile, see Avila Martel, _Esquema_, 39–43.

55. For cabildo discussions of the problem, see AMA, LPA 1, (Feb. 23, 1780, and June 14, 1782); and LEXP 1 (Sept. 22, 1803).

56. ARAR/Int/Crim (15-VII-1789), "Sobre la fuga de Ignacio Zegarra."

57. ARAR/Int/Crim (18-I-1821), "Causa seguida para la aprehensión de Romualdo Quispe profugado de la cárcel."

Republican Fears About Crime

If the deputy for jails in 1820 could be so moved by compassion that "he would start crying with the prisoners, and even wanted to give them his shirt,"[58] a decade later, such a benevolent attitude toward criminals would be difficult to find. Within a year after independence, notices in the local official newspaper—a new forum for public opinion—expressed increasing concern over police services: "Arequipa, which presents the most beautiful potential to be a city lovelier and cleaner than any other, we see it nevertheless turned into a trash heap: without lighting at night, causing robberies, deaths and other disorders under the shelter of darkness."[59] By the end of the decade, fears about rising crime were being voiced by citizens, municipal authorities, court officials, and prefects.

The number of criminal trials increased dramatically from the late colonial to the republican period (see Figure 4.1 and Table 4.1). During the four last decades of the colonial period, there were only 184 reported cases; during the first thirty years after independence, there were 1,021 criminal trials.[60] As shown below, the number of trials began to rise slightly during the last decades of Spanish rule. It was particularly personal-injury lawsuits and disputes with authorities that began to increase, reflecting, perhaps, an initial questioning of the legitimacy of colonial norms. After independence, however, the number of crimes prosecuted accelerated sharply; the increase in violent crimes is particularly striking (see the categories of assault and murder in Table 4.2).

Several factors could account for this burgeoning of criminal trials, a twelve-fold increase in the first decade after independence alone. In the first place, less reliable records for the colonial period may lead to an undercounting of crimes. Cases would have been better preserved after independence, particularly as judicial powers were consolidated under the superior court, which reviewed all cases tried by the judges of first instance. However, a

58. Ibid. For an earlier example, see ARAR/Int/Ped (28-VII-1790), "Informe de Juan de Dios López de Castillo."

59. "Aviso" in *El Republicano*, Jan. 7, 1826. See also "Policía," *El Republicano*, March 11, 1826, 74.

60. For the colonial period, 1784 to 1824, these trials are filed under "Intendencia: Causas Criminales." (I did not count the cases from 1780 to 1783, because they were so few and fell under the older Corregimiento system). For the republican period, 1825 to 1854, the trials can be found in "Corte Superior de Justicia: Causas Criminales." I left the indexes that I made for many *legajos* with the archive, for consultation by future researchers.

Fig. 4.1. Total criminal cases (Valley of Arequipa)

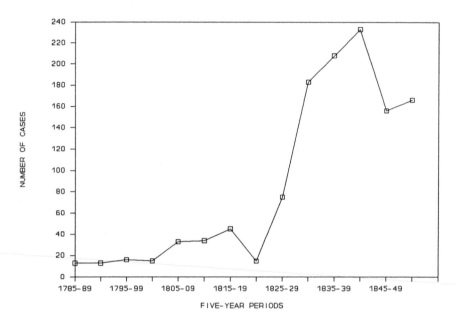

Table 4.1. Total criminal cases by category

Years	Personal	Property	State	Other	Total
1785–1789	11 (84.6%)	1 (7.7%)	1 (7.7%)	0 (0.0%)	13
1790–1794	9 (69.2%)	2 (15.4%)	2 (15.4%)	0 (0.0%)	13
1795–1799	8 (50.0%)	5 (31.3%)	2 (12.5%)	1 (6.3%)	16
1800–1804	9 (60.0%)	5 (33.3%)	1 (6.7%)	0 (0.0%)	15
1805–1809	18 (54.5%)	6 (18.2%)	8 (24.2%)	1 (3.0%)	33
1810–1814	26 (76.5%)	1 (2.9%)	7 (20.6%)	0 (0.0%)	34
1815–1819	34 (75.6%)	6 (13.3%)	5 (11.1%)	0 (0.0%)	45
1820–1824	7 (46.7%)	1 (6.7%)	7 (46.7%)	0 (0.0%)	15
1825–1829	40 (53.3%)	17 (22.2%)	15 (20.0%)	3 (4.0%)	75
1830–1834	101 (55.2%)	43 (23.5%)	35 (19.1%)	4 (2.2%)	183
1835–1839	129 (62.0%)	36 (17.3%)	37 (17.8%)	6 (2.9%)	208
1840–1844	127 (54.5%)	72 (30.9%)	32 (13.7%)	2 (0.9%)	233
1845–1849	89 (57.1%)	39 (25.0%)	21 (13.5%)	7 (4.5%)	156
1850–1854	113 (68.1%)	31 (18.7%)	20 (12.0%)	2 (1.2%)	166

SOURCE: ARAR, Int/Crim (1784–1824) and CS/Crim (1825–1854).

Table 4.2. Cases of personal crimes by category

Years	Injurias	Assault	Sexual	Murder	Total
1785–1789	11 (100.0%)	0 (0.0%)	0 (0.0%)	0 (0.0%)	11
1790–1794	8 (88.9%)	0 (0.0%)	1 (11.1%)	0 (0.0%)	9
1795–1799	8 (100.0%)	0 (0.0%)	0 (0.0%)	0 (0.0%)	8
1800–1804	8 (88.9%)	0 (0.0%)	0 (0.0%)	1 (11.1%)	9
1805–1809	15 (83.3%)	0 (0.0%)	2 (11.1%)	1 (5.6%)	18
1810–1814	16 (61.5%)	6 (23.1%)	2 (7.7%)	2 (7.7%)	26
1815–1819	30 (88.2%)	1 (2.9%)	2 (5.9%)	1 (2.9%)	34
1820–1824	6 (85.7%)	0 (0.0%)	0 (0.0%)	1 (14.3%)	7
1825–1829	16 (40.0%)	9 (22.5%)	5 (12.5%)	10 (25.0%)	40
1830–1834	14 (13.9%)	33 (32.7%)	6 (5.9%)	48 (47.5%)	101
1835–1839	46 (35.7%)	45 (34.9%)	5 (3.9%)	33 (25.6%)	129
1840–1844	20 (15.7%)	41 (32.3%)	9 (7.1%)	57 (44.9%)	127
1845–1849	27 (30.3%)	30 (33.7%)	9 (10.1%)	23 (25.8%)	89
1850–1854	28 (24.8%)	40 (35.4%)	5 (4.4%)	40 (35.4%)	113

SOURCE: ARAR, Int/Crim (1784–1824) and CS/Crim (1825–1854).

more significant—if related—factor is that the republican courts prosecuted crimes that under the colonial system either had gone unheeded or had been handled in oral hearings by local justices of the peace. This change in priorities is also evident in the proportion of cases prosecuted at the initiative of the judge or public prosecutor (*de oficio*) as opposed to those initiated by the injured party (*de parte*) (See Table 4.3). During the colonial period, for example, persons who had been the targets of theft were responsible not only for reporting the crime to the authorities, but also for presenting witnesses and formally accusing the defendant. After independence, the courts were more likely to take over all aspects of the investigation and prosecution after a robbery was reported.

The crime that was most commonly tried in the colonial period, moreover, was also that which was prosecuted almost exclusively de parte: *injurias*. Under Spanish law, "injuries" could be either verbal (*de palabra*)—insults to one's honor or reputation—or physical (*de hecho*), that is, causing bodily harm.[61] Colonial judges were forbidden to prosecute verbal injuries de oficio, and in Arequipa they rarely tried persons for physical injuries. After independence, however, the courts increasingly prosecuted cases of assault— whether or not the injured party wished to press charges—under a new criminal category they called "wounds" (*heridas*).

61. See Avila Martel, *Esquema*, 83–86.

Table 4.3. Criminal cases by type of prosecution

Years	De Parte	De Oficio	Total
1785–1789	12 (92.3%)	1 (7.7%)	13
1790–1794	13 (100.0%)	0 (0.0%)	13
1795–1799	13 (81.3%)	3 (18.8%)	16
1800–1804	12 (80.0%)	3 (20.0%)	15
1805–1809	25 (75.8%)	8 (24.2%)	33
1810–1814	22 (64.7%)	12 (35.3%)	34
1815–1819	39 (86.7%)	6 (13.3%)	45
1820–1824	10 (66.7%)	5 (33.3%)	15
1825–1829	35 (46.7%)	40 (53.3%)	75
1830–1834	31 (16.9%)	152 (83.1%)	183
1835–1839	73 (35.1%)	135 (64.9%)	208
1840–1844	52 (22.3%)	181 (77.7%)	233
1845–1849	53 (34.0%)	103 (66.0%)	156
1850–1854	56 (33.7%)	110 (66.3%)	166

SOURCE: ARAR, Int/Crim (1784–1824) and CS/Crim (1825–1854).

Finally, a case could be made that authorities were responding to a real rise in the crime rate. From a total of six murder cases in the city between 1785 and 1824, the number jumped to ten in only the first five years after independence, and forty-eight between 1830 and 1834. While some murders in the countryside may have gone undetected, it is difficult to believe that those occurring in the city would not have come to the attention of colonial authorities.[62] Even if some colonial cases were simply lost, the increase is still dramatic.

Furthermore, there was a perception among contemporaries that crime was on the rise, especially between 1825 and 1834. As the wealthier inhabitants of the city were more likely to be targets of theft, their concerns focused on the problems of assault and robbery. In 1829, for example, a French merchant was accused of shooting and killing a poor, drunken Spaniard; he claimed the man had been trying to break into his house, and he presented witnesses who testified that there had been a rash of recent robberies. "The city is in a state of fear," affirmed another French merchant, "by the multitude of thieves, who attack the Foreign warehouses and private homes."[63] Witnesses in other trials, when questioned why they carried

62. Comparative work on crime also shows that homicide is the most reliable index of the "real" incidence of crime; see Taylor, *Drinking, Homicide, and Rebellion,* 73–77.
63. ARAR/CS/Crim (22-VI-1829), "Don Santiago LeBris contra Miguel Linares por haber

weapons prohibited by law, claimed that they needed them at night to protect themselves from assault.[64]

While there may have been an actual rise in the number of crimes committed in Arequipa after independence, it would be difficult to pinpoint the cause. The disruption of the economy caused by the wars of independence may have pushed some impoverished plebeians to steal as a way of supporting themselves. Additionally, a growing proportion of those committing violent crimes used knives rather than clubs, rocks, or tools, which may indicate greater availability of such weapons owing to importation or war. Most of the assaults and murders, however, were not premeditated, making it difficult to determine the motives. It is possible that the political chaos and economic crisis during this period put a strain on personal relationships that could erupt into violence.

Finally, the fears of elites about crime may have been intensified by their concern over political instability. Local authorities in the new republic were faced with a crisis of legitimacy, even in the absence of an organized, armed opposition.

The Institutionalization of the Courts

It is difficult to determine how much of the increase in criminal trials after independence was due to better record preservation, increased vigilance by the authorities, and a rise in the real crime rate. It is impossible to deny, however, that the problem of disorder took on a significance for the authorities of the new republic that far surpassed concerns during the last decades of the colonial period.

One of the first responses to the problem of crime in Arequipa was to take full advantage of an increasingly organized and efficient criminal justice system. During the colonial period, political and judicial functions had been combined under the same officials. Mayors (alcaldes) heard cases on the local level, the intendant—assisted by a legal adviser—was the highest judge in the

---

forzado una reja." See also AHMP (CEHMP) Leg. 26, Num. 99, letter from prefect Juan Francisco Reyes to the minister of war, July 5, 1829.

64. ARAR/Pref (20-II-1828), "Contra Don Mariano Arróspide y Don José López por puñaladas a Marselo Arayco"; and ARAR/CS/Crim (17-IV-1833), "Contra Mateo Chávez por el homicidio de Manuel Pacheco."

department, and the real audiencia had the final authority in appeals and oversight. In addition, members of various corporations—such as the church, the military, or the merchant guilds—enjoyed special fueros, that is, the right to be judged in their own courts. Besides the obvious possibility for corruption, this combination of powers considerably slowed the pace of justice.[65]

The republican form of government established after Peru's independence called for the separation of powers among executive, legislative, and judicial branches.[66] While minor disputes between neighbors would still be heard by local justices of the peace, trials for serious crimes (as well as civil litigation) were held under appointed judges of first instance. Sentences, whether or not they were appealed, were reviewed in the second and third instances by regional superior courts, and in the final instance by the supreme court, located in Lima.

The superior court of Arequipa was established by law on February 1, 1825, with jurisdiction over the departments of Arequipa, Tacna, Tarapacá, Moquegua, and Puno.[67] Within a year, local pressure had achieved an increase in the number of justices (*vocales*) from four to six, in addition to the president and *fiscal* (public prosecutor).[68] The courts underwent less turnover in personnel than did other branches of government during regime changes, and such stability contributed to their centrality to the local political culture.

Clearly, the new courts in Arequipa handled many more cases than had those of the colonial period; in addition, a growing proportion of those cases was prosecuted by the state (de oficio). In spite of the heavier workload, trials generally became speedier under the new system; while robbery cases had often lasted several years during the colonial period, for example, it was unusual for such cases to take more than a few months after independence. By 1829, the court was feeling the effects of the rising crime rate not only in an increased case load, but also when one of the justices became the victim of

65. Cooper, "A Short History," 226–38.
66. Ibid., 241–42; and Rubén A. Bustamante Ugarte, *La corte superior de justicia de Arequipa, 1825–1925* (Arequipa: Tipografía Cordova, 1925), 17.
67. Bustamante Ugarte, *La corte superior,* 25–27.
68. Ibid., 57. Under Spanish law, the fiscal was to supervise proceedings in the crown's interest, in order to ensure compliance with the law and to protect royal financial interest. Gradually the fiscal took on a more active role, and in the republic was charged with protecting the public interest. Although the constitutions also called for the establishment of a jury system, it was not implemented during the nineteenth century. See Cooper, "A Short History," 233–61.

an assault.[69] As work piled up on the judges of first instance, the superior justices feared that crimes would go unpunished:

Occupied with the immense dispatch of the civil cases they generally neglect to dedicate to the criminal cases all the attention which the good of society demands, and after long delays, it is not unusual for delinquents to find ways of escaping and thereby eluding the vigor of the laws. We should attribute to this cause the increase in criminality in this town, where robberies, which at another time were very rare, have become all too common.[70]

Their request for a third judge of first instance to handle only criminal trials was approved by the central government on October 8, 1830.[71]

Republican officials in Arequipa did not determine the new structure of the criminal justice system, but their efforts to expand its size and improve its efficiency demonstrated the strong local commitment to maintaining the social order and pursuing criminals. The shifts in penal philosophy, however, were more subtle. Although several constitutions were drafted during the period under study (namely those of 1823, 1826, 1828, 1834, and 1839), civil law was not codified under the republic until 1852, and there was no penal code until 1862. Republican judges, therefore, were still required to base their sentences on the earlier body of Castilian law contained in several compilations: the *Siete Partidas* (circa 1256), the *Nueva Recopilación* (1567), the *Novísima Recopilación* (1805), and the *Recopilación de Leyes de Indias* (1680), which contained laws specifically addressed to the American colonies.[72] This situation created a foundation for continuity in criminal prosecution between the colonial and republican periods.

The flexibility present in colonial law also eased the transition to a republican judicial system. Spanish codes required judges to consider a variety of circumstances accompanying any specific offense before sentencing: the status of the defendant and the victim, their relationship, the type of weapon used, whether there was premeditation, and whether the defendant was affected by alcohol, jealousy, or insanity. Even though various penalties

69. AGN, Corte Superior de Justicia, Leg. 4 (Feb. 19, 1829).

70. Ibid. (Feb. 18, 1830).

71. Ibid.; and Arturo Villegas Romero, *Un decenio de la historia de Arequipa, 1830–1840* (Arequipa: Fundación Gloria, 1985), 314.

72. See Jorge Basadre, *Historia del derecho Peruano* (Lima: Editorial Antena, 1937), 219–75; and Avila Martel, *Esquema*.

were given to meet these situations, both the *Partidas* and the *Recopilación de Indias* recognized local custom when it did not conflict with the law, and both gave wide discretion to judges to make the punishment fit the crime.[73] Despite assertions by defense lawyers after independence, moreover, the Spanish criminal justice system had not been particularly punitive.

In practice, judges in late colonial Arequipa demonstrated both benevolence—by letting off the majority of defendants accused of lesser offenses—and severity, by sentencing to death criminals convicted of premeditated murder. The effect of the pardon or punishment was aimed as much at the general public as at the particular defendant. This trend continued for the first half-decade after independence, although the courts began to use a wider range of punishments. But as concerns about a growing crime wave mounted, judges began to apply harsher penalties in an effort to stem the tide. This crackdown occurred particularly during the 1830s, and against those convicted of theft or murder. It was also in this period that assault was treated as a serious crime. In general, rather than condemning more convicts to the most severe penalty possible (six to ten years in prison for theft, and death for murder), the judges decreased the proportion absolved or let off with the time already served and sentenced them, instead, to intermediate punishments of several years in public works or prison.

While judges quietly used the flexibility of colonial law to pass harsher sentences when public fears about crime were high, attorneys engaged in dramatic debates when those laws came into apparent contradiction with constitutional principles. Republican defense lawyers decried the abuses that had occurred in the courts of their former Spanish "oppressors," which they portrayed as despotic. Some of these jurists would become prominent liberal ideologues who emphasized the protection of civil rights. Prosecutors, on the other hand, lamented the more lenient, "modern" interpretations of the law since independence. They argued for the strict application of the existing (Spanish) body of law, and for the need for public examples to deter crime. The contradictory effects that republican debates about the law had on changes in criminal sentencing are particularly clear in prohibitions against deadly weapons and the imposition of capital punishment.

During the early 1830s, the fiscal of the superior court of Arequipa, Mariano Luna, tirelessly pushed the court to enforce a Spanish law that prohibited carrying any knife with a sharpened point, under pain of six years

---

73. Avila Martel, *Esquema*, 36–38; Basadre, *Historia del derecho*, 268–75.

in a presidio.[74] He based his argument on the need for courts to adhere strictly to the law, but he did not hesitate to add that such a law had never been more important, given the growing number of murders committed: "Since experience teaches that armed men are more bold, and insolent, and the origin of so many tragedies."[75] Defense attorneys generally argued against its application, on the grounds that the use of such knives had become widespread, and that they were necessary in many professions. Casimiro Salazar, for example, appealed such a conviction, arguing that the use of knives had become such "an inalterable custom" that "if a penalty were to be imposed on all those who carried and made use of this weapon there would be very few in Arequipa or outside the city that would remain exempt."[76]

One group of justices took Luna's advice into account when sentencing and even advised the prefect to publish an edict about the prohibition, "considering that we experience daily that the use of such forbidden weapons produces the ills that the said Pragmatic tried to prevent."[77] There is no record of whether such an edict was ever issued, however, and most convictions on weapons possession were overturned on appeal.

The debate between "old" and "modern" interpretations of the law became more heated in the second matter: capital punishment. The first three constitutions called for a moderate use of the death penalty, but the Congress had not specified those cases in which it should or should not be applied.[78] In this case it was the defense lawyers who went on the offensive, reaching high levels of rhetoric in appeals on behalf of their clients condemned to death. They often pointed to the "civilized and humane" powers of Europe, as examples where capital punishment had been limited, and one attorney exclaimed that the courts wanted to "drown the Republic in Blood."[79]

In general the prosecutors kept to the argument of judicial restraint, but, on occasion, fiscal Luna made his own fiery appeals: "The heavens cry out . . . for the blood of the dead, and as long as our modern Laws do not

74. Law 13, Title 6, Book 6 of the *Recopilación*; Avila Martel, *Esquema*, 107.
75. ARAR/CS/Crim (29-VI-1831), "Contra Vidal Jara."
76. ARAR/CS/Crim (12-VII-1831), "Contra Manuel Oliva, José Arrismendi y otros."
77. Ibid.
78. Art. 115 (1823), Art. 122 (1826), and Art. 129 (1828); Juan F. Olivo, ed., *Constituciones políticas del Perú, 1821–1919* (Lima: Imprenta Torres Aguirre, 1922), 57, 100, 137. The more conservative constitutions of 1834 and 1839 included no such provision. See also Pedro L. Alvarez Ganoza, *Origen y trayectoria de la aplicación de la pena de muerte en la historia del derecho Peruano* (Lima: Editorial Dorhca, 1974), 15–20.
79. ARAR/CS/Crim (23-VII-1831), "Contra el indígena Pedro Calderón por haber muerto a Juana Salas."

classify the crimes which call for the death penalty, we should subject our-
selves to the old ones."[80] Although death sentences were common after
independence, more than half of those appealed from 1825 to 1839 were
eventually commuted to lesser penalties; in general the death penalty stood
only when premeditation was clear,[81] if the victim was of higher status than
the offender,[82] or if the crime appeared particularly cruel.[83] Ironically,
however, some of these sentences were overturned only by recourse to an
older Spanish law, which required a chamber of five justices to impose capital
punishment.[84]

   In the end, judicial practice in the late colonial period was neither as harsh,
nor was that of the early republic as lenient, as the critics on either side would
have it. The major change in sentencing in Arequipa after independence was
to decrease the number of defendants let off with little or no punishment and
to mete out moderate punishments instead. Nevertheless, the language of
individual rights marshaled by defense attorneys was new and would have
significant consequences.

The Development of a Police Force

As much as the court system was expanded and reorganized after independence, it could not handle law enforcement in Arequipa on its own. City
officials needed police who could deliver accused criminals to the courts,
patrol the streets to maintain order, and mete out fines and other penalties for

80. ARAR/CS/Crim (4-VII-1831), "Contra Francisco Jorge Gutiérrez."
    81. ARAR/CS/Crim (28-V-1830), "Contra Gregorio Benavides"; and (5-XII-1831), "Contra
Juan Ampuero."
    82. ARAR/CS/Crim (11-VII-1833), "Contra Antonio Lujan por el homicidio del español
Juan Hidalgo"; (9-II-1834) "Contra el negro esclavo Benancio Viscarra por el homicidio de Don
Francisco Pomadera"; and (27-VI-1834), "Contra José Rodríguez por haber herido al Religioso
de la Merced Fray Manuel Muñoz."
    83. For example, killing a pregnant woman or a relative other than a spouse. ARAR/CS/
Crim (30-III-1832), "Contra Mariano Choqueña por el homicidio de Juana Cama, su madre
política"; (21-VIII-1832) "Contra Mariano Macedo por haber dado una puñalada a Manuela
Barrios"; (9-X-1833) "Contra Guillermo García por haber dado una puñalada mortal a su
cuñada Manuela Sedillo"; (20-X-1833) "Contra Agustín Apaza, Fabiana Quispe y María Cayra
por el homicidio de Paula Mamani"; and (8-I-1838), "Contra Francisco Chiri por haber muerto
a su hermana Mercedes Valdés."
    84. Law 16, Title 12, Book 5 of the *Novísima Recopilación*; cited by the justices in
ARAR/CS/Crim (4-VII-1831), "Contra Francisco Jorge Gutiérrez"; and (23-VII-1831), "Contra Pedro Calderón."

minor infractions. The development of the republican police force, however, was a more gradual and uneven process than was the establishment of a judicial system.

Questions of its size, budget, structure, and jurisdiction were negotiated between civilian and military officials, as well as between local authorities and those in Lima. The primary concern of the central government was to maintain armed forces adequate for defending the state against both external and internal threats. Given budgetary restraints, it was reluctant to support additional troops whose main function was to chase down local delinquents. The prefects of Arequipa, on the other hand, wanted a salaried police force of locals that could preserve daily order in the streets and would be under the direct orders of civilian rather than military officials.

On January 7, 1825, Simón Bolívar ordered the establishment of a national guard whose functions would be to conserve public order and be available as a reserve force for the regular army.[85] But difficulties in organizing a civilian militia in Arequipa meant that initially, regular troops quartered in the city went out on patrols.[86] By 1829, frequent reports about rising crime led to calls for a better system, but plans for a municipal police force foundered for lack of funds.[87]

In February, the minister of war ordered the prefect to put a militia company on active duty to maintain order and security until replacements from the regular army could arrive.[88] When orders to deactivate the militia were sent out in June, prefect Juan Francisco de Reyes balked.[89] "The garrison service is of the utmost importance under the current circumstances," he explained, "since the city is plagued by thieves and there is no shortage of other evildoers who have disseminated papers of seditious insolence, [circumstances] that call for the most precautionary measures."[90] He received permission to maintain the militia on salary, but only until the

85. Romulo Merino Arana, *Historia policial del Perú en la república* (Lima: Imprenta del Departamento de Prensa y Publicaciones de la Guardia Civil, 1966), 8; and Art. 165-177 of the 1823 constitution in Olivo, *Constituciones*, 64–65.

86. See ARAR/CS/Crim (13-III-1827), "Contra Carlos Torres por haber estropeado al Comisario de Barrio de San Jerónimo y los soldados de ronda"; (28-IV-1828) "Contra Don Antonio Márquez por haber atropellado a los oficiales de la patrulla"; and (16-XI-1829), "Contra Justo Pastor por cómplice en el maltratamiento que hicieron algunos paisanos a tres soldados."

87. Report published in *El Republicano*, Aug. 1, 1829, 4.

88. Peru had mobilized its regular forces in a war against Colombia. AHMP (CEHMP) J. 16 Libro Copiador (1828–35), letter to the prefect of Arequipa, Feb. 23, 1829.

89. Ibid., letter, June 19, 1829.

90. AHMP (CEHMP) Leg. 26, Num. 99, letter, July 5, 1829.

arrival of troops under the General Commander of the South, Manuel de Aparicio.[91]

After winning the support of General Aparicio to maintain the militia on active duty,[92] prefect Reyes took the further step of creating a special civic police squad to pursue thieves (no mention, this time, of subversives).[93] Although the minister of war approved the measure only until "the indicated malefactors are exterminated,"[94] the new prefect in 1832, Pío Tristán, not only refused orders to disband the force, he even requested its expansion. He pointed to the many duties fulfilled by the force: assisting the sub-prefect in tax collection, carrying out the orders of the justices of the peace and judges of first instance, escorting criminals sentenced to the presidio, pursuing deserters and other criminals, and, in general, enforcing compliance with municipal ordinances. Such services, he insisted, could not be provided by the regular troops who had little knowledge of the area, whose discipline would be compromised by assignments outside their barracks, and who were not available at short notice upon the direct orders of the prefect. In the face of such continued determination, the minister of war finally approved the existence of a permanent police force and increased its members to fifty.[95] Skirmishes between Lima and Arequipa over its size and oversight, however, would continue for several decades.[96]

Although the development of a police force in Arequipa was an uneven process, a permanent force was established, and its tendency was to grow during the first decades of the republican period. The question remains, however, whether the police were effective in maintaining order and deterring crime. The police squad was initially quite small, and even so had difficulty finding recruits. Occasionally delinquents were sentenced to police duty, and it is doubtful that such conscripts did much to improve the effectiveness or morale of the force.

In 1833 the minister of war, referring to a significant loss of equipment and uniforms stolen from the commander's house, censured the police company

91. AHMP (CEHMP) J. 16 Libro Copiador (1828–35), letter, July 19, 1829.

92. AHMP (CEHMP) Leg. 26, Num. 112, letter, July 19, 1829; Leg. 11, Num. 7, letter, Aug. 19, 1829; and J. 16 Libro Copiador (1828–35), letter, Sept. 3, 1829.

93. AHMP (CEHMP) Leg. 26, Num. 114, letter, July 19, 1829.

94. AHMP (CEHMP) J. 16 Libro Copiador (1828–35), letter, Aug. 4, 1829.

95. For the exchange between the prefect and the minister of war, see AHMP (CEHMP) Leg. 25, Num. 21, letter, Mar. 14, 1832; and J. 16 Libro Copiador (1828–35), letter, Apr. 19, 1832.

96. See correspondence between prefects and minister of war from 1839 to 1851, in AHMP (CEHMP) Leg. 6, 8, 13, 14, 18.

for "not simply neglect, but abandonment by its officers."[97] A year later, the police came under criticism from the courts for failing not only to prevent street fighting, but even to find a suspect in the case of a boy who was killed in such a brawl. "This outcome is a disgrace for a cultured town," declared the fiscal, "where the police should be vigilant and prepared to apprehend whomever disturbs the public order."[98] Moreover, security at the jail did not improve significantly, and escapes were common.[99]

Nevertheless, the determination by republican authorities to bring the society under greater control was clear. This zeal included an attack on many aspects of popular culture. One of the first acts of Antonio Gutiérrez de La Fuente as prefect was to issue an edict on June 19, 1825, prohibiting gambling; all those caught would be sent to jail for one month, and the owner of the house would be fined two hundred pesos.[100] In 1832, the departmental junta forbade bullfights, cockfights, and fireworks, and limited the hours when workers could play billiards, although a year later such regulations were eased somewhat, on the grounds that they were "inconvenient."[101] And in 1837, the intendant of police attempted to abolish the custom of "Saint Monday," threatening to fine both the artisans who failed to show up for work and the chicheras who allowed them into their establishments.[102]

Even more interesting than the rules themselves—for the authorities had been issuing similar prohibitions since the conquest—is the language that they used to justify such regulations. In the preamble to his edict on gambling, La Fuente asserted that "the efforts, zeal and the very laws for the prosperity of the Republic will remain in sad theory if the disorders and crimes which cause general misfortune are not attacked with firmness."[103] In

97. See AHMP (CEHMP) Leg. 19, Num. 34, letter, Apr. 1, 1833; and Leg. 19, Num. 58, letter, June 15, 1833.

98. ARAR/CS/Crim (22-IX-1834), "Seguido para indagar las personas que perpetraron el homicidio en el menor Julián Ortega."

99. During the civil wars invading troops sometimes freed prisoners, but others managed to plot their own escapes. See ARAR/CS/Crim (5-I-1829), "Contra Miguel Ramos"; (7-IX-1829) "Expediente sobre un agujero que se había hecho en uno de los calabozos de la cárcel"; (7-IV-1834) "Expediente sobre indagarse el paradero de los presos que fugaron"; (24-XI-1834) "Contra Mariano Villegas"; (10-VI-1836) "Contra Inocencio Pardo"; and Prefectura (23-III-1838), "Sobre la fuga de los presos."

100. BNP doc. D8478, "Bando prohibiendo la práctica del juego de azar."

101. Villegas Romero, Un decenio, 437–38. For the modifications, see El Republicano, May 11, 1833, 5; Aug. 31, 1833, 6; and Sept. 14, 1833, 2–3.

102. Villegas Romero, Un decenio, 447.

103. BNP doc. D8478.

ordering the closure of the cockfighting ring, the departmental junta argued "that cockfights clash directly with the virtue and morals that should be upheld in a Republican Government."[104]

Although it is difficult to judge how effectively such regulations were enforced, there are indications that the authorities were more vigilant than they had been in the late colonial period. Ten days after an 1841 government decree prohibited the unlicensed distillation of liquor from fruit, the police chief in Arequipa was informed of an infraction and dispatched an officer to investigate. The police confiscated twenty sacks of figs and arrested the woman who had begun to make liquor out of them. Three weeks later, she was exonerated on the grounds that the law had not yet been published in Arequipa, but the owner of the still was warned to acquire the proper license.[105]

Republican police officers also exhibited greater zeal than colonial officials by arresting "suspicious" characters without specific charges. Given that the wars of independence had intensified migrations, the growing presence of "strangers"—from other South American nations as well as from the rest of Peru—may have made the authorities more anxious. In 1831, for example, a man was picked up in Yanahuara simply for being in an alley "where thieves surely meet" late at night. The same night, two black men were arrested because "they are not known around here," and reports after the fact asserted that "they live closed in by day so as not to be seen."[106]

Without access to police records, it is difficult to judge effectiveness in routine law enforcement; minor infractions rarely were brought to trial but were sanctioned on the spot, through temporary incarceration or fines. Nonetheless, the authorities certainly gave the impression that they were serious about the enforcement of local ordinances. Regulations governing the whereabouts of outside visitors and controlling public safety and hygiene

104. Quoted in Villegas Romero, *Un decenio*, 445. By contrast, regulations issued for the cockfight ring in 1796 were primarily intended to protect the state's tax base; see ARAR/Int/ Adm (17-IX-1796), "El Intendente Salamanca promulga ordenanzas."

105. ARAR/Pref (16-I-1841), "Contra Doña Francisca Bedoya."

106. ARAR/Pref (21-XI-1831), "Expediente criminal sobre investigarse la conducta de Ramón Llerena, José María Madaleno y José Torres." For other cases of men arrested as "suspicious," see ARAR/CS/Crim (3-VII-1829), "Expediente sobre el encarcelamiento de Pascual Silva sospechado de robo"; (6-VII-1829) "Contra Victoriano Concha por sospecharse que es ladrón"; (1-VIII-1833) "Contra Manuel Crispa por haberse venido de Islay a donde fue conducido para que regresase a su país"; and (10-VI-1836), "Contra Inocencio Pardo por haber herido a Pablo Rosado."

were published in the official newspaper in 1833.[107] Soon thereafter, lists of persons fined for infractions began to appear periodically. Throughout the second half of the year, more than 260 residents were levied between one-half real and six pesos each.

The most frequent violations were the failure of travelers to register or to obtain passports, and of homeowners to light their sections of the streets. But the police also meted out fines for littering, raising animals in the street, drunkenness, cockfighting, and arguing with the officers.[108] In an effort to oversee more serious crimes, the prefect ordered the superior court to submit monthly reports on the progress of all penal cases, which were also printed in the newspaper.[109] It is possible that the leveling off and then decline in the number of criminal trials in the 1840s and 1850s may have reflected a deterrence effect brought about by increased police vigilance.[110]

Whether or not the efforts of police and judges significantly changed behavior in the short run, common people in Arequipa certainly found their daily lives subject to increasing regulation and harassment during the early years of the republic. In one case from 1830 that came to trial because of the refusal of a chichera to obey orders, we get a rare glimpse into the workday of the municipality's deputy of police. Toribio de Linares reported that in the course of his rounds, he confiscated tools from several artisans who refused either to clean up the area around their shops or to pay a city worker to do it for them. He also sent an "insolent" boy to work at the barracks. Finally, he had a woman arrested when she refused to clean up a puddle outside her chichería.[111] This case reveals both the determination of the officer to enforce city ordinances and the resistance by the citizens of Arequipa.

---

107. *El Republicano*, Mar. 30, 1833, 4; July 27, 1833, 1–2; Aug. 10, 1833, 7; Sept. 7, 1833, 7; Nov. 30, 1833, 7; and Dec. 21, 1833, 4–6.

108. *El Republicano*, June 29, 1833, 7; Aug. 3, 1833, 4; Aug. 24, 1833, 7; Sept. 7, 1833, 6–7; Oct. 12, 1833, 6–7; Oct. 26, 1833, 6; Nov. 30, 1833, 7; and Dec. 14, 1833, 7.

109. *El Republicano*, Sept. 28, 1833, 5–6.

110. V. A. C. Gatrell and T. B. Hadden argue that the extension of police control leads, initially, to an increase in arrests, which later decrease as that example leads to deterrence; see Gatrell and Hadden, "Criminal Statistics and Their Interpretation," in E. A. Wrigley, ed., *Nineteenth-Century Society: Essays on the Use of Quantitative Methods for the Study of Social Data* (London: Cambridge University Press, 1972), 353–55.

111. ARAR/CS/Crim (4-I-1830), "Don Toribio de Linares, Diputado de Policía, contra Doña María Escalante por falta de respeto."

Popular Resistance to Police Control

Naturally, the imposition of new controls was not accepted cheerfully by the population of Arequipa. In the first decade after independence, civilians clashed with soldiers patrolling the streets, especially those capturing conscripts. Young men were constantly on the lookout for the *leva* (impressment).[112] In October 1829, for example, a patrol apprehended an alleged deserter, but while they were taking him back to the barracks, they were ambushed by a group of men and women who freed the suspect and harmed the three soldiers.[113]

Furthermore, popular resentment of the military and police was so deeply felt that clashes also occurred when soldiers were not on duty. When police corporal Alejo Taquire was fighting with his mistress, her cries attracted two strangers who came to her defense.[114] Such a case is especially telling given the general reluctance to interfere with a man's "right" to discipline his woman. A couple of weeks later, soldier Ramón Esquivel complained to his commanding officer that three civilians had beaten him up when he had tried to buy some liquor from them.[115]

Resentment of the military and police was not limited to plebeians. Shopkeepers also complained of abuses by soldiers, especially when they were drunk. Andrés Bracamonte, whose wife ran a chichería in their house, said that he did not allow soldiers to enter the establishment.[116] In March 1836, Genaro Benavides complained that a drunken soldier had falsely accused him of taking his rifle and owing him change. Benavides, explaining that the soldier was creating a scene that would hurt his business, unsuccessfully appealed to two officers for their assistance in getting the soldier to

---

112. For references to men hiding from the draft, see ARAR/CS/Crim (7-III-1827), "Contra Francisca y María Josefa Corrales"; (22-VI-1829) "Don Santiago LeBris contra Miguel Linares"; (10-X-1836) "Contra Vicente Salas"; (12-X-1836) "Don José León Dongo contra Juan Salazar por robo."

113. ARAR/CS/Crim (16-XI-1829), "Contra Justo Pastor sobre suponérsele cómplice en el maltratamiento que hicieron algunos paisanos a tres soldados." See also ARAR/CS/Crim (13-III-1827), "Contra Carlos Torres por haber estropeado al Comisario de Barrio de San Jerónimo y los soldados de ronda."

114. ARAR/CS/Crim (5-VII-1833), "Contra Mariano y Pablo Blanco por haber estropeado al cabo de policía Alejo Taquire."

115. ARAR/CS/Crim (22-VII-1833), "Contra Pedro José Madueño por haber estropeado al soldado Ramón Esquivel."

116. ARAR/CS/Crim (16-X-1825), "Contra Cipriano Escobedo por dar un peso falso a un soldado."

leave. Mariano Martín Cañoli, a young clerk, tried to come to Benavides's aid but ended up in a fight with the officers.[117]

Even the city's elite was not completely exempt from military and police surveillance. On a Saturday night in April 1828, the patrol was just finishing its rounds of the city when they heard a noisy party in the house of Don Francisco Valdivia, who was throwing a dance for his cousin's birthday. They stopped to investigate, but some women at the party convinced the officer to join them and brought out drinks for the soldiers. When a quarrel erupted, the officer sided with an acquaintance and ordered the arrest of Antonio Márquez, a Chilean merchant, despite the pleas of some guests. Márquez and other witnesses charged that he and a woman friend were both beaten by the soldiers when they resisted his arrest.[118]

The tension between civilians and soldiers or police was often intensified by differences in social status. Most members of the different branches of the armed forces were poor conscripts, frequently of indigenous or mixed race. A guest at the party where Márquez was arrested, for example, implied that the officer of the patrol and his civilian acquaintance took advantage of the host's hospitality, noting disparagingly that they had chewed coca, an indigenous custom.[119]

Such social differences became dramatically clear in 1836, when a young "gentleman" died from wounds he received during a run in with a night watchman. After a night of drinking, Nicolás Carbajal broke into his lover's house, but her sister called the night watchman, Lorenso Velasco, to evict him. Velasco, who was originally from Cuzco and had worked in Arequipa for only six years, was probably indigenous or mestizo. He whistled for another officer, Andrés Felices, to come help him, and, according to both night watchmen, they politely asked Carbajal to go home. To his protestations that "I am an honorable man, and no one can order me around," Felices replied that "they were appointed to preserve order." Finally the officers got Carbajal to return home, but once there, he called to his brothers and sisters to protect him against the police. A struggle ensued, in which Carbajal tried to grab Velasco's pike and was wounded.

The fiscal charged Velasco with Carbajal's death, for having exceeded his

117. ARAR/CS/Crim (29-III-1836), "Contra Mariano Martín Cañoli por expresiones contra individuos Bolivianos del Ejército."

118. ARAR/CS/Crim (28-IV-1828), "Contra Don Antonio Márquez por haber atropellado a los oficiales de la patrulla."

119. Ibid. The officers who fought with Cañoli were from Bolivia and may have been assumed to be less racially pure.

duties, and called for a punishment that would serve as a warning against "the immorality and arrogance, which to society's misfortune, is the heritage of these kinds of men, who currently carry out the critical function of acting as night sentinels to conserve the public peace." Velasco's lawyer, however, secured his absolution: he argued that the death was accidental and that it was necessary "to protect and assist the night watchmen to maintain their respectability and with it order."[120]

Although this case was unusually dramatic, judges were repeatedly confronted with the problem of upholding the authority of the police and military while, at the same time, protecting people from abuses. With surprising frequency, they favored the latter. In the case where a crowd had freed a "deserter" from three soldiers, the lower court charged Justo Pastor as an accomplice. But the superior court, noting that it had not even been proven that the man in question was, in fact, a deserter, sent the case back for further investigation.[121]

In another case, cited above, in which the soldier Esquivel had been harmed by civilians, the fiscal saw no reason to prosecute, given that Esquivel had provoked the fight.[122] Similarly, when two men were charged with attacking Corporal Taquire while he was arguing with his lover, justice of the peace Mariano Fernández de Pascua sent a letter to the prefect in which he accused Taquire and two other soldiers of being the aggressors: "The crimes that the soldiers of the police commit . . . impels me to turn to Your Lordship as the one charged by Law with conserving order and the security of citizens."[123]

In fact the police force, which was charged with maintaining order, could itself be an agent of disorder and politicization. On the night of March 5, 1833, after elections to the constitutional convention, members of the police gathered in the house of their captain, from where "they left in disguise to

---

120. ARAR/CS/Crim (7-V-1836), "Contra Lorenzo Velasco por heridas mortales a Nicolás Carbajal."

121. ARAR/CS/Crim (16-XI-1829), "Contra Justo Pastor."

122. ARAR/CS/Crim (22-VII-1833), "Contra Pedro José Madueño." Charges were also dropped in ARAR/CS/Crim (29-III-1836), "Contra Mariano Martín Cañoli por expresiones contra Bolivianos del Ejército."

123. ARAR/CS/Crim (5-VII-1833), "Contra Mariano y Pablo Blanco." See also ARAR/CS/Crim (2-VIII-1826), "Sumaria información contra el soldado de la quinta compañía del Batallón Rifles, Manuel Flores"; (23-VI-1838 [incorrectly labeled 23-VII-1838]), "Contra Inocencio Pardo por injurias a los peones de obras públicas y a otros." Linda Arnold found some of the same concerns in Mexico; see Arnold, "Vulgar and Elegant: Politics and Procedure in Early National Politics," *The Americas* 50, no. 4 (1994): 481–500.

disturb the public peace, and attack the innocent population who were celebrating."[124] The clash ended when the soldiers retreated to their barracks, but the civilians, fearing that they had only gone for reinforcements, broke into the house of the police commander to steal arms and other equipment.[125] This incident indirectly gave rise to further disorderly conduct as young men, some wearing the stolen uniforms, committed abuses under the pretense of being police charged with arresting deserters.[126]

In hindsight, it may be that Bishop Chaves de La Rosa was ahead of his time, or at least ahead of contemporary Arequipeños (indeed, an effusive eulogy was belatedly published in 1834, in the local official newspaper).[127] His calls for controls on the "excesses" of popular culture and sexuality, which fell on deaf ears at the end of the colonial period, would have found a more attentive audience among republican leaders attempting to reestablish social order. There was a sense that independence had shattered the ordered colonial world. Feelings among the upper classes that crime had gotten out of control probably were intensified by the sudden presence of strangers in their city, carried from other parts of Peru and even from other nations, by armies that were rarely at peace.[128] This concern also reflected an ideological change; like classical liberals elsewhere, authorities in Arequipa increasingly emphasized the importance of individual discipline.

During the first decades after independence in Arequipa, local officials attempted to establish control over the populace by expanding the systems of criminal justice and law enforcement. There were limits, however, to achieving a new social equilibrium solely through the use of force. Plebeians resisted attempts by authorities to subject them to ever greater regulation,

124. ARAR/CS/Crim (13-VI-1833), "Competencia entre el Juez de Primera Instancia Dr. Don Manuel A. de Ureta y el Juez Militar Don Agustín del Solar."
125. ARAR/CS/Crim (28-II-1834), "Seguida para descubrir los autores del tumulto el cinco de marzo del año pasado."
126. ARAR/CS/Crim (3-VII-1833), "Contra Pablo Aguilar por haberle encontrado con una gorra de soldado de la compañía de policía." For other cases of men impersonating the police, see ARAR/CS/Crim (5-X-1830), "Contra Jerónimo Barriga"; (31-I-1833) "Contra Marcelino Esquivel y otros"; (12-VIII-1833) "Contra Juan Ibáñez y Casimiro Corrales"; (12-VIII-1833) "Contra Calisto Paniagua, Rafael Chávez y Marcelino Esquivel"; and (31-VIII-1843), "Contra Don Manuel Segundo Tapia, el cabo Cipriano Cáceres y el soldado Mariano Quispe Guaman por reclutar sin autorización."
127. El Republicano, Jan. 11, 1834, 5–8; Feb. 1, 1834, 5–8; and Feb. 8, 1834, 4–8.
128. Compare with Mark D. Szuchman, Order, Family, and Community in Buenos Aires, 1810–1860 (Stanford: Stanford University Press, 1988); and David J. Rothman, The Discovery of the Asylum: Social Order and Disorder in the New Republic (Boston: Little, Brown, 1971).

while civilian and military officials themselves did not always agree on the appropriate methods of social control. Members of the popular classes, as victims of abuses committed by policemen and soldiers, may well have joined elites in lamenting the loss of the old social order. Arequipeños from all walks of life were searching for new values and ideas that would help them make sense of their changing world. As we shall see, the quest for a new sense of order and belonging, beyond conflict and repression, would be played out on the field of honor and respectability.

5

From Status to Virtue

The Transformation of the Honor Code

"Que Arequipa se compone de Caballeros, Doctores, Dones, Pendones y
Muchachos sin calzones."[1]

As Arequipa had been relatively isolated from the battles against the Spanish
crown, independence marked a sudden change in local society. In addition to
the political instability, local elites feared that crime and vagrancy were
getting out of control. But when they attempted to regulate the populace
through force, plebeians resisted. There was a sense among most
Arequipeños that their world had been violently disrupted, and they longed
for a reestablishment of public order and social peace. Control could not be
reestablished solely through the use of force, but required a new "social
myth" that could reunite the members of local society.

Broad hegemonic values had served as the foundation of stability in
colonial society and made constant policing unnecessary. In Arequipa, as in
most Spanish American societies, the dominant ideal was honor. As we shall

---

1. "Arequipa is made up of gentlemen, doctors, dons, banners, and boys without breeches."
A Peruvian proverb quoted by Spanish visitor Antonio Pereira y Ruiz; see Carrión Ordóñez, *La
lengua en un texto de la ilustración*, 377.

see, by using conduct as well as status as the standard among their peers, plebeians rejected the elite's exclusive claim to honor. Nevertheless, they abided by a code that recognized and respected hierarchy, particularly important in a society where members of different classes frequently intermingled. It was not merely political unrest and crime that disturbed that relative calm, but also new ideas. Republican discourse, with its emphasis on civic virtue, was, potentially, at odds with a system of inherent privileges. After independence, therefore, plebeians began to reinterpret honor on a more egalitarian basis and used it to resist repression and claim new rights as citizens. In the process, they helped shape the particular form of liberalism promoted by prominent Arequipeños.

The Colonial Code of Honor

The centrality of honor in Mediterranean societies has been widely recognized and studied.[2] It was so important for an individual to be able to claim honor that one author has equated dishonor with social death.[3] And in Spain, an entire body of law (injurias) addressed a variety of offenses against honor.[4] Far from being solely a personal attribute, honor was a social code that governed relations all the way from the family, through the community, to the level of nation. In Spanish society, the king was the font of honor; the nobility, in return for their service and loyalty to the crown, received titles, public offices, and other honorific privileges.[5] Historians have even used the concept as an entry point into analyses of the political transition from

2. For an introduction to the subject, see J. G. Peristiany, ed., *Honour and Shame: The Values of Mediterranean Society* (Chicago: University of Chicago Press, 1966); Julian Pitt-Rivers, *The People of the Sierra*, 2d ed. (Chicago: University of Chicago Press, 1971); Pitt-Rivers, *The Fate of Shechem, or the Politics of Sex* (New York: Cambridge University Press, 1977); and Campbell, *Honour, Family, and Patronage*. See also an anthology that appeared as this book was going to press: Lyman L. Johnson and Sonya Lipsett-Rivera, eds., *The Faces of Honor: Sex, Shame, and Violence in Colonial Latin America* (Albuquerque: University of New Mexico Press, 1998).

3. Julio Caro Baroja, "Honour and Shame: A Historical Account of Several Conflicts," in J. G. Peristiany, ed., *Honour and Shame: The Values of Mediterranean Society* (Chicago: University of Chicago Press, 1966), 85.

4. Jacinto Martín Rodríguez, *El honor y la injuria en el fuero de Vizcaya* (Bilbao: La Diputación Provincial de Vizcaya, 1973).

5. Mark A. Burkholder, "Honor and Honors in Colonial Spanish America," in Johnson and Lipsett-Rivera, eds., *The Faces of Honor*, 18–44.

feudalism to an absolute monarchy.[6] In studies of Spanish America, a focus on sexual honor and racial purity has allowed scholars to demonstrate the key role that marriage played in maintaining a hierarchical social order.[7] Surprisingly, however, little attention has been paid to the role of honor in republican political culture.

The code of honor was certainly alive and well in Arequipa during the eighteenth and nineteenth centuries. Honor was one of the ideological underpinnings that legitimated power, and the city's patricians demonstrated a keen concern over issues of pride and precedence. "A person's honor," asserted Doña Getrudis Vela in an 1830 suit, "is more important that one's existence in the political order."[8] It was more important than wealth to Don José Mariano Bustamante, who vowed to spend his last peso "in defense of honor which is the most precious thing a man has, or rather the only thing."[9] When Don Ramón Sea charged Don José Antonio Berenguel with deflowering his daughter, the latter filed countercharges for slander, claiming that he would demand satisfaction "from beyond the grave," if necessary.[10]

But honor also affected the everyday lives of plebeians. They, too, would have agreed that without a claim to honor, life itself was worth little. The use of the honorific terms of address *Don* and *Doña* was so widespread in Arequipa as to be virtually useless as an indication of social class, in many circumstances. Artisans and chicheras considered themselves to be as entitled to that term of respect as large landowners and public officials, and they used

6. José Antonio Maravall, *Poder, honor y élites en el siglo XVII* (Madrid: Siglo Veintiuno Editores, 1979); and Javier Guillamón Alvarez, *Honor y honra en la España del siglo XVIII* (Madrid: Departamento de Historia Moderna, Facultad de Geografía e Historia, Universidad Complutense, 1981).

7. See Verena Martínez-Alier, *Marriage, Class, and Colour in Nineteenth-Century Cuba: A Study of Racial Attitudes and Sexual Values in a Slave Society* (London: Cambridge University Press, 1974); Ramón A. Gutiérrez, "Honor Ideology, Marriage Negotiation, and Class-Gender Domination in New Mexico, 1690–1846," *Latin American Perspectives* 12, no. 1 (1985): 81–104; Patricia Seed, *To Love, Honor, and Obey in Colonial Mexico: Conflicts over Marriage Choice, 1574–1821* (Stanford: Stanford University Press, 1988); and Susan M. Socolow, "Acceptable Partners: Marriage Choice in Colonial Argentina, 1778–1810," in Asunción Lavrin, ed., *Sexuality and Marriage in Colonial Latin America* (Lincoln and London: University of Nebraska Press, 1989), 209–46. For a comparison with North America, see Bertram Wyatt-Brown, *Honor and Violence in the Old South* (New York: Oxford University Press, 1986).

8. ARAR/CS/Crim (25-II-1830), "Getrudis Vela contra Norberto Laguna."

9. ARAR/CS/Crim (14-XI-1826), "Doña Marta Chávez contra Don Mariano Bustamante por raptar a su hija Doña María Vela."

10. ARAR/CS/Crim (22-II-1833), "Don Ramón Sea contra Don José Antonio Berenguel por el rapto de su hija."

them in official documents.[11] Injurias suits were the most important body of litigation in late colonial Arequipa, and charges were filed by members of different classes and ethnic groups, of both sexes. While their number as a proportion of all criminal cases was highest during the colonial period, such libel suits remained significant after independence (see Table 5.1). But discussions of honor were not limited to libel suits; the documents are filled with references to its importance in virtually every aspect of life.

The literature on honor is careful to acknowledge the variability of the concept both over time and place, and also among different groups within a given society. There are, nevertheless, several key aspects to the concept of honor that should be established before examining the specific case of Arequipa between the colonial and republican periods.

First, honor was as much a social as a personal attribute. That is, an individual's integrity or self-esteem did not translate into honor until those qualities were recognized by others. In societies governed by a code of honor, therefore, reputation was of the utmost importance, and a person had to be prepared to defend his honor before "the court of public opinion," to the point of violence, if necessary.

Table 5.1. Injurias as a percentage of all criminal cases

Years	Injurias	Total
1785–1789	11 (84.6%)	13
1790–1794	8 (61.5%)	13
1795–1799	8 (50.0%)	16
1800–1804	8 (53.3%)	15
1805–1809	15 (45.5%)	33
1810–1814	16 (47.1%)	34
1815–1819	30 (66.7%)	45
1820–1824	6 (40.0%)	15
1825–1829	16 (21.3%)	75
1830–1834	14 (7.7%)	183
1835–1839	46 (22.1%)	208
1840–1844	20 (8.6%)	233
1845–1849	27 (17.3%)	156
1850–1854	28 (16.9%)	166

SOURCE: ARAR, Int/Crim (1784–1824) and CS/Crim (1825–1854).

11. Census takers and priests keeping parish records were more discriminating, but for wills and legal proceedings, notaries seem to have put the title before the name of anyone who claimed it.

In "face to face" societies, a good reputation went beyond considerations of personal pride. A good name was a valuable asset, for example, in the enterprises of merchants and artisans alike. The need for public recognition of honor also explains the significance, in such societies, of physical appearances: titles, emblems, and clothing (especially styles affecting the head) all made the man—or the woman—as much as did any internal character traits. Ritual and ceremony further served to establish and enforce who was to be honored. Finally, as a social attribute, honor could be collective as well as individual. Families, professions, even nations shared a sense of honor symbolized by their head—the patriarch, master, or king.

The second element of honor was its dual—and, potentially, contradictory—meaning of social status and personal virtue. Theoretically, anyone could achieve honor through heroic acts or even socially sanctioned conduct; in a hierarchical society, however, any nobleman was always considered more honorable than the most virtuous commoner. "Respect and precedence," points out Julian Pitt-Rivers, "are paid to those who claim it and are sufficiently powerful to enforce their claim."[12] The legitimacy of those in power, therefore, required that the ambiguity of honor not be publicly recognized. For the Spanish nobility, there could be no conflict between their rank and their merit. Within such a system of "proportional" honor, an insult only threatened one's prestige if it came from an equal. A subordinate could be punished for impudence, but it was not necessary to defend one's honor against affronts from below.

In a hierarchical society, then, one's rank formed the most important claim to respect, and from this follows the third key aspect of honor: lineage. Not only were titles and social position dependent upon one's birth, but even virtue itself was believed to be an inherited trait.[13] In addition to the distinction between "noble" and "low" blood, Spaniards who were descended from converts to the Catholic faith were dishonored by their "impure" blood. The issue of *limpieza de sangre* became even more charged in the multiracial societies of America. In the colonies, an entire vocabulary indicating degrees of racial mixture developed, to distinguish those of

---

12. Pitt-Rivers, "Honour and Social Status," in J. G. Peristiany, ed., *Honour and Shame: The Values of Mediterranean Society* (Chicago: University of Chicago Press, 1966), 24. See also Geoffrey Spurling, "Honor, Sexuality, and the Colonial Church: The Sins of Dr. González, Cathedral Canon," in Johnson and Lipsett-Rivera, eds., *The Faces of Honor*, 45–67.

13. Maravall, *Poder, honor y élites*, 42–43; and Wyatt-Brown, *Honor and Violence*, 64–65.

Spanish heritage from the descendants of Indians and African slaves, populations dishonored by their dependent status.

In order to protect the family from the taint of impurity—and, on a larger scale, to maintain the exclusivity of the dominant class—patriarchs had to be able to arrange marriages with their social equals. Within this context, the final element of the honor system becomes apparent: sexual honor or "shame." In order to make good matches, fathers had to ensure that their daughters remained virgins. Women, therefore, were considered honorable only if they were chaste before marriage and faithful thereafter. Because the dishonor of one woman would extend to her entire family, moreover, it was the duty of men to defend the honor of their female relatives. In practice, nonetheless, what mattered most were appearances; elite women lost honor only if their indiscretions were publicly acknowledged.[14]

Although Arequipa was far from Spain and few of its inhabitants could boast noble titles, concern over honor was great during the colonial period. For members of the elite as well as for those of intermediate groups aspiring to elite status, the claim to be "persons of honor" (*sujetos de honor*) was put forward primarily on the basis of lineage. Those at the very top compiled official documents tracing their genealogy back to noblemen or conquerors, and they held on to as many surnames as possible. Between 1760 and 1785, for example, Don Domingo Bustamante y Benavides presented a series of witnesses testifying to the "noble" descent of his wife, Doña Petronila Diez Canseco Moscoso y Zegarra; he wished to ensure that the rights of his children to certain privileges would be recognized.[15] A few years later, Capt. Pedro de Peralta compiled similar documents to trace his lineage back to a Capt. Diego de Peralta, "one of the first Colonizing and Pacifying Conquerors of these kingdoms."[16] Even those who could not boast such long genealogies still asserted their "illustrious birth," by proving the good repute of their parents and, preferably, also their grandparents. It was especially a

14. Ann Twinam, "Honor, Sexuality, and Illegitimacy in Colonial Spanish America," in Asunción Lavrin, ed., *Sexuality and Marriage in Colonial Latin America* (Lincoln and London: University of Nebraska Press, 1989), 118–55. See also Ann Twinam, "The Negotiations of Honor: Elites, Sexuality, and Illegitimacy in Eighteenth-Century Spanish America," in Johnson and Lipsett-Rivera, eds., *The Faces of Honor*, 68–102.

15. BNP doc. C4007 (1785), "La información seguida por el Coronel Domingo de Bustamante y Benavides."

16. BNP doc. C3989 (1791), "Petición de Pedro de Peralta, para que se le reciba información sobre la filiación de sus hijos."

mark of dishonor to be of "unknown parents," a condition that gave rise to suspicions of illegitimacy and bad blood.[17]

Those who could not claim "noble extraction" went to court to establish their pure blood.[18] In practice determining who was "pure" was often difficult, but such ambiguities could not be acknowledged openly. Limpieza de sangre, an eligibility requirement for many public offices, officially was taken with great seriousness. In 1785, the cabildo's legal representative obtained the intendant's approval for a rule that he should be notified before any such purity-of-blood proceedings were initiated. Without proper attention, he argued, "the nobleman would remain at the same level as the plebeian, the unworthy with the worthy, and finally the meritorious with he who is stripped of this quality."[19]

It was especially crucial for those claiming to be honorable not to have African blood, because of the association with slavery. Persons of African descent were identified as the "base caste, subject to servitude."[20] Cultural stereotype had it, moreover, that mulattoes were inclined to commit thefts and other crimes. Don Juan Joseph de Valcarcel expressed this prejudice when he brought charges of calumny against Bernardo Portugal, a silversmith who rented a room in his house. Portugal had accused him of theft, complained Valcarcel, "without regard to the distinction which exists between us, since my family and descendance is well-known and notorious in this city as well as the nobility of my Blood. . . . The opposite is known of the said Bernardo, since there can hardly be anyone who does not know him as a notorious mulatto, of whom more than of me should be suspected similar and even greater crimes like these."[21]

17. AAA/Civ (20-II-1800), "Don Francisco Ordoñes y Salazar y Doña Melchora Miranda piden que sus hijos sean puestos como legítimos"; and (27-III-1800), "Don Jorge Cayza y Mendoza pide que sea reconocido como legítimo hijo."
18. AAA/Civ (19-II-1805), "Don Antonio de Ybarsena presenta información acerca de su filiación legítima y limpieza de sangre"; (3-XI-1809) "Don José Núñez del Prado pide presentar información acerca de su limpieza de sangre"; and BNP doc. D6556 (1809), "Sobre la limpieza de sangre de Don Antonio Ferrandis."
19. ARAR/Int/Adm (20-XII-1785), "Oficio del Síndico Procurador General Don Manuel Flórez al Intendente."
20. AAA/Pen (9-IV-1791), "Don Diego Llerena contra Calistro Quirós por el rapto de su hija Isidora"; and AAA/Mat (5-III-1800), "Don Julián José Osorio y Doña Francisca Benavides Arana."
21. ARAR/Corregimiento/Crim, Leg. 26, Exp. 433 (21-I-1773), "Don Juan Joseph de Valcarcel contra Bernardo Portugal"; see also Leg. 26, Exp. 434 (18-III-1773), "Antonio Zuñiga y Ignacio Gordillo contra Diego Navarro, mulato, por falsa imputación de robo."

Lineage and racial purity, furthermore, were inextricably bound up with profession. In Arequipa, where class distinctions could be somewhat ambiguous, it was crucial for landowners, merchants, and professionals to be able to distinguish themselves from those who worked with their hands—artisans, laborers, and servants. Within the Spanish tradition, those who worked the land (*labradores*) had never been considered as base as artisans.[22] In order to qualify as a person of honor, in addition to good birth and clean blood, one had to prove that he did not work in one of the "evil and lowly trades" (*oficios viles y bajos*). When Don José Núñez del Prado proved his limpieza de sangre, for example, he presented a witness who testified "that his extraction is clean, without any mixture of bad blood, and therefore he has never been employed in either base or low trades, his occupation being that of commerce in goods from Spain, earning him the esteem and recognition of the principal Persons in this City."[23]

Property or a profession also provided independence. Although indebtedness, both social and monetary, was ubiquitous at all levels of society, to be overly dependent on one person—to have a patron—was dishonorable. One libel suit, in which insults were traded in print between Hermenegildo Garaycochea and Bernardino Cáceres, offers a clear illustration. Cáceres had charged that he could not get justice in a lawsuit because the judge was Garaycochea's patron. In response, Garaycochea challenged anyone who claimed to have patronized or protected him to come forward. While he conceded that Señora Doña María Magdalena Cossío and Doctor Don Raymundo Gutierres had served as the godparents at his wedding, he dared Cáceres to inquire of their servants "to see if at any time we washed plates together, or served at the table with crossed hands and napkins over our shoulders."[24] Although exaggerated, Garaycochea's equation of clientage with servitude accurately reflected the honor code.

Given his attitude toward patrons, Garaycochea was even more insulted when Cáceres asked him to sign a receipt in exchange for a Carnival outfit, stating that the gift was offered out of charity, not obligation. Garaycochea was reported to have said that he would never kneel before Cáceres, and "that if he were dying of hunger and his life depended upon a cup of broth worth

22. Guillamón Alvarez, *Honor y honra*, 61.

23. AAA/Civ (3-XI-1809), "Don José Núñez del Prado presenta información sobre su limpieza de sangre."

24. See first (incomplete) printed article (1827) in ARAR/CS/Crim (7-III-1833), "Bernardino Cáceres contra Hermenegildo Garaycochea."

a half-cent, and Cáceres were to hand it to him, he would surrender his soul to God before accepting it."[25]

The honor of women from all classes was judged primarily on the basis of their sexual conduct. For families attempting to maintain their elite status, it was particularly important to protect the virginity of their daughters. Young couples who did not have parental approval to marry could elope and, thereby, force an unwelcome choice between repairing the woman's sexual honor through marriage and keeping the undesirable suitor out of the family.[26] A patriarch also had the option of bringing charges of *rapto* against the man who had "kidnapped" and deflowered his daughter. In such cases the plaintiff could win monetary retribution, which, technically, served as a dowry for the dishonored woman. Just as important, however, the father hoped to shift the blame for the woman's loss of virginity—and, hence, the dishonor—from himself as an ineffectual patriarch to the perfidious young rogue. Elite men in Arequipa took the violation of their daughters as serious affronts to their own honor, and many of them pressed charges.

Although women of intermediary or elite status had to preserve their reputation in sexual matters, they also had a claim to honor based upon their status. In one of the above cases regarding genealogy, it was precisely the lineage of the wife that brought honor to her husband and children. Women, therefore, felt entitled to demand respect from their inferiors and were prepared to bring charges when it was not forthcoming. When Evarista Arroya was insulted by a mulatta pastry maker, she was able to present several witnesses who were shocked "to see a Lady like Doña Evarista of Illustrious birth which she has proved with abundant documentation as well as notoriety . . . offended in word and deed by a mulatta from such a low sphere."[27]

Good birth, pure blood, and a nonmanual profession were the requirements in Arequipa to join the elite ranks of the honorable; in order for these qualities to count, however, they had to be recognized by the public at large. One was not simply a "well-born Spaniard," for example, but was "known and reputed" as such. One way that persons could establish these characteristics, as we have seen, was to bring forward witnesses to testify to lineage and

---

25. See testimony of Juan José Carvajal on March 9, 1833, in ARAR/CS/Crim (7-III-1833), "Bernardino Cáceres contra Hermenegildo Garaycochea."

26. On *raptos*, see Martínez-Alier, *Marriage, Class, and Colour*; Gutiérrez, "Honor Ideology"; and Seed, *To Love, Honor, and Obey*.

27. ARAR/Int/Crim (17-V-1788), "Doña Evarista Arroyo contra Tomasa, mulata libertina, por injurias."

reputation. Once a certain position or rank was achieved, it was continually reasserted by outward physical signs—such as specific clothing and uniforms, forms of address, or the carrying of a sword—and by participation in the frequent public ceremonies.

This constant need for public recognition explains the preoccupation among colonial officials with questions of precedence, such as the order of seating at the cathedral or in processions.[28] There were ongoing disputes between the cabildo and the cathedral chapter over the fine points of ceremonies: whether councilmen should receive the bishop's blessing standing or on their knees, and whether the mayor or the deacon should have the key to the chest that held the Holy Sacrament on Holy Thursday.[29] Even in death, one's funeral could reflect the honor of both the deceased and the family. When Bishop Chaves de La Rosa made it more difficult for members of religious communities to accompany funeral marches, there was an outcry by the populace. Numerous townspeople filed a legal protest with the intendant, complaining that the bishop had ordered "that the most distinguished persons be conducted to their vault incognito, secretly, and without pomp."[30]

Most assertions of honor, however, occurred in everyday life. Men and women had to be constantly on guard and prepared to defend their reputations against insults and gossip. Because of the outward symbolic nature of honor, verbal affronts were often accompanied by physical shaming. Given the importance of the head, to slap a man in the face or to knock off his hat was considered a serious challenge.[31] As honor was also tied to one's household, it was especially egregious to insult a man in his own home.[32] The

---

28. For examples, see ARAR/Int/Crim (8-VII-1786), "Don Crisóstomo Anco, Alcalde Ordinario del Pueblo de Cayma, contra Domingo Calla y otros por falsa imputación"; ARAR/Int/Ped (4-V-1787), "Don Josef García de San Roque en los autos contra el Alférez Real Don Manuel Flores"; and, on the issue of who was entitled to the title of Your Excellency, see AMA, LCED 6 (Dec. 8, 1788).

29. See AMA, LEXP 1 (Dec. 5 and Nov. 10, 1794); AMA, LAC 26 (especially during 1804, 1805, and 1811); and AMA, LAC 25 (Apr. 27, 1781).

30. BNP doc. D6309 (1805), "Sobre el depósito de cadáveres."

31. See ARAR/Corregimiento/Crim, Leg. 26, Exp. 424 (10-I-1771), "Martín Francisco contra María la Ocoña"; ARAR/Int/Crim (4-VIII-1789), "María Zevallos contra Don Mariano Villanueva"; (30-I-1792) "Don Rafael Contreras contra Don Agustín Herrera"; (1-VI-1792) "Doña María López contra Marcos Torrelio y Pedro Pastor"; and ARAR/CS/Crim (11-XI-1827), "Contra Miguel Ramos por homicidio."

32. See ARAR/Int/Crim (21-II-1785), "Doña Josefa Zegarra y Cáceres contra Juana de Tal"; (3-X-1792) "Don Antonio Acosta en contraquerella con Diego Llerena"; (18-III-1806) "Don Juan Bautista Graci contra Don Pedro Yansen y Don Ramón Hurtado"; (2-VIII-1815) "Doña Luisa Tapia contra Doña Bárbara Rivero"; ARAR/CS/Crim (11-X-1825), "Don Manuel Diez

violation of a patriarch's home was one of the factors that made rapto such a serious affront. Undoubtedly most scores were settled on the spot, either by humbling one's challenger or through violence. Other disputes would have been aired before local justices of the peace, while, a few carried their cases into court with a charge of injurias.

Although in theory only the opinions of peers affected one's honor, Arequipeños who went to court to clear their name—and thereby risked further public scrutiny—were often demanding respect from inferiors. Injurias suits were most likely to arise where the claim to honor was the most tenuous: from men of the intermediary groups and from women who had no men to defend them. Particularly in a society like Arequipa's, where the lines of class and color were not always clearly demarcated, there were borderline cases where the parties involved simply could not agree on their respective statuses. In 1820, for example, the merchant José Pozo contracted with the carpenter Ignacio Severiche to make him a box in which to hold some watches. There was a misunderstanding over how soon the box should be ready, and whether Pozo would pick it up or Severiche would deliver it. The next day, when Severiche discovered that Pozo had bought a box from someone else, he went to reproach him for breaking their contract and they had a heated argument. Ultimately, their dispute escalated into a shaming ritual when Severiche's relatives, armed with sticks and stones and accompanied by musicians from their neighborhood, set siege to the house where Pozo lived.

Severiche brought charges against Pozo for slapping him, chasing him with a sword, and insulting his daughter. Pozo countered that he was the one offended by Severiche, to whom he continually referred as simply "the carpenter," because he had entered his house "with incivility and disrespect, without even greeting him as is customary among honorable people." After their argument, continued Pozo, the carpenter had the arrogance to proclaim "that if he were not in his house he would teach him proper manners with a good kick."[33]

Severiche's daughter also thought Pozo could use a lesson in manners;

Canseco contra su arrendatario Mariano Carbajal"; (12-XII-1832) "Contra Bernarda Torres, Juana Barriga y María Torres por haber herido a María Beltrán"; (22-II-1833) "Don Ramón Sea contra Don José Berenguel"; and (17-IV-1833), "Contra Mateo Chávez por homicidio."

33. ARAR/Int/Crim (22-II-1820), "Don Ignacio Severiche contra Don José Pozo por injurias." On the importance of salutations among men of higher status, see also ARAR/Int/Crim (19-III-1806), "Seguidos por Don Pedro Yansen sobre el robo de pesos."

when he came after her father with a sword, she cried out, "How very ill-bred a man who does not respect an old man like my Father."[34] The witnesses seemed ambivalent in their estimation of the two men; they referred to both as Don, although the merchant Pozo was also identified as a gentleman (*caballero*). At the time of the fight, moreover, the artisan's daughter had been visiting with the mayor, which suggests that her family was not far removed from the social elite. The case was suspended when Pozo left town on a business trip, and, like many libel suits, it was never concluded.

While men of elite status claimed honor as a birthright, plebeians asserted that their conduct earned them honorable reputations.[35] Although there was not always a strict distinction between sujetos de honor and hombres de bien, the former tended to be associated with elite status and the latter with popular notions of good conduct and manliness. On the one hand, conduct was used as a defense against dishonoring charges of criminality, particularly of theft. Aside from racial slurs, the most frequent insult used against men during an argument was the label of "thief." Rather than trying to refute such charges through a presentation of the particular circumstances, men used their reputations as proof of innocence. The defense used by Hermenegildo de Olivera in 1783 was to be repeated by many others throughout the period: "Since in the first place I am a man of notoriously honorable and Christian behavior, known and recognized as such in this City, and therefore the infamous act of theft is not presumable against my conduct."[36]

The defense against charges of theft usually included the presentation of character witnesses, who testified that the accused was, in fact, an hombre de bien. The opinions of others were critical, and the claim to honor was often based on earning the confidence of distinguished persons. A good reputation had material consequences in an economy dominated by credit, especially for artisans and small-scale merchants, whose success depended upon the trust of

---

34. Testimony of Dominga Muñoz on Feb. 22, 1820, in ARAR/Int/Crim (22-II-1820), "Don Ignacio Severiche contra Don José Pozo por injurias."

35. Cheryl English Martin has documented a similar dynamic in eighteenth-century Chihuahua; see Martin, *Governance and Society*, 142–48. Juan Carlos Estenssoro Fuchs has noted that mulattoes in late colonial Lima copied the manners and dances of the nobility; see Estenssoro Fuchs, "La plebe ilustrada: El pueblo en las fronteras de la razón," in Charles Walker, ed., *Entre la retórica y la insurgencia* (Cuzco: CERA Bartolomé de las Casas, 1996), 50–57. See also the following essays in Johnson and Lipsett-Rivera, eds., *The Faces of Honor*: Lipsett-Rivera, "A Slap in the Face of Honor: Social Transgression and Women in Late-Colonial Mexico," 179–200; and Richard Boyer, "Honor Among Plebeians: *Mala Sangre* and Social Reputation," 152–78.

36. ARAR/Corregimiento/Crim, Leg. 26, Exp. 446 (4-IX-1783), "Don Miguel de Cáseres contra Hermenegildo de Olivera por robo." Similar statements can be found in many theft trials.

their clients and customers.[37] In 1808, the master silversmiths requested that the intendant use his authority to ensure that their journeymen complied with the regulations of the guild, especially the prohibition against receiving work independently of a master. The journeymen, particularly outraged at the implication that they received stolen silver pieces, indignantly protested that their honor had been stained. They insisted that they had every right to accept jobs from "any Person who, led by the entire satisfaction which they have in our work as well as in our honorable conduct, place their confidence in us."[38]

As the silversmiths' response implies, dedication and skill in one's occupation was an important element of honorable conduct for plebeians. Even so, simply being employed was a weak defense, and an accused thief's case was much stronger if he could also prove that he owned property or wealth. In 1796, for example, young Calistro Lazo of Socabaya was spreading rumors that the stolen horse with which he had been caught had been given to him by José Alvarez. "Don" José went to court to defend himself before charges had even been filed, declaring: "I am an honorable man [hombre de bien] and recognized as such in all of this city, I have my own property, both personal and real estate, and I manage money, and therefore I am not capable of demeaning myself [grasarme] in robberies."[39] One of his character witnesses was unsure if Alvarez had any property, but he did testify that he rented two plots in Socabaya and was incapable of committing theft because he was a "hardworking man."[40]

When Sebastiana Vera accused the Indian Pascual Calderón of stealing her sheep, he provided a similar defense. Rather than describing his business of slaughtering meat in the sierra and selling it in the city, he claimed to be an "hombre de bien and of moderate conduct," and, furthermore, "with manifest management of property." His neighbors from Miraflores, presumably Spanish gentlemen, backed up his claims, testifying that they had safeguarded Calderón's money.[41]

---

37. ARAR/Int/Crim (17-VIII-1824), "Ignacio Molina de defiende de los cargos puestos por Mariano Goysueta"; and ARAR/CS/Crim (2-V-1832), "Don Enrique Núñez se defiende de la imputación de robo."

38. ARAR/Int/Adm (9-VI-1808), "Expediente sobre que los Maestros Plateros cumplan sus deberes."

39. ARAR/Int/Crim (21-VII-1796), "Don Josef Alvares contra Calisto Lazo por falsa imputación del robo de una yegua."

40. Testimony of Pedro Texada on July 28, 1796, in ARAR/Int/Crim (21-VII-1796), "Don Josef Alvares contra Calisto Lazo por falsa imputación del robo de una yegua."

41. ARAR/Int/Crim (22-VII-1802), "Prueba por parte de Pascual Calderón en la causa que le sigue Sebastiana Vera por robo."

Even though plebeians recognized the respect due their social superiors, they were sensitive to implications of dependence and indebtedness. When Don Vicente Mantilla "politely" reminded Tomás Ortiz of a two-peso debt, he expected deference but, instead, was met with insults and threats.[42] The implication that one had a patron could be taken as an insult. In a dispute over water rights between men who both rented their land, for instance, "Don" Pedro Valdivia picked a fight with Nicolás Quadros by saying to him: "Oh zambo you have a hand for your master."[43] By using the term *master* (*amo*) and labeling Quadros as part African, Valdivia implied that patronage was akin to slavery in its dependence and servitude. When "Don" Pedro Nolasco Murillo tried to marry the daughter of a man from whom he rented land, "Don" Pedro Reynoso vehemently opposed the match on the grounds that Murillo "notoriously has been raised as a *concertado* in my house, as a paid Peon, who has served me in the labor of my hacienda."[44]

In criminal cases, moreover, the accused never appealed explicitly to their "patrons"; it was only the witnesses against them who put such words in their mouths.[45] It is significant that only women—who were considered dependent anyway—explicitly admitted seeking the intercession of a protector.[46] The other group that occasionally admitted having patrons—Indians— was, similarly, stigmatized as servile.[47]

If plebeians appealed to their conduct to define their honor in the eyes of

42. ARAR/Int/Crim (19-XII-1789), "Don Vicente Mantilla contra Tomás Ortís por injurias." For other fights arising from efforts to collect on loans, see ARAR/Int/Crim (30-I-1792), "Don Rafael Contreras contra Don Agustín Herrera"; (8-V-1792) "Don Bernardino de Vera contra Mariano Ticona"; (2-III-1801) "Don Tadeo Torres contra Alexo Paredes"; (5-I-1820) "El Teniente de Cura de Yanahuara Don José Delgado contra Don José León"; ARAR/ CS/Crim (13-IV-1835), "Contra Don Miguel Hernani por heridos a Don Manuel Corrales"; and (10-VI-1835), "Don Miguel Hernani contra Don Manuel Corrales."

43. ARAR/Int/Crim (17-II-1803), "Don Diego Valdivia contra Nicolás Quadros por injurias."

44. A concertado was like an indentured servant. ARAR/Cab/Crim (3-XI-1795), "Por Don Pedro Nolasco Murillo sobre el disenso de Don Pedro Reynoso para contraer matrimonio con su hija."

45. See, for example, the testimony of Isidro Bilca on June 7, in ARAR/Int/Crim (7-VI-1805), "Mariano Solórzano contra el Alcalde de Naturales de Santa Marta"; and that of Pedro Sanches on Oct. 16, in ARAR/CS/Crim (7-X-1838), "Contra Nasario Muñoz por heridas."

46. ARAR/Int/Crim (20-XII-1820), "Paulino Moscoso contra el Alcalde de Tiabaya"; and ARAR/CS/Crim (2-V-1829), "Melchora Ramos hace una petición en autos que le sigue a su hijo por Melchor Rodríguez."

47. Indian "Don" Francisco Pinto appointed his "patron" executor of his will; ARAR, notary M. J. Chávez, Oct. 5, 1845. Esteban Cabana explained that he was identified on the tribute census with the surname Abril because, as a child, he had taken the name of his patron,

their superiors, they particularly expected their peers to recognize them as hombres de bien. The code of manliness included hospitality and generosity. Juan Montoya, a shoemaker from Spain, was outraged when Manuel Lazo kicked him out of his house for swearing at a carpenter. According to one witness, Montoya left in a huff, exclaiming "that everyone had their house, and paid their money, and that he had not shown disrespect in anything."[48] Montoya's words implied that he too had property and, therefore, considered himself to be the social equal of Lazo. When he returned, it was with knife in hand. Montoya's defense lawyer argued that he had been provoked by Lazo, who had shown a complete lack of civilized principles.

Furthermore, an honorable man would never refuse the offer of a drink, and would buy the next round to keep himself on an equal footing.[49] Marcelino Manrique and Gerónimo Ballón were "like brothers" until a fight in which the latter ended up with a broken arm. Ballón testified that when he had declined an invitation to drink, Manrique had retorted that "he was a poor wretch [*un miserable*] and in order not to spend money he doesn't drink."[50]

A man was also expected to be able to control his wife; there was no mark of dishonor more serious than to be cuckolded. In one murder case, even the prosecutor called for a lighter sentence because the deceased had said the defendant prostituted his own wife, "the most serious of the affronts which can be made against an honorable married man."[51]

Hombría ("manly honor") required a man to defend his honor, and fights could begin with the challenge "You are not man enough for me."[52] For this

---

"as most servants are accustomed to do." AGN, Hacienda, H-4-1845, R. 287 (1843), "Matrícula de Indígenas de Arequipa."

48. ARAR/CS/Crim (12-VI-1830), "Contra Juan Montoya por homicidio."

49. For examples, see AAA/Pen (16-XII-1796), "Doña Tadea Gordillo pide divorcio de Pedro Nolasco Espinosa"; (23-IV-1817), "Doña Marta Loayza pide divorcio de Mariano Samatelo"; ARAR/Int/Crim (27-IV-1816), "Contra Martín Muñoz y Bruno Zevallos por robo"; (15-XI-1824) "Expediente sobre la muerte de Manuel Vilca"; ARAR/CS/Crim (11-XI-1827), "Contra Miguel Ramos por homicidio"; (24-IV-1832) "Contra Pablo Villanueva por puñaladas a Paula Muños"; (14-VII-1833) "Contra Andrés Quispe por homicidio"; (7-IV-1836) "Contra Rafael González por dar puñaladas a tres hombres y una mujer en una chichería"; (8-I-1838) "Contra Francisco Chiri por homicidio"; and (14-VII-1851), "Contra Juan Palomino por intento de asesinato."

50. ARAR/CS/Crim (19-XII-1850), "Contra Don Nicolás y Don Marcelino Manrique por romper un brazo a Don Gerónimo Ballón."

51. ARAR/CS/Crim (14-VII-1833), "Contra Andrés Quispe por homicidio."

52. ARAR/CS/Crim (11-XI-1827), "Contra Miguel Ramos por homicidio"; and (10-VI-

reason, many offenses in the plebeian world could be settled only through violence. When journeyman carpenter Agustín Talavera asked his master for a new workbench, his companion Alejo Espinoza joked that he should just turn the old one over. Unamused, Agustín called Alejo a "dog," and, after exchanging racial insults, the two were at blows.[53] Over thirty years later, a similar fight erupted in a tailor's shop. Vicente Salas reported that when he arrived at work, he found the other four journeymen drunk and fooling around. When one tried to draw a cross on his white shirt with charcoal, they got in a fight. The journeyman who tried to pull them apart got stabbed with a pair of scissors.[54]

The teasing was easier to take if it was at the expense of another trade. In 1833, three stonecutters met on the street and began joking with each other. According to Gabriel Llosa, Manuel Pacheco "said to them, as in jest, come and carry, as if implying they were porters, to which the stonecutter Mariano replied, and I also have a [wild] mule to break, at which expression Pacheco laughed."[55] Clearly, artisans claimed and defended ranking among different trades.

Nevertheless, there was a fine line between defending one's own masculine honor and offending that of others. To earn a reputation as querulous and insolent could cost a man the respect of his fellows.[56] Even among the popular classes, moreover, there existed degrees of honor: master artisans expected greater respect from their journeymen, as did parents of their

---

1836), "Contra Inocencio Pardo por heridas a Pablo Rosado." For other analyses of masculine honor, see Cheryl English Martin, "Popular Speech and Social Order in Northern Mexico, 1650–1830," *Comparative Studies in Society and History* 32, no. 2 (1990): 305–24; John Charles Chasteen, "Violence for Show: Knife Dueling on a Nineteenth-Century Cattle Frontier," in Lyman L. Johnson, ed., *The Problem of Order in Changing Societies* (Albuquerque: University of New Mexico Press, 1990), 47–64; Stern, *The Secret History of Gender*, especially 151–88; and Lyman L. Johnson, "Dangerous Words, Provocative Gestures, and Violent Acts: The Disputed Hierarchies of Plebeian Life in Colonial Buenos Aires," in Johnson and Lipsett-Rivera, eds., *The Faces of Honor*, 127–51.

53. ARAR/Int/Crim (15-XII-1803), "Alejo Espinoza contra Agustín Talavera por injurias y heridas."

54. ARAR/CS/Crim (10-X-1836), "Contra Vicente Salas por heridas a Timoteo Vargas."

55. ARAR/CS/Crim (17-IV-1833), "Contra Mateo Chaves y Lucia Torres por heridas a varias personas."

56. See ARAR/Int/Crim (17-V-1788), "Doña Evarista Arroyo contra Tomasa, mulata"; (29-V-1799) "Don Ignacio y Don Ignacio Antonio Delgado contra Pedro Nuñes"; (7-VI-1805) "Mariano Solórzano contra el Alcalde de Naturales de Santa Marta"; (14-XI-1806) "Contra Ignacio Canano por desórdenes de malversación"; (19-IX-1807) "Don Francisco Delgado contra Don Isidro Salas"; and (21-II-1817), "Don José Nuñes contra José Delgado y sus hijos."

children. In 1811, for example, master blacksmith Eugenio Escalera complained that he had paid Pedro Cornejo Sunday morning, but that the latter had come back drunk in the afternoon and asked for two more reals. Escalera pushed him out of his house, "so that he would not give occasion with such an example for the other journeymen to do the same."[57] Another master blacksmith, who was visiting Escalera that afternoon, testified that he was shocked to hear Cornejo shout: "Well I sh— on these sh— faced masters who won't give two reals, tomorrow they can look for me and I won't appear."[58]

Another case demonstrates both the attempt to enforce degrees of respect between near equals and the potential politicization of honor. Antonino Pacheco offered a glass of chicha to a friend, joking "drink Rabbit Eater." Apparently this insult, which referred to followers of rebel general Salaverry, was really aimed at Rafael González, who took revenge by stabbing Pacheco and his companions. González claimed that he had taught Pacheco the cobbling trade, and that they had been enemies since the unfaithful journeyman had begun accepting work without paying González his share, "as if he were the Master." He defended himself against the charges by explaining that he acted "with the authority which Master Shoemakers customarily have with their apprentices and journeymen, and that of being a spiritual *compadre* [co-godparent] with María Gómez, Antonino's mother."[59]

Plebeian women, like elite women, were expected to conform to gendered notions of honor, although sexual fidelity after marriage was more important than chastity beforehand. As long as a single woman was involved in a long-term relationship with a reasonable expectation of marriage, she could still claim that her conduct was honorable.[60] Within popular society, gossip was used to police the sexual conduct of women. Just as the most serious affront to men was to be called a thief, for women it was to be labeled a whore (*puta*).

Married women who were the target of such insults frequently filed

57. ARAR/Int/Crim (12-VIII-1811), "Eugenio Escalera contra Pedro Cornejo por insubordinación."

58. Dashes in original text—apparently the scribe was shocked enough to censor the statement. Testimony of Diego Marroquín, Aug 12, in ARAR/Int/Crim (12-VIII-1811), "Eugenio Escalera contra Pedro Cornejo por insubordinación."

59. ARAR/CS/Crim (7-IV-1836), "Contra Rafael González por puñaladas a cuatro personas en una chichería."

60. AAA/Civ (18-V-1795), "Martina Tapia pide que Rafael Salas cumpla con su palabra de casamiento"; and ARAR/Int/Crim (8-X-1807), "Doña María Tone Esquiagola, Casica de Yanahuara, se defiende de las acusaciones del Alcalde Don Pablo Vera."

charges against the slanderers, in an effort to clear their names. In their petitions to the court, they emphasized the seriousness of such accusations, often claiming that their husbands were threatening to kill them if they did not prove their innocence. A single woman was most likely to come under such attacks if she was involved with a married man, especially if he diverted money from his household to spend it on her. One of the popular nicknames for such women was *come pan ajeno*, or "one who eats another's bread." When Micaela Begaso confronted a young women named María, whom she suspected of adultery with her husband, she blamed María for her husband's abandonment of his responsibilities and asked her: "Is there no single man with whom you can have an affair?"[61] The conduct of widows and women whose husbands were absent came under particular scrutiny. As women without the "protection" and support of a man, it was suspected that they would be after other women's husbands.

Just as in affronts to male honor, verbal accusations against a woman were often accompanied by symbolic physical attacks. As honor was associated with the head, it was considered a serious mark of shame for a woman to have her hair cut.[62] But given the sexual emphasis of female honor, women were also subject to the embarrassing act of having their skirts lifted and their buttocks beaten.[63] Clothing, too, was a reflection of a woman's honor, both of her sexual modesty and her status. A priest who was trying to deny responsibility for paying child support used the strategy of impugning his lover's honor: "She should dress herself in native woolens and cottons like before," he scoffed, "and take off her shawls and dresses."[64]

As such a statement suggests, there was a greater burden of proof upon plebeian women to demonstrate their honor. The assumption, at least among the upper classes, was that plebeian women, particularly chicheras, had loose

61. ARAR/Int/Crim (9-XII-1815), "Doña Micaela Begaso contra María de tal por ilícito comercio con su marido."

62. ARAR/Int/Crim (29-V-1809), "Doña Rafaela Gómez contra Doña María Santos Salazar"; ARAR/CS/Crim (12-VII-1838), "Doña Rosalía Delgado contra Doña Teresa Villalobos"; and (30-VII-1840), "Manuela Veliz contra Nicolasa Benavente y sus hijas."

63. ARAR/Int/Crim (2-II-1804), "Don Sebastian Valencia contra María Laguna y otros por maltratamientos hechos en su mujer"; (5-III-1806) "Don Francisco Alvarado contra Josefa y María Valencia por injurias"; ARAR/CS/Crim (12-XII-1832), "Contra Bernarda Torres y otras por haber herido a María Beltrán"; and (5-III-1838), "Doña Juana Torres contra Don Julian Zegarra por injurias."

64. AAA/Civ (20-XI-1822), "Doña Tomasa Texada contra el Presbítero Don José de Melgar por alimentos." Carlos Champi similarly insulted his wife according to witness Josef Dias de Aragon; AAA/Pen (20-X-1784), "Paula Cáseres contra Carlos Champi por sevicia."

morals. When Martina Tapia requested that Rafael Salas fulfill his promise to marry her, especially since she had maintained her good reputation, he retorted that he could never marry a woman whose occupation was chichera, "which brings with it an unfortunate lifestyle."[65] In 1804, "Doña" María Jacinta Ortis accused José Alvarez of insulting her during a dispute over water rights. He denied the charge but added that it would not be a serious matter anyway, because plebeian women like her drank chicha and called each other "drunkards" every day.[66] Women who were attempting to preserve their reputations, therefore, had to refute the specific charges of sexual misconduct, and, unlike plebeian men, they rarely had recourse to corroborating evidence such as being gainfully employed. Nevertheless, despite elite biases, plebeian women were insistent in their claim to honor.

Plebeians, then, claimed their own version of honor, based upon conduct. A majority of Arequipeños, moreover, were accepted as "Spaniards" despite a probable mixed heritage. Perhaps it was this claim to purity of blood that made so many feel entitled to use the honorific terms of Don and Doña. Furthermore, men of all classes believed that control over women added to their own honor, which is why ritualized marital disputes were taken so seriously. For the most part, nonetheless, plebeians in the colonial period acknowledged that honor was proportional and that one had to show deference—if not servility—to superiors. For example, when a small farmer was questioned during a lawsuit why he had not raised his sons with better manners, he objected that he was an hombre de bien and that he had raised his sons with "respect and subjection to the authorities, and with that due to the other persons according to their classes, status, and conditions."[67] The claim to a good reputation based upon the estimation of more distinguished gentlemen was a recognition that honor existed in degrees.

In Spain, the growing influence of the Enlightenment and fears of economic decline led King Charles III to issue a royal order that recognized artisan trades as "honest and honorable."[68] A small circle of *modernistas*,

65. AAA/Civ (18-V-1795), "Martina Tapia pide que Rafael Salas cumpla con su palabra de casamiento." See also AAA/Mat (9-VI-1790), "Juan Muños y Brígida Valencia"; ARAR/CS/ Crim (4-I-1830), "Don Toribio de Linares contra Doña María Escalante por falta de respeto"; (16-VII-1838) "Don Ildefonso Obando contra Mariano Fuentes por estupro en su hija"; and (3-IX-1848), "Contra Faustino Cuadros y Manuel Delgado por violación en la menor Manuela Bolaños."
66. ARAR/Int/Crim (13-X-1804), "Doña María Jacinta Ortis contra José Alvares."
67. ARAR/Int/Crim (21-II-1817), "Don José Nuñes contra Don José Delgado y sus hijos."
68. Quoted in Guillamón Alvarez, *Honor y honra*, 169.

including several Arequipeños, were also introducing such ideas to Peru by the late colonial period.[69] Nonetheless, the advocates of granting "legal honor" to artisans still believed that it was "a proportional and corresponding honor, each one at his own level, within the social hierarchy."[70] Colonial authorities were also concerned that artisans and other laborers not be discouraged from working. In their eyes, the only thing worse than working in one of the "low and base occupations" (oficios viles y bajos) was not to have any income or occupation at all (*sin oficio, ni beneficio*).

For their part, elites in Arequipa considered the populace of Arequipa— especially when compared with the highland Indians or the coastal blacks and mulattoes—as, generally, well-behaved and honest, if not exactly honorable. Ignacio Paredes, accused of running a gambling house, insisted that only persons of honor such as priests frequented his establishment. "If some Laborers come to buy *aji* [a spicy dish] and chicha, which make up their main nourishment," he continued, "these unfortunate men are not, nor can they be called, vagrants and ne'er-do-wells, since their daily work assures them an honest name among the Folk."[71] The colonial code of honor, therefore, offered a place (albeit unequal) for a large segment of the populace, as well as guidelines for a relatively peaceful coexistence.

Honor for a New Republic

During the colonial period, the code of honor had been based upon the monarchical system. The king, as the head of state, had been not only the most honorable person within the hierarchical ranking, but also the source of honor for all others. With Peruvian independence from Spain, recognized in Arequipa in 1824, that source of honor suddenly vanished. The ideal itself, however, was still considered of the utmost importance. Those who were trying to establish a new state wished to appropriate the power to dispense honors and privileges.[72] Given the instability of officeholders, however, they lacked a symbolic head. The king's role as distributor and guardian of honor

69. Pablo Macera, *Trabajos de historia*, vol. 2 (Lima: Instituto Nacional de Cultura, 1977).
70. Guillamón Alvarez, *Honor y honra*, 21.
71. ARAR/Int/Crim (14-XI-1806), "Contra Ignacio Canano por desórdenes de malversación en su casa."
72. Art. 60 of the constitution of 1823 gave Congress the power to award national honors; in Olivo, *Constituciones*, 46.

passed, instead, to the constitution. The elaborate ceremonies that had earlier reinforced allegiance to the monarch served after independence to legitimate the constitution.

Sensitive to the apparent continuity in civic celebrations, the editors of the official newspaper in Arequipa—*El Republicano*—were quick to point out that the underlying meanings had changed: "It is evident that these same acts have been repeated a thousand times for motives very ominous to the country, and they have become so debased that rightly someone has called them 'sacro-comic functions': but reflective observers . . . will know at a glance when they are effusions of a free soul that rejoices, when the violent services of a slave dragged by the hard law of necessity."[73]

However exaggerated the official descriptions of such festivities, the language on such occasions was radically new. As processions wound their way through the city, criers stopped in the main plazas to read not royal decrees but rather republican constitutions.[74] The crowd heard that all Peruvians were equal before the law, and that hereditary privileges and offices had been abolished.[75] Some learned that they were now citizens, with new rights, including the ability to elect their representatives in the government. When people gathered in shops and chicherías to discuss these changes, someone might read from the newspaper that published and analyzed the constitutions.[76]

Notions of liberty and equality were new to most of the population when they suddenly entered public discourse after 1824. It is perfectly understandable that people would interpret new concepts through ideals with which they were already familiar; in Arequipa, they viewed these changes through the lens of honor, which resonated with the value that republicanism placed on virtue.[77] While lawyers would help people claim their new rights, it is no

73. *El Republicano*, June 30, 1827, 60. See also "Publicación y jura de la constitución Peruana," *El Republicano*, May 17, 1828, 83; July 19, 1834, 7; and letter to the editor signed "Los Libres," July 19, 1834, 8.
74. *El Republicano*, July 19, 1834, 7.
75. Art. 23 (1823); Art. 142, 146, 147 (1826); Art. 157, 158, 159 (1828); Art. 158, 170 (1834); and Art. 160 (1839); in Olivo, *Constituciones*, 39, 103, 140, 180–82, 234.
76. For articles, see *El Republicano*, Aug. 19, 1826, 168–69; Aug. 26, 1826, 172–73; and Dec. 30, 1826, 247–48. The constitution was published in weekly installments in *El Republicano*, from Dec. 1, 1827 through Mar. 15, 1828. Copies of the constitution were also on sale for half a peso (the daily wage of an unskilled laborer); see "Aviso," *El Republicano*, June 27, 1828, 103.
77. For an introduction to the history of republicanism, including the concept of virtue, see J. G. A. Pocock, *The Machiavellian Moment: Florentine Political Thought and the Atlantic Republican Tradition* (Princeton: Princeton University Press, 1975).

coincidence that those most often invoked—such as the right to one's reputation or the inviolability of the home—coincided with long-cherished values.

The early constitutions explicitly recognized every citizen's right to his honor, guaranteeing "the good opinion, or reputation of the individual, as long as he is not declared a delinquent according to the laws."[78] Don José María Portugal cited this article directly in a lawsuit for libel,[79] but more commonly it was used by defendants and their lawyers to win release from jail, since incarceration was considered to be dishonoring. When María Beltran filed charges of injurias against the sisters Bernarda and Juana Torres, bakers in Tiabaya, they claimed that she had been the one to come to their house insulting them and damaging their reputation, "which according to our charter every citizen has the right to conserve as long as he is not declared a delinquent according to the laws." The fiscal (state prosecutor), agreeing that jail was an "offense against honorable families," argued that not only should the women be freed, but that they had the right to sue the justice of the peace for damages.[80]

In 1828, Alberto Anco, a prominent Indian in the parish of Santa Marta, did bring charges against the judge who jailed him during a trial instigated by his wife for adultery. The superior court censured the judge, asserting "that under no circumstances should Don Alberto Anco have been mixed in with the other criminals who occupy the jails, since his conduct and good behavior have constantly made him deserving of public acceptance and because he has been considered worthy of obtaining public offices which he has carried out fully."[81] Such decisions by the courts limited the ability of the police to maintain control by arresting "suspicious" characters. Victoriano Concha, arrested in 1829 on the suspicion of being a thief, was released when the fiscal maintained that the evidence against him was insufficient "to have persecuted a man damaging him in his person and honor."[82]

78. Art. 193 (1823) and Art. 164 (1828); Olivo, *Constituciones*, 68, 141.
79. ARAR/CS/Crim (2-I-1835), "Don Calistro Araujo contra Don José María Portugal."
80. ARAR/CS/Crim (12-XII-1832), "Contra Bernarda Torres, Juana Barriga y María Torres por haber herido a María Beltrán."
81. ARAR/CS/Crim (16-XII-1828), "Don Alberto Anco apela la sentencia que lo ha declarado adúltero." The sentence was also printed in *El Republicano*, Jan. 31, 1829, 3.
82. ARAR/CS/Crim (6-VII-1829), "Contra Victoriano Concha por sospecharse que es ladrón." See also ARAR/CS/Crim (3-VII-1833), "Contra Pablo Aguilar por haberle encontrado con una gorra de policía"; and (2-IX-1834), "Contra Don Diego Begazo y sus yernos por insubordinación a las autoridades."

Even more dishonoring than imprisonment was the punishment of lashes; in the colonial period slaves and Indians had been whipped, but "Spanish" people protested vociferously if subjected to the same treatment.[83] After independence, Arequipeños appealed to a decree passed by Bolívar in 1821, protecting all free people from the lash. When Don Leandro Torres accused Don Gaspar Herrera of whipping his nephew, he asserted that the act was a public crime "because it affects the fatherland and the very society."[84] Although Herrera protested that the youth had tried to seduce his wife, a serious affront to his own honor, he agreed to settle out of court.

Local judicial officials zealously enforced this law as a fundamental republican principle. When the police arrested Don Hermenegildo Rosas for whipping a boy, he was initially put at the disposition of a justice of the peace. Believing such a charge went beyond his jurisdiction, the judge consulted the superior court. Fiscal José Gregorio Paz Soldán agreed that the crime was a serious one, since "with the lashes given to a citizen all the principles were trampled, the entire public was insulted in [the body of] one man, the Government, the Constitution and the dignity of the Republic were violated."[85] Paz Soldán would later become a prominent jurist and politician who defended the notion of civil rights at the national level.

In addition to protecting a person's reputation, the early constitutions guaranteed that "the house of every Peruvian is an inviolable asylum."[86] *El Republicano* cited this protection for particular praise, asserting that "Peruvians, peaceful in the heart of their families will be considered to be defended as if in an impregnable castle."[87] Because to be insulted in one's own home had always been considered a particularly serious affront, Arequipeños seized upon this constitutional guarantee to charge both officials and civilians with illegal breaking and entering.[88] When cacique José Arenaza was charged

83. ARAR/Cab/Civ, Leg. 15, Cuad. 380 (10-VIII-1780), "Bartolomé Cutipa contra Josef Arrenasas, cobrador de los repartos."

84. ARAR/CS/Crim (13-I-1841), "Don Leandro Torres contra Don Gaspar Herrera por haber azotado a su sobrino Manuel Velarde."

85. ARAR/CS/Crim (20-V-1843), "Contra Don Hermenegildo Rosas por haber azotado al menor Mariano Espinoza." For other cases, see ARAR/CS/Crim (2-XI-1839), "Contra Don Mariano Rodríguez"; (3-VIII-1844) "Contra Don José Villegas"; (6-XI-1846) "Contra Don José Franco"; (23-XII-1847) "Contra el Sargento Mayor Don Juan Cornejo"; and (15-III-1848), "Contra Miguel Pas."

86. Art. 145 (1826), Art. 155 (1828), Art. 155 (1834), Art. 158 (1839); Olivo, *Constituciones*, 103, 140, 180, 234.

87. *El Republicano*, Aug. 26, 1826, 173.

88. ARAR/CS/Crim (4-I-1830), "Don Toribio de Linares contra María Escalante"; (12-XII-

with insubordination to the governor of Chiguata, he claimed that he simply had been defending the rights of a poor Indian. Turning the charges around, Arenaza maintained that he had asked the governor: "Why are you coming to insult me in my house, do you not know that this is my sacred asylum?"[89]

In 1832, a group of youths pretending to be the police broke into the home of a shoemaker. The judge cut the case short, but the fiscal protested that the crime was serious: "Whatever the condition and wretchedness of the shoemaker Lázaro may be, and the poverty of his shack or house, it is a haven [*sagrado*] which should be considered according to the law as safe as that of the first magistrate of the Republic."[90] Diego Masías, a key political activist, turned the argument on its head. When charged with attacking the house of Gen. Blas Cerdeña, he asserted that "the breaking of two windows, whether they be those of a Grand Marshall or of a humble artisan, is not a matter to be heard in the courts of first instance."[91]

Finally, with the abolition of hereditary privileges and offices, the constitutions favored the interpretation of honor based upon merit. According to article 158 of the 1828 constitution: "All citizens may be admitted to public employment, without any difference except that of their talents and virtues."[92] Republican authorities, like their colonial predecessors, invoked their honor to legitimize their power; that honor, however, was no longer a birthright, but rather had to be earned from the estimation of the people. As the second prefect of Arequipa, Gen. Antonio Gutiérrez de La Fuente, put it: "The honorable man, within the sphere of his private life, works to make friends among a few: elevated to the rank of public man, he must aspire to become worthy of the consideration of all."[93]

The primary way that politicians earned their honor during the early years of the republic was in military service, that is, defending the honor of the nation. While the press and politicians were effusive in their praise of such

---

1832) "Contra Bernarda Torres y otras por haber herido a María Beltrán"; (6-III-1833) "Don Domingo Santayana contra el Gobernador de Uchumayo"; (17-IV-1833) "Contra Mateo Chávez por homicidio"; (26-V-1834) "Don Domingo Arias contra el Alcalde de Yanahuara"; (25-VIII-1838) "Juan Batista Puma y otros indígenas de Cayma quejan del Gobernador"; and ARAR/Pref (6-IV-1828), "Contra el Dr. Don Francisco Paula Paez por injurias a Feliciana Zegarra."

89. ARAR/CS/Crim (29-IX-1834), "Contra Don José Arenaza por injurias al Gobernador de Chiguata."

90. ARAR/CS/Crim (31-I-1833), "Contra Marcelino Esquivel y otros."

91. ARAR/Pref (10-I-1850), "Para descubrir los autores de la azonada."

92. Olivo, *Constituciones*, 140. See also a letter to the editor asserting that the use of titles was not "republican," in *El Republicano*, Dec. 31, 1825, 24.

93. *El Republicano*, June 27, 1829, 4.

leaders, military commanders were also sensitive to the pride of their troops. In speeches and proclamations, particularly those with a call to arms, leaders addressed Arequipeños as honorable and virtuous citizens.[94] Those who fought in battles, moreover, were rewarded with the right to wear special insignias, the inscription of their names in official books of "meritorious citizens," and membership in Legions of Honor.[95]

Honor, therefore, became linked to patriotism. But if high officers could claim such honor, so could many soldiers and militiamen. Although men in Arequipa evaded forced conscription, many enlisted voluntarily for temporary duty when the city was under attack, and they were ready to claim the rights that accompanied such services. In 1834, the governor and municipality of Sachaca charged Nicanor Chávez with insubordination for refusing to donate a mule to the army. Chávez claimed that prefect Pio Tristán had exempted him from such requisitions as a reward for sheltering soldiers from the enemy forces and helping to retake the city from General San Román. In defense of his claims, he presented a piece of paper on which Tristán had written: "The Governor of Tio shall treat with the highest consideration the citizen Nicanor Chávez, as he is a most honorable patriot."[96] Although the note also stated that Chávez should not be exempted from orders, the governor dropped the charges.

José Arenaza, in his dispute with the governor of Chiguata, said: "I am a Citizen, and I must look out for the unfortunate so that they are not abused, after having fought for the Law."[97] In 1836, a Bolivian officer allegedly provoked an argument when he shouted "that all the Arequipeños were Thieves who had stripped the army of Salaverry and the Bolivians." Shortly afterward he slapped Mariano Martín Cañoli, who retorted: "You must not realize that I am an honorable Citizen, and I have served the fatherland."[98]

As Cañoli's dispute with the Bolivian soldiers implies, Arequipeños also associated their honor as citizens in relation to foreigners. In the wake of

94. *El Republicano*, Mar. 7, 1835, 3–4; Mar. 14, 1835, 6; Dec. 19, 1835, 3–4; and Apr. 23, 1836, 4.

95. See decree of President Orbegoso published in *El Republicano*, Apr. 11, 1835, 1–2; and letter from the military command to the prefect in *El Republicano*, Oct. 8, 1836, 4–5. Compare with Jay M. Smith, "Honour, Royal Service, and the Cultural Origins of the French Revolution: Interpreting the Language of Army Reform, 1750–1788," *French History* 9, no. 3 (1995): 294–314.

96. ARAR/CS/Crim (27-V-1834), "Contra Don Nicanor Chávez por insultos al Gobernador y Municipalidad de Sachaca."

97. ARAR/CS/Crim (29-IX-1834), "Contra Don José Arenaza."

98. ARAR/CS/Crim (29-III-1836), "Contra Mariano Martín Cañoli por expresiones contra individuos Bolivianos del ejército."

independence, "Godo" (a disparaging term for Spaniard) was added to the repertoire of insults. After young Rafael Velarde got into an argument with Cristobal Guillermo Schutte, his father filed charges of injurias against the German merchant. Tying the "honor of the citizen" to his personal security, Jorge Velarde argued indignantly that Schutte's insults deserved rigorous punishment: "If the individuals of a nation have a duty to respect their compatriots, undoubtedly this obligation is even greater in a foreigner who comes to solicit our hospitality. His punishment will be a proof of our respectability and of the decorum which the Laws of a free people deserve. Those who are impudent will also know that they cannot insult with impunity the sons of Peru, without immediately receiving the appropriate punishment."[99] Foreigners were aware that their conduct was under special scrutiny. When an artisan from the United States accused an Irish colleague of theft, he also expressed concern that such behavior threatened the "acceptance and confidence" earned by Anglo citizens residing in the city.[100]

The transition to a republican system of government had set the groundwork for a new sense of national honor. Honor was no longer to be hereditary and hierarchical, but accessible to all citizens according to their merit. Only in this new context could a lawyer argue that "honor is not only tied to the wealthy and powerful, but also to the unfortunate."[101] Or, as another put it, "The people are convinced that it is good works and conduct that constitute nobility, not lineage or titles."[102]

Such ideas weakened colonial customs of deference. Just after independence, Don Manuel Diez Canseco filed charges against one of his tenants, Mariano Carbajal, for insulting and threatening him and his wife. He put down Carbajal's assertion that the rental contract was unfair to mere ignorance, but, indignant that the accusation had been made in front of his peons, he warned that with such an example, "the tenants [*colonos*] could break the bonds of obedience justly owed to their Patrons."[103] Regardless of how

---

99. ARAR/CS/Crim (15-XI-1834), "Don Jorge Velarde contra Don Cristobal Guillermo Schutte."

100. ARAR/CS/Crim (15-VI-1830), "Don Juan Hindman contra David Berri."

101. Pascual Francisco Suero, in ARAR/CS/Crim (15-V-1825), "Contra Julian Zegarra por cuchilladas a Hermenegilda Vera."

102. Mariano Prieto, in ARAR/CS/Crim (7-III-1838), "Entre Doña María Lizarraga y Doña Fernanda Iraula sobre recíprocas injurias."

103. ARAR/CS/Crim (11-X-1825), "Don Manuel Diez Canseco contra su arrendatario Mariano Carbajal por injurias." For a confrontation between humble farmers and two drunk and arrogant gentlemen, see ARAR/CS/Crim (5-X-1830), "Contra Jerónimo Barriga por homicidio."

many followed Carbajal's example, Diez Canseco's concerns were, undoubtedly, shared by other elites.

Similarly, republican authorities faced the challenge of maintaining order
in the midst of a perceived crime wave, with suspects claiming new civil
rights. The possibility of balancing the new egalitarian rhetoric with the need
for social control is suggested by the case of a man who claimed honor based
upon military service. In 1832, Lt. Felipe Escudero was sentenced to ten
years in prison for stealing a brooch and a candelabra while a guest at a party.
His lawyer appealed for a more lenient sentence, arguing that the crime was
not serious, and that after serving his country for eleven years, Escudero's
honor was damaged by the accusations. The fiscal countered that it was
precisely his honor that made the crime—which would have been of little
import if committed by a servant—so serious: "The more decorated a man
finds himself within the rank of his public career, the greater his reputation,
and the stronger the sentiments which remove him from committing certain
kinds of crimes. . . . The officer whose own honor and spirit do not
stimulate him to act well, is worth little for service to the Nation."[104]

The sentence was upheld by the superior court. The republican notion of
civic virtue, with its emphasis on military valor and public conduct, fit well
with the plebeian concept of hombría de bien, but the standards could be
raised. While the meaning of honor was being transformed from below, those
concerned with reestablishing order would try to move it closer to the
concept of respectability and self-discipline.[105]

104. ARAR/CS/Crim (27-V-1832), "Apelación de la causa contra el Alférez Don Felipe
Escudero por dos robos."

105. Judges in Buenos Aires were even more hesitant to uphold civil liberties. See Osvaldo
Barreneche, "Crime and the Administration of Justice in Buenos Aires, Argentina, 1785–1853"
(Ph.D. diss., University of Arizona, 1997). Although there are no comparable studies for this
period in Lima, later in the nineteenth-century, its judicial system was quite punitive; see Carlos
Aguirre, "Criminology and Prison Reform in Lima, Peru, 1860–1930" (Ph.D. diss., University
of Minnesota, 1996). Early republican politicians in Mexico used the term hombre de bien to
refer to the honorable middle class; see Costeloe, The Central Republic, 15–28; and Fernando
Escalante Gonzalbo, Ciudadanos imaginarios (Mexico City: El Colegio de México, 1992).
According to Michael Meranze, judicial sentencing moved from public shame to an emphasis on
individual discipline under the influence of liberalism; see Meranze, Laboratories of Virtue:
Punishment, Revolution, and Authority in Philadelphia, 1760–1835 (Chapel Hill: University of
North Carolina Press, 1996). For an analysis of how traditional honor codes were transformed
by the bourgeoisie in France, see Robert A. Nye, Masculinity and Male Codes of Honor in
Modern France (Oxford: Oxford University Press, 1993).

6

The Limits of Citizenship

Gender and Republican Morality

The transition from colony to nation was marked by two apparently contradictory trends in Arequipa. On the one hand, fearing instability and crime, republican officials increased the use of repressive force through a newly organized police and judicial system. On the other, political leaders and the press introduced a discourse of republicanism that decried tyranny and lauded constitutional rights. Mirroring the frequent rebellions and civil wars, then, were battles over the meanings of both old and new ideals. As part of their resistance to perceived abuses by the military and police, plebeians and their lawyers tried to hold the authorities to their word. In the process of claiming their rights as citizens, they transformed cherished values of honor, by shifting the emphasis away from status toward the more egalitarian concept of virtue. Although judges frequently recognized such claims, they simultaneously tried to reestablish social order by balancing rights with responsibilities. This chapter will explore these limits. Men were held to higher standards of "republican" morality, especially a strict work ethic. Those who could not qualify as proper heads of households—the unemployed, slaves, servants, and all women—were thereby excluded from citizenship.

Although the republican courts limited the ability of the police to arrest suspects by upholding the rights claimed by honorable citizens, justices were selective in identifying those worthy of protection. The constitutions justified this practice of making rights contingent upon responsibilities. Officially, only men who were either married or of majority age (which varied between twenty-one and twenty-five) and who either owned property or exercised an independent profession were granted the privileges of citizenship.[1] In addition to those excluded because of their sex, age, or economic status, notorious gamblers, drunkards, "and others who offend public morals with their scandalous life," were subject to suspension of their citizenship. Such a penalty was also imposed if one was undergoing criminal prosecution, or "for not having employment, an occupation or known way of life."[2] While such duties were codified at a national level, in Arequipa they became part of a dialectic to reinterpret honor. When plebeians claimed honor based upon their conduct, the authorities raised the standards of virtue.

Whereas colonial officials had withheld support from the church in its campaign against the "excesses" of popular culture, republican leaders were quickly converted to the need for a new morality in order to maintain social order. Gambling, although illegal, had been a popular pastime among both plebeians and "persons of honor" during the late colonial period, and authorities, for the most part, had looked the other way. In 1825, however, one of the first decrees emitted by the new prefect of Arequipa not only prohibited games of chance but described them in terms befitting a moral crusade. The vice of gambling, pronounced the preamble, "causes the loss of honor, rectitude and providence; it consumes the life which should be of benefit to the Nation; it upsets the order of public affairs and domestic obligations . . . and prostitutes reason until one sees as hateful the fate of the family, contemptible one's own, and indifferent that of the community."[3] There were also prohibitions against bullfights, cockfights, and fireworks, because they went against "the virtues and morals that should be upheld in a Republican Government."[4]

Whereas inebriation had been considered an extenuating circumstance in criminal cases during the colonial period, republican prosecutors and judges were less inclined to accept it as an excuse and might even consider it as an

1. Art. 17 (1823), Art. 14 (1826), Art. 4 (1828), Art. 3 (1834), Art. 8 (1839); Olivo, *Constituciones*, 38, 78, 110, 150, 205.
2. Art. 24 (1823), Art. 18 (1826), Art. 6 (1828), Art. 4 (1834), Art. 9 (1839); Olivo, *Constituciones*, 39, 79, 111, 151, 206.
3. BNP doc. D8478 (1825), "Bando prohibiendo el juego de azar."
4. Quoted in Villegas Romero, *Un decenio*, 445.

aggravating circumstance. As the fiscal pointed out in the case against Laurencio Salazar for wounding his wife, his drunken state "is one more crime that neither exempts him from the first nor deprives him of the reason to commit it."[5] There are indications that it was in this period that the taverns called chicherías, for the drink consumed in them, began to be referred to by their current name of *picanterías*, for the spicy food they served.[6] Such a change may have reflected the growing concern with respectability.

Finally, republican authorities expressed great alarm over matters related to sexuality. In an unusual case, a French merchant and his Peruvian partner were put on trial for selling "obscene" paintings that, according to the fiscal, would induce "immorality and corruption" and should, therefore, be burned. When their lawyer argued that the paintings were mythological representations similar to those hanging in the salons of Europe, the fiscal indignantly retorted that while such explicit styles might be popular in France, "such frankness is not used on our soil, where there are more pure and religious customs."[7]

French nationality probably also hurt the credibility of Don Carlos Lamarque, when it was discovered that young men were using his café to climb up on the roof and flirt with young women in the adjoining orphanage. The prefect impressed upon the judge the grave nature of the case, because "the seducers have perhaps succeeded in violating the sacred asylum of innocence and in carrying out their lewd and immoral plans." In addition to one-month of detention at the beginning of the trial, Lamarque was fined fifty pesos, in order to build a wall between the two establishments. He thereby narrowly avoided exile, which the fiscal had requested as "the best wall that could be erected."[8]

Had Bishop Chaves de La Rosa lived to see independence, he would have

---

5. ARAR/CS/Crim (30-XI-1852), "Contra Laurencio Salazar por graves heridas a su esposa." See also ARAR/CS/Crim (4-IV-1829), "Contra Manuela Chalcotupa"; (12-VI-1830) "Contra Juan Montoya"; (20-X-1831) "Contra Juan Galiano y Matías Bedoya"; (1-X-1832) "Contra Luis Barrionuevo"; (8-VII-1833) "Contra Julián Martínez"; (3-IX-1833) "Autos seguidos para indagar el autor del robo y heridas inferidas a Don Mariano Espinoza"; (8-I-1838) "Contra Francisco Chiri"; and (29-IX-1841), "Contra Mariano Torrico."

6. For references to picanterías, see ARAR/CS/Crim (27-VI-1834), "Contra José Rodríguez"; (1-II-1849) "Contra Pedro Origuela"; (30-XI-1852) "Contra Laurencio Salazar"; (12-I-1853) "Contra Juan de tal"; and ARAR/Pref (10-I-1850), "Causa criminal seguida para descubrir los autores de la azonada."

7. ARAR/CS/Crim (20-XI-1829), "Contra el Francés Don Alejandro Marsol y Don Mariano Parejo por haberse encontrado en la tienda del primero dos láminas obscenas."

8. ARAR/CS/Crim (18-IV-1853), "Contra Don Carlos Lamarque y cómplices por intento de raptar a una niña."

had no cause to complain of lack of support for his morality campaign. It was not unusual for judges to drop the charges against a defendant for theft or other crimes, for example, yet to impose a penalty or strict warning for carrying on an "illicit" relationship.[9] Indeed, republican judges and prosecutors often went beyond cooperation with the goals of the church, to usurp its role as the arbiter of morality. The secular courts, for example, increasingly heard cases of rapto, which previously would have been tried in ecclesiastical court. Nevertheless, the republican virtues enforced by the courts, like traditional honor codes, varied by sex. Women were more vulnerable to charges of illicit sexuality, while men, as potential citizens, were judged primarily by their conduct within the public sphere.

Hard-Working Citizens

The definition of virtue in Arequipa, as expressed by the official newspaper, drew upon classical republicanism: "Patriotism is a virtue for which man sacrifices all his personal interests to the larger general interest without any limitation: patriotism is the cooperation of the individual in the welfare and prosperity of the society to which he belongs."[10] Among those too humble to hold political office, civic virtue was demonstrated by courage and valor on the battlefield. In Arequipa, military service was both demanded by the state and used by men to justify their rights as citizens.

Nevertheless, there was increasing concern, especially among the region's landowners, that military conscription was contributing to a shortage of labor. Hard work, therefore, was promoted as another way that common citizens could contribute to the public good. As deputy Miguel Abril pointed out when the departmental junta considered draft exemptions for workers in numerous economic sectors: "The citizen with a hoe in his hand is as useful

---

9. ARAR/CS/Crim (20-VI-1831), "Contra Francisco Quiroz y Juana Rivadeneira por robos"; (8-X-1831) "Contra Dominga Rodríguez por haber herido a Antonia Espinoza"; (25-XI-1831) "Contra Victoriano Concha por robos"; (29-II-1832) "Contra Benedicto Muñós por heridas a Antonia Perula"; (12-VII-1832) "Contra María Samudio por heridas al soldado José Valdés"; (22-X-1832) "Contra María Cano por puñaladas a María Miranda"; (16-XI-1832) "Sobre la indagación de la persona que hirió a Bartolomé López"; (7-VI-1833) "Contra Antonio Cotera por el homicidio de José el Colombiano"; (27-XI-1834) "Contra Lucía Llerena por puñaladas a Francisco Rodríguez"; (22-I-1835) "Expediente seguido para averiguar el autor del homicidio de Mariano Trillo"; and ARAR/Pref (23-III-1838), "Contra Benito González por heridas a María del Rosario Condorpusa."

10. "Variedades," *El Republicano*, May 18, 1833, 2.

as he who grasps a sword to defend the Fatherland."[11] The editor of *El Republicano*, similarly, praised the prefect in 1834 for emphasizing the importance of work in his speech marking the anniversary of independence: "With lazy hands, there is nothing but backwardness, and even virtue itself is contemptible when it is not guided by industry and occupation useful to the individual and to the entire society."[12]

Republican authorities in Arequipa looked to a work ethic as one of the most important measures of male respectability, blending traditional expectations of patriarchs as providers and a rising liberal emphasis on labor discipline. And while plebeian men may not have accepted all elements of the new morality, such as temperance, they could take pride in being productive citizens.[13] As during the colonial period, plebeians still invoked their honor as a defense against charges of criminality, but there was a subtle change in their claims. Artisans and laborers bolstered their cases by references to their conduct, particularly their dedication to work, rather than claims to property or wealth.

In 1831, José María Madaleno and José Torres, men of color who had migrated to the city from the coast, were picked up by a patrol in Yanahuara as "suspicious" characters. They both claimed that they had "always maintained themselves with honor [hombría de bien], and by means of their labor." Their character witnesses vouched for their honorable conduct, and one gentleman testified that he had known Madaleno for three years as someone who worked on various farms. Despite their history of temporary jobs and general labor, the judge found them to be "honest men behaving themselves with honor and without any stain on their reputations." Indignant that they had suffered because of an unjust suspicion, he ordered their release, "restoring them to their former good reputations and fame."[14]

Juan Salazar, a zambo from Lima married to a slave in Arequipa, claimed

11. *El Republicano*, supplement to Aug. 29, 1829, 4.

12. "Aniversario de la independencia," *El Republicano*, Aug. 9, 1834, 7.

13. Compare with artisan republicanism; see Sean Wilentz, *Chants Democratic: New York City and the Rise of the American Working Class, 1788–1850* (Oxford: Oxford University Press, 1984); Allan Potofsky, "Work and Citizenship: Crafting Images of Revolutionary Builders, 1789–1791," in Renée Waldinger, Philip Dawson, and Isser Woloch, eds., *The French Revolution and the Meaning of Citizenship* (Westport, Conn.: Greenwood Press, 1993), 185–99; David Sowell, *The Early Colombian Labor Movement: Artisans and Politics in Bogotá, 1832–1919* (Philadelphia: Temple University Press, 1992); and Thomas Krüggeler, "Unreliable Drunkards or Honorable Citizens? Artisans in Search of their Place in the Cusco Society, 1825–1930" (Ph.D. diss., University of Illinois at Urbana-Champaign, 1993).

14. ARAR/Pref (21-XI-1831), "Expediente sobre investigarse la conducta de Ramón Llerena, José María Madaleno y José Torres."

that the charges of theft filed against him in 1836 by Don José León Dongo were libelous. Although trained as a shoemaker, Salazar had been reduced by hard times to working as a laborer in the warehouses of various foreign merchants. One of his character witnesses stated that he had, indeed, seen Salazar in one warehouse, "working with great honor."[15] It is striking that despite their African descent, all three of these men were recognized as honorable.

Although working people were experiencing greater regulation and surveillance of their lives in republican Arequipa, the courts were willing to protect them—and their honor—if they were self-supporting and met the norms of proper behavior. As the cases above demonstrate, judges could be indignant when working people were arrested on mere suspicions, but the opposite was also true. In 1831 Victoriano Concha, who previously had been cleared on charges of suspicious behavior, was arrested a second time for complicity in a theft. As in the earlier case, the prosecutor admitted that there was little evidence against him, but this time argued that his unemployment was proof enough. "A man without an occupation nor a known way of life," he pointed out, "will most likely transgress in all matters."[16] In a similar vein, when Enrique Nuñes complained that he had been illegally imprisoned, judge Pascual Francisco Suero retorted that he was a "vagrant, ne'er-do-well without an occupation, and therefore, not a citizen."[17]

Having employment was necessary, but was not always sufficient to clear a man of charges for vagrancy. The local police ordinances formulated by the prefect in 1835 included a lengthy definition of the term *vagrant*. Minors and those who were too old or disabled to work were not expected to be employed, but they could be arrested if they showed signs of laziness or scandalous conduct. Similarly, artisans and laborers were required not simply to work, but to do so diligently and under the supervision of their employers.[18] Such ambiguity gave leeway to local officials in targeting those residents whom they regarded as undesirable. The military conscription board in the suburban village of Sachaca, for example, was about to hold a lottery because there were no vagrants to draft, when the governor identified Mariano García as without a job or family. The other members agreed,

15. ARAR/CS/Crim (12-X-1836), "Don José León Dongo contra Juan Salazar por robo."
16. ARAR/CS/Crim (25-XI-1831), "Contra Victoriano Concha por robos."
17. ARAR/CS/Crim (2-IX-1826), "Enrique Nuñes contra el Juez de Derecho Pascual Francisco Suero por abusar su autoridad."
18. Art. 64 of the "Reglamento de Policía," *El Republicano*, Nov. 28, 1835, 3.

"according to public opinion and for having witnessed him commit acts foreign to an honorable man that he was a harmful individual in the population."[19] In fact, when they went to capture García, he was irrigating his employer's farm.

Race was one of the factors coloring perceptions of who had the proper work ethic. When the departmental junta considered measures to address the labor shortage, the debate on whether to force Indians to work in the mines was particularly long and heated. Most of the deputies subscribed to the stereotype of Indians as "inclined toward idleness, apathetic, and with only the need to provide themselves a scant and coarse nourishment."[20] Although some expressed the concern that such a measure would violate personal liberty, all agreed that laziness was the "mother of all vices" and that "the Laws required men to be dedicated to their work, and not to idleness, which was the germ of demoralization."[21] Only Miguel Abril, who represented the province of Caylloma, with its large indigenous population, argued that Indians were not lazy and worked when they were paid and treated well. Acknowledging that some abuses had occurred with forced labor in the past, the deputies unanimously passed a resolution that called upon local authorities to make sure that all Indians, as well as vagrants of other races, worked or were drafted—but also to ensure that they were properly paid.[22]

Further responses to the new work ethic—and, possibly, to the labor shortage as well—were the sentences passed out by the courts. Public works had always been one penalty, but the republican courts proposed it as an opportunity for rehabilitation as well as punishment. Such sentences were especially favored for juvenile delinquents in the hope that, by learning a useful trade, they would mend their ways and forsake a life of crime. When thirteen-year-old José Benavides was sentenced to six years' service on a naval ship, his lawyer appealed, arguing that such a punishment would corrupt rather than reform the boy. The superior court apparently agreed: it reduced Benavides's sentence to three years of labor in the hospital run by the order of San Juan de Dios, "so that at the same time that he is providing this service, he shall be instructed in the art of pharmacy to which his Parents had dedicated him, according to their oral deposition." The justices further

19. ARAR/CS/Crim (13-V-1852), "Contra Don Pedro Antonio Zenteno por heridas a Mariano García."

20. El Republicano, Oct. 3, 1829, 3–4.

21. El Republicano, supplement to Oct. 10, 1829, 1.

22. Ibid., 1–2.

ordered the administrator and chaplain of the hospital to oversee the boy's conduct, not allow him to go out onto the streets, and instruct him daily in Christian doctrine.[23]

Justices also took the new step of assigning defendants to work for a master artisan or in an "honorable" house. In 1836 three apprentice tailors, ages twelve to fourteen, were charged with robbing their own master; two of them faced sentences of six months and a year of labor in the hospital. Appealing to the justices' "enlightened" outlook, their lawyer argued that they could better be turned into useful citizens by assigning them to another master tailor, known for his character and good conduct: "Dedicated to their work, there will be engendered in them a love for the conservation of their good names . . . and they will be taught modesty and delicacy."[24] Once again the superior court was persuaded by such an argument: the justices reduced the boys' sentences to thirty and sixty days of public labor, after which they were to be turned over to a master tailor.

Furthermore, the justices' belief in rehabilitation even extended to adults. When Melchor Randes stole some cloth from a petty merchant in 1831, he was originally sentenced to six years in prison. The superior court reduced his punishment to four months of public works, after which time "he shall only be able to leave jail by presenting an honorable person who will take responsibility to teach him a useful way of life, and give him an occupation." If no one was found, his sentence would be increased to two years.[25]

Defense lawyers were quick to catch on to this possibility of commuting their clients' sentences, but the strategy did not always work. In 1836 Pedro Morales, like Randes, was convicted of stealing a trunk of merchandise from a petty vendor in the plaza. His lawyer, arguing that he was a simple laborer with an otherwise clean record, asked that he be turned over to a master shoemaker and that his salary be docked to reimburse the plaintiff. The prosecutor countered that the crime was particularly serious precisely because "he committed the theft in spite of exercising the occupation of shoemaker, the earnings of which are sufficient to satisfy his needs." The defense persisted by appealing the initial sentence of one year of public works, on the grounds that "Morales is dedicated to his work of shoemaking with which he subsists and supports himself, his profession is recognized

---

23. ARAR/CS/Crim (13-VIII-1831), "Contra José Benavides por hurto."

24. ARAR/CS/Crim (5-X-1836), "Contra Narciso Castillo y demás cómplices por robo."

25. ARAR/CS/Crim (4-X-1831), "Contra Melchor Randes por robo." See also ARAR/CS/Crim (12-VII-1831), "Contra Marcelo Paredes por cuchillada a Mariano Perea."

[*conocida*] and honorable." Instead, the superior court increased his sentence to two years, which he served out in the army.[26] Morales did not fit the court's image of an honest working man, and, therefore, his case stirred little sympathy.

If plebeian men had always thought of themselves as hombres de bien, elites in Arequipa were only gradually brought around to the idea of honor based upon work. In the colonial period, authorities acknowledged that it was better at least to have a job, even a "base and low" one, than to lead a life of idleness and vagrancy. Some people even deigned to call manual occupations "honest," if not quite "honorable." After independence, such references became increasingly frequent. Because working the land had never been associated with dishonor to the same extent as other kinds of labor, it was easier for elites to recognize the honor of Arequipa's numerous small farmers. In 1829, for example, the departmental junta praised "our honorable labradores . . . They truly eat the bread that they acquire at the cost of the sweat of their brows; and in their laborious lives, which do not allow them rest, they maintain themselves in virtue and honor."[27] Increasingly, other workers, too, were recognized as honorable, but not without a burden of responsibility. By rewarding those men who worked hard and tried to stay out of trouble, the protections of citizenship could help to reestablish order and stabilize the economy.

While the rights of plebeian citizens were contingent upon their conduct, there were classes of people who were excluded despite their hard work. The Peruvian constitutions, like most in this period, required citizens at least to exercise an independent profession and, in some cases, to own property or pay taxes. The charter of 1823 explicitly added that citizens must work "without subjection to another in the class of servant or day laborer."[28] Such dependents, after all, had also been excluded from the code of honor. Although race did not officially determine citizenship status, the exclusion of servants fell disproportionately on those of African or indigenous descent.

Slaves were denied not only the active rights of citizens, but also the protections officially granted to all Peruvians. They did not even have the opportunity to gain their freedom through military service, a promise that had often been made during the wars of independence.[29] The credit for those

26. ARAR/CS/Crim (28-II-1836), "Contra Pedro Morales por robo."
27. *El Republicano*, Oct. 24, 1829, 2.
28. Art. 17; Olivo, *Constituciones*, 38.
29. Order of commander Ramón Castilla in *El Republicano*, Apr. 18, 1835, 1.

who did fight went, instead, to the masters who had "volunteered" them, like the "meritorious citizen" praised by the prefect in the official newspaper for such a "philanthropic deed."[30] The defense of the institution of slavery within a republican system was so strong that the list of atrocities committed by an enemy force included "the violent extraction of the slaves, leaving the haciendas abandoned and their owners terrified."[31]

The denial of rights to slaves was straightforward, but the freedom of even domestic servants was ambiguous. In 1845, the police reported that they had discovered a "free" boy chained inside a house, "contrary to our institutions and laws." Yet the same justices who could be so indignant when a man was whipped or imprisoned without proof decided that this case was not serious. The twelve-year-old servant, Mariano Parra, had been born in the highlands but raised in the household where he worked. His employers had put the chain on him when they left town because they believed he had stolen from them and were afraid he would run away. Ignoring the caretaker's testimony that the mistress had given explicit instructions to keep the boy chained, the fiscal proposed that what appeared like a "misdemeanor against humanity and the laws" was more likely an oversight. The judge dropped the charges and even ordered that the chain be returned, with a simple warning to report servants who committed serious crimes to the proper authorities for punishment.[32]

Judicial officials displayed a similar lack of concern in the case of a young servant who was stolen from one master and sold to another. Following the fiscal's advice that "the laws have been mitigated" in such matters, the judge released the kidnapper.[33] Race was not the only factor, for in other cases, Indians were granted rights.[34] Nevertheless, the status of both of the above boys as highland Indians, when combined with their youth and dependent positions, likely allayed any qualms that the republican justices may have had in denying them the protections granted to other Peruvians.

Gender was another factor limiting the freedom of domestic servants. Even while defending the right of young women to choose their employers, justices revealed an underlying ambivalence. When Petronila Fuentes com-

30. *El Republicano*, Mar. 28, 1829, 2.

31. "Arequipeños," proclamation of the prefect dated Dec. 10, 1835 (Imprenta del Gobierno por Pedro Benavides), 1. Distributed with *El Republicano*, Dec. 12, 1835.

32. ARAR/CS/Crim (5-VII-1845), "Contra Doña Martina Hurtado por tener un menor con cadena al pie."

33. ARAR/CS/Crim (22-XII-1844), "Contra Gregorio Gonzales por plagio."

34. ARAR/CS/Crim (27-IX-1843), "El Gobernador de Cayma Mariano Paz denuncia al Juez de Paz Juan Bautista Puma por abusos de autoridad."

plained that her employer was trying to force her to remain in her service, for example, the fiscal was quick to support her rights as a free person over the age of eighteen. When Fuentes disappeared, however, the same fiscal demurred that "it should not be allowed that she go about on her own account without being subject to some person who will provide her shelter and protection at an age which still requires another's care and direction."[35] In a similar case, the defender of minors supported the right of a young woman to choose her employer but argued that she must be under the protection of a guardian, "especially when her age and sex puts her at many risks."[36] Clearly the implied risks were sexual, but the concern was likely not only to guard the virtue of poor Indian girls, but also to protect society from women in public who were free from control.

Constitutional protections applied to independent citizens as they acted in the public sphere, but these rights did not extend to the private realm, where patriarchs continued to rule over their dependents. As the fiscal of the superior court argued with respect to the law prohibiting the use of the whip: "It does not penetrate into the domestic household nor put limits on paternal authority."[37] No amount of hard work, therefore, could earn domestic servants the rights of other laborers.

While class and race contributed to the evaluation of who qualified as proper citizens, only slaves and women were excluded as groups regardless of their conduct and status. The justification of women's inherent dependence upon patriarchal authority was a political fiction, given the large numbers of self-supporting women from various classes.[38] But that fiction was compelling enough, in legal deliberations, to render insignificant apparent contradictions. The fiscal's decision cited above, limiting the prohibition of lashes to public establishments, arose not from the punishment of a servant but from accusations that the teacher of a girls' school was whipping her students; presumably, parental consent for such punishment and the students' sex made the school an extension of the domestic realm.

35. ARAR/CS/Crim (22-X-1836), "Petronila Fuentes queja de Doña Getrudis Lisardi por forzarla a quedarse en su servicio."

36. ARAR/CS/Crim (8-I-1841), "Denuncia de Manuela Ampuero contra Doña Petronila Olazabal por falta de pago por su servicio."

37. ARAR/CS/Crim (26-VI-1854), "Contra Doña Carlota La Rosa por haber castigado a sus alumnas."

38. For a similar situation in the United States, see Joan R. Gundersen, "Independence, Citizenship, and the American Revolution," *Signs* 13, no. 1 (1987): 59–77; and Elaine R. Crane, "Dependence in the Era of Independence: The Role of Women in a Republican Society," in Jack P. Greene, ed., *The American Revolution: Its Character and Limits* (New York: New York University Press, 1987), 253–75.

Even though they were denied the rights of citizenship, moreover, women were still expected to meet higher standards of respectability after independence. Theoretically relegated to the private sphere, women in the republic actually found their behavior subject to increasing public scrutiny as officials attempted to curb their influence in neighborhood society and popular culture.

Republican Mothers and Public Women

The linkage of citizenship with honor circumscribed women's place within republican discourse. Compared to its male counterpart, female honor underwent only subtle transformations after independence: women continued to be judged primarily by their sexual purity and domestic virtue. When Doña María Rivera died in 1829, after supervising the foundling home for forty years, a full-page obituary praised her as an example of proper womanhood. At the age of twenty-one she had shut herself off from the world, to dedicate herself entirely to the care of infants whose own mothers had given them up to save their honor: "Austere with herself, sensitive and tender with the family given to her by Christian charity, never was there noted in her that hardness often produced by the effort of closing off the heart to the emotions of love. So it is that she has been the model, not the imitator of maternal tenderness."[39] Notables from the municipality and the church attended her funeral to pay their last respects to this "virtuous" woman.

On the one hand, this tribute reveals a particularly conservative notion of honor, by depicting the ideal woman as both virgin and mother. Nevertheless, it also suggests that women could put their domestic skills to use for the public good.[40] Like mothers, professional women could care for orphans or teach children. One proposal for a private girls' school mirrored the family structure, with a married couple serving as the directors.[41] While women had

39. *El Republicano*, Jan. 17, 1829, 4. See also obituary of María Moscoso y Pérez in *El Republicano*, Apr. 20, 1833, 7.
40. Compare with Linda K. Kerber, *Women of the Republic: Intellect and Ideology in Revolutionary America* (Chapel Hill: University of North Carolina Press, 1980); and Arrom, *The Women of Mexico City*, 259–66.
41. AGN, R. J. (Ministerio de Justicia): Prefectura de Arequipa, Culto, Leg. 143 (1832).

performed such functions before independence, their services gained a new recognition, provided they fulfilled them in an "enlightened" manner. When Doña Cipriana Dueñas advertised her services as a midwife, for example, she emphasized her lengthy professional training in Lima.[42] A local doctor supported her claims and encouraged the women of Arequipa to use her services, "so recommended by modesty and decency and the satisfaction of her knowledge as opposed to the inexperienced women who arrogate this title with nothing but their will, and whom have been tolerated due to the absolute lack of anyone with even some training."[43]

This philosophy of "republican motherhood" comes through most clearly in female education. When young women from two schools demonstrated their mathematical ability before local notables in 1833, the official newspaper covered the events with long and enthusiastic articles. Although the students humbly apologized in advance for the errors they might commit, the reporter was impressed by their skill and "their dedication to a difficult and abstract science which seems reserved for the profound meditations and arduous investigations of the sex endowed with robustness and strength."[44] Both the reporter and the students, in their speeches, contrasted the education of colonial women—limited to learning the rudiments of reading and writing by rote rather than "reflection"—to the new, enlightened curriculum. Nevertheless, the goal was still to prepare them to better fulfill their traditional roles. The lack of education in the colonial period, Rosa Amat pointed out, had made the weak sex a "victim of perversity" and "motive of corruption," who substituted frivolous pleasures for the "true merit of being good wives and mothers."[45] Even arithmetic, pointed out another student, was "necessary for domestic order."[46]

Extending a domestic metaphor into the public realm, the reporter noted that "the Prefect General offered to the spectators the appealing picture of a family patriarch surrounded by his children."[47] During the colonial period, the monarch had been depicted as a father to all his subjects, but in the

42. "Aviso," *El Republicano,* July 11, 1835, 4.

43. "Aviso" signed by the *teniente protomédico* Dr. Juan Manuel Vargas, *El Republicano,* Sept. 5, 1835, 4.

44. "Relación del exámen de aritmética y cálculo analógico en la Universidad de San Agustín," *El Republicano,* supplement to Nov. 23, 1833, 2.

45. Ibid., 4.

46. "Colejio de Educandas," *El Republicano,* Sept. 14, 1833, 5.

47. "Relación del exámen de aritmética y cálculo analógico en la Universidad de San Agustín," *El Republicano,* supplement to Nov. 23, 1833, 2.

republic it was primarily women and children who were under the paternal care of the state. Pupil Juliana Sanches echoed the familial theme in her address to the gathered officials: "Under your auspices, the fair sex will not be, no, a group contemptible for its ignorance, but rather, adorned with knowledge and virtues, it will be the compass that guides the domestic ship along the path of honor, inspiring in the family sentiments of justice and religion."[48]

Though praising their mathematical abilities, moreover, the articles dwelled more on the beauty, modesty, and purity of the students. Indeed, as noteworthy as their earlier efforts at the blackboard was their performance at the banquets given in their honor by the prefect, where the young women, "with their decency and neatness, and their dexterity in the handling of the table setting, gave an idea of the care of their breeding and to their belonging to people of Quality."[49] Such skills were more important than book learning, to many parents; in defending the disciplinary methods of the female teacher accused of whipping her students, several parents praised her particularly for teaching their daughters manners.[50]

Just as the reformed role of women was to nurture republican virtues in members of their families, there were occasions when they were called upon to extend this inspirational role into the public sphere.[51] The editor of *El Republicano* advocated the introduction of French-style salons, where "the ladies distinguish with their esteem only he who demonstrates the most ingenuity and judgment in the resolution of difficult problems."[52] Descriptions of civic celebrations never failed to highlight the presence of the "fair sex," who cried out praises of the parading heroes, threw flowers from balconies, and—in virginal choirs—sang patriotic anthems.[53] Though women had also cheered on royal holidays, they were now admonished by the municipality (rather than the bishop) to adopt a more austere, republican appearance: "Luxury in public functions, the profusion, the disorder in the

48. "Colejio de Educandas," *El Republicano*, Sept. 14, 1833, 4.

49. "Relación del exámen de aritmética y cálculo analógico en la Universidad de San Agustín," *El Republicano*, supplement to Nov. 23, 1833, 3.

50. ARAR/CS/Crim (26-VI-1854), "Contra Doña Carlota La Rosa por haber castigado a sus alumnas."

51. Compare with Ruth H. Bloch, "The Gendered Meanings of Virtue in Revolutionary America," *Signs* 13, no. 1 (1987): 37–58; and Mary P. Ryan, *Women in Public: Between Banners and Ballots, 1825–1880* (Baltimore: Johns Hopkins University Press, 1990).

52. "Estadística," *El Republicano*, Dec. 9, 1826, 234.

53. *El Republicano*, supplement to Dec. 12, 1825, 1; July 26, 1834, 1; Feb. 28, 1835, 7–8; Oct. 3, 1835, 4; Nov. 17, 1838, 2; and Dec. 1, 1838, 2.

dresses of the fair sex, and the tendency toward capricious variety with which the Ladies sometimes insist upon presenting themselves, are fatal obstacles that interfere with the republican character, obstruct prosperity, and hide those charms in which rest good taste. Moderation, decency, and simple uniformity, on the other hand, make up the harmonious enchantment, order and domestic comfort that make society appealing."[54] That this appeal was, apparently, issued in response to their behavior at an earlier event also serves as a reminder that women did not always conduct themselves in the orderly fashion stipulated by the authorities.[55]

While the inspirational role was largely passive, women occasionally took the initiative in making public critiques. The official newspaper, particularly in the early years of the republic, published letters to the editor with myriad complaints about the corruption or inefficiency of government officials. The rare missives signed by women addressed issues of morality and decorum. In 1834 a woman, lamenting that her son had been reduced to stealing silver spoons from his parents to buy lottery tickets, declared: "The Government should not ignore the petition of a poor mother to prohibit such a pernicious game and thereby prevent that so many unwary sons lose their way."[56]

In 1828 the arrival of a theater company was welcomed by the local elite, who aspired to make their city more civilized. But the hopes of many, judging by the letters to the editor, were dashed.[57] Amid complaints of their lack of refinement and skill, the sole woman to contribute her opinion—"La Arequipeña"—limited herself to criticizing men in the audience for smoking, "with discredit to our country and serious annoyance to all those in attendance and particularly the women."[58] Extending to a new medium women's capacity to reform behavior through "gossip," she threatened to publish the names of those who continued.

Women also played a role—albeit a limited one—in the political sphere. Once again they were, officially, to serve primarily as an inspiration to men. Soldiers were exhorted to arms with promises that their sacrifices would be "rewarded with the civic crown of laurels woven by the lovely hands of

54. *El Republicano*, Dec. 3, 1825, 4–5.

55. *El Republicano*, Dec. 17, 1825, 2.

56. *El Republicano*, Sept. 27, 1834, 4. Since letters were published under pseudonyms, it may have been written by a man; if so, it would still illustrate the license given to women to critique public morals.

57. *El Republicano*, Apr. 12, 1828, 65; May 31, 1828, 95; June 21, 1828, 110; Aug. 2, 1828, 135; Oct. 4, 1828, 3; Nov. 1, 1828, 5–6; and Nov. 22, 1828, 4.

58. *El Republicano*, June 14, 1828, 107.

Arequipa's fair sex."[59] Conversely, the specter of what would happen to their wives and children at the hands of the enemy was invoked as a negative incentive.[60] Women were praised, if not called upon, for their financial contributions—most commonly, the symbolic as well as valuable donation of their jewels—to the cause of a particular faction.[61]

In rare cases, women even participated actively in military movements. In 1839, with the restoration of Agustín Gamarra to power, Doña Antonia Torreblanca requested compensation for her services to his cause over the previous five years. She related how she had infiltrated enemy troops under the pretext of selling them food. Then, "in spite of the weakness of my sex and my impotence," she claimed to have crawled on her hands and knees to avoid gunfire and crossed the river in the middle of the night, in order to relay urgent information. Finally, she had solicited donations from "the ladies who I knew were with our party," in order to serve food to the wounded soldiers in the hospital. After several military commanders testified to the truth of her claims, Torreblanca was rewarded with one hundred pesos.

Though an extreme case, Torreblanca's actions and words reveal both the potential and the limitations of women's participation in the republican public sphere. Even if it was economic need that motivated her to request compensation, her account bespeaks a pride in her services and a desire for their recognition. Nevertheless, though she must have heard political rhetoric in numerous speeches, Torreblanca never appropriated the language of republicanism nor of citizenship. Although the prefect remarked upon her "ardent and praiseworthy patriotism," she simply stated that "my spirit and my heart have always been decided on behalf of the present regime so just and beneficent to the fatherland."[62]

Though surprising in this context, the failure to identify women, even figuratively, as citizens or republicans was typical. While the female superior of the foundling home was eulogized solely for her maternal virtues, for example, the priest with whom she served was paid homage as a "good patriot" and "virtuous citizen," dedicated to national independence and

59. Speech by Bruno Murga, *El Republicano*, Aug. 22, 1835, 4.

60. *El Republicano*, July 28, 1838, 4; and Dec. 1, 1838, 2.

61. *El Republicano*, supplement to Mar. 8, 1834, 2; and "Gran Parada del Ejército" (Arequipa: Imprenta del Gobierno, Apr. 29, 1835). Distributed with *El Republicano*, May 2, 1835.

62. AGN, P.L. 19-105 (1839), "El Prefecto de Arequipa acompaña el expediente seguido por Doña Antonia Torreblanca." Seven years earlier, a woman with the same name was charged with theft; see ARAR/CS/Crim (15-II-1832), "Contra Antonia Torreblanca por hurto."

republican institutions.[63] Although some women had been involved in the wars of independence at the national level, they never called for political inclusion in the new state, and male politicians never raised the issue of female suffrage.[64] Either it did not occur to most women to identify themselves as citizens or they realized that such claims would have fallen on deaf ears, as not only the constitutions but the entire discourse of honorable citizenship excluded them.

Instead, women probably realized that they could use the language of domesticity to better advantage. María Seballos, a self-declared merchant, claimed ignorance of a new regulation against distilling alcohol, "as a woman who does not deal with anyone and lives withdrawn in the refuge and care of her family."[65] Despite her rhetoric, her account reveals that she had not heard of the new order because she was away on business, having left her children with tenants in her house.

In a description of her own aunt, Flora Tristan commented ironically on the importance of appearances: "Joaquina's great gift is to persuade everybody, even her husband, shrewd as he is, that she knows nothing, that she is concerned only with her children and her household. Her great piety, her humble and submissive air, the kindness with which she speaks to the poor, the interest she shows in the unimportant people who greet her in the street, all make her seem a modest woman without ambition."[66]

One need not share Tristan's cynicism, nor question the sincerity of women who espoused an ideology of domesticity, to recognize that elite

---

63. "Necrología" of Luís Agustín de La Gala, *El Republicano*, Feb. 9, 1833, 6.

64. A woman in Cuzco who was awarded a pension for her services during independence was still trying to get full payment in 1849; see AGN P.L. 6-285 (1826), "Doña Juana Noín solicita una pensión." Compare with Cherpak, "The Participation of Women in the Independence Movement," 219–234. In Venezuela, where women had been more active in the wars of independence, they did call themselves citizens; see Díaz, "*Ciudadanas* and *Padres de Familia*," 245–88. Nowhere in this period did women win suffrage, but in France women did raise the issue; see William Sewell, "Le Citoyen/la citoyenne: Activity, Passivity, and the Revolutionary Concept of Citizenship," in Colin Lucas, ed., *The Political Culture of the French Revolution* (London: Pergamon Press, 1988), 105–23; the essays in Harriet B. Applewhite and Darline G. Levy, eds., *Women and Politics in the Age of Democratic Revolution* (Ann Arbor: University of Michigan Press, 1990); and Darline G. Levy, "Women's Revolutionary Citizenship in Action, 1791: Setting the Boundaries," in *The French Revolution and the Meaning of Citizenship* (Westport, Conn.: Greenwood Press, 1993), 169–84.

65. ARAR/Pref (16-I-1841), "Contra Doña Francisca Bedoya por la destilación de aguardiente." She rented the still from Ceballos.

66. Tristan, *Peregrinations of a Pariah*, 138–39.

women had a degree of latitude in according their words with their actions.[67] While republican discourse actually increased the standards by which female honor was to be judged, it did, at least, reward virtuous ladies, if not with citizenship, with the right to an education and a recognition of their social value as mothers and arbiters of morality.

While plebeian men asserted their inclusion in the discourse of honorable citizenship, poor women rarely spoke the language of republican mother-hood. Whereas men met and communicated in the work place, the military corps, and the tavern, there were few opportunities, outside of household service, for dialogue among women of different classes. Only families with substantial means could afford to send their daughters to school, where they would be exposed to the new ideas. Even if plebeian women were aware of the subtle shifts in gender ideology, moreover, most forms of employment made it difficult to maintain even the appearance of being retiring keepers of the home and family. Although poor women probably did not accept elite stereotypes, challenging them within the official discourse of republicanism was not an effective strategy.

Poor women had difficulty living up to the image of the republican mother and, therefore, in claiming their parental rights. When her daughter ran away from home and took refuge with her employer, Catalina Aquina filed charges of rapto, claiming that "he has inflicted upon me a violent dispossession, depriving me of the maternal authority conceded to me by the Nature of the laws." But by hiring her daughter out, countered the justice of the peace and the defender of minors, she had exposed the girl to moral corruption and even prostitution. And in profiting from her daughter's labor, they contin-ued, she failed to show the affections of a mother or to "fulfill the duties given her by Nature."[68] In this case the judge, ultimately, upheld the right of Aquina to decide where her daughter should live, but other women were not as fortunate. María Dolores Alcoser was awarded a small pension from the father of her illegitimate daughter, only to have him win a countersuit for custody of the child that he still refused to recognize as his own. To bolster his case, he asserted that as a chichera, Alcoser would likely exploit her

---

67. Amanda Vickery warns against accepting the ideology of domesticity as reflective of women's real lives; see Vickery, "Golden Age to Separate Spheres? A Review of the Categories and Chronology of English Women's History," *Historical Journal* 36, no. 2 (1993): 383–414.

68. ARAR/CS/Crim (17-VIII-1849), "Catalina Aquina contra Don José Santos López por rapto."

daughter's labor, raise her on leftovers and chicha, and expose her to immoral and uneducated people.[69]

The claims of motherhood, similarly, failed to move justices to grant clemency to women convicted of crimes. After serving half of a year's sentence to work in the hospital, María Toledo petitioned for an early release, based upon her good behavior. She appealed especially as an "anguished "mother," whose abandoned children were missing her "caresses" and support.[70] Her request was denied. Juana Pía, convicted of several thefts in 1833, similarly failed to win over the court because she did not live up to the proper norms of womanhood. In an attempt to play upon the justices' sympathies, her lawyer asked mercy for her six children, who, if they lost their mother's support, "would contract a powerful germ of corruption, of idleness and of worse habits than those of lifting items belonging to others." But the fiscal, pointing out that Pía had been unable to support her children even when not in jail, convinced the judges to distance them from their mother's bad example by assigning them, instead, to workshops and domestic service, "in order to avoid in this way a race of bandits."[71]

Not only was it difficult for poor women to base claims upon their rights or duties as mothers, but the mitigating factors used by plebeian men were also denied them. A work ethic failed to redeem women, since their virtue depended upon fulfilling their domestic roles. When Toledo requested an early release, for example, she pointed out that she supported her children on the income she earned as an agricultural laborer. Just months before her request was denied, the sentence of an "honorable" man was reduced on the appeal of his wife, who pointed out that he provided for her and their two children.[72] The role of hardworking provider was reserved for men.

Because women who committed crimes were seen as "unnatural," officials were also less sanguine about their potential rehabilitation. An editorial in *El Republicano* asserted that female prisoners should work not because they would be reformed, but "so that they are not consumed by a sedentary life,

69. AAA/Civ (14-IV-1847), "Seguido por Doña María Dolores Alcoser sobre la filiación de sus hijos"; and (31-III-1849), "Seguido por Don Carlos Arebato sobre que Doña María Dolores Alcoser le entregue su hija natural." Although initiated in ecclesiastical court, the sentences were passed in secular courts.

70. Petition dated Oct. 31, 1845, filed incorrectly with a different case; see ARAR/CS/Crim (3-VIII-1843), "Contra Manuel Gutiérrez por la quiebra fraudulenta."

71. ARAR/CS/Crim (3-VIII-1843), "Contra Juana Pía por robos."

72. Petitions of Borja Cosme dated June 21 and 25, 1845, filed incorrectly with a different case, ARAR/CS/Crim (3-VIII-1843), "Contra Manuel Gutiérrez por la quiebra fraudulenta."

so that they feel in some way the punishment of their crime, so that their passions are not encouraged believing [their crimes] forgotten, and so that the public will have proof that crimes will not increase from impunity or misunderstood compassion."[73] Such a view of women prevented Pía's lawyer from winning her even a transfer from working in the jail to the hospital. The fiscal argued that she had become a habitual thief "due to the perversity of a corrupted heart," and that she would, therefore, "put that holy place in disorder, continuing in her habits and scandalizing the institution."[74]

While men could appeal to their role in defending the nation, military service usually dishonored women—with rare exceptions, such as Torreblanca—because of the assumption that their morals would be corrupted. Despite the critical support that they provided to the troops and their occasional participation in combat, the female camp followers (*rabonas*) were more likely to be scorned than appreciated. The stewards of San Francisco, constrained, perhaps, from complaining about the soldiers quartered in their monastery, did protest to the prefect that "the women who have followed said troops have made the above cited cemetery their permanent home and place of their disorders."[75] According to Flora Tristan, several generals had tried to prohibit women from accompanying the troops, but the soldiers had always rebelled, fearing that the army would be unable to provide for their needs.[76]

Given the difficulty of meeting the high standards of honor and virtue after independence, plebeian women bore the brunt of efforts to enforce the new morality.[77] While it is unlikely that their behavior changed in any significant way, their sexuality was increasingly seen as a threat to public order. When María Samudio was arrested for assaulting her lover, soldier José Valdez, even the prosecutor considered the wounds so inconsequential that the charges should be dropped. He argued, nevertheless, that Samudio should be punished for her loose morals, and that the prefect should take stern measures against women like her, because "this type of crime is repeated daily due to the toleration of the public immorality of these women, who abandoning

73. *El Republicano*, Aug. 24, 1833, 6. See also ARAR/CS/Crim (4-VII-1853), "Contra Marta Cuadros por haber matado a su hijo."

74. ARAR/CS/Crim (3-VIII-1843), "Contra Juana Pía."

75. Petition dated Dec. 29, 1828, in AGN, R.J. (Ministerio de Justicia): Prefectura de Arequipa, Culto, Leg. 143.

76. Tristan, *Peregrinations of a Pariah*, 180.

77. Compare with Christine Stansell, *City of Women: Sex and Class in New York, 1789–1860* (Urbana and Chicago: University of Illinois Press, 1987).

modesty, social considerations, and family obligations, have the impudence to present themselves in public as prostituted persons."[78] The superior court ordered that Samudio be sent home to the port of Arica, with the expressed hope that this separation would end her relationship with Valdez. Additionally, by exiling Samudio, the judges both punished her and rid the city of what they considered her immoral influence.

Similarly, a female target of violence evoked little sympathy if she did not meet elite standards of respectability. When Benedicto Muñós was arrested for stabbing his lover, Antonia Perula, for example, the prosecutor did not believe the charges were much cause for concern, particularly as the fault lay with Perula for her "long concubinage with the aggressor."[79] In some cases, the apparent victim could be recast as the delinquent. When petty vendor Felipa Galdos accused the child of a merchant of stealing a piece of fruit, the indignant father allegedly struck her with a stick, breaking her arm. Although he was initially fined twenty-five pesos to cover her medical expenses, the fiscal requested that the money be paid to the court and that Galdos be made to apologize publicly, "because otherwise, her constant provocations and insults having been fully proved, she would be rewarded instead of punished."[80] Women may have resisted police repression as much as did men, but, given the difficulties of appropriating the language of republicanism, they likely did so primarily through informal channels that were not recorded in official sources.

The differential treatment of men and women by the republican authorities is further exemplified by the official attitude toward domestic violence, which, as we have seen, was a major source of contention in neighborhood disputes. Given the emphasis, after independence, on respectability, one might expect the state to come to the aid of women who complained of dissolute, profligate, and abusive husbands. According to the constitutions, to abandon one's wife or to be at fault in an ecclesiastical separation was considered cause for the suspension of citizenship.[81] Republican officials in Arequipa did increasingly claim the authority to oversee marital affairs, a matter previously left primarily to the church. As judge José Miguel Salazar argued, "The jurisdiction of our Prelates is purely in spiritual matters, and it

78. ARAR/CS/Crim (12-VII-1832), "Contra María Samudio por heridas a José Valdez."
79. ARAR/CS/Crim (29-II-1832), "Contra Benedicto Muñós por heridas a Antonia Perula."
80. ARAR/CS/Crim (19-VI-1854), "Contra Don Antonio Núñez Melgar por haber fracturado un brazo a Felipa Galdos." The final sentence is missing.
81. Art. 24 (1823), Art. 6 (1828), Art. 4 (1834), and Art. 9 (1839); Olivo, *Constituciones*, 39, 111, 151, 206.

is the responsibility of the Government to make sure that its subjects committed to the conjugal state comply with their pacts and do not offend each other."[82]

Nevertheless, the civil authorities were hesitant to interfere with a citizen's patriarchal rights, including his prerogative to "correct" his wife. As one judge optimistically affirmed of a man accused of beating his wife, "The fear of scandalizing the community with actions foreign to an honorable citizen, will be sufficient to moderate in the future the vigor of his temper, and to make him more exact in the fulfillment of his duties in Holy Matrimony."[83]

Not only was it difficult for women to win cases against their husbands, by filing charges they opened their own behavior up to scrutiny as well. When Antonio Vilca was arrested for stabbing his wife, he was not the only one to receive a warning; after "making him understand that he should correct his wife using the moderation prescribed by marital love, and by the considerations due to her weak sex," the court also advised his wife "that she respect and obey her husband avoiding occasions for displeasing him."[84] Anselma López, who accused her husband of pursuing her with a knife and threatening to kill her, complained that the police not only refused to arrest him, but admonished her for not being home that night.[85]

Women did not even enjoy a posthumous protection from public criticism. In 1832, Gaspar Pango was absolved of killing his wife when he hit her with a stone while chasing after her. The fiscal pointed out that he could have killed her earlier, had that been his intention, given "the perverse conduct of that woman, her habit and custom of fleeing from the side of her husband,

---

82. ARAR/CS/Crim (16-XII-1828), "Don Alberto Anco apela la sentencia del Juez de Derecho que lo ha declarado adultero." For similar jurisdictional disputes, see ARAR/Pref (10-II-1827), "Contra Don Juan Rodríguez and Doña María Sánchez por haber sorprendido al Cura del Sagrario"; and ARAR/CS/Crim (22-II-1833), "Don Ramón Sea contra Don José Antonio Berenguel por el rapto de su hija." Strikingly, almost all reported cases of domestic violence in the colonial period can be found in the ecclesiastical archives. After independence such complaints from wives decreased dramatically, suggesting either that priests dealt with them verbally or that they referred the women to secular authorities. Most evidence of domestic violence in the republican period comes from a few complaints by women, seven assault trials, and seventeen murder cases.

83. ARAR/Pref (23-IV-1827), "Doña Faustina Tebes contra Don Juan Antonio Acosta por sevicia."

84. ARAR/CS/Crim (12-VIII-1834), "Contra Antonia Vilca por dos puñaladas a su esposa María Anco."

85. ARAR/CS/Crim (15-V-1849), "Doña Anselma López contra su esposo Don Pedro Ortega por maltratos."

without the singular meekness [*peregrino mansedumbre*] of this man nor his suffering being able to oblige her to reform."[86] Some abusive husbands were caught in the general rise in criminal prosecution, particularly when their drunken or violent behavior threatened public as well as domestic order. In 1852, for example, Laurencio Salazar was arrested for knocking his wife unconscious, and doctors testified that she would require medical treatment for at least one month. During the course of testimony, it became clear that Salazar, having on previous occasions not only mistreated his wife but also killed animals for spite and cut his brother-in-law's hand, was dangerously violent. Even when his wife ran out of money to pursue the case and pardoned her husband on orders from her confessor, the court sentenced him to four months of labor on public works, in addition to the five he had already served in jail.[87] Salazar's case, however, was unusual. In general, the republican courts defined narrowly the degree of violence necessary to constitute assault in domestic cases. When Francisca Obiedo complained that her husband beat her with sticks, stones, and whips and committed incest with her daughter, the fiscal asserted that even if the charges proved true, they would not constitute a public crime that could be tried by the state.[88] The fiscal's remarks are particularly striking if we compare them with official attitudes toward another form of violence against women: only after independence did judges in Arequipa begin actively prosecuting rape.[89]

Although the number of rape trials was small, and only minors were deemed worthy of protection, such cases marked a significant change from colonial practice and reflected the increased concerns over sexuality. When a judge released two defendants because the woman whom they were charged with raping refused to submit to a medical exam, for example, the prefect protested to the superior court, which ordered the trial to continue.[90] About half of the accused rapists were convicted, despite the efforts of their defense lawyers to depict their targets as promiscuous women. Even eighteen-year-old María Núñez, who accused tailor José María Peralta of sneaking into her

---

86. ARAR/CS/Crim (24-VII-1832), "Contra Gaspar Pango por la muerte de su esposa Ilaria Marantes."
87. ARAR/CS/Crim (30-XI-1852), "Contra Laurencio Salazar por graves heridas a su esposa."
88. ARAR/CS/Crim (24-IV-1850), "Contra Carlos Herrera por maltratos a su mujer."
89. Republican justices in Arequipa used the term *estupro* rather than *rapto* when violence was clear and there was no abduction.
90. ARAR/CS/Crim (22-X-1840), "Contra Leandro Delgado, Mariano Manto y otros por estupro de Evarista Yáñez."

room and getting her drunk in order to take advantage of her, convinced the judge of her honorable reputation.[91] Furthermore, the penalties for rape convictions were, generally, more strict than those for simple assault: several months in jail while performing public labor and/or providing a dowry for the young woman.

However limited the definition of rape, it is remarkable that the courts were willing to defend the honor even of poor girls. Indeed, in one case the superior court increased a sentence from the time already served to a one-hundred-peso dowry, precisely because the girl was "an unfortunate one who belongs to the lowest class of the plebe and lacking in fortune deserves more consideration and more legal protection."[92] The language used by judicial officials to describe such crimes provides a stark contrast to their attitude toward plebeian women beaten by their husbands or lovers. In 1834, for example, the justices were outraged when a tailor attempted to rape a seven-year-old girl. Even if he had not been able to consummate the act, argued the fiscal, "he reveals the utmost immorality and corruption which if not repressed and punished, its contagion could upset the order of families and cause serious damages to innocence."[93] When defendants and their lawyers protested that such charges should be pursued only at the initiative of private plaintiffs, the justices countered that rape, like theft or homicide—but apparently not like wife abuse or incest—could be prosecuted by the state as "a true public crime because in addition to damaging the honor and morals of families, it attacks the liberty and the very person of an individual."[94]

The definition of what constituted a "public" crime was key, because the rhetoric of honorable citizenship applied primarily to men's public rather than private conduct. Local police ordinances made commissioners responsible for all the scandals occurring in their neighborhoods, but simultaneously prohibited them from "interfering in the private conduct of the residents [vecinos], unless with their exterior scandalous behavior they attack

91. ARAR/CS/Crim (17-X-1846), "Contra José María Peralta por estupro en María Núñez, menor."

92. ARAR/CS/Crim (11-VIII-1846), "Contra Don Luís Gonsalen por haber violado a la menor Mercedes Murguía."

93. ARAR/CS/Crim (19-VIII-1834), "Contra Mariano Villegas por el rapto y estupro de la menor Teresa Gómez."

94. Fiscal Tomás Dávila, in ARAR/CS/Crim (16-I-1850), "Contra Mariano Jara por haber violado a la menor Manuela Licarde." See also ARAR/CS/Crim (25-V-1844), "Contra Baltazar Cervantes por violación de la hija de Don Silverio Cornejo."

public morals."[95] The courts in republican Arequipa punished men whose violent behavior extended beyond their households, as when they attacked young women over whom they had no patriarchal authority. Indeed, when poor girls were raped, the state often stepped in precisely because they lacked the protection of their own patriarchs.

Only in the most egregious cases, however, was the state willing to intervene in marital relations. This delineation of public and private was often detrimental to women, whose well-being and safety depended upon publicizing their domestic disputes. In a final ironic twist, moreover, it was a matter of some dispute whether chicherías—those spaces managed by women that often protected them from violence—enjoyed the constitutional protection against illegal entry. In 1830, the municipality's police deputy defended himself against charges of violating a woman's home on the grounds that "no chichería deserves the name of sacred [asylum]."[96]

Honorable citizens were expected to be economic providers, but not necessarily kind husbands. Indeed, the emphasis on military service likely reinforced a patriarch's insistence on his right to use violence. The lawyer for one man convicted of killing his wife in a jealous rage explicitly juxtaposed such obligations, in an appeal for clemency to President Orbegoso. "If Your Excellency does not accede," he quoted his client, "you will pay back with death the sacrifice I made of my life for you and your cause."[97]

The transformation of the code of honor under republicanism provided a new hegemonic language but did not, by any means, create an egalitarian or democratic society. On the contrary, repressive forms of social control actually intensified after independence, and republican leaders often fell short of putting liberal principles into practice. Nevertheless, the dialectical tension between elites and plebeians forged a new republican pact, in which some working men were granted the status of citizens. Honorable citizenship drew from plebeian notions of hombría de bien the value placed upon individual conduct and merit rather than lineage and status. But rights carried with them obligations, and citizens were expected to defend their country, to work hard, and to abide by higher standards of respectability.

As in the colonial period, the language of honor served as the basis for

95. *El Republicano*, Nov. 28, 1835, 2.

96. ARAR/CS/Crim (4-I-1830), "Contra Doña María Escalante por resistir al Diputado de Policía Don Toribio de Linares." See also ARAR/CS/Crim (20-X-1831), "Contra Juan Galiano y Matías Bedoya por haber entrado a fuerza a una chichería."

97. Dr. Don Pedro José Gamio y Masías, "Exmo. Señor" (Arequipa: Imprenta del Gobierno por Pedro Benavides, 1835). Distributed with *El Republicano*, either July 1 or July 4, 1835.

dialogue but was not restricted to one meaning. Plebeians did not, necessarily, share elite conceptions about what constituted proper conduct, and they certainly did not behave according to a strict code at all times.[98] They were more likely to emphasize the importance of work than that of moral restraint. When a letter in *El Republicano* accused carpenter Bartolomé Talavera of getting drunk at the Tingo baths, for example, he defended his honor based upon the esteem he earned from his trade, adding that "one should not be surprised that a man in the country drinks a bottle when others in town drink a whole wineskin."[99] Nevertheless, working men did sufficiently acknowledge the new standards, in word and deed, to allay elite concerns about political instability and crime, as reflected in the declining number of criminal convictions.

The recognition of citizenship was not only contingent upon conduct, but was also based upon the exclusion of those identified as dependent. Race continued to color perceptions of honor, as justices denied the protections they so fervently defended for working men to slaves and indigenous domestic servants. But the key factor was that these groups shared with all women the legal subjection to patriarchal control. Though theoretically relegated to the domestic sphere, women found their private virtues subject to increasing public scrutiny. Elite women who were able to maintain the appearance of fulfilling high republican standards of sexual purity, modesty, and maternal nurturing were still denied citizenship but were, at least, recognized as arbiters of morality within the public sphere as well as the home. Poor women, however, who often lived beyond the control of a patriarch and continued to carry out their lives in public, bore the brunt of the repressive campaign against popular culture. Indeed it was only men, whose virtue was judged by their conduct in the public sphere, who truly enjoyed a right to privacy. As long as they worked to support their families and did not threaten the sexuality of women outside of their own homes, they could treat their wives, children, and servants as they saw fit.

Men who could plausibly assert their economic independence gained

---

98. For a cautionary note on working-class respectability in England, see Peter Bailey, " 'Will the Real Bill Banks Please Stand Up?' Towards a Role Analysis of Mid-Victorian Working-Class Respectability," *Journal of Social History* 12, no. 3 (1979): 336–53. See also Roger Kittleson, " 'Ideas Triumph Only After Great Contests of Sorrows': Popular Classes and Political Ideas in Porto Alege, Brazil, 1889–1893," in Vincent C. Peloso and Barbara A. Tenenbaum, eds., *Liberals, Politics, and Power: State Formation in Nineteenth-Century Latin America* (Athens, Ga.: University of Georgia Press, 1996), 235–58.

99. *El Republicano*, Dec. 22, 1827, 164.

rights at the cost of others.[100] They were singled out not simply by constitutional provisions, but because republican authorities in Arequipa needed their labor, their cooperation to maintain social order, and their support in military and political movements. The relatively more stable state institutions established by the middle of the nineteenth century under Ramón Castilla suggest such that efforts were at least partially successful. The alarm over crime in Arequipa began to subside, and judges increasingly remanded less-serious cases to justices of the peace. In this new context, plebeian men probably looked increasingly to political elites rather than to their neighbors to confirm their reputations, with a corresponding decline in the influence of women in popular society. It is striking, for example, that carpenter Talavera defended himself in the press, the central forum of public opinion in a republic.

By the end of the period under study, plebeians were able to articulate their rights as citizens based upon these new requisites, and they began to link them explicitly to politics. In 1850, for example, a shoemaker and a tailor were among those arrested after a riot related to the elections. When they heard that they might be turned over to serve as soldiers in the police force, they indignantly protested their innocence and pointed out "that if the Police are authorized to increase their forces, they should do it with vagrants, and not with honorable and married artisans . . . unless it could be considered a crime to have manifested our opinion as free citizens in favor of the candidacy of General Vivanco."[101]

100. Some argue that the idea of citizenship in France not only excluded women, but was constructed against them; see Joan B. Landes, *Women and the Public Sphere in the Age of the French Revolution* (Ithaca and London: Cornell University Press, 1988); and Dorinda Outram, "Le Langage mâle de la vertu: Women and the Discourse of the French Revolution," in Peter Burke and Roy Porter, eds., *The Social History of Language* (Cambridge: Cambridge University Press, 1987), 120–135. Others are beginning to assert that women did gain political rights; see papers by Suzanne Desan, Stephanie Brown, and Carla Hesse from the panel "Women, Gender, and the French Revolution: From Representations to Practices," at the Tenth Berkshire Conference on the History of Women, Chapel Hill, June 1996.

101. Tomás Peñaranda and Francisco Butrón (who was single, but said he supported his mother), Apr. 5, 1850, in ARAR, Prefectura (27-II-1850), "Seguido sobre una azonada en la otra banda."

7

"Our Opinion As Free Citizens"
Political Culture and Liberalism

On November 13, 1849, police chief Juan Antonio Rivero received reports
that a large group of men was meeting in a picantería on the right bank of the
river. Such a gathering caused concern because the city was in the midst of a
campaign to elect a successor to President Ramón Castilla; the primary
competitors were José Rufino Echenique, who had received Castilla's blessing, and Manuel Ignacio de Vivanco, whose main base of support was in
Arequipa. Upon investigation Rivero found more than eighty supporters of
Echenique, whom he lectured on their duty "to work for their party with
decorum and moderation, without altering public order and tranquility." The
men assured Rivero that "the object of their meeting was to enjoy themselves
and drink a little chicha."[1] But they promised to disperse if supporters of
Vivanco, meeting in a picantería on the other side of the river, did the same.
Rivero received similar assurances from the *vivanquistas*, and quiet settled
over the city.

At nine that night, however, that calm was broken when a crowd gathered

1. ARAR/Pref (10-I-1850), "Causa seguida para descubrir los autores de la azonada que
acaeció el 13 de noviembre."

outside the house of Gen. Blas Cerdeña, a supporter of Echenique. According to various reports, shots fired from the house were answered with stones
from the crowd; a few windows were broken, but no one was hurt. An
investigation implicated Dr. José Genaro Talavera, Dr. Miguel Gomes, and
Diego Masías as leaders of the attack, but they refused to recognize the
authority of the court; Masías even tore up the proceedings related to the
case.

The court was still trying to prosecute the ringleaders of the November
riot when new disturbances broke out. On the night of Sunday, February 24,
1850, many people were returning to the city center from a festival in Cayma.
As one group neared the bridge, they heard a man—later identified as printer
Ignacio Monroy—shouting "Viva Echenique." The crowd of celebrants,
joined by others who were gathered in a nearby shop, responded with cries
of "Viva Vivanco" and "kill him, kill him." The outnumbered Echenique
supporters took refuge in the house of Manuel Amat y Leon, a retired
government official. Once again shots were fired from inside the house, and
the crowd retaliated with rocks.

Meanwhile, on the other side of town, another group of vivanquistas
stopped brothers Francisco Mariano and Melchor Sedillo. The former tried
to calm the crowd by agreeing with them, but the latter, arguing that they
were free to support whomever they wanted, shouted "Viva Echenique." The
crowd chased the Sedillos home and threw stones at their door before
dispersing. Most of those arrested were artisans, including the shoemaker and
tailor, who claimed to be "honorable artisans" expressing their free opinion.
None, however, was successfully prosecuted, as no witnesses were willing to
identify them. Diego Masías was not implicated in this riot but did serve as
bondsman for two defendants.[2]

Vivanco's strong support in Arequipa was not characteristic of the country
at large, and Echenique emerged victorious from the election. In honor of his
inauguration on April 21, 1851, one of his supporters in Arequipa flew a flag
from his house along the alameda. An angry crowd gathered, and, claiming
that the flag was an insult to the people of Arequipa, demanded its removal.
As prefect Alejandro Deustua appealed for calm, someone in the crowd
bumped into a policeman's horse; the officer, interpreting it as an attack,
turned and hit the man with his sword. This brief confrontation sparked a
two-day revolt, far more serious and violent than the earlier disturbances.
Arequipeños armed themselves, set up barricades throughout the city, and

2. ARAR/Pref (27-II-1850), "Sobre una azonada en la otra banda."

engaged the police battalion in battle. At night the shooting temporarily stopped, but several stores were looted. The following day the fighting resumed, until the prefect retreated to the village of Socabaya.[3]

The leaders of the revolt were the same men implicated in 1849: Talavera and the Masías brothers. Once in control of the city, the rebels followed an unusual course of action. They invited the prefect back and proposed that each side send a delegation to Lima. Priest and political activist Juan Gualberto Valdivia, who narrated these events, claimed credit for convincing the caudillos to negotiate. It seems more likely that this particular revolt lacked the support of more prominent citizens, even those who had backed Vivanco. Therefore, the rebels would not have been in a position to coordinate their actions with a broader movement against the new government of Echenique.

Such an interpretation is supported by prefect Deustua's account of the events; he blamed the unrest on the *cholada* and assured his superiors that this cholo mob did not enjoy the backing of "the sensible part of Arequipa including all its notables."[4] It would not be until 1854, when accusations of corruption during Echenique's consolidation of the national debt had provoked enough dissatisfaction among broad sectors of Peruvian society, that another revolt in Arequipa would be carried through to national victory under Castilla's leadership.

Political Culture in Arequipa

Just as the period under study opened in 1780 with Arequipeños rioting in the streets, so too did it close. Traditional accounts point to this string of revolts as evidence of the rebellious spirit of the Pueblo Caudillo. In the search for a logic behind the apparent chaos of the early republican period, historians have uncovered the economic interests of the southern elite that underlay their allegiance to caudillos who advocated free trade.[5] Paul Gootenberg also has begun to move beyond a "personalistic" analysis of

3. Juan Gualberto Valdivia, *Las revoluciones de Arequipa* (Arequipa: Editorial El Deber, 1956), 199–205.

4. AHMP (CEHMP), Leg. 2, Num. 75, letter, April 25, 1851, with a copy of a report from Deustua.

5. Gootenberg, "Beleaguered Liberals," 63–97; and Nils Jacobsen, "Free Trade, Regional Elites, and the Internal Market in Southern Peru, 1895–1932," in Joseph L. Love and Nils

these caudillos, to look at the broader political platforms that they represented.[6]

Nevertheless, popular participation in these movements remains an enigma. The analysis of popular society and culture in the preceding chapters lays the necessary groundwork for a reinterpretation of the political events of the period, with greater attention to the role of plebeians as both soldiers and voters. Further, an analysis of the writings of prominent liberals from Arequipa will reveal the imprint of the rights demanded through the courts by "honorable citizens."

Social networks, forged through daily contacts in neighborhoods, could be mobilized at times of political crisis. When Arequipeños gathered in shops and taverns or gossiped in streets and courtyards, conversation could turn easily from the reputation of their neighbors to politics. Cleric José Mariano Recavarren, for example, was accused of supporting the rebels from Cuzco who occupied the city in 1814. Manuela Briseño, who lived in the same house, was reported to be "in a martyrdom with Recavarren, because she is very royalist, and when there is good news of the King and he sees that she is happy, he takes the contrary position."[7]

After independence, people continued to talk about which caudillo their neighbors supported. They might tease them about it as well, like the shoemaker who called his former master a "rabbit eater" to indicate his support for General Salaverry.[8] Others tried to use the information against their personal enemies.[9] Political leaders were aware of the power of such talk, even if they did not want to acknowledge it as public opinion. A

Jacobsen, eds., *Guiding the Invisible Hand: Economic Liberalism and the State in Latin American History* (New York: Praeger 1988), 145–75.

6. Gootenberg, "North-South," 273–308.

7. BNP doc. D11640 (1815), "Contra Dr. Don José Mariano Recavarren, presbítero, por adicto a la revolución." For testimonies on several men who gathered to drink liquor in a shop and ended up shouting antiroyalist slogans, see BNP doc. D630 (1814), "Contra Don Mariano Nicolás Salazar por rebelión."

8. ARAR/CS/Crim (7-IV-1836), "Contra Rafael González por puñaladas a cuatro personas en una chichería."

9. For examples, see ARAR/Int/Crim (9-XII-1815), "Doña Micaela Begaso contra María de tal 'la Cacepaupaula' por injurias"; ARAR/CS/Crim (2-XI-1838), "Don Matías Rafael Corzo contra Doña Martina Hurtado por injurias"; (13-IV-1835) "Contra Don Miguel Hernani por heridos a Don Manual Corrales"; (17-II-1836) "Dr. Don Mariano Navarro contra Juan de Dios Espejo por injurias"; (25-VIII-1838) "Los indígenas de Cayma quejan contra su Gobernador Don Mariano Salcedo"; (29-V-1839) "Contra Don Juan de Dios Gonzales y Don Vicente Carvajal por imputárseles haber hecho poner en prisión en el Gobierno de Santa Cruz a Don

pro-Gamarra editorial entitled "Malicious Whispers" denounced "false and alarming notices that despite their vulgarity and crudeness, there are always foolish people who believe and publicize them."[10] The article held such rumors responsible for disturbing the peace and, by scaring artisans, paralyzing industry.

Cultural spaces, like community networks of talk, could also become politicized. In 1838, during the Peru-Bolivia Confederation, a Chilean carpenter was attracted to a house by the sounds of people celebrating the holiday of the Holy Cross. When he heard a black man reciting a poem against the Chilean general who had led the failed invasion of Arequipa, the carpenter could not contain his anger and slapped him. In the ensuing fight, the Chilean wounded a hatter who had come to the orator's defense.[11] On such occasions, people also read aloud and discussed partisan broadsheets and newspapers.[12]

Chicherías, moreover, could bring together people from various social classes. When a young merchant was accused of insulting government officials during a party in 1843, witnesses included a master barber, a farmer (labrador), and the chichera at whose establishment the incident occurred.[13] It should come as no surprise, therefore, that the election riots of 1849 and 1850 erupted after members of the respective parties gathered in chicherías or shops.[14] Political skirmishes also frequently coincided with the celebration of holidays, as when the group of vivanquistas returned from a festival in Cayma in 1850.

The broad alliances that appeared both in the 1780 tax revolt and the later civil wars were held together by personal contacts. Just as customs administrator Pando highlighted the presence of gentlemen on horseback to implicate creole leaders in the attack on the customs house, Manuel Amat y Leon

---

José Gregorio Paz"; and (20-IV-1852), "Mariano Origuela y Moscoso contra Don Raymundo Blest y Don Timoteo Muños por homicidio en conato."

10. "Susurros Maliciosos," *El Republicano*, May 10, 1834, 4.

11. ARAR/CS/Crim (13-V-1838), "Contra el Chileno Juan Ramón Asco por heridas a Ambrocio Facundo."

12. For example, ARAR/CS/Crim (10-VI-1835), "Don Miguel Hernani contra Don Manuel Corrales por injurias."

13. ARAR/CS/Crim (26-V-1843), "Contra Don Manuel Delgado por profirir expreciones contra los mandatarios del gobierno."

14. For later links between politics and chicherías, see Belaúnde, *Arequipa de mi infancia*, 290; and Antero Peralta Vásquez, *La faz oculta de Arequipa* (Arequipa: Coop. Ed. Universitaria, 1977), 30–38.

asserted, in 1850, that men rode up to the crowd outside his house "and after speaking to them in secret, they began to operate."[15] The leaders in the street were often minor landowners, priests, shopkeepers, lawyers, and other professionals. These local leaders had connections both to elites—who could incorporate Arequipa into broader national movements—and to the plebeians in their neighborhoods, who presented themselves for service and built the barricades.

Diego Masías and his brothers, who spearheaded the Vivanco movement in Arequipa, for example, were likely landowners, but they were related through marriage to more prominent families such as the Gamios, who had made a fortune in commerce.[16] According to Valdivia (himself a priest and teacher), prefect Deustua knew that the Masías brothers "had great support among the people," and so appealed to their mother to bring them to their senses during the 1851 revolt.[17] Two other leaders prosecuted after the 1849 riot carried the title of doctor, implying that they were professionals of some kind.[18] We know more about those who rallied to the 1854 revolution, because once it was victorious, they were rewarded for their services. Among the leaders cited for their valor were ten professionals, ten landowners (including two named Masías), and two merchants. The "Individuals of the People" who were decorated for their service as petty officers in the various trenches included thirty-three tailors, twenty-two shoemakers, seventeen carpenters, eight small farmers, and numerous artisans from other trades.[19]

Although the networks mobilized during revolts looked remarkably similar from 1780 to 1854, the political context changed dramatically. In 1780, the populace of Arequipa rose up against the imposition of new taxes (customs duties and the threat of an extension of tribute) that would have caused economic hardship for all social classes. The rebels, however, followed a

15. Paz y Guini, *Guerra separatista*, 136; and Amat y Leon, March 9, in ARAR/Pref (27-II-1850), "Expediente seguido sobre una azonada en la otra banda."
16. Eusebio Masías identified himself as the owner of a vineyard; see ARAR/CS/Crim (8-I-1852), "Contra Don Eusebio y Don Manuel Masías por haber insultado al Teniente Coronel de las fuerzas de policía." The political positions and intermarriages of these families from the late eighteenth through the nineteenth century can be traced in Santiago Martínez, *Alcaldes de Arequipa desde 1539 a 1946* (Arequipa, n.p., 1946). Wibel does not mention the Masías family in his discussion of the region's elite; for his description of the Gamios (who were also intermarried with the Goyeneches), see Wibel, "The Evolution of a Regional Community," 138.
17. Valdivia, *Las revoluciones de Arequipa*, 200.
18. ARAR/Pref (10-I-1850), "Causa seguida para descubrir los autores de la azonada."
19. Letter from prefect Francisco Llosa to the minister of government, Feb. 5, 1855, in AHMP (CEHMP), Leg. 12, Num. 2.

common formula of colonial protest: with the cry "long live the king, and death to the bad government," they proclaimed their loyalty to the king who would never harm his subjects, but they opposed the actions of his "disloyal" officials.[20] After independence, there was no monarch to serve as an idealized symbol of authority and justice. The caudillos and politicians—who invoked new ideas, such as liberty and equality, in speeches to those who gathered in the plaza of Arequipa—would have to earn their legitimacy as leaders.

The political education of Arequipeños began with day-to-day negotiations of their rights and responsibilities with the new judicial authorities. With the help of their lawyers, they used the language they heard in patriotic speeches and in public readings of the constitution to protest arbitrary searches and detention. Gradually, their understanding of citizenship expanded from guaranteeing constitutional protections to claiming active political rights.

The specific requirements for suffrage varied with each constitution, but many artisans and small farmers were eligible to vote because they exercised an independent profession or held property, and they paid taxes.[21] Furthermore, in the early republic, literacy requirements were waived for indigenous and mestizo citizens. In 1834, the conservative Gamarristas in Arequipa complained that too many "proletarians" were allowed to vote.[22] Indirect elections for deputies to congresses and constitutional conventions began immediately after independence, and the names of Arequipa's electors were printed in the local newspaper. Elections involved three stages: the election of a supervisory body (*mesa permanente*), the selection of electors, and the electors' subsequent choice of deputies and president. There are stories of competing factions literally fighting to control the *mesa* and thereby favor their candidates in the subsequent elections.[23] Such a process lent itself to

20. Compare with John Leddy Phelan, *The People and the King: The Comunero Revolution in Colombia, 1781* (Madison: University of Wisconsin Press, 1978).

21. For electoral laws, see *El Republicano*, Feb. 23, 1833, 2; Nov. 8, 1834, 1; and Apr. 13, 1853, 1–3; and José Félix Aramburú, *Derecho electoral: Antecedentes históricos y aplicaciones a la nueva ley* (Lima: La Opinión Nacional, 1915). A tailor had been found carrying a knife at a polling place; see ARAR/CS/Crim (8-III-1850), "Contra Don Mariano Bedrigal por andar con puñal." By law, lists of active citizens were formed for electoral purposes; the Revista Cívica of Santa Marta for 1855 (stored in the Archivo Arzobispal de Arequipa) includes numerous artisans.

22. *El Republicano*, May 3, 1834, 4.

23. Jorge Basadre, *Elecciones y centralismo en el Perú* (Lima: Universidad del Pacífico, 1980), 29–32. For an analysis of liberal electoral laws that seriously considers the potential for popular participation and consequent political education, see Vincent C. Peloso, "Liberals, Electoral

corruption, obviously, but it also made the mobilization of popular voters key.

Popular participation in politics did not explode overnight with the declaration of independence. The first elections held in Arequipa had to be extended owing to low turnout; in an attempt to shame people into fulfilling their civic responsibilities, *El Republicano* printed the names of citizens who had failed to vote.[24] Arequipa's liberal representatives in congress, most notably the cleric Francisco Javier de Luna Pizarro, were concerned primarily with establishing a government with limited executive power, working against the authoritarianism first of Simón Bolívar and then of President Agustín Gamarra.[25] Others, such as supporters of Gen. Andrés de Santa Cruz, promoted the reunification of southern Peru with its old trading partner, Bolivia.[26]

The popular classes expressed their opposition to the central authority primarily through passive resistance: evading military conscription and taxes, the burden of which fell increasingly on the urban poor. It would not be long, however, before Arequipeños jumped into the fray of electoral politics and caudillo warfare in an attempt to win more favorable policies from the state.

In contrast to 1825, the editors of *El Republicano* celebrated the turnout for the first round of the 1833 elections: "We have witnessed the council chambers full of citizens casting their votes: and their patriotic enthusiasm on this occasion is worthy of imitation and praise."[27] A subsequent letter to the editor expressed support for a balanced economic program, which would have appealed to several classes, urging the victorious electors to select deputies "who recognize the need to promote industry, the arts and sciences—that of overcoming all the obstacles that hold back the work of

Reform, and the Popular Vote in Mid-Nineteenth-Century Peru," in Vincent C. Peloso and Barbara A. Tenenbaum, eds., *Liberals, Politics, and Power: State Formation in Nineteenth-Century Latin America* (Athens, Ga.: University of Georgia Press, 1996), 186–211. For the case of Mexico, see also Richard Warren, "Elections and Popular Political Participation in Mexico, 1808–1836," in Peloso and Tenenbaum, eds., *Liberals, Politics, and Power*, 30–58.

24. *El Republicano*, Dec. 31, 1825, 22.

25. See Francisco Javier de Luna Pizarro, *Escritos políticos*, ed. Alberto Tauro (Lima: Universidad Nacional Mayor de San Marcos, 1959); Benito Laso, *El poder de la fuerza y el poder de la ley* (1858; reprint, Lima: Ediciones Hora del Hombre, 1947); and speeches by Laso and Vigil reprinted in Raúl Ferrero, *El liberalismo Peruano* (Lima: Biblioteca de Escritores Peruanos, 1958), 113–82.

26. *El Republicano*, supplement to Aug. 8, 1829; Aug. 15, 1829; Aug. 29, 1829; and Sept. 5, 1829; and Wibel, "The Evolution of a Regional Community," 324–25.

27. *El Republicano*, Jan. 19, 1833, 5.

Agriculture and Mining—that of balancing imports and exports—that of providing a living [*modo de vivir*] to all classes—that of making indigence unknown, and finally—that of providing us with machinery, chemical laboratories, artisans, and all that contributes to the independence of a country where there exist the elements for all kinds of manufactures."[28]

The electoral colleges met on March 5 and chose liberal deputies to the National Convention, including Luna Pizarro, José Luis Gómez Sánchez, and Francisco de Paula González Vigil of Tacna, who were in opposition to the existing conservative regime of Agustín Gamarra. As people "were occupied in the innocent pleasure of acclaiming their elected deputies with music in the streets," according to the denunciation of Gómez Sánchez, the crowd was attacked by disguised soldiers from the police battalion. The people subsequently regrouped, however, and acquired arms by raiding the police station. Gómez Sánchez reported that he and other "notables" were unable to disperse the three thousand citizens. Prefect Pio Tristán and the local military commander, members of the current regime, tried to play down the significance of the riot, but it was a sign of things to come.[29]

The subsequent presidential elections were widely seen as corrupted, so when Gamarra's term ended in December, the national convention elected José Luis de Orbegoso as interim president. In January 1834, Gamarra staged a coup in Lima against his successor, and it was in defense of Orbegoso that Arequipa's broad regional alliance reemerged in open rebellion. "Recent events had completely changed the atmosphere of the town," wrote Flora Tristan, "calm, monotonous and intolerably boring before the revolution, it was now extraordinarily lively and in a state of perpetual noise and bustle."[30]

Even the leaders of the revolt initially seemed surprised at the support they received from the populace. "The barracks became crowded," reported a special edition of *El Republicano*, "and by some kind of magic spell, the people that have viewed military enlistments with horror, were transformed into a town of soldiers."[31] Poems lauded the contributions of common Arequipeños and emphasized local unity:

28. "Electores," *El Republicano*, Feb. 9, 1833, 7.
29. *El Republicano*, May 11, 1833, 1–3; and June 1, 1933, 3–5.
30. Tristan, *Peregrinations of a Pariah*, 165. See also Valdivia, *Las revoluciones de Arequipa*, 22–35; and Wibel, "The Evolution of a Regional Community," 309–10, 386.
31. *El Republicano*, supplement to Jan. 23, 1834, 3. Another article contrasted the mobilization to the population's inaction during the wars of independence; see "Para la historia," *El Republicano*, July 26, 1834, 8.

The sad farmer leaves his field
Covered, with the grains he has harvested
And prefers the lance
To field, harvests, children, and cattle.

The artisan quickly leaves
The work undertaken by his hand
And aspires only to the pleasure
Of staining his sword with the tyrant's blood.

In short all is valor among the people
Who want only to be Republican;
Valor breathes the youth
The child, the woman, and even the old man.

Oh Arequipa, fortunate city!
Model of heroism and virtues,
Soon you will find yourself free,
Or you will be without doubt another Sparta.[32]

The liberal constitution drafted by the National Convention in 1834 included the right of habeas corpus and increased civilian control over military conscription, measures that would have enjoyed popular support. The city remained loyal to Orbegoso through sieges by generals Miguel de San Román and Felipe Salaverry, whose efforts to raise recruits and provisions only deepened hostility among the populace.[33] Orbegoso, on the other hand, rewarded his followers in June 1835 by proclaiming "that all the farmers should return to their homes in the security that today an order has been given that none of them can be enrolled in the ranks and that the army corps cannot recruit in the countryside."[34] In 1836 Arequipeños benefited further, from Orbegoso's abolition of personal and urban property taxes and his return of the milling tax to municipal control.[35] Finally, the citizens' com-

32. "Lamentos de la patria," *El Republicano*, Mar. 1, 1834, 3. See also the poem in *El Republicano*, Feb. 8, 1834, 4.
33. Valdivia, *Las revoluciones de Arequipa*, 39–67; and Wibel, "The Evolution of a Regional Community," 391–402.
34. Letter, June 10, 1835, in BNP doc. D10190 (1835), "Correspondencia con el Sr. Prefecto de este departamento."
35. AGN, Hacienda H-1-1, O.L. 270, Num. 218, letter, Oct. 22, 1839; and ARAR/Pref (8-IV-1836), "Remate del impuesto a las moliendas de trigo y guiñapo."

mitment to the constitutional process earned Arequipa yet another title: "The Department of the Law."

Despite the steadfast support of Arequipa, Orbegoso could not triumph on his own, and in 1835 he joined forces with Santa Cruz. The ultimate consequence of the pact with the Bolivian caudillo was the reunification of the southern Andean territories in the Peru-Bolivia Confederation. From 1836 to 1839, Arequipeños exerted a strong influence within the Southern Peruvian State and gained a degree of autonomy from Lima.[36] The region's merchants and landowners benefited from the liberal policies of Santa Cruz, such as low tariffs and the sale of public lands.[37]

Santa Cruz, reportedly, was also very popular among the populace of the White City.[38] The majority stood by him when the Chileans, fearful that the enlarged Andean republic would grow in power as well as territory, invaded the valley in October 1837. Among the letters supporting the war with Chile in 1836 were those from numerous artisan guilds, whose members served in the national guard as well as donating their labor for military needs.[39] Rather than completing an almost certain victory over the invading expedition, however, Santa Cruz negotiated a peace treaty with the Chileans.

A second invasion from Chile in 1839 restored Gamarra to power and reestablished centralized control from Lima; the new constitution, for example, abolished all elected bodies at the local level.[40] In further revenge against Arequipa, Gamarra removed from its jurisdiction the province of Moquegua. Opposition to Gamarra's autocratic methods soon resurfaced, however, and in 1840, even his handpicked prefect in Arequipa, Pedro José Gamio, resigned in protest rather than impose yet another forced loan on the local elite.[41] The arrival in early 1841 of his successor, Manuel Ignacio de Vivanco, marked the beginning of a new political love affair for the White City.

It was an unlikely alliance, since Vivanco had earlier supported Gamarra and Salaverry, while opposing the confederation. Nevertheless, the new prefect restored several fiscal policies from the confederation that had

36. The presidents of the assemblies in both southern and northern Peru were natives of Arequipa; see Wibel, "The Evolution of a Regional Community," 303–4. See also Phillip T. Parkerson, *Andrés de Santa Cruz y la Confederación Perú-Boliviana, 1835–1839* (La Paz: Librería Editorial Juventud, 1984).

37. Wibel, "The Evolution of a Regional Community," 408–10.

38. *El Republicano*, Oct. 3, 1835, 4; and Valdivia, *Las revoluciones de Arequipa*, 146.

39. *El Republicano*, Dec. 17, 1836, 5–6.

40. Basadre, *Historia de la República del Perú*, vol. 2, 197–201.

41. Wibel, "The Evolution of a Regional Community," 423.

benefited Arequipa, and soon he declared open opposition to Gamarra.[42] Within a few months, General Castilla routed Vivanco from the city. In January 1843, however, a military revolt in Arequipa proclaimed the former prefect their chief, and by March he was established in Lima as the self-titled Supreme Director of Peru.

Vivanco's "Regeneration" movement opposed Gamarra and the 1839 constitution not out of disdain for authoritarianism, for the supreme director would also claim strong executive control. Rather, vivanquistas wanted government "in the hands of the capable and cultured."[43] After years of warfare, some Arequipeños were undoubtedly attracted to an "enlightened despot," who would both restore order and defend the region's economic interests. Throughout the decade, Vivanco brought together at least some prominent Arequipeños from both the liberal and more conservative ends of the political spectrum who had been at odds under the confederation, such as José Luís Gómez Sánchez, Manuel Toribio Ureta, Andrés Martínez, and members of the Gamio family. This was also the period in which fears about crime began to decline, which perhaps both contributed to and reflected a climate of conciliation.

Vivanco's plans to reduce the military, abolish internal tariffs, promote national industry and commerce, and support educational and cultural programs appealed to the southern elite, but they also included elements that could attract popular support.[44] Nevertheless, the Regeneration would be short-lived. As rival caudillos rallied their forces throughout Peru, Vivanco retreated to his beloved Arequipa, where he was again defeated by his nemesis, Castilla, in July 1844.

Under President Castilla, Peruvians enjoyed their first period of stability since independence. He took advantage of this space and the country's newfound wealth in guano to strengthen the state and extend its control over the national territory. Stability won by force was maintained through the incorporation of former enemies, including vivanquistas, and the adoption of many of the liberal policies that Castilla had previously opposed.[45] The only thorn in the president's side was the continuing affair between Vivanco and the White City.

During the presidential campaign of 1849 to 1850, pitting Vivanco against

42. Ibid., 428.
43. Basadre, *Historia de la República del Perú*, vol. 2, 207.
44. Ibid., vol. 3, 45–46.
45. Ibid., vol. 4, 123–56; and Gootenberg, "Beleaguered Liberals," 80–81.

Castilla's handpicked successor, Echenique, Arequipa's political maneuvering shifted from the military back to the electoral sphere, and plebeians, especially artisans, began to play an increasingly active role. The 1833 election riot revealed early signs of that mobilization in Arequipa, but it reached even higher levels in the numerous partisan clashes from 1849 to 1852. In addition to the three major riots, minor skirmishes in the streets frequently erupted when someone shouted slogans on behalf of one candidate or the other.[46] The politicization of the population even infiltrated the city jail, where a riot broke out when the guards, supporters of Echenique, began throwing stones at the prisoners who were expressing their support for Vivanco.[47]

Political leaders such as Diego Masías may have wooed supporters by throwing parties, buying drinks, and even buying votes, as would be documented in later elections.[48] Nevertheless, artisans like the young shoemaker Pedro Orellano, who testified that Masías had tried to get him to reveal who had told him to support Echenique, insisted that their political choices reflected their own opinions.[49] The majority of Arequipeños placed their hope in Vivanco, whose 1849 platform retreated even further from his earlier authoritarianism and included more measures to attract popular support, such as the establishment of direct elections, widespread suffrage, and the protection of civil liberties. He continued to advocate the reduction of the regular army and the establishment, instead, of civil guards. And his economic proposals combined the promotion of free trade with protection for some national industries, the extension of education in the arts and sciences, the development of irrigation systems, and the abolition of indigenous tribute.[50] Vivanco's defeat at the national level by Echenique triggered yet another revolt in the White City.

It seems ironic, therefore, that when Arequipa rose up again against President Echenique in January 1854, it was Castilla who rode into town and

46. ARAR/CS/Crim (1-XI-1849), "Don Diego Masías contra Pedro Orellano por homicidio en conato"; (16-I-1850) "Contra Baltasar Castillo por haber tirado a Don Estanislao Reynoso"; (16-I-1850) "Contra varios por atacar a Don Diego Masías"; (9-III-1850) "Contra los individuos que quebraron la casa del Gobernador de Miraflores"; and (29-III-1852), "Contra reos fugados por haber herido de bola al Alferes Don José Manuel Alfaro."
47. ARAR/CS/Crim (22-I-1850), "Sobre insubordinados en la cárcel."
48. For such practices in 1871 and 1872, see Carmen E. McEvoy, "Estampillas y votos: El rol del correo político en una campaña electoral decimonónica," Histórica 18, no. 1 (1994): 117–22.
49. Nov. 3, 1849, in ARAR/CS/Crim (1-XI-1849), "Don Diego Masías contra Pedro Orellano por homicidio en conato."
50. Basadre, Historia de la República del Perú, vol. 3, 288–89.

claimed the banner of the revolution.[51] When Vivanco set siege to the city the following November, the population that had once acclaimed him instead repulsed him, during twelve hours of fierce fighting. Recognizing, perhaps, that Castilla had incorporated many of their demands into his platform, they pragmatically chose to be on the victorious side, for once. In his second term Castilla enacted further reforms, including the abolition of Indian tribute and African slavery. Nevertheless, he frequently clashed with the congress, and many liberals, including those from Arequipa, found themselves once again in the opposition by 1856. Although the city would continue to be the scene of several more rebellions, regional politicians increasingly sought the best possible terms for incorporation into the national project, rather than directly challenging Lima's hegemony.

Independence did not create an ideal democracy, but it did set in motion a gradual process of politicization among the popular classes. The artisans, small farmers, and traders who took to the streets from 1849 to 1854 expressed their adherence to a particular party and its platform. This type of political consciousness distinguished them from their forebears who had risen up against taxes in 1780. Even more significantly, however, this generation justified their political activism in terms of their rights as citizens in a republic. Their great-grandparents in colonial times had followed their own code of honor but accepted a social hierarchy in which elites had looked down on them as the "lowly plebe."

After independence, whatever the leaders of republican Arequipa thought in private, in public they had to acknowledge at least some men of the popular classes as their fellow citizens, who had earned honor through respectable conduct and service to the nation. Therefore, caudillos included proposals in their political platforms that would appeal to small farmers and artisans: limits on forced military conscription, the promotion of local industry, and the protection of civil liberties. Finally, popular concepts of honorable citizenship influenced the political philosophies of prominent liberals from Arequipa.

---

51. Corruption during Echenique's "consolidation" of the national debt had triggered opposition throughout Peru; see Alfonso W. Quiroz, *La deuda defraudada: Consolidación de 1850 y dominio económico en el Perú* (Lima: Instituto Nacional de Cultura, 1987).

Arequipeño Liberalism

In the wake of the 1854 revolution, direct elections based upon universal male suffrage brought a new generation of liberals to power.[52] Prominent representatives to the National Convention from the department of Arequipa, including José Simeón Tejeda, Manuel Toribio Ureta, and Juan Gualberto Valdivia, were among those passing the short-lived liberal constitution of 1856, which abolished the death penalty and hereditary privileges, imposed congressional oversight upon the army, established national guards, prohibited military conscription, and reestablished departmental juntas and municipal councils.

The influence of Arequipa's liberals at the national level was particularly strong in the area of law. By the late 1830s, a majority of the justices on Peru's supreme court had been educated and begun their careers in Arequipa. Several of the high court's most notable fiscals, such as José Gregorio Paz Soldan and Manuel Toribio Ureta, also hailed from the White City.[53] More than half the members of the commission that drafted the first republican civil code in 1852 were Arequipeños, including its vivanquista chair, Andrés Martínez.[54] Eight years later, Francisco García Calderón, a young law professor in Arequipa, wrote the legal dictionary that would be consulted by lawyers and jurists throughout the rest of the century.[55]

Many justices from the White City had a direct impact on national politics, as elected deputies and appointed officials, including Evaristo Gómez Sánchez, Manuel Toribio Ureta, Toribio Pacheco, Juan Manuel Polar, Pedro José Bustamante, Ezequiel Rey de Castro, and José María Pérez Franco. Finally, other prominent politicians were related to jurists; the defense lawyer

52. For general studies of liberalism in Peru, see Ferrero, *El liberalismo peruano*; Daniel Michael Gleason, "Ideological Cleavages in Early Republican Peru, 1821–1872" (Ph.D. diss., University of Notre Dame, 1974); Hector Ballón Lozada, *Las ideas socio-políticas en Arequipa, 1540–1900* (Arequipa: PubliUnsa, 1986); Alberto Adrianzén, ed., *Pensamiento político peruano* (Lima: DESCO, 1987); and Hugo Garavito Amézaga, *El Perú liberal: Partidos e ideas de la ilustración a la república aristocrática* (Lima: Ediciones El Virrey, 1989).

53. For the supreme court, see Wibel, "The Evolution of a Regional Community," 449. For fiscals, see Alfredo Gastón, *Compilación de las vistas fiscales*, 2 vols. (Lima: Imprenta del Estado, 1873).

54. Basadre, *Historia de la República del Perú*, vol. 3, 307–15.

55. Ibid., vol. 5, 37–40; and Francisco García Calderón, *Diccionario de la legislación peruana* (Lima: Imprenta de Eusebio Aranda, 1864).

who appealed to President Orbegoso on behalf of the soldier who had killed his wife, for example, was related to both the Masías and Gamio families.[56] The political philosophy of Arequipa's liberals was strongly influenced by their education and exposure to European ideas, but was also rooted in their interactions with the popular classes, both through the courts and in local politics. All were trained in law and many, like their professors in Arequipa, worked in the local courts as lawyers for plebeian defendants or as judges who passed sentences protecting the civil guarantees of respectable male citizens. Ureta, for example, who held successive positions as a lawyer, rector of the University of San Agustín, congressional deputy and, ultimately, fiscal on the national supreme court, had in 1850 served as a bondsman for the two artisans claiming their right to express their support for Vivanco in the elections.[57] In both theory and practice, Arequipa's liberals consistently and strongly defended the tenets of classical political liberalism as well as free trade.

José Simeón Tejeda was from the generation educated after independence at the University of San Agustín in Arequipa. Upon graduation, in 1851, he practiced law and edited *El Republicano*. A major supporter of the 1854 revolution, he was elected a deputy from the province of Condesuyos, and in 1864 he served as minister of justice and education. Tejeda is remembered particularly for his defense of free-market liberalism, but his famous speech in 1852 to Arequipa's Academia Lauretana, "The Emancipation of Industry," dealt primarily with the problems of artisans. He opposed guild restrictions that prevented journeymen from working independently out of their own homes, "the sacred place of the individual."[58]

As we have seen, many artisans were taking such work illegally and were, no doubt, heartened to hear Tejeda assert that they should be treated as

56. Dr. Don Pedro José Gamio y Masías, "Exmo. Señor" (Arequipa: Imprenta del Gobierno por Pedro Benavides, 1835). Distributed with *El Republicano* either July 1 or July 4, 1835. Biographical information has been gleaned from Martínez, *Alcaldes de Arequipa*; Carlos Milla Batres, *Diccionario histórico y biográfico del Perú, siglos XV–XX* (Lima: Editorial Milla Batres, 1986); P. Emilio Dancuart, *Crónica parlamentaria del Perú* (Lima: Imprenta de la Revista, 1906–); Ismael R. Echegaray Correa, *La cámara de diputados y las constituyentes del Perú* (Lima: Imprenta del Ministerio de Hacienda y Comercio, 1965); and Wibel, "The Evolution of a Regional Community." On the importance of lawyers to early republican politics in Colombia, see Victor M. Uribe, "The Lawyers and New Granada's Late Colonial State," *Journal of Latin American Studies* 21, no. 3 (1995): 517–50.
57. ARAR/Pref (27-II-1850), "Sobre una azonada en la otra banda."
58. José Simeón Tejeda, *Libertad de la industria* (1852; reprint, Lima: Ediciones Hora del Hombre, 1947), 49.

honorable workers rather than criminals.[59] Tejeda shared the concern of other authorities over morality and discipline, but he offered as a cure for Saint Monday "to awake the interest of all classes of journeymen by elevating them to the category of masters, without any requirement other than their own desire and that the public, the most competent examiner since it is the consumer, judge their skill and ability."[60] Such words echoed the plea of the journeymen silversmiths of Arequipa to be allowed to accept jobs from "any Person who, led by the entire satisfaction which they have in our work as well as in our honorable conduct, place their confidence in us."[61] Finally, Tejeda's criticism of abuses committed by the police and soldiers doubtless struck a chord with plebeians in Arequipa. He asserted that given adequate work, the poor would rise up only in defense of their own rights. "The army that has merit in a Republic," he declared, "is the entirety of its employed men."[62]

One of the most prominent jurists from Arequipa was José Gregorio Paz Soldán (1808–75). Paz Soldán began his education at the Seminary of San Jerónimo under such professors as Luna Pizarro and Andrés Martínez, and later he received his law degree from the University of San Agustín. In the 1830s he began his career in the local courts, moving through the ranks from court reporter to judge of first instance and, finally, fiscal. His national prominence began in 1845, when he was appointed by Castilla as minister of foreign relations, a post he subsequently held under several other administrations. Best known for his diplomatic work, he also served as fiscal to the supreme court between 1851 and 1875. Although Paz Soldán did not always ally with the caudillos most popular in Arequipa, his judicial philosophy consistently defended both economic and civil liberty and bore the stamp of Arequipa's popular republicanism.[63]

Paz Soldán advocated free trade, advising the government to abolish all monopolies and special privileges.[64] Yet, like Tejeda, he simultaneously defended the freedom of work. Before the abolition of slavery, he defended

---

59. Ibid., 55.
60. Ibid., 44.
61. ARAR/Int/Adm (9-IV-1808), "Expediente sobre que los Maestros Plateros cumplan sus deberes." See Chapter 5.
62. Tejeda, *Libertad de la industria*, 64.
63. For a biography, see José Pareja Paz Soldán, *José Gregorio Paz Soldán: Diplomático y jurista* (Lima: Ediciones Peruanas, 1964).
64. See, for example, Gastón, *Compilación de las vistas fiscales*, vol. 1, 10–11, 16–17, 60–62, 66–67.

the slave trade and depicted the conditions in Peru in a rosy light.[65] Nevertheless, he later opposed efforts to reestablish various forms of coerced labor. In 1861, he advised the government to overturn a labor code from the northern coastal province of Lambayeque (an economic rival of Arequipa) that included the conscription of vagrants and fines for missed work, on the grounds that "society does not have the right to obligate a man to work more time than is necessary to earn his daily bread."[66]

His advice that "if they want permanent laborers, they should stimulate them with a salary and good treatment" was reminiscent of Miguel Abril's defense of indigenous workers before Arequipa's departmental junta in 1829.[67] As for the urban poor, what they needed was not charity, but jobs: "Before being able to contemplate enriching man's spirit, it is necessary to first assure his existence through work."[68] When populist political movements were reinvigorated in Lima in the 1860s, Paz Soldán expressed his support, hosting a meeting of three hundred artisans at the Club Progresista.[69] And his legal advice to the government on free trade included protecting artisans from state regulation.[70]

Paz Soldán was also quick to denounce, in fiery language, the oppression of the indigenous population by corrupt officials and greedy landlords (who were never from Arequipa). After an indigenous uprising in Huancané, Puno, shocked the country, Paz Soldán scoffed that it was no "caste war," but rather "the resistance of the oppressed against their oppressors."[71] He lamented the rebels' ignorance and their state of degradation, but was confident that they could be reformed. "The Indians are no more savage or ferocious than other peoples who have been attracted to a social and civilized life," he paternalistically pointed out.[72]

Finally, Paz Soldán enthusiastically promoted the civil liberties of common folk, in a language that echoed the appeals of defendants in Arequipa's courts. In 1868 he acknowledged the need to reform the penal code, because "the

65. José Gregorio Paz Soldán, "Memoria sobre la esclavitura en el Perú" (Jan. 12, 1846), in Ricardo Aranda, ed., *Colección de los tratados*, vol. 8 (Lima: Imprenta del Estado, 1905), 195–215.

66. Gastón, *Compilación de las vistas fiscales*, vol. 1, 12.

67. Ibid., 13. See Chapter 2.

68. Ibid., 405.

69. Paul Gootenberg, *Imagining Development: Economic Ideas in Peru's "Fictitious Prosperity" of Guano, 1840–1880* (Berkeley and Los Angeles: University of California Press, 1993), 149.

70. Gastón, *Compilación de las vistas fiscales*, vol. 1, 122–23, 475–76.

71. Ibid., 45.

72. Ibid., 47. For further defenses of the indigenous population, see 65–66, 70.

personal liberty and honor of citizens are not sufficiently guaranteed."[73] Although he lamented that crimes often went unpunished, he still advocated due process and advised judges to be cautious, because "they should be friends of liberty."[74] Therefore, Paz Soldán frequently defended the independence of the judiciary by denouncing abuses by prefects and police officers.[75]

One of the youngest liberals who supported the 1854 revolution was José María Quimper. Born in the province of Camaná in 1828, he was educated in Arequipa, where he received degrees in letters, theology, and law. In 1852, he served as fiscal in a case against two of the Masías brothers for insulting a police officer; his advice that the charges were not serious enough for the state to pursue may be an early indication of his political sympathies.[76] Quimper served in various national administrations, but he is best known for his political writings. After publishing several short books aimed at (in his own words) "enlightening the masses of Peru in the knowledge of their political rights and duties," he compiled his philosophy of government in the two-volume *Derecho político general.*[77]

As a classical nineteenth-century liberal, Quimper emphasized the principles of order and morality, defended the free market, and warned that the sacred principle of liberty should not be carelessly invoked "before the uneducated [*inconsciente*] masses to irritate their passions."[78] Nevertheless, the core of his theory of government consisted of a defense of individual liberty and civil guarantees that certainly would have resonated with the popular classes of Arequipa. He emphasized the inviolability of the home, where "a man is the only sovereign."[79] A man should be protected from arbitrary arrest, and his detention limited to the absolute minimum time required for a trial.[80] If convicted, continued Quimper, a man's life was still sacred; rather than the death penalty, "the true interest of society is in

73. Ibid., 349.
74. Ibid., 560 (quotation), 414–15, 449–50.
75. Ibid., 609, 615.
76. ARAR/CS/Crim (8-I-1852), "Contra Eusebio y Manuel Masías por haber insultado al Teniente Coronel de policía."
77. José María Quimper, *Derecho político general*, vol. 1 (Lima: Editorial Benito Gil, 1887), 17. For one of his books aimed at artisans, see Quimper, *Instrucción política y reformas para el pueblo* (Arequipa: Imprenta de Francisco Ibañez, 1854). Another of his early works was republished as *El principio de la libertad* (Lima: Ediciones Hora del Hombre, 1948).
78. Quimper, *El principio de la libertad*, 28.
79. Quimper, *Derecho político general*, vol. 1, 313.
80. Ibid., 312.

reforming the delinquent, purifying his soul and in rooting out crime from his heart."[81]

In addition to physical security, Quimper emphasized the guarantee to honor, "because any harm that affects it ends the social existence of an individual."[82] For private citizens or government officials who violated any of these guarantees, he called for severe penalties. True order, asserted Quimper, did not rest upon the actions of the police or a standing army, but rather upon the effective defense of civil rights.[83] "Sustain therefore these rights and defend them with determination," he declared, "in them lies your life, your honor."[84] Defendants in the courts of Arequipa would have agreed that such rights were not merely abstract.

Quimper's defense of civil liberties reflected judicial practice in Arequipa. So too was it, effectively, limited to men. In theory, Quimper recognized the injustice of allowing men to act in the name of their wives and children and advocated equal rights for women, based upon the image of republican motherhood: "If the woman's influence [acción] on the customs, education, and moral and physical force of the citizens is recognized as so powerful, she should have an equal status to the man."[85] Nevertheless he feared that, in practice, to protect the potential freedoms of women and children could lead to the violation of men's basic right as heads of households to inviolability of the home. In the end, therefore, he came down in support of absolute patriarchal authority: "In political society, the family remains for the individual as it existed in the society of nature. The [civil] pact did not alter in this respect the rights and duties of men."[86] Quimper's position on this issue was undoubtedly influenced, in part, by his experience in Arequipa, where authorities rewarded men's loyalty to the republic and proper conduct by reinforcing their power within the household.

Even the region's most radical political philosopher, Francisco de Paula González Vigil, supported patriarchal authority. Vigil had studied theology in Arequipa before independence and served as a priest in his native province of Tacna. In 1826 he was elected a deputy to the National Convention, and in 1831 he returned to Arequipa for a doctorate in law. He subsequently represented Tacna in the legislature for many terms, where he frequently spoke out against abuses by the executive branch and served as the director of the

81. Ibid., 200.
82. Ibid., 205.
83. Ibid., 60; and vol. 2, 197–200, 281–83.
84. Quimper, *El principio de la libertad*, 56.
85. Quimper, *Derecho político general*, vol. 2, 10; see also vol. 1, 396.
86. Quimper, *El principio de la libertad*, 55–56.

national library under Castilla. The bulk of his published work developed a critique of the Catholic church as an institution, earning him the condemnation of ecclesiastical authorities, including his former ally Luna Pizarro. Unlike the classical liberals, Vigil's political philosophy emphasized the importance of community and civic associations. He advocated a work ethic for the poor, but also encouraged the rich to share their wealth with the less fortunate and contributed to the populist newspaper *El hijo del pueblo*.[87] He praised the positive influence that mothers could have on the virtues of their children and, therefore, called for the education of women. But he was emphatic that their place was in the home: "Far from us is the idea of vindicating women in the exercise of political rights or to make her appear casting her vote in the popular elections and disputing man for posts and magistracies."[88] His fear of the conservative influence of priests upon women led him to assert that patriarchal authority, divinely ordained, preceded that of governments, which were, by contrast, based upon popular sovereignty.[89]

Paz Soldán, Quimper, and Vigil, like many liberals, advocated the separation of church and state and the ascendancy of secular over canon law. Throughout the eighteenth and nineteenth centuries, moreover, first the crown and then republican officials eroded the church's sphere of authority. Although republican officials were not anticlerical, they did insist on the right to exercise control over ecclesiastical appointments and repeatedly used forced loans, clerical taxes, and the nationalization of church property to make up for chronic revenue shortfalls. By contrast, bishop José Sebastián Goyeneche of Arequipa (later archbishop of Peru) was the most vigorous defender of church privileges in Peru, though his moral indignation was balanced by a pragmatic need to come to terms with the various political administrations.[90] Although disputes between the church and state in Are-

---

87. Francisco de Paula González Vigil, *Importancia de las asociaciones, importancia de la educación popular* (1858; reprint, Lima: Ediciones Hora del Hombre, 1948); and Gootenburg, *Imagining Development*, 148.

88. Francisco de Paula González Vigil, *Importancia de la educación del bello sexo* (Lima: Instituto Nacional de Cultura, 1976), 50.

89. Ibid., 78.

90. The leader of the 1834 rebellion, Gen. Domingo Nieto, denounced the bishop as an "enemy of the people" for allegedly cooperating with the opposition and refusing to pay a forced loan; see *El Republicano*, July 5, 1834, 5–6. For examples of moderately anticlerical articles in the local official newspaper, see *El Republicano*, Jan. 7, 1826, 26–28; Oct. 21, 1826, 206–8; June 21, 1828, 109; and May 16, 1835, 3–4. For an overview of church-state relations in this period, see Pilar García Jordán, "¿Poder eclesiástico frente a poder civil? Algunas reflexiones sobre la iglesia Peruana ante la formación del estado moderno, 1808–1860," *Boletín Americanista* 26, no. 34 (1984): 45–74; García Jordán, "La iglesia Peruana ante la formación del estado moderno,

quipa were usually resolved before escalating into serious rifts, judicial officials frequently upheld individual rights over the bishop's objections.

In a dramatic incident that entered local lore, a young nun set fire to a cadaver to give the impression that she had died, and she subsequently escaped from the convent of Santa Rosa. Although the ecclesiastical court refused to grant her secularization, Paz Soldán restored her civil rights, winning praise from the editors of *El Republicano*, who denounced religious despotism.[91] A few years later he similarly overrode a case of ecclesiastical censorship, with the assertion that "the republic recognizes no laws other than those that it has given or adopted."[92]

The strength of the church is often cited as the reason for Arequipa's social conservatism, but its role in early republican politics is ambivalent and needs further study. Although the bishops of Arequipa were royalist and conservative, priests like Mariano de Arce, Luna Pizarro, González Vigil, and Valdivia were at the forefront of the independence movements and liberal politics.

Furthermore, little is known about popular religious beliefs.[93] At least in the late colonial period, bishops were frustrated in their efforts to mold their flock into "proper" Catholics. There are also hints that in the heat of political activism, common Arequipeños did not always respect ecclesiastical authority. In 1834, for example, a crowd of men and soldiers occupied the cathedral when the bishop refused to say mass for a political occasion.[94] Similarly, when the prefect complained that the ringing of church bells at odd hours was disturbing the peace, the bishop responded that it was dificult to resist crowds that forced their way into the bell towers.[95]

Nevertheless, a growing desire for order and shared grievances against the

---

1821–1862," *Histórica* 10, no. 1 (1986): 19–43; and García Jordán, *Iglesia y poder en el Perú contemporáneo, 1821–1919* (Cuzco: CERA Bartolomé de Las Casas, 1991).

91. *El Republicano*, Dec. 21, 1833, 6–7. Paz Soldán was also a thorn in side of Archbishop Luna Pizarro; see *Escritos políticos*, 117, 120–22, 124–26, and 129.

92. Decision dated Aug. 26, 1840, in BNP doc. D8323, "Apuntamientos sueltos . . . de José Gregorio Paz Soldán," ff. 197–99.

93. Jeffrey Klaiber believes that until the latter part of the nineteenth century, common Peruvians did not have a strong identification with the church as an institution separate from their general beliefs in Catholicism; see Klaiber, *La iglesia en el Perú* (Lima: Pontificia Universidad Católica del Perú, 1988).

94. Letter of the cathedral chapter to the minister of government, Oct. 9, 1834, in AGN, R.J. (Ministerio de Justicia): Leg. 162.

95. Letters dated Nov. 23 and Nov. 25, 1841, in AAA, Libro Copiador de Oficios (1841–1843).

central state may have permitted a renewed alliance between religious and civil authorities in Arequipa during the second half of the nineteenth century.[96] In 1868, for example, the city's officials refused to swear loyalty to a new liberal constitution that contained anticlerical provisions. Significantly, it was primarily women—excluded from the terms of honorable citizenship, and who looked to the church for help with domestic problems—who crowded into the cathedral to protest the heretical document.

The White City

Popular concepts of rights, developed first within the early republican courts and then expressed politically during the intense mobilization during the elections of 1849 to 1851, subsequently influenced the theories of liberalism advocated by prominent Arequipeños at the national level. These liberals consistently called for the protection of civil liberties, advocated the right of journeymen artisans to work independently, and favored voluntary civic militias over a standing army. The same process led to the emergence of the myth of the White City.

The Masías family, chief instigators of the pro-Vivanco riots, continued to dominate local politics throughout the nineteenth century. Diego Masías y Calle (possibly the same politician whose name has come up repeatedly in this chapter, but more likely his younger second cousin) wrote poems and plays that conveyed an image of Arequipa as liberal—in both the political and economic spheres. In 1876, he composed an allegory to be performed as part of the celebrations for Independence Day. When the character representing the nation laments the passing of the generation of valiant soldiers from the wars of independence, Glory replies: "I can be found not only crowning combatants / But also in work." La Patria decides, therefore, to seek help in Arequipa, the "town [*pueblo*] of progress." Her search is rewarded in the final scene, when Work and Industry come to the rescue.

A longer play of the same year, entitled "Clotilde," reveals the importance of gender with a lesson for women about the importance of both political and personal loyalty. The work also highlights changing meanings of honor. The

---

96. In contrast to the earlier hesitancy to endorse censorship, in 1853 the fiscal of Arequipa alerted the prefect to a planned student speech that might promote the freedom to choose any faith; see *El Republicano*, Sept. 28, 1853, 3–4.

hero, before departing to join the fight for independence upon the urging of his beloved, declares: "If there was a time in which I believed / In the noble cradle, today I see / No more titles of nobility / Than virtue and talent." Although unpublished, these plays, potentially, could have reached a wide audience within Arequipa.[97]

Fifteen years later, Jorge Polar dedicated his book *Arequipa: Description and Social Study* to Diego Masías y Calle, who was, at that time, mayor of the city. An unusual mixture of scientific and poetic observations, this book may be the first published expression of the myth of the White City.[98] "The People of Arequipa are, above all, honorable," wrote Polar, "with an honesty carried to the extreme of sacrifice, to heroism."[99] He asserted that the absence of a true aristocracy mitigated class conflict in Arequipa and offered social mobility "for the man who has heart and talent."[100] For these reasons, he maintained, Arequipa was particularly well suited for democracy and progress.

Nonetheless, Polar did not spare his homeland from all criticism. In order to reach its destiny, Arequipa's population would need to shake off its colonial heritage and develop a greater sense of individualism and drive for success. The women of Arequipa, with their skin "the color of pearls," could serve as an inspiration towards this end; in order to gain the hand of such a bride, "man improves himself, he avoids impure contacts, he wants to grow, to be strong and have honor, to have glory."[101]

The link between the pro-Vivanco riot, which opened this chapter, and María Nieves y Bustamante's 1892 regionalist novel, *Jorge, or the Son of the People*, is particularly striking. The story opens on the morning of April 21, 1851, with the wedding of José Flórez, "an honorable artisan."[102] The nuptial celebrations in the "modest home" are interrupted by a heavy pounding on the door; "Here you are very calm," chides the *paisano* who enters, while "the *echeniquistas* supported by the police are assassinating the people."[103]

97. I would like to thank Nils Jacobsen of the University of Illinois at Urbana-Champaign for providing me copies of the manuscript versions of these plays.

98. Jorge Polar, *Arequipa: Descripción y estudio social*, 3d ed. (1891; reprint, Arequipa: Primer Festival del Libro Arequipeño, 1958). Or perhaps the title of first should go to the lengthy and effusive chapter on Arequipa in Mateo Paz Soldán, *Geografía del Perú* (Paris: Fermin Didot, 1862), 432–66.

99. Polar, *Arequipa*, 203.

100. Ibid., 202.

101. Ibid., 198.

102. María Nieves y Bustamante, *Jorge, o el hijo del pueblo*, vol. 1 (1892; reprint, Arequipa: Librería Editorial Ibero Americana, 1958), 11.

103. Ibid., vol. 1, 15.

The women weep and pray, while the men run to the bridge to join the crowd calling for the lowering of the flag hoisted for Echenique's inauguration. When a policeman wounds a civilian, it is José's orphaned nephew Jorge, the hero of the novel, who cries out: "To arms!"[104] Nieves y Bustamante's description of the ensuing battle closely follows Juan Gualberto Valdivia's account, with the notable exception of any references to looting (forty years had assuaged the qualms of eyewitnesses). By the end of the second day, the city has been liberated, but the patriarch of the Flórez family, Don Raimundo, lies mortally wounded. On his deathbed, he reveals to his son José a secret that he must vow to keep silent: Jorge, whom everyone believes to be illegitimate, is really the offspring of a clandestine marriage.

The numerous chapters that follow interweave the personal stories of the characters, descriptions of Arequipa's landscape and customs, and the political events of the period. The villain of the novel is, not surprisingly, an arrogant and conniving military officer from Lima, named Alfredo Iriarte. Nevertheless, two Arequipeños are also the object of criticism. Señor Don Guillermo de Latorre and his sister Doña Enriqueta are depicted as relics of the colonial period: ambitious, obsessed with titles and appearances, and disdainful of those beneath them.

It was no coincidence that Nieves y Bustamante chose that family name for her characters; the La Torre family was descended from one of the founders of the city. But, fortunately for Arequipa, they were a dying breed, and by the end of the novel a new generation has come to the fore. Don Guillermo's saintly daughter Isabel, unlike the rest of her family, treats servants and workers with the respect they deserve. After being deceived by Iriarte with false promises of marriage, she enters the convent of Santa Catalina. Thus, reflecting the patriarchal nature of Arequipa's myth, even in this version written by a woman, the heroine of the novel is a cloistered and virginal member of the elite.[105] Just as the potential threat posed by real rioters in 1851 is elided by idealizing the artisan characters, plebeian women in the novel are very distinct from the active and assertive women who populate the archives. Isabel's maid, Cecilia, and José's bride, Rosa, who do not even have

---

104. Ibid., vol. 1, 19.

105. For analyses of representations of gender, nationalism, and republicanism in fiction, see Doris Sommer, *Foundational Fictions: The National Romances of Latin America* (Berkeley and Los Angeles: University of California Press, 1991); Francine Masiello, *Between Civilization and Barbarism: Women, Nation, and Literary Culture in Modern Argentina* (Lincoln: University of Nebraska Press, 1992); and Lynn Hunt, *The Family Romance of the French Revolution* (Berkeley and Los Angeles: University of California Press, 1992).

last names, literally play supporting roles in the novel. There may have been room for chicherías in the myth of the White City, but not for chicheras. It is, therefore, men and masculine honor who take center stage. Ironically, the reader's expectation of a marital union between Isabel and Jorge is thwarted when it is revealed that the two are half-siblings. Rather, the hero alone unifies the various strands of regional identity. As the son of aristocratic Latorre but raised by the "people," Jorge represents a literal embodiment of honor as status *and* virtue. In a dramatic final scene, however, Jorge renounces both his name and his inheritance: "The fruit of the honorable work of the artisan is enough for me to live; there is no bread sweeter than that earned by the sweat of one's brow."[106]

Polar's ideal Arequipeño and the fictional Jorge, respectable men who worked hard, supported their families, and defended their homeland, bear remarkable resemblance to the image of the honorable citizen asserted by plebeian men during the transition from the colonial to republican period. However, what became increasingly absent, as this worldview was elevated to the level of social mythology, were its origins in the daily interactions and conflicts between living plebeians and local authorities. It was precisely that combination of sufficient credibility with idealization that held together regional cross-class alliances into the next century. Politicians from Arequipa continued to be major players in both national elections and armed revolts, including the progressive dictatorship of Mariano Ignacio Prado in 1865, the *civilista* movement of Manuel Pardo in 1872, the 1894 revolution of Nicolás de Piérola, the decentralist revolt against Augusto B. Leguía in 1930, and protests against military dictator Manuel Odría in 1950 and 1955. And repeatedly, the leaders of these movements published poems, plays, and memoirs that contributed to the mythic image of Arequipa as a white, middle-class, patriarchal democracy.[107]

---

106. Nieves y Bustamante, *Jorge, o el hijo del pueblo*, vol. 3, 284.

107. In addition to the works of Masías and Polar, see Belaúnde, *Arequipa de mi infancia*; Manuel J. Bustamante de La Fuente (a leader of the 1930–31 movements), *La Monja Gutiérrez y la Arequipa de ayer y de hoy* (Lima: n.p., 1971–72); and Mario Polar (active in the opposition to Odría), *Viejos y nuevos tiempos* (Lima: Francisco Moncloa Editores, 1968). In 1958 the city held the First Festival of the Arequipeño Book, which released new editions by Arequipa's eighteenth- and nineteenth-century authors.

Conclusion

The White City Revisited

Enduring social myths are powerful, not as precise reflections of reality but because, through continual processes of negotiation, key versions incorporate enough elements to ring true for a critical mass. Elites promote myths to mobilize support, but in so doing must contend with constant contestation and redefinition. The elements of conflict that myths erase in order to promote unity and harmony, historians can partially recover. The striking resemblance between Bustamante's fictional Jorge and the very real Tomás Peñaranda and Francisco Butrón—who defended their right as "honorable and married artisans" and "free citizens" to support the candidate of their choice in 1850—is no coincidence.[1] Nor should we forget those excluded from, rather than incorporated into, the myth of the White City. Chichera María Escalante vociferously defended her rights as a "mujer de bien" before the police in 1830,[2] but her counterparts in Bustamante's novel were softened into anonymous barmaids cheerfully serving drinks to masculine heroes.

1. ARAR/Pref (27-II-1850), "Seguido sobre una azonada en la otra banda." See Chapter 6.
2. ARAR/CS/Crim (4-I-1830), "Contra Doña María Escalante por resistir el Diputado de Policía." See Chapter 3.

The process by which the myth of the White City became hegemonic challenges us to rethink the role of the popular classes in shaping the political transition from colonial to republican forms of rule. Republicanism and liberalism did not originate in Latin America, but these ideologies were transformed in distinctive ways after their introduction with independence. Intellectuals and politicians had the means to articulate political philosophies, but the preceding chapters have revealed the mark left by members of the popular classes as they transformed themselves from subjects to citizens, by negotiating meanings of honor within the courts.

On the one hand, elites from Arequipa could promote their agenda on a national level because they had gained support for it at home, and, when necessary, the city's artisans and small farmers would take to the streets in defense of their leaders. Even more importantly, however, tensions in local society had shaped the agenda itself by adding to free-trade liberalism the defense of individual liberties and support for honest working men.

The degree of change following independence and the significant role of the popular classes only become apparent, however, if we broaden our view of politics to include everyday negotiations of rule. The division between public and private spheres posited by republican states was largely artificial. Indeed, in Arequipa the degree of state intervention in popular culture and the household, arenas where gender dynamics were central, increased after independence. The granting of rights to "honorable" male citizens and the repression of women deemed without virtue, therefore, were interrelated processes. Moreover, common folk heard about new political concepts and laws in speeches, but they continued to interpret their meanings during the course of discussions and arguments about honor with neighbors and family members. Finally, direct interactions with agents of the state were most likely to occur in court, a forum that allowed at least some negotiation over rights.

Culture and Politics in Arequipa

The regional solidarity evident in Arequipa was rooted in local social relations. An economy based upon agriculture, trade, and small-scale manufacturing provided occupations that allowed many Arequipeños to consider themselves worthy of the title Don or Doña. Commercial farming, in particular, was dominated by landowners of small and medium-size farms and by renters. Like any Spanish American city of that period, Arequipa had both rich and poor inhabitants, but neither local authorities nor travelers noted the stark contrasts frequently commented upon in larger capitals. Once elite families fell on hard times and their sons entered the professions, they were likely to come into contact with modestly successful artisans, small farmers, and traders, who aspired to join the ranks of "respectable" society. There were certainly numerous servants and workers who were excluded from such social and political networks; nevertheless, it is striking that even some nonwhite day laborers claimed—and were recognized as having— honorable reputations.

Regional solidarity was further facilitated by ambiguous ethnic boundaries. To most outsiders, including officials from Lima, the majority of Arequipeños seemed mestizo or cholo; even prominent ladies were described as having skin the color of gingerbread. It is understandable, therefore, that the city's inhabitants preferred not to dwell upon racial labels. Even when they were called upon to classify their neighbors by caste, Arequipeños rarely agreed on the precise terminology. Ethnic identity depended upon a variety of factors beyond the color of one's skin, such as language, dress, customs, and occupation. As long as there was still communal land available in the late colonial period, for example, the children of mixed marriages might claim an indigenous identity to justify their membership in a community. By the mid-nineteenth century, on the other hand, the number of villagers willing to declare themselves to census takers as Indians had declined. Even more striking than the apparent ambiguity of ethnic identity was the widespread acceptance by officials of claims to whiteness.

Blurred lines of race and class laid the groundwork for a broad popular culture in Arequipa, which shaped interpretations of honor and facilitated political mobilization. People with varying degrees of social and economic status lived, worked, and socialized in close quarters. Under such conditions, Arequipeños gained a familiarity with their neighbors that often extended to intimate details of their personal lives. Although these shared experiences built up a sense of community, it was not free from conflict. Gender relations, in particular, were an arena of discord; while men and women seemed to agree on a general picture of marital roles, for example, they often differed in their interpretation of those responsibilities. Therefore, the reinforcement of patriarchal rights by republican officials helped them secure support among men of the popular classes for the new state. The language and ritual of neighborhood disputes, moreover, carried over into political actions, and the values invoked most often increasingly bore the stamp of middling respectability.

As throughout Spanish America, honor played a central role in Arequipa's culture, both at its elite and more plebeian levels. In the colonial period, notions of honor were hierarchical; members of elite families based their claims to status upon noble—or at least "pure"—lineages, and they reinforced those claims in ostentatious displays of finery and public ritual. Popular notions of honor, on the other hand, emphasized personal conduct over innate traits. Men, in particular, desired the recognition of their peers as fellow hombres de bien, while they treated their clear social superiors with respect, if not subservience. Independence, however, created a new context, in which the code of honor was transformed significantly. As titles to nobility went the way of the monarchy, status gave way, increasingly, to virtue. A new, more egalitarian and republican sense of honor formed the basis for the definition of the rights and obligations of citizenship.

Nevertheless, just as popular culture in Arequipa was suffused with conflict, republican honor emerged out of real contradictions and tensions during the transition from the colonial order. Civil authorities during the late colonial period had relied upon neighborhood networks of surveillance and a common acceptance of social hierarchies to mitigate disorder. Therefore, they saw the bishop's morality campaign as unnecessary and even intrusive. The turbulent years of the early republic, however, shattered that relative calm. Fearing crime and espousing liberal doctrines of discipline, police and military officers increased repressive methods of social control but met widespread resistance.

In the major capitals of Spanish America, efforts to repress crime and popular culture had begun under the Bourbons in the late eighteenth century, but their association with the transition to republicanism in a provincial city like Arequipa had important consequences. The transformation of honor had its roots in the Enlightenment, but the language of rights was new. Many plebeians protested that they were not criminals or vagrants, but honorable citizens. Those who were able to support their claims with proof of hard work and respectable conduct were granted some constitutional rights.

But such political gains were limited, and they did not necessarily improve the economic position of common folk. Indeed, the willingness of elites to grant honor to those beneath them may reflect a growing belief that wealth, not status, was the primary social marker. Moreover, as social and cultural activities gradually became more segregated by class, the need for a strict code of manners to govern behavior in mixed company declined. Finally, common men, who served as militia soldiers, workers, and, sometimes, voters, gained at the expense of women of their class, who were forced to meet more stringent standards of moral conduct without earning any corresponding status as citizens.

Whatever the limits, legal rights that allowed plebeian men to protect themselves from arbitrary conscription or criminal prosecution and to govern their own households were not merely abstract principles. It is understandable, therefore, that they would be willing to follow liberal politicians and caudillos who included the defense of civil liberties on their platforms. That republican leaders were responsive to such demands from below, moreover, indicates that popular support—whether on the battlefield or at the ballot box—was a crucial factor in determining which political faction would emerge dominant from the turbulent years of the early republic.

Arequipa in Comparative Perspective

This research on popular politics during the crucial, but little-studied, transition from colonial to republican rule helps resolve apparent paradoxes of Arequipa's ongoing role in Peruvian history. Historians have identified the region's dominant classes as simultaneously bourgeois and feudal, and its politicians as socially conservative, even as they promoted economic liberalism. By the second half of the nineteenth century, the earlier demands of the region's elites for free trade paid off in a profitable export economy based upon wool.[3] When prices for wool on the international market later declined, during the 1920s, the commercial elite recognized a need to modernize production and strengthen the internal market through the promotion of local industries.[4]

Even those who identify the southern elite as a new class of upwardly mobile exporters, however, see its "seigniorial" worldview as an anachronistic holdover from the colonial period.[5] What these scholars have missed is the

---

3. Flores Galindo, *Arequipa y el sur andino*; Burga and Reátegui, *Lanas y capital mercantil en el sur*; Alberto Flores Galindo, Orlando Plaza, and Teresa Oré, "Oligarquía y capital comercial en el sur Peruano, 1870–1930," *Debates en sociología* 3 (1978): 54–66; Baltazar Caravedo Molinari, "Poder central y descentralización: Perú, 1931," *Apuntes* 5, no. 9 (1979): 112–15; and Jacobsen, *Mirages of Transition*.

4. Caravedo Molinari, "Poder central," 117–21; and Jacobsen, "Free Trade, Regional Elites, and the Internal Market," 168–69.

5. Flores Galindo, Plaza, and Oré, "Oligarquía y capital comercial," 68; José Luis Rénique,

significant transformation in the meaning of honor and *señorío* that took place during the early republican period. Similarly, the recurrent conservative elements, such as emphases on morality, labor discipline, and "traditional" gender roles, in the platforms of political movements emerging from Arequipa were not simple colonial legacies, but the outcome of attempts after independence to simultaneously incorporate and contain demands from below.

The evidence from Arequipa that popular engagement in politics began soon after independence can also deepen our understanding of important national political movements, such as *civilismo*, that developed in the second half of the nineteenth century. The political clique of cousins—Diego Masías, Domingo Gamio, and Juan Mariano Goyeneche (Jr.)—that became dominant in Arequipa in 1854 mobilized local voters for Manuel Pardo during his campaign for the presidency in 1871 and 1872.[6] Recent research has highlighted the populist elements of Pardo's civilismo, previously seen primarily as the epitome of bourgeois economic liberalism.[7] In light of this study of Arequipa, it becomes apparent that the civilistas' use of republican symbols in civic rituals and their appeal to order, work, and honorable citizenship were rooted in the daily negotiations of rule that had been developing since independence. Finally, Pardo's promotion of both exports and simple manufacturing echoed earlier economic proposals from Arequipa that had appealed to the economic elite without alienating artisans and small farmers.

In addition to reshaping interpretations of elite ideology, this study provides a foundation for historicizing popular participation in politics. On May Day 1906, workers, most of them still artisans, marched through the streets of Arequipa in support of a resurgent liberal movement. The previous lack of research on the early republican period made the participation of artisans in this liberal movement look like a "sudden change" in direction and a "leap in their consciousness."[8] Their organization into formal associations was new, but when carpenter Mariano E. Valencia, the treasurer of the Social Center of the Worker, addressed the crowd in the plaza, his words echoed

---

"Los descentralistas arequipeños en la crisis del año 30," *Allpanchis* 12 (1979): 54; and Francisco Villena, "La sociedad arequipeña y el Partido Liberal, 1885–1920," *Análisis* 8–9 (1979), 82.

6. McEvoy, "Estampillas y votos," 122.

7. Carmen E. McEvoy, "The Republican Utopia: Ideals and Realities in the Formation of Peruvian Political Culture, 1871–1919 (Ph.D. diss., University of California at San Diego, 1995), 79–176; and Paul Gootenberg, *Imagining Development*, 71–89.

8. Villena, "La sociedad arequipeña," 91.

those of artisans fifty years earlier: "My companions: Workers all, I see joy in your faces, because we are celebrating the Festival of Labor, of labor, which every honorable man exercises because it ennobles him and makes him useful to society; because intelligent workers mean the enhancement of the nation in which they live."[9]

In addition to an acknowledgement of their honor and protection of civil rights, however, artisans at the turn of the century also called for a share of the material benefits of progress. Just as nineteenth-century liberals had extended their call for economic freedom to include the protection of independent artisans from state (and guild) intervention, important fractions of the regional bourgeoisie maintained their hegemony in the twentieth century by recognizing the need for moderate labor reform.[10]

Politicians from Arequipa throughout the nineteenth and twentieth centuries would emphasize their region's exceptionalism in order to claim a leading role in the nation, but a broader view reveals connections both within Peru and throughout Latin America. Although the results were not identical, the role of the urban popular classes in shaping the political transition from colonial to republican rule was important far beyond Arequipa. Even scholars who have called attention to their role, however, have often made their assertions upon a thin basis of evidence.[11] The preceding chapters have shown how we can go beyond demonstrating the presence of plebeians in rioting crowds to uncovering elements of their political consciousness. Studies of nineteenth-century artisans have, briefly, noted the centrality of honor in popular republicanism, but have focused primarily on the educated leaders and not analyzed in depth the underlying discourses of the rank and file.[12] An examination of judicial records from other regions, therefore, might reveal how proclamations in newspapers and pamphlets were rooted in artisans' encounters with the officials of the state.[13]

9. Quoted in Raúl Fernández Llerena, *Los orígenes del movimiento obrero en Arequipa: El Partido Liberal y el primero de mayo de 1906* (Arequipa and Lima: Amauta and Tarea, 1984), 207.

10. Baltazar Caravedo Molinari, *Desarrollo desigual y lucha política en el Perú, 1948–1956* (Lima: Instituto de Estudios Peruanos, 1978).

11. Torcuato S. Di Tella, for example, asserts that the masses were crucial, but he focuses almost entirely upon the writers who attempted to mobilize them. See Di Tella, *National Popular Politics in Early Independent Mexico*.

12. Sowell, *The Early Colombian Labor Movement*, 94–98; Gootenberg, *Imagining Development*, 143–63; and Krüggeler, "Unreliable Drunkards or Honorable Citizens?"

13. See Richard Warren, "Vagrancy and Political Order in Nineteenth-Century Mexico," paper presented at the annual meeting of the American Historical Association, 1994.

Nonetheless, there were also differences between provincial cities and capitals. Artisan associations in Lima, Bogotá, and Santiago were able to form political alliances with liberal parties, yet such a strategy tied their fate closely to the fortunes of particular political factions. Once those movements were defeated, often in the wake of riots, dominant groups tended to depict artisans as unruly and lazy, rejecting rather than incorporating their claims to respectability.[14]

The insistence of artisan associations on protective tariffs became the key point of contention with political parties, most of which espoused free trade by mid-century. Yet divisive conflicts over trade never erupted in early republican Arequipa, Peru's "bastion" of economic liberalism. Perhaps the competition from imports seemed less direct in the provinces and could be blamed upon the capital. Moreover, guilds were weak, and alternative artisan organizations did not develop until the end of the nineteenth century. While artisans were a strong presence in Arequipa's political movements, they did not yet assert a clear identity apart from other members of the popular classes. Class tensions in Arequipa, rather than manifesting themselves as conflict between economic elites and a united and relatively autonomous group of artisans, were more individualized and resolved on a case-by-case basis through the courts. Furthermore, such divisions could be bridged in movements that emphasized a united regional front against the central state in Lima. Further research may reveal similar alliances in other provincial cities throughout Latin America.

Although the urban popular classes in nineteenth-century provincial cities have received less attention than their counterparts in the capitals, historians have begun to explore the role of peasants in national politics. Challenging the stereotype of the peasant as isolated and backward-looking, they have revealed ways in which rural folk engaged republican and liberal ideologies. In general, peasants asserted their rights not through a language of individual honor, but through one resting on communal rights. In Peru, in particular, they refashioned the colonial pact to base their claim to citizenship upon the payment of the national head tax.[15] In Mexico, both the important role

14. In addition to works cited above, see L. A. Romero, *La Sociedad de la Igualdad: Los artesanos de Santiago de Chile y sus primeras experiencias políticas, 1820–1851* (Buenos Aires: Instituto Torcuato Di Tella, 1978); Peter Blanchard, *The Origins of the Peruvian Labor Movement, 1883–1919* (Pittsburgh: University of Pittsburgh Press, 1982); and Francisco Quiroz Chueca, *La protesta de los artesanos: Lima-Callao, 1858* (Lima: Universidad Nacional Mayor de San Marcos, 1988).

15. See Contreras, "Estado republicano y tributo indígena," 9–44; Héctor Omar Noéjovich,

played by peasant militias in defeating foreign invasions, as well as the key alliances between particular peasant communities and factions of the liberals, resulted not in democracy but in keeping peasant demands at least on the national political agenda.[16] In Peru, by contrast, political elites rarely recognized peasants as citizens and, therefore, failed to construct a hegemonic nation-state.[17]

Like the artisan associations in the capitals, peasant communities were problematic allies for political elites. Though internally differentiated, their representation by a relatively autonomous corporate body could make peasant demands difficult to subsume within broader movements. Moreover, critical economic resources were at stake: land, labor, and fiscal revenue. Surrounded by a large rural indigenous population, early republican authorities in Cuzco dreamed of becoming political and economic mediators, but were frustrated in their attempts to intervene in the relatively autonomous communities. Hence there were no strong alternatives in Cuzco to a neocolonial discourse that depicted Indians as "unambitious and infantile" and, therefore, incapable of becoming citizens.[18] The erosion of first the land base and subsequently the tribute-paying population of indigenous communities in the valley of Arequipa, by contrast, made them seem less threatening.

The social construction of race, therefore, is another element underlying the degree of hegemony achieved at either national or regional levels. Only the elite tier of artisans in Cuzco, several of the most prominent being migrants from Arequipa, were able to win official recognition as "honorable citizens," while the rest were seen as lazy and "unreliable drunkards." Whites, who dominated the higher status trades, constituted only 4 percent

"Las relaciones del estado peruano con la población indígena en el siglo XIX a través de su legislación," *Histórica* 15, no. 1 (1991): 43–62; Peralta Ruíz, *En pos del tributo en el Cusco rural*; Méndez G., "Los campesinos, la independencia y la iniciación de la república," 165–88; Cecilia Méndez G., "República sin indios: La comunidad imaginada del Perú," in Henrique Urbano, ed., *Tradición y modernidad en los Andes* (Cuzco: CERA Bartolomé de las Casas, 1992), 15–42; Christine Hunefeldt, "Circulación y estructura tributaria: Puno, 1840–1890," in Henrique Urbano, ed., *Poder y violencia en los Andes* (Cuzco: CERA Bartolomé de las Casas, 1991), 189–210; Charles Walker, "Los indios en la transición de colonia a república: ¿Base social de la modernización política?" in Urbano, *Tradición y modernidad en los Andes*, 1–14; and Thurner, *From Two Republics to One Divided.*

16. Peter Guardino, "Identity and Nationalism in Mexico: Guerrero, 1780–1840," *Journal of Historical Sociology* 7, no. 3 (1994): 314–42; and Guardino, *Peasants, Politics, and the Formation of Mexico's National State.*

17. For a comparison, see Mallon, *Peasant and Nation.*

18. Walker, "Peasants, Caudillos, and the State in Peru."

of the population, according to an 1862 census. The remaining population was identified as 74 percent mestizo and 22 percent Indian.[19] In Lima, the perceived threat from unruly mobs of protectionist artisans was compounded by fears of the city's significant population of African descent (38 percent in 1818). Although the number of slaves declined steadily—from about 25 percent of the urban population in 1792 to 12 percent in 1839—they consistently formed a larger presence than slaves in Arequipa (about 4.5 percent in 1792). Conflicts between individual masters and slaves were, undoubtedly, as common in Arequipa as elsewhere, but elites did not explicitly express the fears of potential slave rebellions and gangs of black bandits that were often voiced by their counterparts in Lima.[20]

The relationship between race and hegemonic alliances, however, was not mechanical nor automatic. Arequipa's relatively larger "white" population was not simply a demographic fact, but a result of ideologies and practices among both elites and members of the popular classes that de-emphasized racial identities. Elites in Arequipa were no less racist than others, but, based upon their interactions with the local indigenous population, they believed that assimilation was possible. An anonymous article serialized in the local newspaper in 1833 promoted a policy, which would later become dominant throughout much of Latin America, of "whitening" by "diluting and homogenizing" the *castas*. Significantly, the author connected racial policy to liberal politics, asserting that the indigenous population was held back not by inherent defects, but lack of education and true legal equality. To assuage the frustration of the lower classes, whose labor seemed to go unrewarded, he proposed making "practical" the "theoretical" guarantees and freedoms.[21]

Indeed, members of the popular classes in Arequipa did demand such rights, as citizens in the new republic. Class and ethnic conflict, therefore, could be contained (and later erased by myth making) through a combination of repression against criminality and incentives toward respectable behavior. This process laid the groundwork for a variant of liberalism that called for citizen militias rather than standing armies and advocated the protection of individual liberty, tempered by respect for the law and morality. Or, as

19. Krüggeler, "Unreliable Drunkards or Honorable Citizens?" 45. I am interpreting Krüggeler's evidence contrary to his own analysis that race was not a primary determinant of status.

20. Hunefeldt, *Paying the Price of Freedom*; Aguirre, *Agentes de su propia libertad*; and Peter Blanchard, *Slavery and Abolition in Early Republican Peru* (Wilmington: Scholarly Resources, 1992).

21. "Sobre las relaciones del Perú con la Europa, y consigo mismo," *El Republicano*, Sept. 28, 1833, 7; and Oct. 5, 1833, 7–8.

Belaúnde put it, liberalism "in the noble sense of the word, that is to say in the respect of individual rights, without utopias nor Jacobin radicalism."[22]

Of the regional elites who played a key role in nineteenth-century Peruvian politics, Arequipeños justified their influence by asserting a particular identity as white, hardworking, and democratic. But if we apply the insights from this analysis to other Latin American countries, we will find similar "white cities." In Colombia, Antioqueños have been identified as white—especially in contrast to the neighboring black province of Cauca—as well as hardworking (or "miserly," by their detractors). Although mining played a greater role than agriculture in Antioquia, small farming plots were distributed widely, and all white males of legitimate descent claimed the title of Don. Like Arequipa, its late colonial elite was successful in commerce, but on a more modest scale than merchants of viceregal capitals.[23] With slaves constituting almost 20 percent of its late colonial population, the region's nineteenth-century reputation of racial purity, like Arequipa's, relied upon both miscegenation and ideological whitening.[24] Finally, gender was a central component of Antioquia's mythic identity. In contrast, again, to the perceived sensuality of Cauca's African population, Antioqueños claimed to defend the "traditional" family. Women who did not conform to proper notions of sexual virtue, by the mid-nineteenth century, found themselves subject to arrest under vagrancy laws.[25] Antioqueños mobilized their myth to claim a role in national politics. Although its elites increasingly allied with the conservative (rather than liberal) party, their use of symbols from popular culture, such as the typical outfits of small farmers, suggests their success in forging a cross-class regional alliance.

Far from Arequipa, in the north of Mexico, the rural inhabitants of Chihuahua similarly asserted their identity as hardworking, entrepreneurial, and egalitarian, although their particular myth was rooted in the frontier experience. The Apache became the sign of ethnic barbarity, against which settlers of mixed descent defined themselves as civilized and, hence, de facto "white." In return for fighting the Apache, colonists gained access to land that tempered economic inequalities. Masculine honor—based upon military

22. Belaúnde, *Arequipa de mi infancia*, 131.

23. Ann Twinam, *Miners, Merchants, and Farmers in Colonial Colombia* (Austin: University of Texas Press, 1982).

24. Peter Wade, *Blackness and Race Mixture: The Dynamics of Racial Identity in Colombia* (London and Baltimore: Johns Hopkins University Press, 1993), 74–77.

25. Nancy Appelbaum, "Remembering Riosucio: Region, Race, and Community in Colombia, 1850-1920," (Ph.D. diss., University of Wisconsin at Madison, 1997).

prowess, the defense of virtuous white women, and productive labor—was a key component of *norteño* identity, one that would become a battle cry in this politically rebellious region.[26] As in Arequipa, this egalitarian myth was constructed in the heat of conflict, rather than reflecting uncontested social harmony. In Chihuahua, the critical turning point was not independence, but the end of the Indian wars in 1886. In response to the repeal of privileges by the central state that no longer needed militiamen, and because of conflicts with local elites over land and labor, smallholders and laborers rose up in repeated rebellions to defend their honor. The victory of northern factions in the 1910 revolution suggests that local elites were able to harness this rebelliousness within a hegemonic process.[27]

Prominent liberals from Arequipa based their political philosophies on European models; but their emphasis on certain elements, such as the inviolability of the home, and their addition of a right to honor, echoed the pleas of defendants they heard in court. That such appeals to masculine honor were also expressed in Antioquia and Chihuahua, as well as by artisans in cities throughout Spanish America, suggests that Arequipa may be less distinctive than it appears. However, in order to uncover the role played by both the urban and rural popular classes throughout Latin America during the transition from colonialism to republicanism, we need to look beyond the narrow sphere of formal politics.

It was in homes, taverns, and on street corners that key political concepts were adopted and reinterpreted before they could serve as a basis for mobilization. And the courts, those central institutions of Spanish American governance that linked state and society, provided arenas where common folk, lawyers, and judges negotiated the rights and obligations of colonial subjects who were becoming republican citizens.

---

26. Ana María Alonso, *Thread of Blood: Colonialism, Revolution, and Gender on Mexico's Northern Frontier* (Tucson: University of Arizona Press, 1995).

27. In addition to Alonso, see Daniel Nugent and Ana María Alonso, "Multiple Selective Traditions in Agrarian Reform and Agrarian Struggle: Popular Culture and State Formation in the *Ejido* of Namiquipa, Chihuahua," in *Everyday Forms of State Formation*, ed. Gilbert M. Joseph and Daniel Nugent (Durham: Duke University Press, 1994), 209–46; and Paul Vanderwood, "Region and Rebellion: The Case of Papigochic," in *Mexico's Regions: Comparative History and Development*, ed. Eric Van Young (San Diego: Center for U.S.–Mexican Studies, University of California at San Diego, 1992), 167–89.

Bibliography

Archives

Archivo Arzobispal de Arequipa (AAA), Arequipa
    Causas Civiles (AAA/Civ)
    Causas Penales (AAA/Pen)
    Matrimonios (AAA/Mat)
    Pedimentos (AAA/Ped)
Archivo del Palacio Arzobispal de Arequipa, Arequipa
    Libros de Bautismos
    Libros de Entierros
    Libros de Matrimonios
Archivo General de la Nacion (AGN), Lima
    Sección Colonial
        Campesinado: Derecho Indígena and Juzgado de Aguas
        Real Audiencia: Causas Civiles and Causas Criminales
        Superior Gobierno
    Sección Republicana
        Corte Superior de Justicia de Lima
        Ministerio de Gobierno y Relaciones Exteriores
        Ministerio de Hacienda
        Ministerio de Justicia
Archivo Histórico-Militar del Perú (Centro de Estudios Histórico-Militares del Perú) (AHMP [CEHMP]), Lima
        Correspondencia del Ministerio de Guerra
        Libros Copiadores
Archivo Municipal de Arequipa (AMA), Arequipa
    Libros de Actas de Cabildo (LAC)
    Libros de Aranceles (LAR)
    Libros de Cédulas de su Magestad (LCED)
    Libros de Expedientes (LEXP)
    Libros de Propios y Arbitrios (LPA)

Archivo Regional de Arequipa (ARAR), Arequipa
 (formerly Archivo Departamental de Arequipa)
  Cabildo, Justicia Ordinaria: Administrativo (Cab/Adm), Causas Civiles
  (Cab/Civ), and Causas Criminales (Cab/Crim)
  Corregimiento: Causas Civiles and Causas Criminales
  Corte Superior de Justicia: Causas Criminales (CS/Crim)
  Intendencia: Administrativo (Int/Adm), Causas Criminales (Int/Crim),
  Pedimentos (Int/Ped)
 Notarios Públicos:
  Pedro de Figueroa (1780)
  Manuel González de la Fuente (1785)
  Ramón Bellido (1790)
  Rafael Hurtado (1795)
  Mariano de Tapia (1800)
  Josef Alberto de Gómez (1805)
  Hermenegildo Zegarra (1810)
  Rafael Hurtado (1815)
  Francisco Xavier de Linares (1820)
  José Nazario de Rivera (1825)
  Pedro Mariano Araujo (1830)
  Francisco de Linares (1835)
  Casimiro Salazar (1840)
  Miguel José de Chávez (1845)
  Francisco Paula Gonzales (1850)
 Prefectura (Pref)
Biblioteca Denegri Luna, Lima (private library)
 José María Blanco, "Diario del viaje del Presidente Orbegoso al sur del Perú."
Biblioteca Nacional del Perú (BNP), Lima
 Colección de Manuscritos

Newspaper

El Republicano. Arequipa, Peru

Published Primary Sources

Aranda, Ricardo, ed. *Colección de los tratados.* 14 vols. Lima: Imprenta del Estado, 1905.
Barriga, Víctor M., ed. *Arequipa y sus blasones.* Arequipa: Editorial La Colmena,1940.
— — —. *Memorias para la historia de Arequipa.* 4 vols. Vols. 1–3, Arequipa: Editorial La Colmena, 1941, 1946, 1951. Vol. 4, Lima: Imprenta Portugal, 1952.

Belaúnde, Víctor Andrés. *Arequipa de mi infancia: Memorias, primera parte.* Lima: Imprenta Lumen, 1960.

———. *Meditaciones Peruanas.* Lima: Biblioteca Perú Actual, 1933.

———. *Peruanidad.* 3d ed. Lima: Ediciones Librería Studium, 1965.

Bermejo, Vladimiro, ed. *Historiadores y Prosistas.* Arequipa: Primer Festival del Libro Arequipeño, 1958.

Bolívar, Simón. *Decretos del Libertador.* 3 vols. Ed. Sociedad Bolivariana de Venezuela. Vol. 1, *1813–1825* Caracas: Imprenta Nacional, 1961.

Bonilla, Heraclio, ed. *Gran Bretaña y el Perú.* 5 vols. Vol. 4, *Informes de los cónsules: Islay, Mollendo, Arica e Iquique, 1855–1913.* Lima: Instituto de Estudios Peruanos, 1976.

Bustamante de La Fuente, Manuel J. *La Monja Gutiérrez y la Arequipa de ayer y de hoy.* 2 vols. Lima: n.p., 1971–72.

Carrasco, Eduardo. *Calendario y guía de forasteros de la república peruana para el año de 1847.* Lima: Imprenta de Instrucción Primaria, 1846.

Carrión Ordóñez, Enrique. *La lengua en un texto de la ilustración: Edición y estudio filológico de la noticia de Arequipa de Antonio Pereira y Ruiz.* Lima: Pontificia Universidad Católica del Perú, 1983.

Cossío, Matheo de. "Razón circunstanciada que Don Matheo Cossío diputado del comercio de Arequipa produce al Real Tribunal del Consulado de Lima con relación a los ramos de industria de aquella provincia (1804)." *Revista del Archivo Nacional* 28 (1964): 219–33.

Echeverría y Morales, Francisco Xavier. "Memoria de la Santa Iglesia de Arequipa." In *Memorias para la historia de Arequipa,* ed. Víctor M. Barriga. Vol. 4. 1804. Reprint, Arequipa: Imprenta Portugal, 1952.

Fisher, John R., ed. *Arequipa 1796–1811: La relación del gobierno del intendente Salamanca.* Lima: Seminario de Historia Rural Andina, 1968.

García Calderón, Francisco. *Diccionario de la legislación Peruana.* Lima: Imprenta de Eusebio Aranda, 1864.

Gastón, Alfredo, ed. *Compilación de las vistas fiscales.* 2 vols. Lima: Imprenta del Estado, 1873.

González Vigil, Francisco de Paula. *Importancia de la educación del bello sexo.* 1858, 1872. Reprint, Lima: Instituto Nacional de Cultura, 1976.

———. *Importancia de las asociaciones, importancia de la educación popular.* 1858. Reprint, Lima: Ediciones Hora del Hombre, 1948.

Haigh, Samuel. "Bosquejos del Perú, 1825–1827." In *Viajeros en el Perú republicano,* ed. Alberto Tauro. Lima: Universidad Nacional Mayor de San Marcos, 1967.

Humboldt, Alexander von. *Ensayo político sobre el reino de la Nueva España.* Ed. Juan A. Ortega y Medina. Mexico City: Editorial Porrua, 1966.

Laso, Benito. *El poder de la fuerza y el poder de la ley.* 1858. Reprint, Lima: Ediciones Hora del Hombre, 1947.

Loayza, Francisco A. *Preliminares del incendio: documentos del año de 1776 a 1780.* Lima: Librería e Imprenta D. Miranda, 1947.

Luna Pizarro, Francisco Javier de. *Escritos políticos.* Ed. Alberto Tauro. Lima: Universidad Nacional Mayor de San Marcos, 1959.

Middendorf, Ernst W. *Perú.* 3 vols. Lima: Universidad Nacional Mayor de San Marcos, 1973–74.
Nieves y Bustamante, María. *Jorge, o el hijo del pueblo.* 3 vols. 1892. Reprint, Arequipa: Librería Editorial Ibero Americana, 1958.
Olivo, Juan F., ed. *Constituciones políticas del Perú, 1821–1919.* Lima: Imprenta Torres Aguirre, 1922.
Paz Soldán, Mariano Felipe. *Atlas geográfico del Perú.* Paris: Fermin Didot, 1865.
Paz Soldán, Mateo. *Geografía del Perú.* Ed. Mariano Felipe Paz Soldán. Paris: Fermin Didot, 1862.
Paz y Guini, Melchor de. *Guerra separatista: Rebeliones de indios en Sur America.* 2 vols. Ed. Luis Antonio Eguiguren. Lima: Imprenta Torres Aguirre, 1952.
Polar, Jorge. *Arequipa: Descripción y estudio social.* 3d ed. 1891. Reprint, Arequipa: Primer Festival del Libro Arequipeño, 1958.
Polar, Mario. *Viejos y nuevos tiempos.* Lima: Francisco Moncloa Editores, 1968.
Quimper, José María. *Derecho político general.* 2 vols. Lima: Editorial Benito Gil, 1887.
― ― ―. *Instrucción política y reformas para el pueblo.* Arequipa: Imprenta de Francisco Ibáñez, 1854.
― ― ―. *El principio de la libertad.* Lima: Ediciones Hora del Hombre, 1948.
Sartiges, Etienne Gilbert Eugène, comte de. "Viaje a las repúblicas de América del Sur." In *Viajeros en el Perú,* ed. Raul Porras Barrenechea, trans. Emilia Romero. Vol. 2, *Dos viajeros franceses en el Perú republicano.* 1834. Reprint, Lima: Editorial Cultura Antártica, 1947.
Tejeda, José Simeón. *Libertad de la industria.* 1852. Reprint, Lima: Ediciones Hora del Hombre, 1947.
Tepaske, John J., and Herbert S. Klein, eds. 4 vols. *The Royal Treasures of the Spanish Empire in America.* Vol. 1, *Peru.* Durham: Duke University Press, 1982.
Travada y Córdova, Ventura. *El suelo de Arequipa convertido en cielo.* 1752. Reprint, Arequipa: Primer Festival del Libro Arequipeño, 1958.
Tristan, Flora. *Peregrinations of a Pariah: 1833–1834.* Trans. Jean Hawkes. 1874. Reprint, Boston: Beacon Press, 1986.
Valdivia, Juan Gualberto. *Las revoluciones de Arequipa.* 1874. Reprint, Arequipa: Editorial El Deber, 1956.
Witt, Heinrich. *Diario y observaciones sobre el Perú, 1824–1890.* Lima: COFIDE, 1987.
Zamácola y Jáuregui, Juan Domingo de. *Apuntes para la historia de Arequipa.* 1804. Reprint, Arequipa: Primer Festival del Libro Arequipeño, 1958.

Secondary Works

Adrianzén, Alberto, ed. *Pensamiento político peruano.* Lima: DESCO, 1987.
Aguirre, Carlos. *Agentes de su propia libertad: Los esclavos de Lima y la desintegración de la esclavitud, 1821–1854.* Lima: Pontificia Universidad Católica del Perú, 1993.

— — —. "Cimarronaje, bandolerismo y desintegración esclavista: Lima, 1821–1854." In *Bandoleros, abigeos y montoneros: Criminalidad y violencia en el Perú, siglos XVIII-XX*, ed. Carlos Aguirre and Charles Walker. Lima: Instituto de Apoyo Agrario, 1990.

— — —. "Criminology and Prison Reform in Lima, Peru, 1860–1930." Ph.D. dissertation, University of Minnesota, 1996.

Alonso, Ana María. *Thread of Blood: Colonialism, Revolution, and Gender on Mexico's Northern Frontier*. Tucson: University of Arizona Press, 1995.

Alvarez Ganoza, Pedro L. *Origen y trayectoria de la aplicación de la pena de muerte en la historia del derecho Peruano*. Lima: Editorial Dorhca, 1974.

Amussen, Susan Dwyer. *An Ordered Society: Gender and Class in Early Modern England*. New York: Basil Blackwell, 1988.

Anderson, Benedict. *Imagined Communities: Reflections on the Origin and Spread of Nationalism*. London: Verso, 1983.

Anderson, Rodney D. "Race and Social Stratification: A Comparison of Working-Class Spaniards, Indians, and Castas in Guadalajara, Mexico in 1821." *Hispanic American Historical Review* 68, no. 2 (1988): 209–43.

Andrews, George Reid. *The Afro-Argentines of Buenos Aires, 1800–1900*. Madison: University of Wisconsin Press, 1980.

— — —. "Spanish-American Independence: A Structural Analysis." *Latin American Perspectives* 12, no. 1 (1985): 105–32.

Anna, Timothy E. *The Fall of the Royal Government in Peru*. Lincoln: University of Nebraska Press, 1979.

Appelbaum, Nancy. "Remembering Riosucio: Region, Race, and Community in Colombia, 1850–1920." Ph.D. dissertation, University of Wisconsin at Madison, 1997.

Applewhite, Harriet B., and Darline G. Levy, eds. *Women and Politics in the Age of Democratic Revolution*. Ann Arbor: University of Michigan Press, 1990.

Aramburú, José Félix. *Derecho electoral: Antecedentes históricos y aplicaciones a la nueva ley*. Lima: La Opinión Nacional, 1915.

Arnold, Linda. "Vulgar and Elegant: Politics and Procedure in Early National Politics." *The Americas* 50, no. 4 (1994): 481–500.

Arrom, Silvia M. *The Women of Mexico City, 1790–1857*. Stanford: Stanford University Press, 1985.

Avila Martel, Alamiro de. *Esquema del derecho penal indiano*. Santiago, Chile: Seminario de Derecho Público de la Escuela de Ciencias Jurídicas y Sociales de Santiago, 1941.

Bailey, F. G., ed. *Gifts and Poison: The Politics of Reputation*. Oxford: Basil Blackwell, 1971.

Bailey, Peter. " 'Will the Real Bill Banks Please Stand Up?' Towards a Role Analysis of Mid-Victorian Working-Class Respectability." *Journal of Social History* 12, no. 3 (1979): 336–53.

Ballón Lozada, Héctor. *Las ideas socio-políticas en Arequipa, 1540–1900*. Arequipa: PubliUnsa, 1986.

Barnadas, Josep M. "The Catholic Church in Colonial Spanish America." In *The*

Cambridge History of Latin America, ed. Leslie Bethel. Vol 1. Cambridge: Cambridge University Press, 1984.

Barreneche, Osvaldo. "Crime and the Administration of Justice in Buenos Aires, Argentina, 1785–1853." Ph.D. dissertation, University of Arizona, 1997.

Barthes, Roland. *Mythologies*. New York: Hill and Wang, 1972.

Basadre, Jorge. *Historia de la República del Perú*. 6th ed. 17 vols. Lima: Editorial Universitaria, 1968.

— — —. *Historia del derecho Peruano*. Lima: Editorial Antena, 1937.

— — —. *La multitud, la ciudad y el campo en la historia del Perú*. 3d ed. Lima: Ediciones Treintaitres and Mosca Azul Editores, 1980.

Beezley, William H., Cheryl English Martin, and William E. French, eds. *Rituals of Rule, Rituals of Resistance: Public Celebrations and Popular Culture in Mexico*. Wilmington: Scholarly Resources, 1994.

Betalleluz, Betford. "Fiscalidad, tierras y mercado: Las comunidades indígenas de Arequipa, 1825–1850." In *Tradición y modernidad en los Andes*, ed. Henrique Urbano. Cuzco: Centro de Estudios Regionales Andinos (CERA) Bartolomé de las Casas, 1992.

Blanchard, Peter. *The Origins of the Peruvian Labor Movement, 1883–1919*. Pittsburgh: University of Pittsburgh Press, 1982.

— — —. *Slavery and Abolition in Early Republican Peru*. Wilmington: Scholarly Resources, 1992.

Bloch, Ruth. "The Gendered Meanings of Virtue in Revolutionary America." *Signs* 13, no. 1 (1987): 37–58.

Bonilla, Heraclio, ed., *La independencia en el Perú*. Lima: Instituto de Estudios Peruanos, 1972.

Bowser, Frederick P. *The African Slave in Colonial Peru, 1524–1650*. Stanford: Stanford University Press, 1974.

Boyer, Richard. "Honor Among Plebeians: *Mala Sangre* and Social Reputation." In *The Faces of Honor: Sex, Shame, and Violence in Colonial Latin America*, ed. Lyman L. Johnson and Sonya Lipsett-Rivera. Albuquerque: University of New Mexico Press, 1998.

— — —. "Women, *La Mala Vida*, and the Politics of Marriage." In *Sexuality and Marriage in Colonial Latin America*, ed. Asunción Lavrin. Lincoln and London: University of Nebraska Press, 1989.

Brading, D. A. *Miners and Merchants in Bourbon Mexico, 1763–1810*. Cambridge: Cambridge University Press, 1971.

Brading, D. A., and Celia Wu. "Population Growth and Crisis: León, 1720–1866." *Journal of Latin American Studies* 5 (1973): 1–36.

Brennan, Thomas. *Public Drinking and Popular Culture in Eighteenth-Century Paris*. Princeton: Princeton University Press, 1988.

Brown, Kendall W. *Bourbons and Brandy: Imperial Reform in Eighteenth-Century Arequipa*. Albuquerque: University of New Mexico Press, 1986.

Burga, Manuel, and Wilson Reátegui. *Lanas y capital mercantil en el sur: La casa Ricketts, 1895–1935*. Lima: Instituto de Estudios Peruanos, 1981.

Burkholder, Mark A. "Honor and Honors in Colonial Spanish America." In *The Faces of Honor: Sex, Shame, and Violence in Colonial Latin America*, ed. Lyman

L. Johnson and Sonya Lipsett-Rivera. Albuquerque: University of New Mexico Press, 1998.

Bustamante Ugarte, Rubén A. *La corte superior de justicia de Arequipa, 1825–1925.* Arequipa: Tipografía Córdova, 1925.

Cahill, David. "Colour by Numbers: Racial and Ethnic Categories in the Viceroyalty of Peru, 1532–1824," *Journal of Latin American Studies* 26, no. 2 (1994): 325–46.

— — —. "Taxonomy of a Colonial 'Riot': The Arequipa Disturbances of 1780." In *Reform and Insurrection in Bourbon New Granada and Peru,* ed. John R. Fisher, Allan J. Kuethe, and Anthony McFarlane. Baton Rouge: Louisiana State University Press, 1990.

Cahill, David, and Scarlett O'Phelan Godoy. "Forging Their Own History: Indian Insurgency in the Southern Peruvian Sierra, 1815." *Bulletin of Latin American Research* 11, no. 2 (1992): 125–67.

Calhoun, Craig, ed. *Habermas and the Public Sphere.* Cambridge: MIT Press, 1992.

Campbell, J. K. *Honour, Family, and Patronage: A Study of Institutions and Moral Values in a Greek Mountain Community.* Oxford: Clarendon Press, 1964.

Caravedo Molinari, Baltazar. *Desarrollo desigual y lucha política en el Perú, 1948–1956.* Lima: Instituto de Estudios Peruanos, 1978.

— — —. "Poder central y descentralización: Perú, 1931." *Apuntes* 5, no. 9 (1979): 111–29.

Caro Baroja, Julio. "Honour and Shame: A Historical Account of Several Conflicts." In *Honour and Shame: The Values of Mediterranean Society,* ed. J. G. Peristiany. Chicago: University of Chicago Press, 1966.

Carpio Muñoz, Juan Guillermo. "Rebeliones arequipeñas del siglo XIX y configuracion de la oligarquía 'nacional.'" *Análisis* 11 (May–Aug. 1982): 33–45.

— — —. *El Yaraví arequipeño: Un estudio histórico-social.* Arequipa: Editorial La Colmena, 1976.

Chambers, Sarah C. "Crime and Citizenship: Judicial Practice in Arequipa, Peru, During the Transition from Colony to Republic." In *Reconstructing Criminality in Latin America,* ed. Carlos Aguirre and Robert Buffington. Wilmington: Scholarly Resources, 1999.

— — —. "The Limits of a Pan-Ethnic Alliance in the Independence of Peru: The Huánuco Rebellion of 1812." M.A. thesis, University of Wisconsin at Madison, 1987.

— — —. " 'To the Company of a Man Like My Husband; No Law Can Compel Me': Women's Strategies Against Domestic Violence in Arequipa, Peru, 1780–1854." *Journal of Women's History* 11, no. 1 (1999), 31–52.

Chance, John K. *Race and Class in Colonial Oaxaca.* Stanford: Stanford University Press, 1978.

Chance, John K., and William B. Taylor. "Estate and Class in a Colonial City: Oaxaca in 1792." *Comparative Studies in Society and History* 19 (1977): 454–87.

— — —. "Estate *and* Class: A Reply." *Comparative Studies in Society and History* 21 (1979): 434–42.

Chasteen, John Charles. *Heroes on Horseback: A Life and Times of the Last Gaucho Caudillos.* Albuquerque: University of New Mexico Press, 1995.

— — —. "Violence for Show: Knife Dueling on a Nineteenth-Century Cattle Frontier," In *The Problem of Order in Changing Societies*, ed. Lyman L. Johnson. Albuquerque: University of New Mexico Press, 1990.

Cherpak, Evelyn. "The Participation of Women in the Independence Movement in Gran Colombia, 1780–1830." In *Latin American Women: Historical Perspectives*, ed. Asunción Lavrin. Westport, Conn.: Greenwood Press, 1978.

Contreras, Carlos. "Estado republicano y tributo indígena en la sierra central en la post-independencia," *Histórica* 13, no. 1 (1989): 9–44.

Cook, David Noble. *The People of the Colca Valley: A Population Survey*. Boulder: Westview Press, 1982.

— — —. "La población de la parroquia de Yanahuara, 1738–1747: Un modelo para el estudio de las parroquias coloniales peruanas." In *Collaguas I*, ed. Franklin Pease G. Y. Lima: Pontificia Universidad Católica del Perú, 1997.

Cooper, H. H. A. "A Short History of Peruvian Criminal Procedure and Institutions." *Revista de derecho y ciencias políticas* 32 (1968): 215–67.

Cope, R. Douglas *The Limits of Racial Domination: Plebeian Society in Colonial Mexico City, 1660–1720*. Madison: University of Wisconsin Press, 1994.

Corrigan, Phillip, and Derek Sayer. *The Great Arch: English State Formation As Cultural Revolution*. New York: Basil Blackwell, 1985.

Costa, Emília Viotta da. *The Brazilian Empire: Myths and Histories*. Chicago: University of Chicago Press, 1985.

Costeloe, Michael P. *The Central Republic in Mexico, 1835–1846: Hombres de Bien in the Age of Santa Anna*. Cambridge: Cambridge University Press, 1993.

Crane, Elaine F. "Dependence in the Era of Independence: The Role of Women in a Republican Society." In *The American Revolution: Its Character and Limits*, ed. Jack P. Greene. New York: New York University Press, 1987.

Curcio-Nagy, Linda A. "Giants and Gypsies: Corpus Christi in Colonial Mexico City." In *Rituals of Rule, Rituals of Resistance*, ed. William H. Beezley, Cheryl English Martin, and William E. French. Wilmington: Scholarly Resources, 1994.

Dancuart, P. Emilio. *Crónica parlamentaria del Perú*. Lima: Imprenta de la Revista, 1906–.

Davies, Keith A. *Landowners in Colonial Peru*. Austin: University of Texas Press, 1984.

Davis, Natalie Zemon. *Society and Culture in Early Modern France*. Stanford: Stanford University Press, 1975.

Desan, Suzanne. "Crowds, Community, and Ritual in the Work of E. P. Thompson and Natalie Davis." In *The New Cultural History*, ed. Lynn Hunt. Berkeley and Los Angeles: University of California Press, 1989.

Díaz, Arlene Julia. "*Ciudadanas* and *Padres de Familia*: Liberal Change, Gender, Law, and the Lower Classes in Caracas, Venezuela, 1786–1888." Ph.D. dissertation, University of Minnesota, 1997.

Díaz Rementería, Carlos J. *El cacique en el Virreinato del Perú: Estudio histórico-jurídico*. Sevilla: Universidad de Sevilla, 1977.

Di Tella, Torcuato S. *National Popular Politics in Early Independent Mexico, 1820–1847*. Albuquerque: University of New Mexico Press, 1996.

Durand, Francisco. "Movimientos sociales urbanos y problema regional: Arequipa, 1967–1973." *Allpanchis* 12, no. 13 (1979): 79–108.

Echegaray Correa, Ismael R. *La cámara de diputados y las constituyentes del Perú.* Lima: Imprenta del Ministerio de Hacienda y Comercio, 1965.

Escalante Gonzalbo, Fernando. *Ciudadanos imaginarios.* Mexico City: El Colegio de México, 1992.

Estenssoro Fuchs, Juan Carlos. "Modernismo, estética, música y fiesta: Elites y cambio de actitud frente a la cultura popular, Perú 1750–1850." In *Tradición y modernidad en los Andes,* ed. Henrique Urbano. Cuzco: CERA Bartolomé de las Casas, 1992.

— — —. "La plebe ilustrada: El pueblo en las fronteras de la razón." In *Entre la retórica y la insurgencia,* ed. Charles Walker. Cuzco: CERA Bartolomé de las Casas, 1996.

Felstiner, Mary Lowenthal. "Kinship Politics in the Chilean Independence Movement." *Hispanic American Historical Review* 56, no. 1 (1976): 58–80.

Fernández Llerena, Raúl. *Los orígenes del movimiento obrero en Arequipa: El Partido Liberal y el primero de mayo de 1906.* Arequipa and Lima: Amauta and Tarea, 1984.

Ferrero, Raúl. *El liberalismo peruano: Contribución a una historia de las ideas.* Lima: Biblioteca de Escritores Peruanos, 1958.

Fisher, John R. *Government and Society in Colonial Peru: The Intendant System, 1784–1814.* London: Athlone Press, 1970.

— — —. "Royalism, Regionalism, and Rebellion in Colonial Peru, 1808–1815." *Hispanic American Historical Review* 59, no. 2 (1979): 232–57.

Flores Galindo, Alberto. *Arequipa y el sur andino, siglos XVIII–XX.* Lima: Editorial Horizonte, 1977.

— — —. *Aristocracia y plebe: Lima, 1760–1830.* Lima: Mosca Azul Editores, 1984.

— — —. *Buscando un Inca.* Lima: Editorial Horizonte, 1988.

— — —, ed. *Independencia y revolución.* 2 vols. Lima: Instituto Nacional de Cultura, 1987.

— — —, ed. *Túpac Amaru II: 1780.* Lima: Antología Retablo de Papel, 1976.

Flores Galindo, Alberto, Orlando Plaza, and Teresa Oré. "Oligarquía y capital comercial en el sur Peruano, 1870–1930." *Debates en sociología* 3 (1978): 53–75.

Galdos Rodríguez, Guillermo. *Comunidades prehispánicas de Arequipa.* Arequipa: Fundación M. J. Bustamante de La Fuente, 1987.

— — —. *La rebelión de los pasquines.* Arequipa: Editorial Universitaria, 1967.

Gallagher, Mary. "Imperial Reform and the Struggle for Regional Self-Determination: Bishops, Intendants, and Creole Elites in Arequipa, Peru, 1784–1816." Ph.D. dissertation, City University of New York, 1978.

Garavito Amézaga, Hugo. *El Perú liberal: Partidos e ideas de la ilustración a la república aristocrática.* Lima: Ediciones El Virrey, 1989.

García Jordán, Pilar. "La iglesia Peruana ante la formación del estado moderno, 1821–1862." *Histórica* 10, no. 1 (1986): 19–43.

— — —. *Iglesia y poder en el Perú contemporáneo, 1821–1919.* Cuzco: CERA Bartolomé de las Casas, 1991.

— — —. "¿Poder eclesiástico frente a poder civil? Algunas reflexiones sobre la iglesia peruana ante la formación del estado moderno, 1808–1860." *Boletín Americanista* 26, no. 43 (1984): 45–74.

Garrioch, David. *Neighborhood and Community in Paris, 1740–1790.* London: Cambridge University Press, 1986.

Gatrell, V. A. C., and T. B. Hadden. "Criminal Statistics and Their Interpretation." In *Nineteenth-Century Society: Essays on the Use of Quantitative Methods for the Study of Social Data,* ed. E. A. Wrigley. London: Cambridge University Press, 1972).

Gleason, Daniel Michael. "Ideological Cleavages in Early Republican Peru, 1821–1872." Ph.D. dissertation, University of Notre Dame, 1974.

Góngora, Mario. "Urban Stratification in Colonial Chile." *Hispanic American Historical Review* 55, no. 3 (1975): 421–48.

Gootenberg, Paul. "Beleaguered Liberals: The Failed First Generation of Free Traders in Peru." In *Guiding the Invisible Hand: Economic Liberalism and the State in Latin American History,* ed. Joseph L. Love and Nils Jacobsen. New York: Praeger, 1988.

— — —. *Between Silver and Guano: Commercial Policy and the State in Postindependence Peru.* Princeton: Princeton University Press, 1989.

— — —. *Imagining Development: Economic Ideas in Peru's "Fictitious Prosperity" of Guano, 1840–1880.* Berkeley and Los Angeles: University of California Press, 1993.

— — —. "North-South: Trade Policy, Regionalisms, and *Caudillismo* in Post-Independence Peru." *Journal of Latin American Studies* 23, no. 2 (1991): 273–308.

— — —. "Population and Ethnicity in Early Republican Peru: Some Revisions." *Latin American Research Review* 26, no. 3 (1991): 109–57.

— — —. "Social Origins of Protectionism and Free Trade in Nineteenth-Century Lima." *Journal of Latin American Studies* 14, no. 2 (1982): 329–58.

Gramsci, Antonio. *Selections from the Prison Notebooks.* Ed. and trans. Quintin Hoare and Geoffrey Nowell Smith. New York: International Publishers, 1971.

Grieshaber, Erwin. "Survival of Indian Communities in Nineteenth-Century Bolivia: A Regional Comparison." *Journal of Latin American Studies* 12, no. 2 (1980): 223–69.

Guardino, Peter. "Identity and Nationalism in Mexico: Guerrero, 1780–1840." *Journal of Historical Sociology* 7, no. 3 (1994): 314–42.

— — —. *Peasants, Politics, and the Formation of Mexico's National State: Guerrero, 1800–1857.* Stanford: Stanford University Press, 1996.

Guardino, Peter, and Charles Walker. "The State, Society, and Politics in Peru and Mexico in the Late Colonial and Early Republican Periods." *Latin American Perspectives* 19, no. 2 (1992): 10–43.

Guillamón Alvarez, Javier. *Honor y honra en la España del siglo XVIII.* Madrid: Departamento de Historia Moderna, Facultad de Geografía e Historia, Universidad Complutense, 1981.

Gundersen, Joan R. "Independence, Citizenship, and the American Revolution." *Signs* 13, no. 1 (1987): 59–77.

Gutiérrez, Ramón A. "Honor Ideology, Marriage Negotiation, and Class-Gender Domination in New Mexico, 1690–1846." *Latin American Perspectives* 12, no. 1 (1985): 81–104.

— — —. *When Jesus Came, the Corn Mothers Went Away: Marriage, Sexuality, and Power in New Mexico, 1500–1846*. Stanford: Stanford University Press, 1991.

Habermas, Jürgen. *The Structural Transformation of the Public Sphere*. Trans. Thomas Burger. Cambridge: MIT Press, 1989.

Haitin, Marcel Manuel. "Late Colonial Lima: Economy and Society in an Era of Reform and Revolution." Ph.D. dissertation, University of California at Berkeley, 1983.

Hamnett, Brian R. "Dye Production, Food Supply, and the Laboring Population of Oaxaca, 1750–1820." *Hispanic American Historical Review* 51, no. 1 (1971): 51–78.

Haslip, Gabriel James. "Crime and the Administration of Justice in Colonial Mexico City, 1696–1810." Ph.D. dissertation, Columbia University, 1980.

Hoberman, Louisa Schell, and Susan Migden Socolow, eds. *Cities and Society in Colonial Latin America*. Albuquerque: University of New Mexico Press, 1986.

Holloway, Thomas H. *Policing Rio de Janeiro: Repression and Resistance in a Nineteenth-Century City*. Stanford: Stanford University Press, 1993.

Hunefeldt, Christine. "Circulación y estructura tributaria: Puno, 1840–1890." In *Poder y violencia en los Andes*, ed. Henrique Urbano. Cuzco: CERA Bartolomé de las Casas, 1991.

— — —. *Lucha por la tierra y protesta indígena: Las comunidades indígenas del Perú entre colonia y república, 1800–1830*. Bonn: Bonner Amerikanistische Studien, BAS 9, 1982.

— — —. *Paying the Price of Freedom: Family and Labor Among Lima's Slaves, 1800–1854*. Berkeley and Los Angeles: University of California Press, 1994.

Hunt, Lynn. *The Family Romance of the French Revolution*. Berkeley and Los Angeles: University of California Press, 1992.

Jackson, Robert H. "Race/Caste and the Creation and Meaning of Identity in Colonial Spanish America." *Revista de Indias* 55, no. 203 (1995): 149–73.

Jacobsen, Nils. "Free Trade, Regional Elites, and the Internal Market in Southern Peru, 1895–1932." In *Guiding the Invisible Hand: Economic Liberalism and the State in Latin American History*, ed. Joseph L. Love and Nils Jacobsen. New York: Praeger, 1988.

— — —. *Mirages of Transition: The Peruvian Altiplano, 1780–1930*. Berkeley and Los Angeles: University of California Press, 1993.

— — —. "Taxation in Early Republican Peru, 1821–1851: Policy Making Between Reform and Tradition." In *América Latina en la época de Simón Bolívar*, ed. Reinhard Liehr. Berlin: Colloquium Verlag, 1989.

Johnson, Lyman L. "Dangerous Words, Provocative Gestures, and Violent Acts: The Disputed Hierarchies of Plebeian Life in Colonial Buenos Aires." In *The Faces of Honor: Sex, Shame, and Violence in Colonial Latin America*, ed. Lyman L. Johnson and Sonya Lipsett-Rivera. Albuquerque: University of New Mexico Press, 1998.

— — —. "Manumission in Colonial Buenos Aires." *Hispanic American Historical Review* 59, no. 2 (1979): 258–79.

Johnson, Lyman L., and Sonya Lipsett-Rivera, eds. *The Faces of Honor: Sex, Shame, and Violence in Colonial Latin America*. Albuquerque: University of New Mexico Press, 1998.

Joseph, Gilbert M. and Daniel Nugent, eds. *Everyday Forms of State Formation: Revolution and the Negotiation of Rule in Modern Mexico*. Durham: Duke University Press, 1994.

Karasch, Mary C. *Slave Life in Rio de Janeiro, 1808–1850*. Princeton: Princeton University Press, 1987.

Kerber, Linda K. *Women of the Republic: Intellect and Ideology in Revolutionary America*. Chapel Hill: University of North Carolina Press, 1980.

Kittleson, Roger. " 'Ideas Triumph Only After Great Contests of Sorrows': Popular Classes and Political Ideas in Porto Alegre, Brazil, 1889–1893." In *Liberals, Politics, and Power: State Formation in Nineteenth-Century Latin America*, ed. Vincent C. Peloso and Barbara A. Tenenbaum. Athens, Ga.: University of Georgia Press, 1996.

Klaiber, Jeffrey. *La iglesia en el Perú*. Lima: Pontificia Universidad Católica del Perú, 1988.

— — —. "Los partidos católicos en el Perú." *Histórica* 7, no. 2 (1983): 157–78.

Klarén, Peter F. *Modernization, Dislocation, and Aprismo: Origins of the Peruvian Aprista Party, 1870–1932*. Austin: University of Texas Press, 1973.

Kristal, Efraín. *The Andes Viewed from the City: Literary and Political Discourse on the Indian in Peru, 1848–1930*. New York: P. Lang, 1987.

Krüggeler, Thomas. "Unreliable Drunkards or Honorable Citizens? Artisans in Search of their Place in the Cusco Society, 1825–1930." Ph.D. dissertation, University of Illinois at Urbana-Champaign, 1993.

Kubler, George. *The Indian Caste of Peru, 1795–1940*. Washington, D.C.: U.S. Government Printing Office, 1952.

Ladd, Doris M. *The Mexican Nobility at Independence, 1780–1826*. Austin: Institute of Latin American Studies at the University of Texas, 1976.

Landes, Joan. *Women and the Public Sphere in the Age of the French Revolution*. Ithaca and London: Cornell University Press, 1988.

Larson, Brooke. *Colonialism and Agrarian Transformation in Bolivia: Cochabamba, 1550–1900*. Princeton: Princeton University Press, 1988.

— — —, and Olivia Harris, eds. *Ethnicity, Markets, and Migration in the Andes: At the Crossroads of History and Anthropology*. Durham: Duke University Press, 1995.

Lavrin, Asunción, ed. *Sexuality and Marriage in Colonial Latin America*. Lincoln and London: University of Nebraska Press, 1989.

Lavrin, Asunción, and Edith Couturier. "Dowries and Wills: A View of Women's Socioeconomic Role in Colonial Guadalajara and Puebla, 1640–1790." *Hispanic American Historical Review* 59, no. 2 (1979): 280–304.

Leonard, Irving A. *Baroque Times in Old Mexico: Seventeenth-Century Persons, Places, and Practices*. Ann Arbor: University of Michigan Press, 1959.

Levy, Darline Gay. "Women's Revolutionary Citizenship in Action, 1791: Setting the Boundaries." In *The French Revolution and the Meaning of Citizenship*, ed. Reneé Waldinger, Philip Dawson, and Isser Woloch. Westport, Conn.: Greenwood Press, 1993.

Lincoln, Bruce. *Discourse and the Construction of Society: Comparative Studies of*

Myth, Ritual, and Classification. New York and Oxford: Oxford University Press, 1989.

Lipsett-Rivera, Sonya. "A Slap in the Face of Honor: Social Transgression and Women in Late-Colonial Mexico." In *The Faces of Honor: Sex, Shame, and Violence in Colonial Latin America,* ed. Lyman L. Johnson and Sonya Lipsett-Rivera. Albuquerque: University of New Mexico Press, 1998.

Lomnitz-Adler, Claudio. *Exits from the Labyrinth: Culture and Ideology in the Mexican National Space.* Berkeley and Los Angeles: University of California Press, 1992.

Lynch, John. *Caudillos in Spanish America, 1800–1850.* Oxford: Clarendon Press, 1992.

— — —. *The Spanish American Revolutions, 1808–1826.* 2d ed. New York: W. W. Norton, 1986.

Macera, Pablo. *Trabajos de historia.* 4 vols. Lima: Instituto Nacional de Cultura, 1977.

MacLachlin, Colin. *Criminal Justice in Eighteenth-Century Mexico: A Study of the Tribunal of the Acordada.* Berkeley and Los Angeles: University of California Press, 1974.

Málaga Medina, Alejandro. *Arequipa: Estudios Históricos.* 3 vols. Arequipa: Biblioteca Arequipa, 1981, 1985, 1986.

Malamud, Carlos D. "El fin del comercio colonial: Una compañía comercial gaditana del siglo XIX." In *Independencia y revolución,* ed. Alberto Flores Galindo. Lima: Instituto Nacional de Cultura, 1987.

— — —. "Relaciones familiares, comercio y guerra de independencia (1808–1828), Los Goyeneche." Tésis de licenciatura, Universidad Complutense, Madrid, 1978.

Mallon, Florencia E. *The Defense of Community in Peru's Central Highlands: Peasant Struggle and Capitalist Transition, 1860–1940.* Princeton: Princeton University Press, 1983.

— — —. "Economic Liberalism: Where We Are and Where We Need to Go." In *Guiding the Invisible Hand: Economic Liberalism and the State in Latin American History,* ed. Joseph L. Love and Nils Jacobsen. New York: Praeger, 1988.

— — —. *Peasant and Nation: The Making of Postcolonial Mexico and Peru.* Berkeley and Los Angeles: University of California Press, 1995.

— — —. "Peasants and State Formation in Nineteenth-Century Mexico: Morelos, 1848–1858." *Political Power and Social Theory* 7 (1988): 1–54.

Mannarelli, María Emma. *Pecados públicos: La ilegitimidad en Lima, siglo XVII.* Lima: Ediciones Flora Tristán, 1993.

Maravall, José Antonio. *Poder, honor y élites en el siglo XVII.* Madrid: Siglo Veintiuno Editores, 1979.

Martin, Cheryl English. *Governance and Society in Colonial Mexico: Chihuahua in the Eighteenth Century.* Stanford: Stanford University Press, 1996.

— — —. "Haciendas and Villages in Late Colonial Morelos." *Hispanic American Historical Review* 62, no. 3 (1982): 407–28.

— — —. "Popular Speech and Social Order in Northern Mexico, 1650–1830." *Comparative Studies in Society and History* 32, no. 2 (1990): 305–24.

Martín Rodrígez, Jacinto. *El honor y la injuria en el fuero de Vizcaya*. Bilbao: Diputación Provincial, 1973.

Martínez, Santiago. *Alcaldes de Arequipa desde 1539 a 1946*. Arequipa, n.p., 1946.

Martínez-Alier, Verena. *Marriage, Class, and Colour in Nineteenth-Century Cuba: A Study of Racial Attitudes and Sexual Values in a Slave Society*. London: Cambridge University Press, 1974.

Masiello, Francine. *Between Civilization and Barbarism: Women, Nation, and Literary Culture in Modern Argentina*. Lincoln: University of Nebraska Press, 1992.

McAlister, Lyle N. "Social Structure and Social Change in New Spain." *Hispanic American Historical Review* 43, no. 3 (1963): 349–70.

McCaa, Robert. "*Calidad, Clase*, and Marriage in Colonial Mexico: The Case of Parral, 1788–1790." *Hispanic American Historical Review* 64, no. 3 (1984): 477–501.

McCaa, Robert, and Stuart B. Schwartz. "Measuring Marriage Patterns: Percentages, Cohen's Kappa, and Log-Linear Models." *Comparative Studies in Society and History*, 25 (1983): 711–20.

McCaa, Robert, Stuart B. Schwartz, and Arturo Grubessich. "Race and Class in Colonial Latin America: A Critique." *Comparative Studies in Society and History* 21 (1979): 421–33.

McEvoy, Carmen E. "Estampillas y votos: El rol del correo político en una campaña electoral decimonónica." *Histórica* 18, no. 1 (1994): 95–134.

— — —. "The Republican Utopia: Ideals and Realities in the Formation of Peruvian Political Culture, 1871–1919." Ph.D. dissertation, University of California at San Diego, 1995.

Méndez G., Cecilia. "Los campesinos, la independencia y la iniciación de la república: El caso de los iquichanos realistas." In *Poder y violencia en los Andes*, ed. Henrique Urbano. Cuzco: CERA Bartolomé de las Casas, 1991.

— — —. "República sin indios: La comunidad imaginada del Perú." In *Tradición y modernidad en los Andes*, ed. Henrique Urbano. Cuzco: CERA Bartolomé de las Casas, 1992.

Meranze, Michael. *Laboratories of Virtue: Punishment, Revolution, and Authority in Philadelphia, 1760–1835*. Chapel Hill: University of North Carolina Press, 1996.

Merino Arana, Romulo. *Historia policial del Perú en la república*. Lima: Imprenta del Departamento de Prensa y Publicaciones de la Guardia Civil, 1966.

Merry, Sally Engle. "Rethinking Gossip and Scandal." In *Toward a General Theory of Social Control*, ed. Donald Black. Vol. 1, *Fundamentals*. New York: Academic Press, 1984.

Milla Batres, Carlos. *Diccionario histórico y biográfico del Perú, siglos XV–XX*. Lima: Editorial Milla Batres, 1986.

Millones Santa Gadea, Luis. "Los ganados del señor: Mecanismos de poder en las comunidades andinas, siglos XVIII y XIX." *América Indígena* 39, no. 1 (1979): 107–45.

Minchom, Martin. "The Making of a White Province: Demographic Movement and Ethnic Transformation in the South of the Audiencia de Quito, 1670–1830." *Bulletin de l'Institut Français d'Etudes Andines* 12, no. 3–4 (1983): 23–39.

— — —. *The People of Quito, 1690–1810: Change and Unrest in the Underclass.* Boulder: Westview Press, 1994.

Mörner, Magnus. *Race Mixture in Latin America.* Boston: Little, Brown, 1967.

Mosse, George L. *Nationalism and Sexuality: Middle-Class Morality and Sexual Norms in Modern Europe.* Madison: University of Wisconsin Press, 1988.

Neira Avendaño, Máximo, Guillermo Galdos Rodríguez, Alejandro Málaga Medina, Eusebio Quiroz Paz Soldán, and Juan Guillermo Carpio Muñoz. *Historia general de Arequipa.* Arequipa: Fundación M. J. Bustamante de La Fuente, 1990.

Noéjovich, Héctor Omar. "Las relaciones del estado peruano con la población indígena en el siglo XIX a través de su legislación." *Histórica* 15, no. 1 (1991): 43–62.

Nye, Robert A. *Masculinity and Male Codes of Honor in Modern France.* Oxford: Oxford University Press, 1993.

O'Phelan Godoy, Scarlett. *Rebellions and Revolts in Eighteenth-Century Peru and Upper Peru.* Cologne: Böhlau Verlag, 1985.

Outram, Dorinda. "Le Langage mâle de la vertu: Women and the Discourse of the French Revolution." In *The Social History of Language*, ed. Peter Burke and Roy Porter. Cambridge: Cambridge University Press, 1987.

Pareja Paz Soldán, José. *José Gregorio Paz Soldán: Diplomático y jurista.* Lima: Ediciones Peruanos, 1964.

Parkerson, Phillip T. *Andrés de Santa Cruz y la Confederación Perú-Boliviana, 1835–1839.* La Paz: Librería Editorial Juventud, 1984.

Pease G. Y., Franklin, ed. *Collaguas I.* Lima: Pontificia Universidad Católica del Perú, 1977.

Peloso, Vincent C. "Liberals, Electoral Reform, and the Popular Vote in Mid-Nineteenth-Century Peru." In *Liberals, Politics, and Power: State Formation in Nineteenth-Century Latin America*, ed. Vincent C. Peloso and Barbara A. Tenenbaum. Athens, Ga.: University of Georgia Press, 1996.

Peralta Ruíz, Víctor. *En pos del tributo en el Cusco rural, 1826–1854.* Cuzco: CERA Bartolomé de las Casas, 1991.

Peralta Vásquez, Antero. *La faz oculta de Arequipa.* Arequipa: Coop. Ed. Universitaria, 1977.

Peristiany, J. G., ed. *Honour and Shame: The Values of Mediterranean Society.* Chicago: University of Chicago Press, 1966.

Phelan, John Leddy. *The People and the King: The Comunero Revolution in Colombia, 1781.* Madison: University of Wisconsin Press, 1978.

Pitt-Rivers, Julian. *The Fate of Shechem, or the Politics of Sex.* New York: Cambridge University Press, 1977.

— — —. "Honour and Social Status." In *Honour and Shame: The Values of Mediterranean Society*, ed. J. G. Peristiany. Chicago: University of Chicago Press, 1966.

— — —. *The People of the Sierra.* 2d ed. Chicago: University of Chicago Press, 1971.

Platt, Tristan. *Estado boliviano y ayllu andino.* Lima: Instituto de Estudios Peruanos, 1982.

— — —. "Simón Bolívar, the Sun of Justice and the Amerindian Virgen: Andean Conceptions of the *Patria* in Nineteenth-Century Potosí." *Journal of Latin American Studies* 25 (1993): 159–85.

Pocock, J. G. A. *The Machiavellian Moment: Florentine Political Thought and the Atlantic Republican Tradition.* Princeton: Princeton University Press, 1975.

Ponce, Fernando. "Social Structure of Arequipa, 1840–1879." Ph.D. dissertation, University of Texas at Austin, 1980.

Potofsky, Allan. "Work and Citizenship: Crafting Images of Revolutionary Builders, 1789–1791." In *The French Revolution and the Meaning of Citizenship*, ed. Renée Waldinger, Philip Dawson, and Isser Woloch. Westport, Conn.: Greenwood Press, 1993.

Powers, Karen Vieira. "The Battle for Bodies and Souls in the Colonial North Andes: Intra-ecclesiastical Struggles and the Politics of Migration." *Hispanic American Historical Review* 75, no. 1 (1995): 31–56.

Quiroz, Alfonso W. *La deuda defraudada: Consolidación de 1850 y dominio económico en el Perú.* Lima: Instituto Nacional de Cultura, 1987.

———. "Estructura económica y desarrollos regionales de la clase dominante, 1821–1850." In *Independencia y revolución*, ed. Alberto Flores Galindo. Vol. 2. Lima: Instituto Nacional de Cultura, 1987.

Quiroz Chueca, Francisco. *La protesta de los artesanos: Lima-Callao, 1858.* Lima: Universidad Nacional Mayor de San Marcos, 1988.

Quiroz Paz Soldán, Eusebio. "La intendencia de Arequipa: Organización y problemas económicos." *Histórica* 8, no. 2 (1984): 151–75.

———. "La rebelión de 1780 en Arequipa: Reflexiones para una interpretación." In *La Revolución de los Túpac Amaru: Antología*, ed. Luis Durand Flórez. Lima: Comisión Nacional del Bicentenario de la Rebelión Emancipadora de Túpac Amaru, 1981.

Remy, María Isabel. "La sociedad local al inicio de la república: Cusco, 1824–1850." *Revista Andina* 6, no. 2 (1988): 451–84.

Rénique, José Luis. "Los descentralistas arequipeños en la crisis del año 30." *Allpanchis* 12 (1979): 51–78.

Rodgers, Daniel T. "Republicanism: The Career of a Concept." *Journal of American History* 79, no. 1 (1992): 11–38.

Romero, L. A. *La Sociedad de la Igualdad: Los artesanos de Santiago de Chile y sus primeras experiencias políticas, 1820–1851.* Buenos Aires: Instituto Torcuato di Tella, 1978.

Rothman, David J. *The Discovery of the Asylum: Social Order and Disorder in the New Republic.* Boston: Little, Brown, 1971.

Ryan, Mary P. "Gender and Public Access: Women's Politics in Nineteenth-Century America." In *Habermas and the Public Sphere*, ed. Craig Calhoun. Cambridge: MIT Press, 1992.

———. *Women in Public: Between Banners and Ballots, 1825–1880.* Baltimore: Johns Hopkins University Press, 1990.

Sabean, David Warren. *Power in the Blood: Popular Culture and Village Discourse in Early Modern Germany.* London: Cambridge University Press, 1984.

Safford, Frank. "Race, Integration, and Progress: Elite Attitudes and the Indian in Colombia, 1750–1870." *Hispanic American Historical Review* 71, no. 1 (1991): 1–33.

Saignes, Thierry. "Indian Migration and Social Change in Seventeenth-Century

Charcas." In *Ethnicity, Markets, and Migration in the Andes*, ed. Brooke Larson and Olivia Harris. Durham: Duke University Press, 1995.

Sala i Vila, Núria. "Gobierno colonial, Iglesia y poder en Perú: 1784-1814." *Revista Andina* 11, no. 1 (1993): 133–61.

———. *Y se armó el Tole Tole: Tributo indígena y movimientos sociales en el Virreinato del Perú, 1790–1814*. Huamanga: Instituto de Estudios Regionales José María Arguedas, 1996.

Sánchez-Albornoz, Nicolás. *Indios y tributos en el Alto Perú*. Lima: Instituto de Estudios Peruanos, 1978.

———. "Migración urbana y trabajo: Los indios de Arequipa, 1571–1645." In *De historia e historiadores: Homenaje a José Luis Romero*. Mexico City: Siglo Veintiuno Editores, 1982.

Scarano, Francisco A. "The Jíbaro Masquerade and the Subaltern Politics of Creole Identity Formation in Puerto Rico, 1745–1823." *American Historical Review* 101, no. 5 (1996): 1,398–1,431.

Scardaville, Michael C. "Alcohol Abuse and Tavern Reform in Late Colonial Mexico City." *Hispanic American Historical Review* 60, no. 4 (1980): 643–71.

———. "Crime and the Urban Poor: Mexico City in the Late Colonial Period." Ph.D. dissertation, University of Florida, 1977.

———. "(Hapsburg) Law and (Bourbon) Order: State Authority, Popular Unrest, and the Criminal Justice System in Bourbon Mexico City." *The Americas* 50, no. 4 (1994): 501–25.

Scott, James C. *Domination and the Arts of Resistance: Hidden Transcripts*. New Haven: Yale University Press, 1990.

Scott, Joan Wallach. *Gender and the Politics of History*. New York: Columbia University Press, 1988.

Seed, Patricia. "Social Dimensions of Race: Mexico City, 1753." *Hispanic American Historical Review* 62, no. 4 (1982): 569–606.

———. *To Love, Honor, and Obey in Colonial Mexico: Conflicts over Marriage Choice, 1574–1821*. Stanford: Stanford University Press, 1988.

Seed, Patricia, and Philip F. Rust. "Estate and Class in Colonial Oaxaca Revisited." *Comparative Studies in Society and History* 25 (1983): 703–10.

Sewell, William. "*Le Citoyen/la citoyenne*: Activity, Passivity, and the Revolutionary Concept of Citizenship." In *The Political Culture of the French Revolution*, ed. Colin Lucas. London: Pergamon Press, 1988.

Smith, Jay M. "Honour, Royal Service, and the Cultural Origins of the French Revolution: Interpreting the Language of Army Reform, 1750–1788." *French History* 9, no. 3 (1995): 294–314.

Socolow, Susan M. "Acceptable Partners: Marriage Choice in Colonial Argentina, 1778–1810." In *Sexuality and Marriage in Colonial Latin America*, ed. Asunción Lavrin. Lincoln and London: University of Nebraska Press, 1989

Sommer, Doris. *Foundational Fictions: The National Romances of Latin America*. Berkeley and Los Angeles: University of California Press, 1991.

Sowell, David. *The Early Colombian Labor Movement: Artisans and Politics in Bogotá, 1832–1919*. Philadelphia: Temple University Press, 1992.

— — —. " 'La teoría i la realidad': The Democratic Society of Artisans of Bogotá, 1847–1854." *Hispanic American Historical Review* 67, no. 4 (1987): 611–30.

Spalding, Karen. *Huarochirí: An Andean Society Under Inca and Spanish Rule.* Stanford: Stanford University Press, 1984.

— — —. "*Kurakas* and Commerce: A Chapter in the Evolution of Andean Society." *Hispanic American Historical Review* 53, no. 4 (1973): 581–99.

Spurling, Geoffrey. "Honor, Sexuality, and the Colonial Church: The Sins of Dr. González." In *The Faces of Honor: Sex, Shame, and Violence in Colonial Latin America*, ed. Lyman L. Johnson and Sonya Lipsett-Rivera. Albuquerque: University of New Mexico Press, 1998.

Stansell, Christine. *City of Women: Sex and Class in New York, 1789–1860.* Urbana and Chicago: University of Illinois Press, 1987.

Stern, Steve J. *Peru's Indian Peoples and the Challenge of Spanish Conquest: Huamanga to 1640.* Madison: University of Wisconsin Press, 1982.

— — —, ed. *Resistance, Rebellion, and Consciousness in the Andean Peasant World.* Madison: University of Wisconsin Press, 1987.

— — —. *The Secret History of Gender: Women, Men, and Power in Late Colonial Mexico.* Chapel Hill: University of North Carolina Press, 1995.

Stevens, Donald. *Origins of Instability in Early Republican Mexico.* Durham: Duke University Press, 1991.

Szuchman, Mark D. *The Middle Period in Latin America: Values and Attitudes in the Seventeenth–Nineteenth Centuries.* Boulder: Lynne Rienner, 1989.

— — —. *Order, Family, and Community in Buenos Aires, 1810–1860.* Stanford: Stanford University Press, 1988.

Tandeter, Enrique, Vilma Milletich, María Ollier, and Beatríz Ruibal. "Indians in Late Colonial Markets: Sources and Numbers." In *Ethnicity, Markets, and Migration in the Andes*, ed. Brooke Larson and Olivia Harris. Durham: Duke University Press, 1995.

Taylor, William. *Drinking, Homicide, and Rebellion in Colonial Mexican Villages.* Stanford: Stanford University Press, 1979.

Thurner, Mark. *From Two Republics to One Divided: Contradictions of Nationmaking in Andean Peru.* Durham: Duke University Press, 1997.

Tibesar, Antonine. "The Peruvian Church at the Time of Independence in the Light of Vatican II." *The Americas* 26, no. 4 (1970): 349–75.

Tord, Luis Enrique. *Arequipa artística y monumental.* Lima: Banco del Sur del Perú, 1987.

Trazegnies, Fernando de. *La idea de derecho en el Perú republicano del siglo XIX.* Lima: Pontificia Universidad Católica del Perú, 1992.

Twinam, Ann. "Honor, Sexuality, and Illegitimacy in Colonial Spanish America." In *Sexuality and Marriage in Colonial Latin America*, ed. Asunción Lavrin. Lincoln and London: University of Nebraska Press, 1989.

— — —. *Miners, Merchants, and Farmers in Colonial Colombia.* Austin: University of Texas Press, 1982.

— — —. "The Negotiation of Honor: Elites, Sexuality, and Illegitimacy in Eighteenth-Century Spanish America." In *The Faces of Honor: Sex, Shame, and Violence in*

Colonial Latin America, ed. Lyman L. Johnson and Sonya Lipsett-Rivera. Albuquerque: University of New Mexico Press, 1998.

Urbano, Henrique, ed. *Modernidad en los Andes*. Cuzco: CERA Bartolomé de las Casas, 1992.

———. *Poder y violencia en los Andes*. Cuzco: CERA Bartolomé de las Casas, 1991.

Uribe, J. Jaramillo. "Mestizaje y diferenciación social en el Nuevo Reino de Granada en la segunda mitad del siglo XVIII." *Anuario Colombiano de historia social y de la cultura* 2, no. 3 (1965): 21–48.

Uribe, Victor M. "The Lawyers and New Granada's Late Colonial State." *Journal of Latin American Studies* 21, no. 3 (1995): 517–50.

Van Deusen, Nancy Elena. "*Recogimiento* for Women and Girls in Colonial Lima: An Institutional and Cultural Practice." Ph.D. dissertation, University of Illinois at Urbana-Champaign, 1995.

Van Young, Eric. "Recent Anglophone Scholarship on Mexico and Central America in the Age of Revolution." *Hispanic American Historical Review* 65, no. 4 (1985): 725–44.

Vickery, Amanda. "Golden Age to Separate Spheres? A Review of the Categories and Chronology of English Women's History," *Historical Journal* 36, no. 2 (1993): 383–414.

Villegas Romero, Arturo. *Un decenio de la historia de Arequipa, 1830–1840*. Arequipa: Fundación Gloria, 1985.

Villena, Francisco. "La sociedad arequipeña y el Partido Liberal, 1885–1920." *Análisis* 8–9 (1979): 82–108.

Viqueira Albán, Juan Pedro. *¿Relajados o reprimidos? Diversiones públicas y vida social en la ciudad de México durante el Siglo de las Luces*. Mexico City: Fondo de Cultura Económica, 1987.

Voekel, Pamela. "Peeing on the Palace: Bodily Resistance to Bourbon Reforms in Mexico City," *Journal of Historical Sociology* 5, no. 2 (1992): 183–208.

Vollmer, Günter. *Bevölkerungspolitik und Bevölkerungsstruktur im Vizekönigreich Peru zu Ende der Kolonialzeit, 1741–1821*. Bad Homburg: Gehlen, 1967.

Wade, Peter. *Blackness and Race Mixture: The Dynamics of Racial Identity in Colombia*. London and Baltimore: Johns Hopkins University Press, 1993.

Waldron, Kathy. "The Sinners and the Bishop in Colonial Venezuela: The *Visita* of Bishop Mariano Martí, 1771–1784." In *Sexuality and Marriage in Colonial Latin America*, ed. Asunción Lavrin. Lincoln and London: University of Nebraska Press, 1989.

Walker, Charles. "Los indios en la transición de colonia a república: ¿Base social de la modernización política?" in *Tradición y modernidad en los Andes*, ed. Henrique Urbano. Cuzco: CERA Bartolomé de las Casas, 1992.

———. "Peasants, Caudillos, and the State in Peru: Cusco in the Transition from Colony to Republic, 1780–1840." Ph.D. dissertation, University of Chicago, 1992.

———. "Rhetorical Power: Early Republican Discourse on the Indians in Cusco." Paper presented for the Conference on Latin American History during the Annual Meeting of the American Historical Association, Chicago, Dec. 27–30, 1991.

―――. "Voces discordantes: Discursos alternativos sobre el indio a fines de la colonia." In *Entre la retórica y la insurgencia: Las ideas y los movimientos sociales en los Andes, siglo XVIII*, ed. Charles Walker. Cuzco: CERA Bartolomé de las Casas, 1996.

Warren, Richard. "Elections and Popular Political Participation in Mexico, 1808–1836." In *Liberals, Politics, and Power: State Formation in Nineteenth-Century Latin America*, ed. Vincent C. Peloso and Barbara A. Tenenbaum. Athens, Ga.: University of Georgia Press, 1996.

―――. "Vagrancy and Political Order in Nineteenth-Century Mexico." Paper presented at the Annual Meeting of the American Historical Association, San Francisco, Jan. 6–9, 1994.

Wibel, John Frederick. "The Evolution of a Regional Community Within Spanish Empire and Peruvian Nation: Arequipa, 1780–1845." Ph.D. dissertation, Stanford University, 1975.

Wightman, Ann M. *Indigenous Migration and Social Change: The Forasteros of Cuzco, 1570–1720*. Durham: Duke University Press, 1990.

Wilentz, Sean. *Chants Democratic: New York City and the Rise of the American Working Class, 1788–1850*. Oxford: Oxford University Press, 1984.

Williams, Raymond. *Marxism and Literature*. Oxford: Oxford University Press, 1977.

Wu, Celia. "The Population of the City of Querétaro in 1791." *Journal of Latin American Studies* 16, no. 2 (1984): 277–307.

Wyatt-Brown, Bertram. *Honor and Violence in the Old South*. New York: Oxford University Press, 1986.

Zulawski, Ann. *They Eat from Their Labor: Work and Social Change in Colonial Bolivia*. Pittsburgh: University of Pittsburgh Press, 1994.

Index